EMBODIMENT, IDENTITY, AND GENDER IN THE EARLY MODERN AGE

Embracing a multiconfessional and transnational approach that stretches from central Europe, to Scotland and England, from Iberia to Africa and Asia, this volume explores the lives, work, and experiences of women and men during the tumultuous fifteenth to seventeenth centuries.

The authors, all leading experts in their fields, utilize a broad range of methodologies from cultural history to women's history, from masculinity studies to digital mapping, to explore the dynamics and power of constructed gender roles. Ranging from intellectual representations of virginity to the plight of refugees, from the sea journeys of Jesuit missionaries to the impact of Transatlantic economies on women's work, from nuns discovering new ways to tolerate different religious expressions to bleeding corpses used in criminal trials, these essays address the wide diversity and historical complexity of identity, gender, and the body in the early modern age.

With its diversity of topics, fields, and interests of its authors, this volume is a valuable source for students and scholars of the history of women, gender, and sexuality as well as social and cultural history in the early modern world.

Amy E. Leonard (Associate Professor of History at Georgetown University) focuses on women, gender, and sexuality in Reformation Germany. She is the author of *Nails in the Wall: Catholic Nuns in Reformation Germany*. She is currently working on a book that compares and contrasts changing views of female sexuality during the Reformations.

David M. Whitford (Professor of Reformation Studies at Baylor University) is a senior editor of *The Sixteenth Century Journal*. He is the author of *A Reformation Life* and *The Curse of Ham in Early Modern Europe*. He is currently working on the construction of masculinity during the Reformations.

EMBODIMENT, IDENTITY, AND GENDER IN THE EARLY MODERN AGE

Edited by Amy E. Leonard and David M. Whitford

LONDON AND NEW YORK

First published 2021
by Routledge
2 Park Square, Milton Park, Abingdon, Oxon OX14 4RN

and by Routledge
52 Vanderbilt Avenue, New York, NY 10017

Routledge is an imprint of the Taylor & Francis Group, an informa business

© 2021 selection and editorial matter, Amy E. Leonard and David M. Whitford; individual chapters, the contributors

The right of Amy E. Leonard and David M. Whitford to be identified as the authors of the editorial material, and of the authors for their individual chapters, has been asserted in accordance with sections 77 and 78 of the Copyright, Designs and Patents Act 1988.

All rights reserved. No part of this book may be reprinted or reproduced or utilised in any form or by any electronic, mechanical, or other means, now known or hereafter invented, including photocopying and recording, or in any information storage or retrieval system, without permission in writing from the publishers.

Trademark notice: Product or corporate names may be trademarks or registered trademarks, and are used only for identification and explanation without intent to infringe.

British Library Cataloguing-in-Publication Data
A catalogue record for this book is available from the British Library

Library of Congress Cataloging-in-Publication Data
Library of Congress Cataloging-in-Publication Data
Names: Leonard, Amy, 1966-editor. | Whitford, David M. (David Mark), editor.
Title: Embodiment, identity, and gender in the early modern age/edited by Amy E. Leonard and David M. Whitford.
Description: Abingdon, Oxon; New York, NY: Routledge, 2021. | Includes bibliographical references and index.
Identifiers: LCCN 2020037237 | ISBN 9780367507350 (hbk) | ISBN 9780367507336 (pbk) | ISBN 9781003051046 (ebk)
Subjects: LCSH: Gender identity--History. | Women--History. | Sex--History.
Classification: LCC HQ18.55 .E65 2021 | DDC 305.309--dc23
LC record available at https://lccn.loc.gov/2020037237

ISBN: 978-0-367-50735-0 (hbk)
ISBN: 978-0-367-50733-6 (pbk)
ISBN: 978-1-003-05104-6 (ebk)

Typeset in Bembo
by MPS Limited, Dehradun

CONTENTS

List of tables viii
List of contributors ix
Foreword: a reflection on Merry Wiesner-Hanks xiv
Natalie Zemon Davis

Acknowledgments xx

Introduction 1

PART I
The body and manifestations of gender 11

1 The strange survival of the bleeding corpse 13
   Joel F. Harrington

2 Martin Luther and the Reformation of virginity 24
   Amy E. Leonard

3 Martin Luther's gendered reflections on Eve 36
   David M. Whitford

4 A "Prodigal son" remembers John of the cross 48
   Jodi Bilinkoff

5 Women, conflict, and peacemaking in German villages 59
   Marc R. Forster

6 James I and unruly women   70
   Carole Levin

PART II
Women between reform, subversion, and self-determination   **83**

7 Protestant and Catholic nuns confronting the Reformation   85
   Marjorie Elizabeth Plummer

8 Female religious communities during the Thirty Years' War   97
   Sigrun Haude

9 Conflicts between male reformers and female monastics   109
   Elizabeth A. Lehfeldt

10 Anna Maria van Schurman: poetry as exegesis   122
   John L. Thompson

11 Sacral systems: the challenge of change   135
   Raymond A. Mentzer

12 Catholic women in the Dutch Golden Age   148
   Christine Kooi

13 Women and religious expression in Calvin's Geneva   160
   Jeffrey R. Watt

PART III
Gendered dynamics of displacement, migration, and conflict   **173**

14 Women, gender, and religious refugees   175
   Nicholas Terpstra

15 Refugee wives, widows, and mothers   187
   Timothy G. Fehler

16 Did the Jesuits introduce "Global Studies"?   197
   Kathleen M. Comerford

17 Devotion at sea: ship voyages and Jesuit masculinity   210
   Ulrike Strasser

18 Spanish women, work, and the early modern Atlantic economy 223
    Allyson M. Poska

    Afterword: looking backwards and forward *235*
    Susan Karant-Nunn

    Index *241*

TABLES

5.1 Involvement of women in the minutes (*Verhörprotokolle*) of the lower court of the Deutschordenskommende Mainau 60

CONTRIBUTORS

Jodi Bilinkoff (PhD, Princeton) is Professor of History at the University of North Carolina at Greensboro. She is the author of *The Avila Of Saint Teresa: Religious Reform in a Sixteenth-Century City*, *Related Lives: Confessors and Their Female Penitents, 1450–1750*, and coeditor (with Allan Greer) of *Colonial Saints: Discovering the Holy in the Americas, 1500–1800*. The essay in this collection forms part of her current book project, tentatively titled *John of the Cross: The History, Mystery, and Memory of a Spanish Saint*.

Kathleen M. Comerford (PhD, Wisconsin) is Professor of History at Georgia Southern University. She is the author of three monographs, including *Jesuit Foundations and Medici Power, 1532–1621*, 12 articles/chapters, including two in books she coedited, and ten encyclopedia articles. She is the Associate Editor of the *Journal of Jesuit Studies* and frequently reviews submissions for other journals. She has received grants from the University of Wisconsin-Madison Libraries, the American Historical Association, the Andrew W. Mellon Foundation, the Renaissance Society of America, the Folger Shakespeare Library, the Newberry Library, the Beinecke Library at Yale University, and Princeton University Libraries. She is a former president of the Sixteenth Century Society.

Natalie Zemon Davis (PhD, Michigan) is the Henry Charles Lea Professor Emeritus at Princeton University and Professor of History at the University of Toronto. She is the author of over 200 articles and eight books, including *The Return of Martin Guerre* and *Trickster Travels: A Sixteenth-Century Muslim Between Worlds*. All of her books have been translated into several foreign languages. In 2010, the Norwegian government awarded her the Ludwig Holberg International Prize in the Humanities.

x   Contributors

Timothy G. Fehler (PhD, Wisconsin) is the William E. Leverette, Jr., Professor of History at Furman University. His research interests and publications have centered primarily around questions of poor relief, religious refugees, and toleration and coexistence among various religious communities, particularly in northwestern Germany and the Netherlands in the sixteenth century. He is the author of *Poor Relief and Protestantism: the Evolution of Poor Relief in Early Modern Emden* and has coedited *Religious Diaspora in Early Modern Europe: Strategies of Exile* and *Signs and Wonders in Britain's Age of Revolution*.

Marc R. Forster (PhD, Harvard) is the Henry B. Plant Professor of History at Connecticut College. He is the author of three books on German Catholicism, *The Counter-Reformation in the Villages*, *Catholic Revival in the Age of the Baroque*, and *Catholic Germany between the Reformation and the Enlightenment*. He is the coeditor of several volumes and is a former president of the Sixteenth Century Society. He has earned several NEH Fellowships and a Guggenheim Fellowship.

Joel F. Harrington (PhD, Michigan) is Centennial Professor of History at Vanderbilt University. He has published seven books, including *Dangerous Mystic: Meister Eckhart and His Path to the God Within*, which has been recognized with a 2020 Literature Award from the American Academy of Arts & Letters, and *The Faithful Executioner: Life and Death, Honor and Shame in the Turbulent Sixteenth Century*, which has been translated into 13 languages and was named one of the best books of 2013 by *The Telegraph* and *History Today*. He is currently at work on books about the sixteenth-century robber baron Götz von Berlichingen and the mercenary adventurer Hans Staden.

Sigrun Haude (PhD, Arizona) is Walter C. Langsam Professor of European History at the University of Cincinnati. She is the author of *In the Shadow of "Savage Wolves": Anabaptist Münster and the German Reformation During the 1530s* as well as several chapters and articles on the Thirty Years' War, Anabaptism, and gender. She is the coeditor of *Challenging Orthodoxies: The Social and Cultural Worlds of Early Modern Women*, and her monograph *Coping with Life During the Thirty Years' War (1618–1648)* is forthcoming.

Susan C. Karant-Nunn (PhD, Indiana) is Emerita Director, Division for Late Medieval and Reformation Studies, and Emerita Regents' Professor of History at the University of Arizona. Her most recent authored monograph is *The Personal Luther: Essays on the Reformer from a Cultural Historical Perspective*. She is a former president of the Sixteenth Century Society and is the proud recipient of their Medal of Honor, which she received alongside Merry Wiesner-Hanks.

Christine Kooi (PhD, Yale) is a professor of History at Louisiana State University. She is the author of numerous articles, as well as of *Liberty and Religion: Church and State in Leiden's Reformation* and *Calvinists and Catholics in Holland's Golden Age*. She is a former president of the Sixteenth Century Society, and is working on a survey of the Reformation in the Low Countries between 1500 and 1620.

Amy E. Leonard (PhD, Berkeley) is Associate Professor of History at Georgetown University. Her research focuses on women, gender, and sexuality in Reformation Germany. Her main publications include *Nails in the Wall: Catholic Nuns in Reformation Germany*; with Karen Nelson, eds, *Masculinities, Childhood, Violence*; "Female Religious Orders," in *A Companion to the Reformation World*, ed. R. Po-Chia Hsia; "The Personal is Political: Convents in the Holy Roman Empire," in *Politics and Reformation: Studies in Honor of Thomas A. Brady, Jr.* Christopher Ocker, ed.

Elizabeth A. Lehfeldt (PhD, Indiana) is Professor of History and Mandel Professor in Humanities at Cleveland State University. She is the founding dean of the Jack, Joseph and Morton Mandel Honors College at Cleveland State and former vice president of the Teaching Division of the American Historical Association and a former president of the Sixteenth Century Society. She has published extensively on the subject of female monasticism including *Religious Women in Golden Age Spain: the Permeable Cloister*, various essays, and articles in the *Journal of Medieval and Early Modern Studies*, *Sixteenth Century Journal*, and *Archive for Reformation History*.

Carole Levin (PhD, Tufts) is Willa Cather Professor of History at the University of Nebraska. She is the author or editor of eighteen books, including *The Heart and Stomach of a King: Elizabeth I and the Politics of Sex and Power*, *Dreaming the English Renaissance*, and *Shakespeare's Foreign Worlds*, coauthored with John Watkins. She has held fellowships at the Newberry Library, the Folger Shakespeare Library, and the Institute of Advanced Study at the University of Warwick, and was a Fulbright Scholar at the University of York.

Raymond A. Mentzer (PhD, Wisconsin) holds the Daniel J. Krumm Family Chair in Reformation Studies in the Department of Religious Studies, University of Iowa. His most recent publications are *Les registres des consistoires des Églises réformées de France, XVIe–XVIIe siècles: un inventaire* and *A Companion to the Huguenots*, coedited with Bertrand Van Ruymbeke. He is a former president of the Sixteenth Century Society. He is currently preparing a study of material culture and the liturgy in the French Reformed tradition.

Marjorie Elizabeth Plummer (PhD, Virginia) is the Susan C. Karant-Nunn Professor of Reformation and Early Modern European History in the Division for Late Medieval and Reformation Studies at the University of Arizona. Her publications include *From Priest's Whore to Pastor's Wife: Clerical Marriage and the Process of Reform in the Early German Reformation*, and articles on marriage, gender, historical memory, monasticism, and Protestant nuns. She is coeditor of *Ideas and Cultural Margins in Early Modern Germany*, *Archeologies of Confession: Writing the German Reformation, 1517–2017*, *Topographies of Tolerance and Intolerance: Responses to*

Religious Pluralism in Reformation Europe, Names and Naming in Early Modern Germany, and *Cultural Shifts and Ritual Transformations in Reformation Europe.*

Allyson M. Poska (PhD, Minnesota) is Professor of History at the University of Mary Washington in Fredericksburg, Virginia and the author of four books: *Gendered Crossings: Women and Migration in the Spanish Empire; Women and Authority in Early Modern Spain: The Peasants of Galicia,* winner of the 2006 Roland H. Bainton Prize for best book in early modern history; *Women and Gender in the Western Past* (coauthored with Katherine French), and *Regulating the People: The Catholic Reformation in Seventeenth-Century Spain.* She is also the coeditor of *The Ashgate Research Companion to Women and Gender in Early Modern Europe.* She has served as a member of the executive council of the Sixteenth Century Society, the executive board of the Society for Spanish and Portuguese Historical Studies, and as president of the Society for the Study of Early Modern Women.

Ulrike Strasser (PhD, Minnesota) is Professor of History at the University of California, San Diego. She held previous appointments at the University of California at Irvine and as a Clark Professor at UCLA. Strasser is the author of the award-winning monograph *State of Virginity: Gender, Politics, and Religion in a Catholic State.* She is coeditor of the Routledge volume *Gender, Kinship, Power: A Comparative and Interdisciplinary History*; *Cultures of Communication: Theologies of Media in Early Modern Europe and Beyond*; and *Explorations and Entanglements: Germans in Pacific Worlds From the Early Modern to the Modern Period.* Her new monograph *Missionary Men in the Early Modern World: German Jesuits and Pacific Journeys* is scheduled to be released in fall 2020.

Nicholas Terpstra (PhD, Toronto) is Professor and Chair of History at the University of Toronto. He has written numerous books on topics at the intersection of politics, religion, gender, and charity, including *Religious Refugees in the Early Modern World: An Alternative History of the Reformation,* and *Cultures of Charity: Women, Politics, and the Reform of Poor Relief in Renaissance Italy,* which won awards from the American Historical Association and the Renaissance Society of America. He has also edited a number of collections that look at some of the global contexts and implications of early modern religious reform movements, including *Global Reformations: Transforming Early Modern Religions, Societies, and Cultures,* and *Global Reformations Sourcebook: Convergence, Conversion, and Conflict in Early Modern Religious Encounters.*

John L. Thompson (PhD, Duke) is Professor Emeritus of Historical Theology and the Gaylen and Susan Byker Emeritus Professor of Reformed Theology at Fuller Theological Seminary. His research and writing interests address exegetical history and gender issues, especially with reference to the history of biblical interpretation. He has contributed to *A Companion to Paul in the Reformation* and *The Cambridge Companion to John Calvin,* and has written popular essays for *Sacred History* magazine and *Modern Reformation.* His study of the "texts of terror" in the history of exegesis appeared as *Writing the Wrongs: Women of the Old Testament among Biblical Commentators from Philo through the Reformation*, and he continued this line of inquiry in a more popular vein in *Reading the Bible with the Dead: What You Can Learn from the History of Exegesis That You Can't Learn from Exegesis Alone*.

Jeffrey R. Watt (PhD, Wisconsin) is the Kelly Gene Cook, Jr. Professor of History at the University of Mississippi. He is the author of *The Scourge of Demons: Possession, Lust, and Witchcraft in a Seventeenth-Century Italian Convent*, *Choosing Death: Suicide and Calvinism in Early Modern Geneva*, *The Making of Modern Marriage: Matrimonial Control and the Rise of Sentiment in Neuchâtel, 1550–1800*. He is also the editor of *From Sin to Insanity: Suicide in Early Modern Europe* and the coeditor (with Isabella M. Watt) of the *Registres du Consistoire de Genève au temps de Calvin*, vols. 6–10. He is a former president of the Sixteenth Century Society.

David M. Whitford (PhD, Boston) is Professor of Reformation Studies at Baylor University. He is a senior editor of *The Sixteenth Century Journal*. He is the author of *A Reformation Life* and *The Curse of Ham in Early Modern Europe* and has edited a number of volumes including *Martin Luther in Context* and (with Brian Brewer) *Calvin and the Early Reformation*.

FOREWORD: A REFLECTION ON MERRY WIESNER-HANKS

Natalie Zemon Davis

"I want you to meet an extraordinary graduate student!" So the late Robert Kingdon exclaimed about Merry Wiesner in the 1970s, when she was doing her doctorate at the University of Wisconsin. She was then deep in the research that would lead to her 1979 doctoral dissertation on "Birth, Death, and the Pleasures of Life: Working Women in Nuremberg, 1480–1620" and then, expanded by research in several other German cities, to her 1986 book *Working Women in Renaissance Germany*.[1] This was pioneering work. Those of us teaching the new history of women in the 1970s were still falling back on Alice Clark's 1919 classic, *Working Life of Women in the Seventeenth Century*, which was limited to England. The late Louise Tilly and Joan W. Scott were laying out a structure for treating women's place in the economy in their *Women, Work and the Family* of 1978, but its focus was on modern times. Olwen Hufton had opened the field for eighteenth-century France, especially in regard to rural women and the poor; Liliane Mottu-Weber and I were offering pictures of urban women at work respectively in sixteenth-century Geneva and Lyon; Heide Wunder was sketching a plan for the study of women in the labor force of early modern Germany.[2]

Wiesner's book was among the first, if not the first, to provide that study for Germany. She showed how the often-hidden history of women's work could be unearthed in the archives. The women were present throughout the city economy—domestic work and prostitution, the healing arts, trade in markets and streets, and in weaving and other crafts. With learning and clarity, Wiesner traced women's work as it changed over the life cycle and placed women in relation to men—as they worked in the household under the aegis of husbands, as they were the target of journeymen who refused to work at their side, and as they suffered more than men when town councils required additional training for certain employ. Yet the women were resilient, finding ways to have "continued involvement in [economic life] despite barriers and restrictions. As they were progressively excluded from the skilled crafts, they turned to sales and services or to those crafts which were informally organized."[3]

With characteristic breadth of interest, Wiesner began early to explore the relation of gender to religion. Along with Lyndal Roper and Susan Karant-Nunn, she centered women and the family in the history of the Reformation in German-speaking lands. In an early paper (1987) on "Luther and Women," Wiesner showed how problematic Luther's teachings were for the religious status of women: if men were to relinquish their celibacy in favor of a wife they should love, women were consigned to the role of obedient wife in a patriarchal household. She soon branched out into essays on the women themselves, where Protestant women, wives though they were, took initiative in shaping their religious lives and learning, and celibate women in convents, both Catholic and Lutheran, made decisions in defiance of clerical authority. Anticipating the historiographical element so powerful in her subsequent scholarship, Wiesner-Hanks reviewed the growing literature in the field in an essay "Towards a Gender Analysis of the Reformation." Accounts of women must not be left in a side channel, however. Instead, the history of women must be integrated into the main narrative of religious change.[4]

Wiesner-Hanks went on to do precisely that herself. She began in 1993 with the centuries and region she knew well from her own research: *Women and Gender in Early Modern Europe*.[5] Written for a large audience, including undergraduate students, the book had an elegant structure. Wiesner-Hanks opened it with an introduction on the prescriptive ideas and laws governing women's lives in the early modern period and then organized the book around the themes central in the western philosophical tradition: Body (the women's life cycle, women's work); Mind (women's literacy, writing, and the creation of culture); and Spirit (religion and witchcraft). A prize-winner and soon appearing in later editions, *Women and Gender* was among the books leading to an invitation to write an entire volume on the early modern period for the Cambridge History of Europe (2006). It exists today with a companion website, created by Wiesner-Hanks so that readers can have access to sources, maps, and much more.[6]

Meanwhile Wiesner-Hanks had decided to deepen and expand her early picture of the regulation of women's conduct by looking at the realm of male and female sexual behavior in all its expressions. *Christianity and Sexuality in the Early Modern World: Regulating Desire, Reforming Practice* appeared in 2000.[7] Moved by a new interest in world history, Wiesner-Hanks set her account not only in Europe but also in Latin and North America, Africa, and Asia, where missionaries, soldiers, and settlers had taken their Catholic and Protestant sentiments and institutions. In each setting, she looked at attitudes and practices in regard to sex, both within and outside of marriage, before early modern Christian reformers got to work. She then moved to the teachings, pressures, and institutions established to keep human sexuality strictly within the boundaries of lawful marriage. No sexual adventures were to be had before marriage or outside of the marriage bed, and certainly no sexual encounters with someone of the same gender. Indeed, within marriage itself the sex should not be limitless but contained within proper and moderate limits.

On the whole, Wiesner-Hanks found the early modern Christian enterprise relatively successful in winning assent to the centrality of marriage, especially when it coincided with the interests of families themselves and their plans for inheritance. As for societies that practiced polygamy, marriage was important, but Christian missionaries were not going to persuade the men to give up their multiple—and to them legitimate—wives. Early modern Christianity lost the battle of stamping out sex before marriage and between persons of the same gender, so Wiesner-Hanks showed, but the opprobrium cast upon these intimacies and the punishment wrought upon them, especially the latter, intensified the guilt with which they were practiced. Wiesner-Hanks's *Christianity and Sexuality*, with its down-to-earth detail on sermons, courts, and behavior, was an important corrective to the schema of Michel Foucault's volumes on the history of sexuality and, in its geographical breadth, a complement to the new histories of sexuality in Europe.[8]

Merry Wiesner-Hanks had consulted myriad studies for her books on early modern times and had deftly woven their findings into her broad comparative portraits. This mastery and her enthusiasm for the sources for historical study led her to produce a remarkable series of books to be used in the classroom. These were often done in collaboration with others, exhibiting a scholarly style that was especially inspiring when put to the use of the history of women. Already in 1996, she and Joan Skocir had published a set of translated texts on *Convents Confront the Reformation: Catholic and Protestant Nuns in Germany*. *Luther on Women: A Sourcebook*, prepared with Susan Karant-Nunn, followed in 2003. *A Companion to Gender History*, coedited with Teresa Meade, was published in 2004. About the latter, Bonnie Smith, a pioneer in the history of women and gender, has commented, "One of my go-to books (were it not blasphemous, I'd say my Bible) is the *Companion to Gender History* [Wiesner-Hanks] created with Teresa Meade. Each essay is a gem, useful and brilliant."[9]

The essays chosen by Meade and Wiesner-Hanks for that volume were written by historians of Africa, Asia, Europe, and the Americas, and ranged in time from prehistory through the present. For Wiesner-Hanks, the collection reflected her transformative entrance into world history, not only in early modern times but also over the millennia. Her interest in gender and religion surely facilitated this transnational move: as she herself said, through migration and intermarriage, "women acted as intermediaries between local and foreign cultures" in many parts of the world, while sixteenth-century religious movements readily jumped political borders.[10] In 2005, in her *Age of Voyages, 1350–1600*, Wiesner-Hanks constructed European travel to different parts of the globe as a central thread in her narrative. She was soon working with others to create volumes on world history and was then herself named editor in chief of the seven volumes of the prestigious *Cambridge World History*, appearing in 2015.[11] There she ensured the participation of at least some non-western scholars in an interdisciplinary account of humankind from Paleolithic times to our own day. In the early modern volume, Wiesner-Hanks herself wrote the essay on "Gender and Sexuality." She stressed the social and cultural themes that had been her hallmark: migration and intermarriage and their consequences; third gender and transgenders; and gender and sexuality in religious transformation, with examples from Europe, India, Korea, and Japan. The evidence confirmed, so she suggested, the "fluid and performative nature of gender and sexuality."[12]

Meanwhile, Wiesner-Hanks had written two books of her own, which show her remarkable range and her commitment to making the human past available to many readers. One was *A Concise History of the World* (2015), a vivid account compressed in less than four hundred pages.[13] Wiesner-Hanks followed changes over the centuries in production, colonization and its unraveling, the shapes of hierarchical social structures, and the like. Throughout, the family, gender, and sexuality are part of the story. These subjects are now an accepted inclusion in global history, for which Merry Wiesner-Hanks can be accredited as the major agent.

I conclude, however, with one of my favorites, *The Marvelous Hairy Girls: The Gonzales Sisters and their Worlds* (2009).[14] Here Wiesner-Hanks returned to the kind of local, in-depth study she had done earlier on women at work in sixteenth-century German cities, but enriched by her wider perspectives. Petrus Gonzalez and his family are the center of her book. Born in the Canary Islands with his face covered with hair (*hypertrichosis*), Gonzalez was taken as a boy to the court of the French king Henri II, and—oddity though he was—was educated with the other court children. Catherine de Medici married him off to a smooth-faced woman, who gave him several children, including three hairy-faced daughters and two hairy-faced sons. Wiesner-Hanks puts their story together, especially from the paintings and woodcuts made of them by artists of the day, and also ties the contemporary fascination with them to other European beliefs. Hairy-faced people could be linked to old beliefs about wild men and the current fascination with monsters, strange births, and other curiosities. God, of course, could always be the source of such miracles. And then there was the question of gender, treated in delicious lines in this book:

> When people looked at the Gonzales sisters, or their pictures, they saw beasts or monsters as well as young women, but this was also true when they looked at most women. The ancient Greek philosopher Aristotle, whose ideas were still powerful in the sixteenth century, had described women as monsters because they were not as perfect as men.[15]

Merry Wiesner-Hanks has major books on gender and its cultural implications, more gifts from the bounty of her scholarship.[16] With her characteristic modesty, in her "Preface" to the *Cambridge World History*, she echoed two historians of India in her hope to stimulate discussion and the quest for new knowledge. As can be attested by her many readers and others touched by her teaching, she has more than delivered in those hopes. Lyndal Roper has commented on "that sense of life imbuing all her scholarship, which is deeply generous. Merry has been a feminist activist in the academy and she has changed it."[17] I think back to Christine de Pizan's *City of Ladies,* the first book I read on the history of women and then used to open every course I taught on that subject. How Christine would have marveled at Merry Wiesner-Hanks's contribution! How she would have welcomed Merry into that honored City!

Notes

1 Merry E. Wiesner-Hanks, *Working Women in Renaissance Germany* (New Brunswick, NJ: Rutgers University Press, 1986).
2 Alice Clark, *Working Life of Women in the Seventeenth Century* (London: Routledge, 1919); Louise A. Tilly and Joan W. Scott, *Women, Work and Family* (New York and Toronto: Holt, Rinehart and Winston, 1978); Olwen Hufton, *The Poor of Eighteenth-Century France* (Oxford: Clarendon Press, 1974); Heide Wunder, "Zur Stellung der Frau im Arbeitsleben une ind der Gesellschaft des 15–18 Jahrhunderts: Eine Skizze," *Geschichtsdidaktik* 3 (1981): 239–251; Liliane Mottu-Weber, "Les femmes dans la vie économique de Genève," *Bulletin de la société d'histoire et d'archéologie de Genève* 16 (1979): 381–401; Natalie Zemon Davis, "Women in the Crafts in Sixteenth-Century Lyon," *Feminist Studies* 8, no. 1 (Spring 1982): 46–80.
3 Wiesner-Hanks, *Working Women*, 194.
4 Merry E. Wiesner-Hanks, "Luther and Women: The Death of the Two Marys," in Jim Obelkevich, Lyndal Roper and Raphael Samuel, eds. *Disciplines of Faith. Studies in Religion, Politics and Patriarchy* (London and New York: Routledge and Kegan Paul, 1987), 295–310; "The Reformation of the Women," originally published in 1993 in the *Archiv für Reformationsgeschichte. Sonderband Washington* (Gütersloh: Gerd Mohn, 1993), 193–208, and reprinted in Merry E. Wiesner-Hanks, *Gender, Church, and State in Early Modern Germany. Essays by Merry E. Wiesner* (London: Longman, 1997) 63–78. "Ideology Meets the Empire: Convents and the Reformation," originally published in 1992 in *Germania Illustrata: Essays Presented to Gerald Strauss*, ed. Andrew Fix and Susan C. Karant-Nunn (Kirksville, MO: Sixteenth-Century Essays and Studies, 1992), 181–196, and reprinted in Wiesner-Hanks, *Gender, Church and State*, 47–62. Merry E. Wiesner-Hanks, "Beyond Women and the Family: Towards a Gender Analysis of the Reformation," *The Sixteenth-Century Journal* 18, no. 3 (1987): 311–321.
5 Merry E. Wiesner-Hanks, *Women and Gender in Early Modern Europe* (Cambridge: Cambridge University Press, 1993), second edition, 2000; third edition, 2008. *Women and Gender in Early Modern Europe* was given the 1995 Choice Outstanding Academic Books Award.
6 Merry E. Wiesner-Hanks, *Early Modern Europe, 1450–1789*, Cambridge History of Europe, vol. 2 (Cambridge: Cambridge University Press, 2006; 2nd ed. 2013); Cambridge University Press Online Resources, Supplementary website for the second edition of Merry E. Wiesner-Hanks, *Early Modern Europe, 1450–1789*. See http://www.cambridge.org/features/wiesnerhanks/default.html
7 Merry E. Wiesner-Hanks, *Christianity and Sexuality in the Early Modern World: Regulating Desire. Reforming Practice* (London: Routledge, 2000; 2nd ed. 2010).
8 Michel Foucault, *Histoire de la sexualité*, 3 vols. (Paris: Gallimard: 1976–1984).
9 Merry E. Wiesner-Hanks, ed. and Joan Skocir and Merry E. Wiesner-Hanks, trans., *Convents Confront the Reformation: Catholic and Protestant Nuns* (Milwaukee: Marquette University Press, 1996); Susan C. Karant-Nunn and Merry E. Wiesner-Hanks, ed., *Luther on Women: A Sourcebook* (Cambridge: Cambridge University Press, 2003); Teresa A. Meade and Merry E. Wiesner-Hanks, eds., *A Companion to Gender History* (Malden, MA: Blackwell, 2004). Email communication of Bonnie Smith, 2 April 2018.

10 Merry E. Wiesner-Hanks, "Early Modern Women and the Transnational Turn," *Early Modern Women. An Interdisciplinary Journal* 7 (Fall 2012): 191–202, quotation 199. See also her essays "Women's History and World History Courses," *Radical History Review* 91 (Winter 2005): 133–150 and "World History and the History of Women, Gender and Sexuality," *Journal of World History* 18 (March 2007): 53–68.

11 Merry E. Wiesner-Hanks, *An Age of Voyages, 1350–1600* (New York: Oxford University Press, 2005). In 2000, Merry E. Wiesner-Hanks was coauthor, along with Paul V. Adams, Peter Stearns, Erik Langer, and Lily Hwa of *Experiencing World History* (New York: New York University Press, 2000). *Cambridge World History*, editor in chief, Merry E. Wiesner-Hanks, 7 vols. (Cambridge: Cambridge University Press, 2015), "Preface" by Wiesner-Hanks, 1:xv–xx, and reprinted in all volumes.

12 Merry E. Wiesner-Hanks, "Gender and Sexuality," *Cambridge World History,* vol. 6, Part I, ed. Jerry H. Bentley, Sanjay Subrahmanyam, and Merry E. Wiesner-Hanks, 133–156, quotation on 154.

13 Merry E. Wiesner-Hanks, *A Concise History of the World* (New York: Cambridge University Press, 2015).

14 Merry E. Wiesner-Hanks, *The Marvelous Hairy Girls: The Gonzalez Sisters and their Worlds* (New Haven and London: Yale University Press, 2009).

15 Wiesner-Hanks, *Hairy Girls*, 10.

16 Urmi Engineer and Merry Wiesner-Hanks, *A Primer for Teaching Women/Gender/Sexuality in World History* (Duke University Press, September 2018), and Merry Wiesner-Hanks, ed., *Gendered Temporalities in the Early Modern World* (University of Amsterdam Press, May 2018).

17 Email communication from Lyndal Roper, 18 April 2018.

ACKNOWLEDGMENTS

Merry Wiesner-Hanks has spent her career looking at the lives of people; women and men living their lives in all of its complexity and richness, in times of triumph and adversity. This book is our tribute to her scholarship—but also, on a deeper level—to Merry the person. A mentor. A generous colleague. A friend. The idea for the book was hatched in the most appropriate of places—in an evening chat with friends at the Sixteenth Century Studies Conference. Merry has been a member of the SCSC since its early days. She is a former president, recipient of its prestigious SCSC Medal, and is a senior editor of the society's journal—*The Sixteenth Century Journal*. That evening, the group of 8–10 quickly settled on the major themes such a hoped-for volume would include. We settled on editors. We even began to narrow down possible contributors. Contributors were easy to enlist. We should say that one contributor who heartily agreed and had even begun to draft an essay is not included here. Anne Jacobson Schutte passed away before she could complete her essay and we are sorry we could not include it. Other life events, including a significant illness and a pandemic, colluded to delay this volume a bit longer than we had hoped. But we are pleased with the depth and breadth of the completed volume. We hope you, and Merry, are likewise pleased.

We owe a debt of gratitude to the clandestine organizing committee from that evening at SCSC. You know who you are. We do as well, and we thank you for helping us to get this ball rolling. Two graduate students from Baylor helped proof-read and copy-edit all of the essays. The book would have considerably more typographical errors and mistakes without the close attention of Scott Prather and Erik Lundeen. Isabel Voice and the team at Routledge and Taylor and Francis were a pleasure to work with and helped ensure a quality product of which all of us can be proud. The blind reviewers for Routledge recommended a number of very helpful changes to the volume and made it much stronger. We do not know who you are, but we offer you our deepest thanks.

Finally, some personal thanks. To Merry's husband Neil and their sons Kai and Tyr, thanks for keeping our secret for so long and making the surprise so fantastic. Well done! We also wish to thank our spouses, who have heard a lot about Merry over the time we have worked on this and who patiently let us edit and fiddle and bring this about. They probably felt like she was a member of the family on more than one occasion. Stiff and Laurel enrich our lives and, honestly, our scholarship as well.

INTRODUCTION

In 1973, when Merry Wiesner-Hanks began graduate school at the University of Wisconsin-Madison, the study of women in the Reformation and early modern period was in its infancy. To some degree, Roland Bainton's 1971 book, *Women in the Reformation: Germany and Italy*, had offered an important corrective to the scholarship focused on men, but its attention to mostly nobility and reformers' wives left many women out of the story. The important and field-defining work in the early 1970s of Miriam Chrisman, Natalie Zemon Davis, Olwen Hufton, and Nancy Roelker provided different models for Wiesner-Hanks, which questioned traditional assumptions and broadened the lens of inquiry.[1] Her dissertation and subsequent book, *Working Women in Renaissance Germany*, pioneered new methods and materials for the study of early modern women.[2] Her advisor, Robert Kingdon, would later remark that his book *Adultery and Divorce in Calvin's Geneva* would never have been written—or even considered—had it not been for Wiesner-Hank's dissertation and the influence of her questions on his thinking.[3] In this, as with everything in her career, Wiesner-Hanks showed herself to be ahead of the curve, leading the way in transforming a discipline.

This introduction will show how the field of women and gender studies has developed, where it is going, and how that evolution is reflected in the work and influence of Wiesner-Hanks. With 21 books (including coauthored works and editions) and over one hundred articles, Wiesner-Hanks has defined a field and opened innumerable doors of inquiry. In this collection, however, we have chosen to trace the development of the field through one of Wiesner-Hanks' most transformative works: *Women and Gender in Early Modern Europe*.[4] More than just a textbook, *Women and Gender* both represented and molded a field, with each new edition responding to the rapidly evolving scholarship on women and gender studies. Between 1993 and 2019, the bibliography grew so dramatically that Wiesner-Hanks had to move it online so as not to overwhelm the print version.

She also added new chapters on gender and power and gender and the colonial world to better represent the directions of new research. The many editions of this book, which Cambridge University Press almost did not publish because so many board members thought of gender as a passing fad, embodies the development of our field.[5]

One of the primary concerns of the first edition was periodization. Returning women to the historical record raised questions about the accepted historical trajectory. Though Jacob Burkhardt could write with confidence in 1878 that during the Renaissance "women stood on a footing of perfect equality with men," Joan Kelly was closer to the mark when she answered her own question about whether or not women had a Renaissance with a resounding no.[6] Following Kelly's lead, Wiesner-Hanks questioned the traditional periodization and meaning of the Renaissance in terms of its relevance for women's history, leading to one of the most innovative aspects of her text: its organization. Rather than structuring the book chronologically, she split it into three sections—Body, Mind, and Spirit, divisions that better embraced the totality of the female experience. In addition to moving beyond chronology to structure the book, Wiesner-Hanks reconsidered chronological labels, preferring the term "early modern," over the traditionally masculine conceptions of Renaissance and Reformation, noting "every development of the [early modern] era brought change to the lives of many women and stunning transformation to the lives of others."[7]

Embracing women's lives and lived experiences, though, raised questions for some and concerns for others. The introductions to the first two editions, thus, focused on explaining the origins of women's history, including the uneasy relationship between a history focused solely on women and more traditional ones. Women's history first gained prominence in the late 1960s and early 1970s, inspired by social history and the second wave of feminism. The focus of this early generation of scholars was self-consciously on women, though with, as Bainton exemplifies, most of the attention paid to those already famous—monarchs, queens, and the wives of notable men. This approach, a history only of "women worthies" (in Natalie Zemon Davis' words) or "add women and stir," (as Wiesner-Hanks described it) often marginalized the women brought into the historical record; they were incorporated but the mainstream narrative was still overwhelmingly male. Indeed, many of these women were only in the new narrative because of the men in their lives. What made the work of Chrisman, Zemon Davis, and Wiesner-Hanks so important was that it broke from this model; they wrote history that tried to look at *all* women, regardless of class or relationship to men.

Soon there were calls to broaden women's history (and by some accounts, make it more relevant) by looking at gender, not just women. Already in 1976, Zemon Davis had noted that women's historians "should be interested in the history of both women and men" in order to understand the full spectrum of life as it was lived and experienced.[8] A decade later, Joan Scott would build on this foundation and offer a powerful argument for a more theoretically inclusive focus of inquiry. In her famous essay (currently the most downloaded article ever published in the *American Historical Review*) she stated that "women and men were defined in terms of one another, and no understanding of either could be achieved by entirely separate study."[9] Gender, along with race and class, needed to be understood as a construct that affected every sphere in history.

It may be hard now to remember how controversial the idea of gender history seemed initially, and not just to traditional, male-focused historians. Among a number of women's historians resentment was high, with many noting that it had taken years to insert women into the conversation, and that the effort to broaden the subject and make it more "inclusive," would simply end in their exclusion, once again. As Joan Hoff wrote, this new focus would only "eliminate the category of woman."[10] Unfortunately, the new gender research could also be overly theory-laden and impenetrable, embracing what has been called the linguistic turn, with a focus on discourse rather than actions. Some worried the cultural construction of gender downplayed historical context and ignored material reality, taking away female agency and obscuring women yet again.[11]

Wiesner-Hanks made a powerful intervention in these intellectual debates by using both Women *and* Gender in the title of her text, making clear that she saw benefits to both approaches. She embraced gender, seeing it as "a new lens" that helps us "ask the large questions, the ones that make us rethink all that has been learned until now."[12] Translating the theory for her audience, she showed how the linguistic turn opened new avenues for interpretation, while never losing sight of her female actors. Over the years, women, gender, and theory have come to a truce; as Lynn Hunt concluded in 2015 "most historians have simply moved on, incorporating insights from postmodern positions but not feeling obliged to take a stand on its epistemological claims."[13]

By the time the second edition of *Women and* Gender appeared in 2000, the field had been further transformed by more sustained studies on sexuality and masculinity. Many who studied women and gender often used the terms interchangeably, with the tacit understanding that the gender they were talking about was always female. Men were often left out of the conversation, as though their gender was static and universal and did not need to be deconstructed and analyzed. However, the new historians of masculinity argued that we gain a deeper understanding of the real power of gender over people's actions when we study *both* men and women. Indeed, gender history's call for inclusivity was fortified and invigorated by the development of masculinity studies, which has done much to broaden our understanding of the impact of gendered structures and ideologies on early modern women and men.

Not surprisingly, the renewed focus on men's experience often worried women's historians, with some warning against any separation of women and gender studies from an explicitly political/feminist agenda.[14] There were similar concerns with sexuality studies. Many noted that the field of women's history was overwhelmingly heteronormative and needed to move away from a strict binary view of male and female, to understand the more fluid nature of gender and sexuality.

Some questioned whether or not the male and female sexes even existed as separate entities; just as language and discourse needed to be deconstructed, so too did bodies and sex.[15] The very act of study did damage to the female "subject" and further undermined her existence. Scholars needed to acknowledge their own "disfigurement" of the historical record when they tried to reconstruct the past.[16] These "body wars" roiled the field with many arguing that this deconstruction not only took away women's agency and voice, but also denied them one aspect central to historical analysis: their physical nature.

Wiesner-Hanks had already intervened in this contentious debate in 1993, and in 2000 continued this work by showing how women's history and gender history could both be enriched by embracing a wider lens—including both masculinity and sexuality—and looking beyond Europe and North America. *Christianity and Sexuality in the Early Modern World* displays her deepening interest in world history and provides a breathtaking synthesis of religion and sexuality in Europe, Latin America, North America, Asia, and Africa.[17] In doing so, she showed how interrogating sexuality in a global context helped to broaden the field and pushed scholars to ask bigger and more complicated questions.

By 2008, Wiesner-Hanks, like many in the profession, had completely embraced the "global turn," which posits that we cannot understand Europeans, including the role of women and gender, without acknowledging their interaction with the non-European world. As Durba Ghosh writes, the "global turn" involves "our urgent need to understand and historicize our own globalized condition from the perspective of many locales."[18] Even though the text was still titled *Women and Gender in Early Modern Europe*, Wiesner-Hanks realized that nothing could be looked at with such geographic specificity. She added a new chapter on Gender in the Colonial World, and integrated non-European contexts throughout the book. The global turn, and its attention to non-Europeans, went hand in hand with intersectional analysis and critical race theory. Legal scholar Kimberlé Crenshaw coined the term intersectionality in 1989, though it has roots going back to the nineteenth century, and argues that one cannot separate race, class, or gender (or ethnicity, age, or sexuality) but rather they must be studied and understood together, to truly understand how they intersect.[19] By studying non-noble women Wiesner-Hanks was already taking an intersectional approach in her first book, before intersectionality had been developed as a framework; this work only deepened over her career.

Although the global turn is perhaps the most significant shift from the 1993 edition, Wiesner-Hanks describes other interdisciplinary turns (or rather lenses, denoting not a turning away but a shift in perspective) that have fundamentally transformed the field and her own work.[20] We see the spatial turn, which brings renewed focus to borders, frontiers, migration, and the natural and built environment.[21] The long-held spatial dichotomy of private (female) versus public (male) has been properly debunked as overly simplistic, but as we will see in many of the essays collected here, the tension between domestic/enclosed/female spaces and what are seen as more properly male spheres is still a potent area of historical inquiry.

In addition, Wiesner-Hanks' work has been informed by the study of material culture and the history of emotions.[22] Material possessions such as clothing and household goods are critical sources for understanding women's lives. Looking at the expression or performance of love, hate, anger opens new ways to see gender in action. The stereotypical designation of reason as male and the emotions as female exemplifies the importance of analyzing emotions from a gendered perspective.

The final debate currently agitating the field is in many ways a throwback to the main question of early women's history: how pervasive is/was patriarchy? The word "patriarchy" was not mentioned in Wiesner-Hanks' first introduction, although it informed much of the literature being reviewed and the lives of the women described throughout. The standard assumption was that patriarchy was such an overwhelming force in women's lives in early modern Europe that women could only succeed in exceptional circumstances. More recently, however, some gender historians have started to downplay the role of patriarchy, opting for descriptors such as "hegemonic masculinity." The many examples of women's agency cast doubt on the potency of patriarchy. Allyson Poska has argued that we need a more "agentic" model for women, allowing for a world that accepted women's power and autonomy in certain situations.[23] It is probably not yet time to reject the patriarchal model, but any notion that women did not have some flexibility and agency in the past, even as their lives were certainly constrained, is belied by the research. As Wiesner-Hanks notes, we need to "make patriarchy more complex, intersectional and dialectic."[24]

Beyond her scholarship, Wiesner-Hanks has led the expansion of women's and gender history. She has promoted the field in a variety of forums, for many years organizing and even hosting *Attending to Early Women,* a triennial symposium established in 1990, and serving on the editorial board of *Early Modern Women: An Interdisciplinary Journal.* More recently, as coeditor of the book series "Gendering the Late Medieval and Early Modern World," at Amsterdam University Press, she has been a driving force behind new and innovative scholarship. She has skillfully navigated scholarly conflicts and debates over how women, gender, sexuality and the myriad turns can all be best deployed to understand the past. And through it all, she has provided enduring support and calm leadership and been a mentor to a generation of scholars.

This volume, with its diversity of topics, fields, and interests of its authors, is a testament to her body of work. Not everyone in the volume describes themselves as a historian of women, gender, and/or sexuality, but that is somehow the point; Wiesner-Hanks has transformed the field so fundamentally that she made women and gender integral to any understanding of the early modern world. We have organized the 18 essays gathered here into three sections that harken back to the tripartite divisions of Women and Gender in Early Modern Europe, but the themes and topics raised cover the spectrum of women and gender studies, with cross-currents throughout. Although they do not explore all of the issues raised by Wiesner-Hanks over her career (race, in particular, is underrepresented), agency, space, masculinity, oppression, the body and sexuality, and above all, the myriad ways that gender informed early modern life take center stage.

The essays of Section One focus primarily on the body and sexuality and accept Wiesner-Hanks's challenge to see the body as a site of negotiation, power, constructed gender, and oppression. Joel Harrington shows the importance of the body for legal judgment, as a site of torture but also of justice performance, literally embodied in the physical corpse. The body has power, even in death, to affect the living beyond the purely spiritual or sentimental. Amy Leonard argues that the Reformation had a profound impact on views of the female body, as Martin Luther devalued virginity and defined a woman as a purely passive vessel, with no physical worth beyond what she brings to the marriage bed. Wiesner-Hanks was one of the first historians to study the importance of Luther's views of and on women, but as we see in David Whitford's essay, women also had a profound impact on Luther.[25] Whitford examines the reformer's sermons and lectures with careful attention to gender, sexuality, and masculinity. He shows how Luther's role as husband and father affected his personal and professional identity, transforming the sacred theologian into the embodied man. Following Merry Wiesner-Hanks's interest in the history of emotions, Jodi Bilinkoff examines the feelings of her monastic subjects and their masculine relationships. She shows the psychological, intellectual, and physical connections between protégé and presumptive saint in the preservation and promotion of the cult of St. John of the Cross.

Marc Forster describes the tension between female agency and patriarchal control, centered on female sexuality. Though Forster's women subjects felt empowered to use the German courts for their own purposes, there was still a danger in publicizing their complaints; women venturing into the public sphere often faced attacks, especially in sexual terms, as accusations of whore were ubiquitous. Carole Levin demonstrates male uneasiness with unruly women, especially when they venture into the public realm. Her essay is a story of both the continuing power of patriarchy as well as one of anxious masculinity, as men were pressured to control the women in their families.

The classic tension between public and private is even more pronounced in the next section, whether it be in the ambiguous space of the convent or the complicated relationship between home and outside world. The first three essays describe a particular type of female space, the convent, which, as we learned from Wiesner-Hanks, had more complexity and female autonomy than previously understood or acknowledged.[26] Again we see the tension between female agency and the particulars of patriarchy, as women (and men) navigated the gender norms of their time and resisted and/or were punished for their self-determination. The monastic space and its fraught relationship with enclosure, especially for women, was a powerful arena of negotiation, community, and identity-formation. Marjorie Elizabeth Plummer's nuns created a hybrid, multiconfessional institution, often at odds with the lay and religious authorities outside the cloister.[27] Plummer examines the decisions these women made regarding whether to stay or leave their convents. Many of the nuns praised for rejecting the "godless" cloister actually returned later, showing the enduring appeal of these communities. Sigrun Haude shows the fundamental importance of space and community for nuns, especially those under attack during the Thirty Years' War. These nuns desperately cling to, and modify, their enclosed spaces as a way to reaffirm their religious community in a time of great duress. Elizabeth Lehfeldt's essay looks more deeply at nuns and their agency transregionally and ultimately cross-confessionally. She describes the often-contentious relationship between male reformers and female religious in England and Spain and shows that the nuns were both pragmatic and at times deeply passionate about protecting their religious and personal prerogatives.

John Thompson's essay takes us to a different interior space, the private poetry of Anna Maria van Schurman. Her poems embrace the exegetical history of Genesis, but more importantly reflect a deeply embodied and gendered reading. While remaining deeply pious, there is a grittiness and emotional register in van Schurman that separates her from the men who proceeded her. Raymond Mentzer continues an analysis of gender and religious piety by examining the complicated nature of the public and private spheres in France. Women, whether Protestant or Catholic, were crucial religious actors in the private domestic sphere, collaborating with their husbands' public persona. Mentzer highlights the degree to which women created what can really only be called an alternate—even syncretic—vision of reform in the sixteenth century. Public and private had a different valence in the Dutch Republic where Protestantism was the public religion and Catholicism grudgingly tolerated in private. Christine Kooi shows again how women, as keepers of the home, were critical mediators. Dutch families navigated the intricacies of their confessional world with a careful negotiation between husband and wife and their public and domestic worlds; in the end, the home was a woman's realm of influence and power. Beyond the family, policing the boundaries of belief remained the prerogative of men alone. That is not to say that gender did not matter. Indeed, in the essay by Jeffrey Watt, the opposite becomes glaringly obvious. Watt demonstrates that gender affected not just who appeared before the religious tribunals in Geneva, but also what happened once a person arrived there.

In the final section, our contributors demonstrate how migration, religious persecution, and overseas travel defined and redefined gender roles. In Nicholas Terpstra's piece on the demographics of Christian exiles, women are again the arbiters and protectors of what happens in the private sphere. Much like Jewish and Muslim exiles, these female refugees became the preservers of a communal, religious identity as their households became sites of a "cultural confessionalism" despite their mobility. Timothy Fehler builds on Terpstra's work with a quantitative analysis of female refugees. We see how the fact that women were usually identified by their relationship to men (wife, widow, mother) and almost never by an occupation, could have severe economic repercussions. Fehler shows how the explosion of the refugee population affected the social welfare system in noticeably gendered ways.

The final three essays reveal the possibilities of the global turn. In Kathleen Comerford's contribution, the Jesuits define themselves by a spiritual mission geared toward world expansion. She stresses the ways these young men were trained for their futures in the mission field and how that training shaped their masculine identities as soldiers of Christ. Ulrike Strasser also notes the transregional aspect of the Jesuits, calling them "one of the first global organizations of the early modern world." Strasser's Jesuits, like the nuns of section two, interact in a particular enclosed space—the ships carrying them on foreign mission—where Jesuits molded and created their own unique brand of masculinity. They then translated these views about masculinity and femininity to their mission territories. We end the collection with a contribution by Allyson Poska, who argues that gendered analysis forces us to rethink both the nature of women's work and the evolution of the Atlantic economy. This chapter highlights the intersection of Wiesner-Hanks's deep influence on the history of women's work and her focus on global history. That intersection reveals how a new gendered and racialized view of agricultural work and expanded economic opportunities for women transformed European empires.

The essays collected here show what Merry Wiesner-Hanks has been teaching us for almost four decades: women are everywhere, gender affects everyone, and the early modern exists beyond Europe. We cannot understand religion, politics, economics, or any part of culture in general without considering women, gender, and sexuality. Every contributor to this volume has been guided or inspired by her, either as a mentor or as a supportive fellow scholar. We are very honored to present this volume in appreciation for an outstanding career that has changed both our lives and our profession.

Notes

1. Miriam U. Chrisman, "Women and the Reformation in Strasbourg 1490–1530," *Archive for Reformation History* 63 (1972): 143–68; Natalie Zemon Davis, "City Women and Religious Change in Sixteenth-Century France," in *A Sampler of Women's Studies*, ed. Dorothy Gies McGuigan (Ann Arbor: University of Michigan, Center for Continuing Education of Women, 1973), 17–45; Olwen Hufton, "Women in Revolution 1789–1796," *Past & Present* 53 (1971): 90–108; Nancy Lyman Roelker, "The Appeal of Calvinism to French Noblewomen in the Sixteenth Century," *The Journal of Interdisciplinary History* 11, no. 1 (1971): 391–418. Historians often point to Alice Clark, *Working Life of Women in the Seventeenth Century* (Augustus M. Kelley, 1968 (1919)) as the first sustained analysis of women in early modern Europe.
2. Merry E. Wiesner, *Working Women in Renaissance Germany* (New Brunswick, N.J: Rutgers University Press, 1986).
3. Robert Kingdon, *Adultery and Divorce in Calvin's Geneva*, Harvard Historical Studies 118 (Cambridge, Mass: Harvard University Press, 1995).
4. Merry E. Wiesner, *Women and Gender in Early Modern Europe* (Cambridge: Cambridge University Press, 1st edition: 1993; 4th ed. 2019).
5. Wiesner-Hanks, "Adjusting Our Lenses to Make Gender Visible," *Early Modern Women: An Interdisciplinary Journal* 12, no. 2 (Spring 2018): 6.
6. Jacob Burckhardt, *The Civilisation of the Renaissance in Italy*, trans. S. G. C. [Samuel George Chetwynd] (NY: MacMillan, 1890), 395; Joan Kelly, "Did Women

Have a Renaissance?," in *Becoming Visible: Women in European History*, ed. Renate Bridenthal and Claudia Koonz (Boston: Houghton Mifflin, 1977), 137–64.
7 Merry E. Wiesner-Hanks, "Do Women Need the Renaissance?" *Gender & History* 20, no. 3 (November 2008): 551.
8 Natalie Zemon Davis, "'Women's History' in Transition: The European Case," *Feminist Studies* 38, no. 3/4 (Spring-Summer 1976): 90.
9 Joan Wallach Scott, "Gender: A Useful Category of Historical Analysis," *American Historical Review* 91, no. 5 (1986): 1054.
10 Joan Hoff, "Gender as a Postmodern Category of Paralysis," *Women's History Review* 3, no. 2 (1994): 150. For more on this dispute see the introduction to Attending
11 Claudia Koonz, "Review: Joan Scott, Gender and the Politics of History," *The Women's Review of Books* 6, no. 4 (Jan 1989): 20; Christine di Stefano, "Who the Heck Are We? Theoretical Turns Against Gender," *Frontiers* 12, no. 2 (1991): 87–88; Tilly, "Gender, Women's History, and Social History," 452.
12 Merry E. Wiesner, "Beyond Women and the Family: Towards a Gender Analysis of the Reformation," *Sixteenth Century Journal* 38 (1987): 320, 321.
13 Lynn Hunt, *Writing History in the Global Era* (New York: W. W. Norton & Company, 2015), 39.
14 Mary Libertin, "The Politics of Women's Studies and Men's Studies," *Hypatia* 2, no. 2 (Summer 1987): 143–152. Judith Bennett makes a similar argument in *History Matters: Patriarchy and the Challenge of Feminism* (Philadelphia: University of Pennsylvania Press, 2006), 8.
15 Judith Butler, *Bodies That Matter: On the Discursive Limits of "Sex"* (New York: Routledge, 1993); Monique Wittig, "One is Not Born a Woman," in *The Straight Mind* (New York: Beacon Press, 1992), 9–20.
16 Kathleen Biddick, *The Shock of Medievalism* (Durham: Duke University Press, 1998), 187.
17 Merry E. Wiesner, *Christianity and Sexuality in the Early Modern World: Regulating Desire, Reforming Practice* (London: Routledge, 2000). The third edition just appeared in June of this year.
18 Durba Ghosh, "Another Set of Imperial Turns?," *The American Historical Review* 117, no. 3 (June 1, 2012): 778.
19 Michele Tracy Berger and Kathleen Guidroz, *Intersectional Approach: Transforming the Academy through Race, Class, and Gender* (Chapel Hill: The University of North Carolina Press, 2010).
20 Merry E. Wiesner-Hanks, "Adjusting Our Lenses to Make Gender Visible," *Early Modern Women: An Interdisciplinary Journal* 12, no. 2 (Spring 2018): 3–32.
21 Jo Guldi, "What Is the Spatial Turn?" at Spatial Humanities: University of Virginia Library, https://spatial.scholarslab.org/spatial-turn/what-is-the-spatial-turn/.
22 "AHR Conversation: The Historical Study of Emotions," with Nicole Eustace, Eugenia Lean, Julie Livingston, Jan Plamper, William M. Reddy, and Barbara H. Rosenwein, *The American Historical Review* 117, no. 5 (December 1, 2012): 1487–1531; "AHR Conversation: Historians and the Study of Material Culture," with Leora Auslander, Amy Bentley, Halevi Leor, H. Otto Sibum, and Christopher Witmore, *The American Historical Review* 114, no. 5 (December 1, 2009): 1355–1404.
23 Allyson M. Poska, "The Case for Agentic Gender Norms for Women in Early Modern Europe," *Gender & History* 30, no. 2 (2018): 354–365.
24 Merry Wiesner-Hanks, "Forum Introduction: Reconsidering Patriarchy in Early Modern Europe and the Middle East," *Gender & History* 30, no. 2 (2018): 320–330.
25 Merry E. Wiesner, "Luther and Women: The Death of Two Marys," in *Disciplines of Faith: Studies in Religion, Politics and Patriarchy*, ed. Jim Obelkevich, Raphael Samuel, and Lyndal Roper (New York: Routledge & Kegan Paul, 1987), 295–308; Susan C. Karant-Nunn and Merry E. Wiesner-Hanks, eds., *Luther on Women: A Sourcebook* (Cambridge: Cambridge University Press, 2003).

26 Merry E. Wiesner, "Ideology Meets the Empire: Reformed Convents and the Reformation," in *Germania Illustrata: Essays on Early Modern Germany Presented to Gerald Strauss*, ed. Andrew C. Fix and Susan C. Karant-Nunn (Kirksville, Mo.: Sixteenth Century Essays and Studies, 1992), 181–96.
27 What Wiesner-Hanks now describes as "queer." Merry E. Wiesner-Hanks, "Adjusting Our Lenses to Make Gender Visible," *Early Modern Women: An Interdisciplinary Journal* 12, no. 2 (Spring 2018): 4.

PART I
The body and manifestations of gender

1

THE STRANGE SURVIVAL OF THE BLEEDING CORPSE

Joel F. Harrington

In 1503, the village of Ettiswil, in the canton of Luzern, was scandalized by the brazen murder of a young woman, Margarete Spiessin, found strangled in her own bed. Almost immediately, according to chronicler Diebold Schilling, "many people began to murmur and suspect" the dead woman's husband, Hans Spiess, a mercenary with a local reputation as a "whoremonger, gambler, and spendthrift."[1] Spurred by the public uproar, the local *Schultheiss*, knight Peter Feren, ordered Spiess arrested, imprisoned in the local tower, and later interrogated with torture. When, after several sessions, the young mercenary still refused to confess, many villagers clamored for further torture, even to the death if necessary. Instead, Feren turned to an ancient means of adjudication in unresolved murder cases, in this instance suggested by Spiess himself. The body of the deceased, already in the ground for three weeks, was exhumed, washed with wine and water, and placed on a bier in the town square. The accused, naked and shorn, was escorted to the bier, which he ritually circled three times on his knees. In the presence of "seven trustworthy men"[2] (and many other eager spectators), Spiess then placed two fingers on the breast of his dead wife and swore a ritual oath: "As I hereby see and touch this dead body, I ask God, if I am in any way or form guilty of any encouragement, deed, favor, support, or help in her murder or death, that God Almighty make a public sign here of my guilt or innocence ... so help me God and all the saints."[3] Suddenly, according to the chronicler, "a foam began to flow out of her mouth, and the closer he came to her, the more steadily it foamed; and when he came still closer, a red mark suddenly appeared on her chest." When Spiess kneeled down and further protested his innocence, the corpse began to bleed, the blood running down the side of the bier. Upon this "miracle," Spiess finally broke down and confessed to the murder, for which he was later executed with the wheel. "Thus, one clearly sees that God lets no murder go unpunished," concludes the chronicler, and "no one should wonder or question whether there is a heaven or a hell."[4]

Cruentation, known to jurists as *ius cruentationis*, and more popularly as "the bier test" (*Barhprobe; l'épreuve du cercueil*), was ubiquitous in early modern Europe, particularly in northern regions, including France and the British Isles. A supposedly ancient Germanic method for identifying unknown murderers, this curious form of trial by ordeal enjoyed an exceptionally long lifespan in parts of Europe and North America, well into the nineteenth century. How do we account for this longevity, especially given the demise of most other forms of trial by ordeal by the thirteenth century? Even if cruentation were merely a spectacularly resilient popular superstition, its thriving in the midst of dramatic shifts in the early modern intellectual landscape bears closer examination. In fact, I suggest, it was cruentation's very murky epistemological foundation that made it useful to legal procedures of the time and thus insured its survival into the modern era.

Legal historians of the nineteenth century, the very time that the popular belief in cruentation was finally breathing its last breath, looked to the practice's origins to help explain its durability.[5] Trial by ordeal, in general, was absent from Roman law and appears to have originated among the Franks, whence it was later promulgated by Charlemagne.[6] Unlike the iron glove or boiling cauldron or even the duel, however, there is no mention of cruentation in any surviving source until some twelfth-century sagas. Most famously, in the *Niebelungenlied*, when Hagen approaches the corpse of the slain Siegfried on his bier, the dead body begins to bleed, thereby unveiling its murderer. Even here, though, as in other literary sources, the perpetrator was not actually suspected before the bleeding, but rather surprisingly revealed by the event.[7] The same is true of the first apparent real-life application during the murder investigation of a French abbot, Petrus Monoculus, in 1180.[8] There is in fact no reference to the practice in German law until the *Freisinger Rechtsbuch* of 1328, more than a hundred years after Lateran IV's prohibition of all trials by ordeal.[9] The circumstances of this delayed and curious "created tradition" is a worthy subject for another exploration.

Although the relatively late-appearing cruentation was thus probably not formally a trial by ordeal[10]—again, an ecclesiastically-banned legal procedure since 1215—it shared some important traits with the latter. The building of a popular consensus on guilt, for instance, was an integral aspect of all trials by ordeal, with the so-called facts of the event always open to the interpretation of spectators (not unlike the twelve traditional "oath-helpers"). Like other trials by ordeal, it also contained an oath of purgation and an appeal to divine intervention.

More importantly from the popular perspective, cruentation also allowed a deceased victim to accuse his or her murderer directly. The legal standing of dead persons was a particularly deeply entrenched legal concept in German lands, dating back to before Christianization and helps explain the broad appeal of cruentation.[11] Well into the fifteenth century, legal authorities permitted corpses to be brought to courtrooms, where they "participated" as either defendant or plaintiff.[12]

(There's actually an illustration of this in the most famous manuscript of the thirteenth-century *Sachsenspiegel*). By the later middle ages, many German courts began to bring merely the chopped-off right hand to the trial, so as to proceed with a "complaint with the dead hand." By the sixteenth century, this custom had been modified still further to allow for a wax facsimile of the dead hand or other "body signs" (*Lebenzeichen*), such as a finger, lock of hair, or favorite shirt.

Cruentation thus retained the miraculous aspect of other trials by ordeal, but also allowed the victim to play a part in examples of divine justice. Margarete Spiessin's dramatic exposition of her murderer husband carried enormous popular appeal in a culture still deeply shaped by the Mosaic Law's life-for-a-life justice. In his 1597 *Demonology*, James VI gives voice to this visceral attraction of the cruentation spectacle: "… for as in a secret murther, if the deade carcase be at any time thereafter handled by the murtherer, it wil gush out of bloude, as if the blud wer crying to the heaven for revenge of the murtherer, God having appointed that secret super-natural signe, for tryall of that secrete vnnaturall crime."[13]

Yet once more we return to the central question of why this particular popular custom survived the skepticism or condemnation that learned critics of the sixteenth and seventeenth centuries leveled against other allegedly supernatural means of resolving legal disputes. Why did Protestants in particular—among them learned jurists, physicians, and theologians—not just tolerate cruentation but in some cases actually endorse it—while simultaneously rejecting the miracles associated with saints and holy objects as either superstitious or diabolical? What was different about the bleeding corpse?

In the instance of early modern jurists, cruentation found a sweet spot in the gap between the commonly higher expectations for legal, and especially criminal, procedures and the commonly inadequate means of implementation, particularly in the nature of evidence and proof. During the sixteenth century, many legal jurisdictions throughout Europe established new civil and criminal codifications, which were intended to insure both greater consistency and greater efficiency among their respective courts. Roman-canonical principles shaped much of the new legislation, even in more resistant German lands. Emperor Charles V's 1532 imperial criminal code, or *Carolina*, for instance, allowed the Empire's constituent jurisdictions to retain many local customs in personnel and punishments, but at the same time it attempted to standardize procedure along inquisitorial—canonical—lines. Stymied by the frequent absence of two eye-witness accusers in many criminal cases—the standard Roman legal definition of proof—the *Carolina*'s drafters encouraged judges to aggressively gather as many other constitutive elements of proof as possible, what they called *indicia*, or indices, especially physical evidence (bloody clothing or weapons, burglary tools, etc.) or confession.[14] Yet recognizing that these indices themselves were often lacking, the code's authors felt impelled to provide detailed instructions for local legal authorities on one other means of building evidence: special inquisition, aka torture. Although the *Carolina* urged great restraint in relying on this "last resort," the code's unintended legacy turned out to be an unprecedented spread of what might be called enhanced interrogation throughout the Empire in a variety of criminal cases, most infamously in the pursuit of alleged witches.

The incomplete shift from an accusatorial to an inquisitorial form of criminal justice evident in the *Carolina* and most sixteenth-century criminal codifications in turn yielded a convenient niche for the medieval practice of cruentation. What laypeople clearly still viewed as a kind of divine intervention, most sixteenth-century jurists instead perceived as a valuable, constitutive indicator of proof. In other words, while earlier courts had treated the bleeding corpse as either a means of resolving disputed guilt (an *Entscheidungsmittel*) or as proof itself (a *Beweismittel*), sixteenth- and seventeenth-century jurists saw the psychologically-charged bier test as another form of enhanced interrogation, offering one more indicator of guilt or innocence. As a sole decider of guilt, cruentation had no standing among jurists; as part of a cumulative process of establishing proof, however, it could continue to play a role.

Most commonly, sixteenth-century jurists addressed whether an instance of apparent cruentation might be considered a *magnum indicium* of guilt, justifying torture, an *indicium remotum*, requiring other supplemental proof (*indicium ad inquirendum*), or no indicator at all (*indicium falsum*). Most Italian, French, and German jurists before 1550 agreed that such bleeding should be considered a major indicator, also known as an *indicium perfectum*, although they differed on whether the cause was natural or supernatural.[15] The Neapolitan Matteo d'Afflitto (d. 1510), for instance, considered cruentation the result of divine intervention, while the Cypriot Hieronymus Maggius (d. 1572) believed that the murderer gave special power to the blood of the victim, and the Bourges jurist Nicolas Boerius (1469–1539) thought that the enmity between two spirits triggered the effusion. Marcus Antonius Blancus (Marcantonio Bianchi; 1498–1548), displayed more profound skepticism about the validity of cruentation itself, but was in a distinct minority among legal experts.[16]

The legal role was thus consistently an ambiguous one, neither officially endorsed nor prohibited by most jurists or codes before the modern era. Neither the *Carolina*, nor its predecessor the *Bambergensis*, mentions cruentation at all—a significant omission considering other popular practices that were specifically condemned.[17] Yet it was clearly practiced widely, and not just in German lands.[18] Sometimes, as in the case of Hans Spiess, the ritual was requested by accused parties eager to clear their names, functioning as a kind of "purification oath" (*Reinigungseid*) before witnesses—and usually without it backfiring so spectacularly as it did for Spiess. On other occasions, suspected murderers were forced to undergo the ritual against their wills, sometimes successfully exonerating themselves and other times confessing in the face of apparent bleeding or movement by the cadaver. During the seventeenth century, cruentation's reinforcement of popular consensus made it an especially compelling weapon against accused witches. The famous trials of the English witch Jennet Preston of Pendle (1612) and the Scottish witch Christine Wilson of Dalkeith (1661) both included eyewitness accounts of alleged victims of their magic posthumously bleeding upon the women's approach of the corpses.[19] German witch prosecutors of the period also occasionally made use of similar evidence to authorize torture, citing cruentation's passing endorsement by the famous *Malleus Maleficarum*.[20]

Criminal prosecutors readily embraced eyewitness accounts of bleeding corpses when it suited their purposes. The English jurist Thomas Potts found cruentation "a great argument to induce a Jurie to hold him guiltie that shall be accused of murther, and hath seldome, or never, fayled in the Tryall."[21] Yet in no legal or literary account I have come across was cruentation in any form treated by a legal court as sufficient proof in the manner of a medieval trial by ordeal. Even Potts only cited one case where he considered evidence of posthumous bleeding decisive; in most other English cases, a failed or disputed instance of cruentation resulted in diminished sentences or outright acquittals.[22] In one German case described by the sixteenth-century Nuremberg executioner Frantz Schmidt, a suspected child murderer was brought before the body of a dead infant and even though the baby's cadaver apparently moved and began to bleed, the accused woman—who did not confess—was not tortured and received only a public flogging, not the usual death sentence for infanticide.[23] In other words, the sixteenth-century move towards professional judges, and inquisitorial procedure provided a check against the mob rule tendencies of late-medieval cruentation, even in cases of alleged witchcraft. At the same time, the door remained open to use of the practice as a possible indicator of guilt, somewhere between *mala fama* (bad reputation) and full confession under torture.

In typical lawyerly fashion, the informal inclusion of cruentation among the indices of innocence or guilt did not require jurists to take a position on whether the phenomenon itself was genuine. Most judges clearly harbored some doubts about the so-called miraculous revelation of a bleeding corpse and were wary about a return to medieval ordeals. Yet just as obviously, many learned people before the eighteenth century did believe in the reality of cruentation, that is, that for some natural or supernatural reason, the bodies of murder victims genuinely bled or otherwise altered in the presence of their murderers. To understand this credulity, we must turn to the other two groups of professionals who kept the bleeding corpse alive throughout the early modern period: physicians and theologians.

Natural explanations for what physicians called *cruentatio cadaverum* abounded during the sixteenth and seventeenth centuries.[24] Both legal and medical experts appeared sufficiently persuaded by multiple published accounts to agree with the physician and alchemist Andreas Libavius (1550–1616) that "it is not impossible for something of this kind to happen."[25] Contrary to their Italian counterparts, most northern Europeans viewed death as a gradual process, whereby a corpse became "more dead" during the weeks after a person's last breath. "During this liminal period," Katherine Park writes, the recently dead body is considered "active, sensitive, or semi-animate, possessed of a gradually fading life."[26] Francesco Paolo de Ceglia considers this north/south distinction to have been more determinative in the cruentation positions of early modern professionals than any religious or even philosophical factors.[27] Many northern natural philosophers, for instance, shared the opinion of the Dutch physician Lemnius (1503–1568) that a certain vegetable force remained in dead bodies, evidenced in the continued growing of hair and nails or the response of a cadaver's skin to moisture.[28] Perhaps, Lemnius speculated, powers of sympathy and antipathy remained in the blood after death, "so great is the force of secret nature."

Libavius concurred that "there is some force or power from nature in the cadaver by which, when friend or enemy is present, the spirit and the blood are moved."[29] But he firmly rejected the explanation of Paracelsus and his fellow chemical doctors, whose theory relied on the power of signs and words to alter nature—something Libavius decried as diabolical magic if it worked, superstition when it did not. The medical theories proposed by Libavius and other Aristotelians instead focused on the occult powers of human blood. Unlike the forensic use of swords and other murder weapons smeared with a special salve to identify culprits—another practice Libavius considered diabolical magic—cruentation worked because of the lingering passion in the victim's blood. It was, he stressed, a completely natural process that was triggered by a physical contact between a murderer's hand or breath and the residual vital spirit in the victim's blood. That process remained mysterious, thus occult, but was not in any way magical or supernatural.

Not all physicians agreed with Libavius. Many, such as the Coburger Andreas Livius (d. 1616) took the Paracelsan line on invisible spiritual forces at work.[30] But unanimity was not necessary for cruentation to retain a necessary degree of plausibility among learned men, or at least possibility. Early modern jurists did not need to know or understand such medical theorizing in order to come to the conclusion that their physician counterparts were not willing to rule out either the reality of cruentation or possible natural explanations for the phenomenon. Many would have sided with the physician François Ranchin (1560–1641), who concluded that the proximate cause of cruentation was simply unknowable: "God does not always adapt to our desires: He manifests his power when He pleases, and the miracles of His goodness we sometimes see by grace."[31] Most importantly for its remarkable longevity, cruentation did not rely on any magical explanations. The Restoration physician John Webster, a noted skeptic of witchcraft, firmly believed that "through the vehement desire of revenge, the irascible and concupiscible faculties do strongly move the blood ... to motion and ebullition."[32]

Meanwhile, the average layperson continued to see the bleeding corpse as fundamentally supernatural, a "controlled miracle," an instance of God allowing a dead spirit to achieve vengeance against an unpunished murderer. This perception, threatening a return to the medieval trial by ordeal, was hardly welcomed by most jurists, but it was nevertheless actively encouraged by a third group of professionals: pastors and other clerics. Most Protestant and Catholic theologians remained reticent on the subject, but Philip Melanchthon enthusiastically endorsed cruentation as a *signa ... divinitus addita*.[33] Melanchton's outlier position among learned divines was apparently widely shared at the parish level. As we have known at least since the early work of Keith Thomas, Protestant abolition of purgatory did not eliminate continuing apparitions of the unhappy dead, in both dreams and waking visions.[34] Murder victims could be especially relentless in their pursuit of justice, bent on exposing their murderers in various imaginative ways. Here, too, was a natural niche for cruentation, systematically exploited by religious authors eager to prove the hand of God at work in their own midst.

Popular pamphlets and sermons, often written as disguised sermons, made the most of such beliefs, underscoring their illustration of divine providence at work. Tiny scraps of incriminating evidence miraculously survive a devastating house fire; on a whim a farmer drains a pond and discovers two skeletons; evidence of poison is discovered when a dog or pig dies after eating a victim's vomit.[35] Here, too, was a natural niche for cruentation, systematically exploited by religious authors eager to prove the hand of God at work in their own midst. In one especially gruesome English account, a fortune-seeking father has his own three children murdered so that he can be free to marry a wealthy widow. When the hired killer is taken back to the house where the bodies are buried under the floorboard,

> the father being there also, the wondes began to bleede afresh, which the Crowner sawe, hee commanded the partie apprehended to looke upon the children, which hee did, and called them by their names, whereupon, behold the wonderfull works of God, for the fact being still denied, the bodies of the children, which seemed white like unto soaked flesh laid in water, sodainely received their former colour of bloude, and had such a lively countenance flushing in theyr faces, as if they had been living creatures lying asleepe.[36]

Significantly, the miraculous event causes the assassin to confess and implicate the children's father as well.

The bloodthirsty and avenging murder victim was of course also a staple of Elizabethan and Jacobean theater.[37] Shakespeare was especially fond of the topos and made frequent use of the accusing dead and guilty living in such works as *Richard III, Hamlet*, and *Macbeth*. As in explicitly moralistic pamphlets, divine providence often works through the guilty conscience of the murderer, recognizing the psychological dimension of cruentation and revenants that jurists exploited. In the anonymous *A Warning to Fair Women* (1599), observers to the bleeding corpse of John Beane interpret the event as providential, but the playwright is careful to introduce the powerful force of guilt at work in one of the murderer's asides to the audience:

> I gave him fifteen wounds,
> Which now be fifteen mouths do accuse me.
> In every wound there is a bloody tongue
> Which will all speak, although he hold his peace;
> By a whole jury I shall be accused.[38]

The discrediting of cruentation among learned professionals was a gradual process, with some physicians and theologians, such as the Berlin professor of medicine Michael Alberti (1682–1757), vigorously defending the phenomenon well into the eighteenth century.[39] Yet as early as 1519, Spaniard Antonio Gómez (d. ca. 1550) had begun to question the sufficiency of cruentation as a basis for torture.[40] One of the most devastating attacks on the internal logic of cruentation came from the Tuscan polymath Girolamo Maggi (1523–1572), whose treatise posed such questions as:

> Why does cruentation not occur in animals? Why does it not happen to a person who is injured, but not killed in battle? … Why does it also happen to those who, for example, are killed in their sleep and are unable to develop a desire for revenge against the killer? Why does it also take place when someone has been killed from a long distance (for example with a bullet)? … Why do animals not bleed in front of the butcher and the executed in front of the executioner? Why, on the contrary, do children bleed in the presence of mothers and the drowned in front of friends and relatives?[41]

Over the course of the sixteenth century, learned consensus shifted to the skeptical position, including the influential papal jurist Propsero Farinseius (1544–1618), Phillip II's legal advisor Giulio Claro (1525–1575), and leading jurists from the universities of Rostock, Wittenberg, and Tübingen.[42] In 1621, the law faculty of Tübingen unanimously rejected an appeal based on cruentation, thereby jeopardizing the ritual's legal standing in the 1609 Württemberg Criminal Ordinance.[43] According to Christoph Besold (1577–1638), "to proceed with torture based on this *indicium* alone would be an injustice."[44] The last German code to even mention cruentation was the Hessen-Darmstädtische Landesordnung of 1639.

The most decisive legal blow against cruentation in Germany was delivered by Benedict Carpzov in his 1635 magnum opus on Saxon criminal law, where he emphatically rejected cruentation as a reliable indicator of guilt and thus as a basis for torture or any other sanctions. Like most jurists of his day, Carpzov based his objection less on the practice's alleged occult nature than its susceptibility to popular manipulation. Writing during the waning days of the witch craze, he lamented the use of the bleeding corpse and other questionable indicators as justification for torture—another source of evidence that he found problematic to be used only in "extraordinary" cases.[45] Trained judges and their legal consultants, not frenzied lay spectators, should determine what constitutes proof in a murder case, and by this time few legal authorities were willing to enmesh themselves in the medieval spectacle of the bleeding corpse.

Like many intellectually discredited popular practices, cruentation continued to find its believers long after university-trained lawyers and doctors deemed it pure superstition. There are in fact a few accounts of the practice in nineteenth-century U.S. murder cases, as well as a famous episode in Mark Twain's *Adventures of Tom Sawyer*.[46] As the remarkably long life of the bleeding corpse finally drew to an end, however, the cause was less some vague disenchantment of the world than a final definitive shift from popular, accusatorial justice to professional courts and sophisticated legal codes. Cruentation had enjoyed a shadowy niche during that long early modern transition, not least because of the shortcomings of forensic investigations and evidence. With the decline of judicial torture in the eighteenth century and the simultaneous rise of modern police methods, the last medieval trial by ordeal lost not just its intellectual credibility but also its usefulness. As Malcolm Gaskill has written, "in modern murder trials, forensic evidence speaks for the dead; in early modern [Europe] the dead had to speak for themselves"—as bleeding corpses or accusatory ghosts.[47] Whether the murdered Margarete Spiessin or countless other historical victims would share such confidence in the effectiveness of modern law enforcement and justice is another question.

Notes

1 "Nu fieng mengcklich an murmeln und meynen…krieger, hurer, spiler, prasser." Alfred A.Schmid, ed., *Die Schweizer Bilderchronik des Diebold Schilling*, (Luzern: Faksimile-Verlag, 1981), 328–331. See also *Valerius Anshelm's, genannt Rüd, Berner-Chronik von Anfang der Stadt Bern bis 1526* (Bern: Haller, 1827), 254; Petermann Etterlin, *Kronica von der loblichen Eidgenossenschaft* (Aarau: Sauerländer, 1965), 319–320.
2 "Sieben gloupsamer mannen." *Die Schweizer Bilderchronik*, 330.
3 "Wie ich hie sich und berüere disen toten lib, so bitt ich gott, ob ich, in umbracht oder in sinem tode schuldig, rat, that, gunst, fürderung oder hilf than hab in inig wis oder gestalt, dass dann gott der allmächtig hie ein offenlich zeichen thüej miner schuld oder unschuld … und mir gott also helfe und alle heiligen." From the Luzerner Formelbuch of 1542, as cited in Jakob Baechtold, "Ueber die Anwendung der Bahrprobe in der Schweiz," *Romanische Forschungen, Festschrift Konrad Hofmann zum 70sten Geburtstag* (Erlangen: Junge, 1890), vol. 5:224.
4 "da fieng sy angendsan, warff ein schum zum mund uss, und je näher er zuohin kam, je vester sy anfieng shumen, und da er noch hinzuo kam, da entsprang is ein roter fleck an der styrnen … wunderzeichen…Darby man wol mag erkennen, das Gott kein mort ungestraffet lat und soll keiner wundern oder fragen, ob ein himmel oder ein hell syg." *Die Schweizer Bilderchronik*, 330.
5 The single best overview of premodern cruentation that I have encountered is the recent Francesco Paolo de Ceglia, "Saving the Phenomenon: Why Corpses Bled in the Presence of Their Murderer in Early Modern Science," in *The Body of Evidence: Corpses and Proofs in Early Modern European Medicine*, ed. Francesco Paolo de Ceglia (Leiden/Boston: Brill, 2020), 23–52. More valuable from the legal perspective is Hubert Ewers, "Die Bahrprobe," (Law dissertation: University of Bonn, 1951).
6 Robert Bartlett, *Trial by Fire and Water* (Oxford: Clarendon Press, 1988), 4–12.
7 Karl Lehmann, "Das Bahrgericht," in *Germanistische Abhandlungen zum LXX. Geburtstag Konrad von Maurers* (Göttingen: Dieterich, 1893), 28. Another early appearance is in Hartmut von Aue's adaptation of the *Yvain* of Chrétien de Troyes (ca. 1203). De Ceglia, "Saving the Phenomenon," 24.
8 Ewers, "Die Bahrprobe," 4. Cruentation is also discussed in the *Stadtrecht* of Visby (1341) and the *Landrecht* of Schwyz (1342); Ewers, 8.
9 Article 273; Lehmann, "Das Bahrgericht," 23.
10 For a summary of the debate among nineteenth-century German legal historians, see Lehmann, "Das Bahrgericht," 25–27.
11 See especially H. Brunner, "Das rechtliche Fortlebendes Toten bei den Germanen," *Deutsche Monatshefte für das gesamte Leben der Gegenwart* 12 (1907): 18–32.

12 Wolfgang Schild, "Zur strafrechtlichen Behandlung der Toten," in Norbert Stefenelli, ed., *Körper ohne Leben. Begegnung und Umgang mit Toten* (Vienna/Cologne/Weimar: Böhlau, 1998), 852–61.
13 *King James the First, Daemonologie (1597)*, ed. G. B. Harrison (London: John Lane, 1924), 80.
14 See especially articles six and twenty-two of the *Carolina*, discussed in Bernhard Heitsch, "Beweis und Verurteilung im Inquisitionsprozess Benedikt Carpzovs: zur Geschichte des Inquisitionsprozesses von der Constitutio Criminalis Carolina bis zu Benedikt Carpzovs Practica nova imperialis Saxonica rerum criminalium" (Law dissertation: University of Göttingen, 1964), 1–6.
15 Ewers, "Die Bahrprobe," 17–24. For further examples of this position among jurists, see De Ceglia, "Saving the Phenomenon," 36–37.
16 Marcus Antonius Blancus, *Tractatus de indiciis homicidii et proposito commissi; et de aliis indiciis homicidii & furti, ad legem finale ff. de quaestionibus* (Lyons, 1547).
17 See the few sixteenth-century legal codes cited in Lehmann, "Das Bahrgericht," 24.
18 For sixteenth-century cases, see Malcolm Gaskill, "Reporting Murder: Fiction in the Archives in Early Modern England," *Social History* 23, no. 1 (January 1998): 8–13; Baechtold, "Ueber die Anwendung," 225–230; Lehmann "Das Bahrgericht," 30ff.
19 David Pickering, *Lexikon der Magie und Hexerei* (Augsburg: Bechtermünz, 1999), 24.
20 Katrin Moeller, *Dass Willkür über Recht ginge. Hexenverfolgung in Mecklenburg im 16. und 17. Jahrhundert* (Bielefeld: Verlage für Regionalgeschichte, 2007), 186; "Teil I, Zweite Frage: Ob der Dämon mit dem Hexer mitwirke," *Malleus Maleficarum*, trans. Montague Summers (New York: Cosimo, 2007), 13.
21 Original cited in Gaskill, "Reporting Murder," 10.
22 The 1612 Lancaster conviction of Jenet Preston, where Potts claimed that evidence of cruentation decisively swayed the jury towards a guilty verdict. Thomas Potts, *The Wonderfull Dicouerie of Witches in the Covntie of Lancaster* ... (London: W. Stansby for John Barnes, 1612), 96.
23 Joel F. Harrington, *The Faithful Executioner: Life and Death, Honor and Shame in the Turbulent Sixteenth Century* (New York: Farar, Straus & Giroux, 2013), 56.
24 See the excellent discussion of medical explanations, both natural and occult, in De Ceglia, "Saving the Phenomenon," 39–47.
25 Bruce T. Moran, *Andreas Libavius and the Transformation of Alchemy* (Sagamore Beach, MA: Science History Publications, 2007), 282.
26 "The Life of the Corpse: Division and Dissection in Late Medieval Europe," *Journal of the History of Medicine and Allied Sciences* 50 (1995): 115. See also Norbert Stefenelli, "Sonderstellung des toten Körpers während seiner Anwesenheit im Bereiche der Lebenden," in Stefenelli, *Körper ohne Leben*, 31–33.
27 De Ceglia, "Saving the Phenomenon," 51–52.
28 Moran, *Libavius*, 285.
29 Moran, *Libavius*, 282–283.
30 Ewers, "Die Bahrprobe," 25–29.
31 *Opuscules ou traictes divers et curieux en medicine* (1640), 758, translated by Margaret Louise Ingram in her thesis, "Bodies That Speak: Early Modern Gender Distinctions in Bleeding Corpses and Demoniacs" (M.A. thesis, University of Oregon, 2017). I am grateful to Ms. Ingram for sharing her unpublished research with me.
32 John Webster, *The Displaying of Supposed Witchcraft* (London: J.M., 1677), 308.
33 De Ceglia, "Saving the Phenomenon," 40.
34 Keith Thomas, *Religion and the Decline of Magic* (New York: Scribner, 1971).
35 Gaskill, "Reporting Murder," 6.
36 *Sundrye Strange and Inhumaine Murthers, Lately Committed* (London, 1591), sig. A4v, cited in Lesel Dawson, "In Every Wound There is a Bloody Tongue," in *Blood Matters: Studies in European Literature and Thought, 1400–1700*, eds. Bonnie Lander Johnson and Eleanor Decamp (Philadelphia: University of Pennsylvania Press, 2018), 154.

37 See Dawson, "In Every Wound There is a Bloody Tongue," 151–166; also Mary Floyd-Wilson, *Occult Knowledge, Science and Gender on the Elizabethan Stage* (Cambridge: Cambridge University Press, 2013), 58ff.
38 4.4.138-142, quoted in Dawson, "In Every Wound There is a Bloody Tongue," 163.
39 *Iurisprudentia medica* (Leipzig: 1736–1747), 188.
40 Ewers, "Die Barhprobe," 36.
41 As summarized in De Ceglio, "Saving the Phenomenon," 47.
42 Ewers, "Die Barhprobe," 37–45.
43 Lehmann, "Das Bahrgericht," 24.
44 Ewers, "Die Bahrprobe," 45.
45 Benedikt Carpzov, *Practica nova imperialis Saxonica rerum criminalium* (Wittenberg, 1635), 128. See also Heitsch, "Beweis und Verurteilung," 48.
46 1818 case in Sharonville, Ohio; 1833 case in Philadelphia; 1874 case in South Carolina. Robert P. Brittain, "Cruentation in Legal Medicine and in Literature," *Medical History* 9, no. 1 (1965): 85–86.
47 Gaskill, "Reporting Murder," 25.

2

MARTIN LUTHER AND THE REFORMATION OF VIRGINITY[1]

Amy E. Leonard

Ideals of virginity in Germany were embraced and denigrated throughout the sixteenth century and had various values for the different sides of the confessional debate. There was no one view, within or between the confessions; male, female, religious, lay, Protestant, and Catholic all used and manipulated discourses around virginity in their own ways and for their own purposes. Actual physical virginity was hard to verify for women (and impossible for men), so the virgin and virginity took on great metaphorical and spiritual power, which opens up new ways of seeing the effects of the Reformation, in theory and in daily life.[2]

This new way of seeing particularly affects the history of women. Views of sex and sexuality were very male-based before and during the Reformation.[3] The phallus ruled, and licit versus illicit sex was defined by its procreative value. Many claimed women were created solely for reproduction; their needs, desires, and identity were not often taken into the equation in the prescriptive literature. This male focus explains the religious and legal preoccupation with penetration as defining sex and the relative disinterest in female same-sex relations. Scholars of the history of sexuality and queer studies initially reinforced this male emphasis, with most studying primarily men; but recent work has broadened the question and pushed scholarship to understand premodern sexual identity more broadly from a multi-gendered perspective.[4]

Studying virginity more closely can help push the discussion even further. Virginity was a sexual category for both men and women, but it was generally defined by the woman. Putting virgins and virginity at the forefront of a study can refocus our views of sexuality and give women more importance. Previous studies often emphasized the negative aspects of virginity discourse; that is, the ideal of virginity undermined female sexual agency and made the body's intactness women's main defining characteristic. There is certainly much misogyny associated with Church views of female virginity; but virginity can also be empowering, as seen in the lives and writings of numerous nuns, mystics, and other educated women. There was no one set view of virginity, by either men or women in the Reformation era. This essay looks to tease out some of the different views of female virginity and what effect the Reformation had by looking at the main German reformer, Martin Luther. His views on virginity must be read within the context of his criticism of the Catholic Church and monasticism in general, as well as his antipathy for nuns and their supposed elite status as Brides of Christ. But they tell us more than just how he felt about celibacy and perpetual virginity; they get at the heart of his view of gender roles, especially for how women should be protected and confined within the private, domestic sphere.

The study of virginity offers a window into the Reformation and a way to compare and contrast Protestant confessions. Protestant anticlericalism was often based in sex and sexuality, and both Catholics and Protestants were intimately concerned with what went on in the bedroom.[5] Sexualized language permeated the Reformations. Protestants attacked Catholics for their sexual debauchery and hypocrisy and Catholics responded by accusing Protestants of unrestrained lust, claiming their clerics were too weak to remain celibate. All confessions wanted to control sexuality, especially female sexuality (though their rhetoric and methods differed), with church and state working together to regulate marriage and sexual patterns.[6]

Virginity had meaning both for the individual (in physical and spiritual ways) and symbolically for society at large. Everyone was born a virgin, but the designation only began to matter after puberty, and usually only in reference to women. The most basic category of virgin was the young maid, post-puberty but before marriage. Virgins who never married (generally viewed as spinsters or old maids) held precarious positions in society, looked upon with suspicion and always just one step away from whoredom.[7] Some women embraced virginity and became perpetual virgins, choosing (in theory) to remain unmarried for spiritual reasons.[8] These women were often associated with an enclosed religious community, though not necessarily.[9] And finally, there were what I am calling "born-again virgins," those whose virginity had been "restored," through penance and redemption, faith, or divine intervention.[10]

Early Christian writers and medieval theologians discussed and dissected all these types of virginity, often focused on female purity and how women could overcome their inherently sinful nature; numerous Church Fathers wrote lengthy treatises on the topic, some to the point of obsession.[11] The praise of virginity and its elevation above marriage marked a distinct difference between Christianity and previous Classical and Jewish cultures. The pre-Christian world saw perpetual virginity as abnormal; virginity was rather a temporary state before marriage. Even those who embraced it as a vocation (like the Vestal Virgins or Essenes) did not view it as desirable for large numbers to follow their example. In Peter Brown's words, "it was an elaborately contrived suspension of the normal process."[12] Perpetual virginity would not have been an acceptable choice for most non-Christians, even if they had been given that choice. Christianity transformed the ideal, in theory if not in general practice; what we will see is that Luther wanted to change it back.

The German word for virgin is *Jungfrau*, literally young woman or maiden, and generally needs a masculine qualifier when referring to men. In sixteenth-century Germany, virginity, perpetual or temporary, monastic or lay, was more associated with women than men.[13] Rather than virginity, chastity (*Keuschheit*) or purity (*Reinheit*) were more frequently used when describing men who abstained from sex. Chastity refers to behavior and attitudes, habits of thought and practice, vis-à-vis sex. All Christians in theory were held to certain standards of chastity, but those standards varied according to one's state of life. The monastic took a vow of chastity, a stronger vow with more weight than the secular clergy's vow of celibacy (i.e. unmarried).[14] While monks embraced chastity, German nuns usually took a vow of *Jungfräulichkeit*, or virginity; thus chastity and perpetual virginity became completely wedded for religious women.[15] Virginity was a state of being while chastity was chosen; perpetual virginity, however, began as a gift from God but became a choice, a choice that was superior to all others for women in the Middle Ages.

Luther strongly differentiated between chastity and virginity, always praising chastity more. He emphasized the voluntary aspect of chastity (the hallmark of any good marriage) and refused to accept perpetual virginity as a freely chosen vocation. But he had to walk a careful line where he condemned the virginity of the Catholic Church and its nuns but still praised Mary and the virgin birth of Christ. He also wanted to value virginity more than Judaism did, which dismissed it as barrenness. This led Luther to a tripartite view. The first part saw virginity as a metaphor for the church, which for Luther was the only accepted form of spiritual (rather than physical) virginity. This metaphor had nothing in common with the second, wrong kind of spiritual virginity: the false and corrupt elitism of monasticism and the nun. The final, and for Luther the most important aspect of virginity, was in its bodily sense, as something precarious and vulnerable for the majority of women in their lived reality. The fragile nature of female virginity meant that, for Luther, the best virgin was a married one.

Looking first at spiritual versus physical or bodily virginity, Luther saw them as separate entities, with no real relation to each other. Physical virginity had a temporal, social, and material benefit completely removed from any spiritual or religious aspect. Spiritual virginity was not associated with the body but rather included all of Christendom, based in faith and the soul. It was not gendered or sexed. Luther dismissed any attempt to put a spiritual value on physical virginity as works not faith. There could be individual, spiritual virgins, but they were rare.

This view of spiritual virginity provided the basis for Luther's most positive depictions of virginity, as a metaphor for Christians and the pure church. While this metaphor was common in the Bible and throughout the Judeo-Christian tradition, Luther strongly differentiated his version from both the Catholic and Jewish ones.[16] According to Luther, Jews saw virginity as "the greatest kind of disorder," a form of barrenness, and saved all their praise for fertility and marriage.

"Today, however," Luther wrote, "we praise virginity as a gift from God, and we do not curse it."[17] But even as he took pains to distance himself from these negative views, Luther still mocked virginity. In his discussion of the Sixth Commandment in his Large Catechism he explained that among the Jews "the virgin estate was not valued; public prostitution and dissolute lifestyles were also not allowed (as now). Therefore, adultery was the most common form of unchastity among them."[18] Luther could not help this swipe against the Catholic Church, which accepted public prostitution, putting that and lewdness in the same breath as the virgin state and hinting that they were all deviant forms of sexuality.

Spiritual virginity was no special province of women or any way to gain status or respect in the temporal realm (as the Catholics argued); instead, it denoted every Christian. This virgin was the true bride of Christ (not the nun), but she (like the physical virgin maiden) was sexually vulnerable: "Now the devil seeks to seduce the bride, so that she will lose her chastity and virginity, in which she was betrothed to Christ."[19] The sexual metaphor continued with faith: "For the soul is called a spiritual virgin and a bride of God only because of faith, by which it receives the word of God and becomes pregnant with the Holy Spirit."[20]

The pure virgin was the faithful Christian, but association with the corrupt Catholic Church sullied this true Christian, leading to her fall from the virginal state.

> This whore, who before was a pure virgin and dear bride, is now an apostate, erring, married whore, a house-whore, a bed-whore, a key-whore, being the mistress of the house, having the key, the bed, the kitchen, the cellar, and everything at her command. Yet she is so evil that beside her the common unattached whores, the pimp-whores, the whores of the field, the country, and the army are almost holy. For she is the true arch-whore and the true whore of the devil.[21]

By classifying the female virgin as a universal for all Christians, Luther could use his favorite gendered, sexual slur (whore) to attack the Catholic Church. Anyone at odds with true Christianity was sexually deviant: "Therefore faith is the spiritual virginity through which we are married to Christ… Thus, Jews and bad Christians in the prophets are always accused of fornication, that is, unbelief."[22] Those who fail in this faith "fall into adultery."[23]

The Catholic Church corrupted the virgin and turned her into a whore by emphasizing works over faith. Luther complained that virginity had become a spiritual commodity, when its true worth was only of this world. "Thus, they have made a trade out of their virginity, hoping to gain something with it before God, not being satisfied with the temporal advantage of chastity and the eternal gain of faith."[24] Luther also defined virginity as a commodity, but one tied to marriage, not salvation. Virginity was a woman's "best dowry" (*optima dote*).[25] It gained its greatest power for Luther right after marriage, as the token of exchange between bride and bridegroom, representing her purity and worthiness. "For the feeling of love in a bridegroom is most tender and impatient, especially at the very moment of marriage, when the embrace and the nuptial joy are at hand."[26] Only in that moment did Luther truly see it as active, but only as it benefited the man; it was still a passive commodity for the woman. This was a virginity of potential, and its loss was ruinous. "If someone should take your money, gold, silver, and cattle, it is a small loss; but to take a virgin, a beautiful and beloved wife from whom you expect offspring with your whole heart and from whom you hope for the seed of the promised descendants, this is surely a wrong and insult that surpasses all wrongs."[27] In this way, virginity only had meaning in relation to marriage and procreation.

Virginity was a commodity and, along with her dowry, formed part of what the bride brought to the marriage. German women still traditionally received a *Morgengabe* ("morning-gift") the day after their marriage, in recompense for their maidenhead.[28] This gift, which became the property of the bride, was typically worth 10–20% of the dowry and clearly showed that one's virginity had an economic value, though more so for the husband than the wife since his profit was greater.[29]

Luther prized most this material value of virginity, one which fit within his larger focus on marriage. He criticized the traditional Catholic hierarchy of chastity that put the virgin on top, above married people and the widowed.[30] Since virgins existed in all religions, how could they have some special spiritual edge that makes them better than everyone else? Virginity and marriage were states of being, not belief; they were stations in life created by God.[31] He separated out an individual's spiritual virginity (remaining a virgin without lust) from the physical (a more temporary state before marriage). To remain a spiritual virgin for life was nigh impossible; because lust was so strong, one had to have a gift from God to mitigate it. And if one lusted at all, one's spiritual virginity was clearly absent or voided. Though Luther acknowledged this gift existed, he stressed that it was exceedingly rare; more often he saw it as impossible. "There has never been either a virgin or a celibate in this life who has been without lust."[32] Anyone feeling carnal desire (or experiencing "fluxes and pollutions," *fluxus et pollutiones*) clearly did not have the gift and should get married.[33] In fact, the virgin was *more* sinful than the wife, since she was fooling herself. Because her lust was not channeled and controlled by marriage, she was more in its thrall and beneath the married woman. This meant that the chastity found in marriage was "far above virginity."[34] This chastity was also private—a matter for the family, headed by the patriarch, not for the public. This domestic chastity was directly at odds with the monastic life.

Luther's dismissal of spiritual virginity as a feasible choice for women informed his critique of the nuns' vocation. Luther's attacks on monasticism are well-known, but I want to place them within his configuration of physical, public virginity versus a private, marital chastity. The problem with the nuns' virginity was how showy and yet empty it was. Virginity was not something to be proud of or to flaunt. Praising the biblical Sarah, Luther noted that her "chastity is without show and without glory before the world, it is secret and hidden by a cover because she is a married woman. This cover deceives the celibates."[35] She might be married but "her chastity surpasses the virgins."[36] The good pure virgin was the one who asked nothing of God, did not need to be showered with praise, and was confident in her faith; she did not draw attention to herself like the "lazy virgin accustomed to leisure and luxury."[37]

There are seeming contradictions in Luther's writings on marriage and virginity. On the one hand, as we have seen, he felt the married woman was better than the virgin maiden.[38] But in the same text, he made clear that marriage came second: "For when one compares marriage and virginity [*Jungfrawschafft*], then of course chastity [*Keuschayt*] is a nobler gift than marriage."[39] First, note the term gift. Only when one's lust has been taken away by God can pure chastity and virginity exist. But more importantly, Luther differentiated between virginity and the virgin. While freely-given perpetual virginity might be better for Luther, he did not have much respect or praise for the actual virgin. The state of virginity was better than marriage, but the wife was better than the nun. For Luther, the virgin (spiritual or physical) did not benefit society; she had a great gift, but it was ultimately selfish, even if God-given. Virgins had done nothing for this gift (it should not be work for them, since it came from God) and they were able to avoid all the labor and strife the wife and mother had to endure.

> For whoever lives unmarried and a celibate is relieved of all the labor and disgust which are a part of the married state. In short: It is a beautiful, delightful, and noble gift for him to whom it is given... Still one must not deny that before God a married woman is better than a virgin, although the married woman has much labor and trouble here on earth, and the virgin much happiness, ease, and comfort.[40]

The married woman worked, helped her neighbor, and created the next generation; the virgin did nothing.

There was of course one virgin whom Luther consistently accepted and praised, in both her spiritual and physical aspect: Mary. Mary's virginity was a core part of her identity and was absolutely fundamental to Christianity. Luther retained an affection and attachment to Mary beyond what many other Protestants felt. He defended her perpetual virginity, the immaculate conception, and even, to a degree, her bodily assumption.[41] It can seem contradictory that Luther emphasized Mary's virginity as much as he did, while downplaying it everywhere else for women, but it was critically important to him. Mary was a pure virgin before, during, and after the birth of Christ and remained eternally a perpetual virgin because of God's power and the miracle of Christ's birth.[42] On a more pragmatic and patriarchal note, if Mary was not a virgin, then the true father of Jesus was unclear, though of course Luther did not put it in those terms. It was also important for Luther that Mary's virginity was not a choice, nor did it bring salvation; it was a gift from God. She was saved through Christ, not her state of virginity.[43]

Mary's perpetual virginity held such weight for Luther for the precise reason that it was unique: she was the exception that proved the rule. Responding to supposed Turkish beliefs about the virgin birth (that in fact many women had done it), Luther made clear that only Mary could remain a virgin after giving birth. "Those virgins who bear children become women. A virgin who gives birth to a child cannot remain a virgin. We do not believe their yarn, and we do not want them to spread it in our homes; otherwise our daughters would all become whores."[44] Virginity here acts as social and gendered control. If maidens thought they could retain their virginity after childbirth, there would be one less reason for them to avoid fornication. Here we see how vulnerable and fragile female virginity was for Luther. Mary's virginity should not be taken in any way as a model or guide for other women, women without the necessary divine support.[45] Her singularity was key and only reinforced Luther's main argument: perpetual virginity was unnatural.

Luther wrote about other virgin saints, but emphasized that their virginity was not a selling point. In discussing virgin martyrs such as Saints Agatha and Agnes, Luther praised them as active agents of resistance and downplayed their physical attributes; rather, they were "universal models of evangelism."[46] Their sexual purity was irrelevant and just a product of their youth—they were too young to marry anyway; it was their proclamation of the Word that mattered and made them martyrs. Thus, these women could become examples for both men and women as they "exercise[d] the vocation of the priesthood of all believers."[47]

One category of virgin differs from all the others; what I am calling the "born-again" virgin. Many Catholics wrote that virginity could be restored, not just symbolically but physically as well. Symbolic "revirginization" was epitomized by Mary Magdalene and the series of houses founded in her name to redeem fallen women, especially prostitutes. Through penance the woman was restored to an earlier state and rebranded pure and ready for marriage.[48] This process went beyond just spiritual redemption; many wrote that God had the power to restore the physical rupture, especially if that rupture had come against the virgin's will.[49] Augustine argued that a rape victim's body was not physically damaged by the assault so long as she felt no lust during the attack. Christian women who suffered such assault "have within them the glory of chastity, the witness of their conscience."[50] Aquinas, following Augustine, wrote that true virginity is not "situated in the flesh."[51] Not surprisingly, Luther dismissed this as magical thinking and Catholic abuse. While spiritual virginity could be restored, bodily virginity was a black and white issue: once penetrated, it was gone. He was outraged by rape, and did not always blame the victim, but her loss was permanent.[52]

Because the loss of virginity was so traumatic and unalterable for Luther, he believed that virgins needed to be protected; just not the way the Catholic Church had been doing. He condemned what he saw as the rampant abuse of forced monachization—putting women in convents against their will—and the discourse of marriage as lesser than celibacy and perpetual virginity. He was particularly horrified by the acceptance of prostitution and civic brothels and dismissed the argument that these were antidotes to homosexuality or the violation of pure maidens and honest matrons.[53] Brothels did not protect women, since any man so immodest as to visit one would have no compunction about propositioning anyone else.[54] The only real protection for the virgin was to transfer her from the protection of her father to that of her husband. Defending the virgin benefited the future bridegroom, too. Virginity was a dangerous time for women, but it also held perils for men. How could one truly know if your betrothed was untouched? "Who can guarantee or say that he is really getting a virgin?… 'The road goes past the door' (as they say)."[55] A virgin must be removed from society, looking on no man, not even her bridegroom. She was in a waiting pattern, until she mattered. Virginity's true worth and meaning existed more after it was gone: when the honorable maiden married and had children. Then her modest upbringing and virginity had been positively fulfilled and literally brought to fruition, as opposed to the fallen woman who had sex outside of wedlock and came to ruin; her virginity, her greatest commodity, wasted. Thus, the virgin must be hidden, protected, and, as quickly as possible, married off.

Luther discarded the traditional Catholic view of virginity—as something better, having both physical and spiritual merit—and embraced one firmly grounded in the temporal world. For Luther, the virgin embodied potential. The state of virginity was a waystation between too young to marry and should be married. Virginity was just the precondition of motherhood. In his lectures on Isaiah, Luther claimed that the section on virgins referred to their youth, not their virginity. It is about "the hope of producing offspring."[56] Virgin was synonymous with unmarried woman or maiden and the loss of virginity (if done appropriately) equaled marriage. Thus, virginity and marriage were conflated; the loss of one meant the procurement of the other.

Returning now to the nuns and their virginity, I want to suggest that here is where Luther and the Reformation brought real change. The convents were often on the frontlines in the battle over reform, as the women within were told to convert and leave. And yet, these women fought back, usually in greater numbers than their male counterparts, and often succeeded in remaining in their houses. Even as Luther transformed the way Protestants viewed sexuality, tying its licit and accepted expression completely to marriage, the nuns refused that reconfiguration. While Luther saw the state of virginity as a waystation or only embodying procreative potential, the nuns saw it as a representation of their faith, community, and female sexual identity. Luther insisted they were wrong and he sapped female virginity of all its power. In his view, it was not an active agent; the only real spiritual virginity was universal, representing all true Christians, married or not. This disempowered those admittedly few who did get agency and a voice from their perpetual virginity. By refusing to accept that women could choose to remain virgins, he denied them an active sexuality separate from men and consigned them forever more to the private, domestic sphere.

Virginity is often the forgotten stepchild in the history of sexuality. While discussed and noted, especially for differences between Catholic and Protestant theology, it is usually couched in terms of shunning "normal" sexuality and not taken seriously as a category of its own. But this misses an opportunity. Because virginity has so many manifestations—physical, metaphorical, symbolic, and spiritual—and represents something both inherently biological (one is born a virgin) *and* socially constructed (one can choose to become a perpetual virgin) it becomes a blank slate on which historical actors could express their deepest sexual and societal views.

Notes

1 Translations are my own except where indicated. I would like to thank the Georgetown Faculty Research Seminar for their helpful comments.
2 There are many discussions throughout the premodern period about how to test for virginity and the role of the hymen. See Kathleen Coyne Kelly, *Performing Virginity and Testing Chastity in the Middle Ages* (New York: Routledge, 2000).
3 For relevant reviews of the literature, see Katherine Crawford, *European Sexualities, 1400–1800* (Cambridge: Cambridge University Press, 2007); Ruth Mazo Karras, *Sexuality in Medieval Europe: Doing Unto Others*, 2nd ed. (London: Routledge, 2012); Helmut Puff, "Martin Luther, die sexuelle Reformation und gleichgeschlechtliche Sexualität: Ein Christ zwischen Reformen und Moderne (1517–2017)," in *Martin Luther: Christ Zwischen Reformen und Moderne (1517–2017)*, ed. Alberto Melloni (Berlin: De Gruyter, 2017); Rüdiger Schnell, *Sexualität und Emotionalität in der vormodernen Ehe* (Köln: Böhlau Köln, 2002); Merry E. Wiesner-Hanks, *Christianity and Sexuality in the Early Modern World: Regulating Desire, Reforming Practice*, 3rd ed. (London: Routledge, 2020).
4 Merry Wiesner-Hanks, "Sexual Identity and Other Aspects of 'Modern' Sexuality: New Chronologies, Same Old Problem?," in *After the History of Sexuality: German Genealogies with and beyond Foucault*, eds. Scott Spector, Helmut Puff, and Dagmar Herzog (New York: Berghahn Books, 2012), 31–42.
5 Marjorie Elizabeth Plummer, *From Priest's Whore to Pastor's Wife: Clerical Marriage and the Process of Reform in the Early German Reformation* (Burlington, VT: Ashgate, 2012); Helmut Puff, *Sodomy in Reformation Germany and Switzerland, 1400–1600* (Chicago: University of Chicago Press, 2003); Hans-Christoph Rublack, "Anticlericalism in German Reformation Pamphlets," in *Anticlericalism in Late Medieval and Early Modern Europe*, eds. Heiko A. Oberman and Peter A. Dykema (Leiden: Brill, 1993), 461–490; Wiesner-Hanks, *Christianity and Sexuality*.
6 Sheilagh Ogilvie, *A Bitter Living: Women, Markets, and Social Capital in Early Modern Germany* (Oxford: Oxford University Press, 2003); Ulinka Rublack, "Interior States and Sexuality," in *After the History of Sexuality*; Ulrike Strasser, *State of Virginity: Gender, Religion, and Politics in an Early Modern Catholic State* (Ann Arbor, MI: University of Michigan Press, 2004).
7 Ruth Mazo Karras, *Common Women: Prostitution and Sexuality in Medieval England* (New York: Oxford University Press, 1996).
8 How much actual choice they had in the matter is debatable. See Anne Jacobson Schutte, *By Force and Fear: Taking and Breaking Monastic Vows in Early Modern Europe* (Ithaca, NY: Cornell University Press, 2011).
9 Catholic authorities increasingly preferred them behind walls. See Elizabeth M. Makowski, *Canon Law and Cloistered Women: Periculoso and Its Commentators, 1298–1545* (Washington, D.C.: Catholic University of America Press, 1997); Heike Uffmann, "Inside and Outside

the Convent Walls: The Norm and Practice of Enclosure in the Reformed Nunneries of Late Medieval Germany," *The Medieval History Journal* 4, no. 1 (April 1, 2001): 83–108; Alison Weber, ed., *Devout Laywomen in the Early Modern World* (Burlington, VT: Routledge, 2016).
10 Maeve B. Callan, "Of Vanishing Fetuses and Maidens Made-Again: Abortion, Restored Virginity, and Similar Scenarios in Medieval Irish Hagiography and Penitentials," *Journal of the History of Sexuality* 21, no. 2 (2012): 282–296; Lucia Ferrante, "Honor Regained: Women in the Casa Del Soccorso Di San Paolo in Sixteenth-Century Bologna," in *Sex and Gender in Historical Perspective*, eds. Edward Muir and Guido Ruggiero, trans. Margaret A. Galluci (Baltimore: Johns Hopkins University Press, 1990), 73–109.
11 Kelly, *Performing Virginity*, 3. Church Fathers who specifically addressed virginity include Ambrose, Augustine, Basil of Caesarea, Cyprian of Carthage (two works), Gregory of Nyssa, Jerome (six works), John Chrysostom (three works), Methodius of Olympus (two works), Sulpicius Severus, and Tertullian. See further Roger Steven Evans, *Sex and Salvation: Virginity as a Soteriological Paradigm in Ancient Christianity* (Lanham, MD: University Press of America, 2003).
12 Peter Brown, *The Body and Society: Men, Women, and Sexual Renunciation in Early Christianity* (New York: Columbia University Press, 1988), 9.
13 Luther did use *Jungfrau*, without masculine qualifiers, to refer to men, usually biblical exemplars like Noah and Paul, and stressed that the term was not tied to any one sex. WA 12:109, *1 Korinther 7* (1523); WA 42:266, *Die Genesisvorlesung* (1535/38). The majority of his discussion of virgins and virginity, however, referred to women, with virgin often synonymous with maiden.
14 I would like to thank David Collins for his help in clarifying this for me.
15 These sexual categories were reflected in the convent hierarchy: the top, elite tier of veiled, choir nuns were reserved (except in rare cases) for virgins; widows and other non-virgins could only attain lay nun status. Only a virgin was worthy (and pure enough) to be a Bride of Christ. See further Julie Hotchin, "The Nun's Crown," *Early Modern Women* 4 (2009): 187–194.
16 Virginity was important in Judaism but only as a symbol of purity before marriage. Unlike many patristic writings (as well as Greek and Roman), Jewish ones often directed their comments on virginity to both men and women, with the consistent theme that young Jews were expected to marry and have children; even the raped woman must marry her rapist (Deuteronomy 22:28–29 and Exodus 22:16–17). Virginity was important, especially to the high priest, who must marry a virgin from his own people (Leviticus 13–14), but not as a permanent arrangement. See further Evans, *Sex and Salvation*, 17–19; Shalom M. Paul and Louis Isaac Rabinowitz, "Virgin, Virginity," in *Encyclopedia Judaica*, ed. Michael Berenbaum and Fred Skolnik, 2nd ed., vol. 20 (Macmillan Reference, 2007), 539–41; Tikva Simone Frymer-Kensky, "Virginity in the Bible," in *Gender and Law in the Hebrew Bible and the Ancient Near East*, eds. Victor Harold Matthews, Bernard M. Levinson, and Tikva Simone Frymer-Kensky (Sheffield, England: Sheffield Academic Press, 1998), 79–96.
17 WA 31/2:443–444, *Vorlesung über Jesaja* (1527).
18 WA 30/1:160, *Großer Katechismus* (1529).
19 WA 47:159, *Predigten über Johannis* (1539).
20 WA 10/2:121, *Wider den falsch genannten geistlichen Stand des Papstes und der Bischöfe* (1522).
21 WA 51:502–503, *Wider Hans Worst* (1541). Translation from *LW* 41:207-208.
22 WA 3:89, *Psalmenvorlesungen* (1513–1515).
23 WA 31/2:471, *Vorlesungen über Jesaja* (1527–1530).
24 WA 12:135–136, *Predigten, Korinther* (1523). Translation from *LW* 28:50.
25 WA 43:640, *Genesisvorlesung* (1535–1545).
26 WA 43:633, *Genesisvorlesung*; *LW* 5:297.

27 *WA* 43:633, *Genesisvorlesung*; *LW* 5:296.
28 Widows also received a Morgengabe, but there is some evidence that it was lesser and that symbolically it still represented an exchange for virginity.
29 Laurent Feller, "'Morgengabe', dot, tertia: rapport Introductif," in *Dots et Douaires dans le Haut Moyen Âge*, eds. Laurent Feller, François Bougard, and Regine Le Jan, vol. 295 (Rome: École Française de Rome, 2002), 1–25; Joel F. Harrington, *Reordering Marriage and Society in Reformation Germany* (Cambridge: Cambridge University Press, 1995), 192–193; Judith J. Hurwich, "Marriage Strategy Among the German Nobility, 1400–1699," *Journal of Interdisciplinary History* 29, no. 2 (1998): 169–195; cf. Diane Owen Hughes, "From Brideprice To Dowry in Mediterranean Europe," *Journal of Family History* 3, no. 3 (September 1, 1978): 262–296.
30 *WA* 17/2:157–160, *Fastenpostille* (1525).
31 *WA* 17/2:158, *Fastenpostille* (1525).
32 *WA* 8:858, *De votis monasticis* (1521).
33 *WATr* 3:607, (1538).
34 *WA* 17/2:159, *Fastenpostille* (1525).
35 *WA* 43:24, *Genesisvorlesung* (1535–1545).
36 *WA* 43:26, *Genesisvorlesung* (1535–1545).
37 *WA* 43:329, *Genesisvorlesung* 1535–1545).
38 Throughout his commentary on 1 Corinthians 7. *WA* 12:88–142 (1523).
39 *WA* 12:104, *Predigten, Korinther*.
40 *WA* 12:99. Translation from *LW* 28:11.
41 For more on Luther and the other reformers' views on the Virgin Mary, see Bridget Heal, *The Cult of the Virgin Mary in Early Modern Germany: Protestant and Catholic Piety, 1500–1648* (Cambridge: Cambridge University Press, 2007); Peter Meinhold, "Die Marienverehrung im Verständnis der Reformatoren des 16. Jahrhunderts," *Saeculum* 32, no. 1 (1981): 43–58.
42 *WA* 20:357.
43 *WA* 17/2:294.
44 *WA* 46:153, *Predigten, Johannes*.
45 See further the Gospel for Christmas Eve, Luke 2:1–14, *WA* 10.I.2:58–94.
46 Margaret Arnold, "'To Sweeten the Bitter Dance': The Virgin Martyrs in the Lutheran Reformation," *Archiv für Reformationsgeschichte* 104 (October 2013): 115.
47 Arnold, "To Sweeten the Bitter Dance," 121.
48 Sherrill Cohen, *The Evolution of Women's Asylums since 1500: From Refuges for Ex-Prostitutes to Shelters for Battered Women* (New York: Oxford University Press, 1992); Lucia Ferrante, "Honor Regained"; Rachel L. Geschwind, "Magdalene Imagery and Prostitution Reform in Early Modern Venice and Rome, 1500–1700" (PhD Dissertation, Case Western Reserve University, 2011).
49 See Callan, "Of Vanishing Fetuses and Maidens Made-Again" for examples throughout the Middle Ages of the miraculous repair of the hymen.
50 Augustine, *De Civitate Dei*, 1:19. Quoted in Joy A. Schroeder, *Dinah's Lament: The Biblical Legacy of Sexual Violence in Christian Interpretation* (Minneapolis: Fortress Press, 2007), 66.
51 Thomas Aquinas, *Summa Theologica*: Virginity (II-II, Q. 152, Art. 1). New Advent, accessed October 9, 2013, http://www.newadvent.org/summa/3152.htm.
52 Joy A. Schroeder, "The Rape of Dinah: Luther's Interpretation of a Biblical Narrative," *Sixteenth Century Journal* 28, no. 3 (Fall 1997): 775.
53 For more on prostitution in Europe and Germany, see Ruth Mazo Karras, "Prostitution in Medieval Europe," in *Handbook of Medieval Sexuality*, eds. Vern L. Bullough and James A. Brundage (New York and London: Garland Publishing, 1996), 243–260; Lyndal Roper, "Discipline and Respectability: Prostitution and the Reformation in Augsburg," *History Workshop* 19 (April 1, 1985): 3–28; Merry E. Wiesner, "Paternalism in Practice: The Control of Servants and Prostitutes in Early

Modern German Cities," in *The Process of Change in Early Modern Europe: Essays in Honor of Miriam Usher Chrisman*, eds. Phillip Bebb and Sherrin Marshall (Athens: Ohio University Press, 1988), 179–200.
54 *WA* 43:60, *Genesisvorlesung* (1535–1545).
55 *WA* 50:640, *Von den Konziliis und Kirchen* (1539).
56 *WA* 31/2:128, *Vorlesungen über Jesaja* (1527–1530).

3

MARTIN LUTHER'S GENDERED REFLECTIONS ON EVE

David M. Whitford

Cleaning out her father's things after his death, a friend discovered a telegram her father sent to his mother. It was just a sentence long, "grandson arrived 10 lbs 9 oz mother and son doing fine." In the era before international calling, or the internet, such telegrams were commonplace. Before that, letters did the same thing, only slower. In June 1526, Martin Luther wrote just such a letter to one of his closest friends. It is, like that telegram, just about a sentence long. It announced the birth of his son, Hans. He thanked God that mother and child were both well.[1] He must have written a similar letter, now lost, to his parents because his mother arrived in Wittenberg a week or so after Hans was born to help Katherina with the newborn. In the months that followed, Luther's letters are full of small, joyful anecdotes about his son—whom he almost always calls Hanschen—or Johnny.[2] Eighteen months later, however, the doting father's joy turned to terror.

In late summer 1527, the plague struck Wittenberg. By October it had reached Luther's house, his family, and his friends. Katherina Luther was pregnant with their second child and was bed-ridden with the disease. Hanschen was likewise stricken. Luther's young aide's wife, Hanna Rörer, was—like Katherina—pregnant and sick with plague. On 2 November, Rörer delivered a still-born son. Worn out by the delivery and the plague, she died shortly thereafter. In a remarkably personal letter to one of his closest friends, Luther recorded his feelings as Katherina's pregnancy drew to its conclusion, "I am so anxious about the delivery of my wife, so greatly has the example of the deacon's [i.e., Georg Rörer] wife terrified me." He continued, sharing his anxiety—but also a small glimmer of hope—regarding Hans's health, "My Johnny cannot now send his greetings to you because of his illness, but he desires your prayers for him. Today is the twelfth day that he has eaten nothing, but he has somehow been sustained only on liquids. Now he is beginning to eat a little bit. It is wonderful to see how this little infant wants to be happy and strong as usual, but he cannot because he is too weak."[3]

On 10 December, Katherina Luther gave birth to their second child—a girl they named Elisabeth. A few weeks later, Luther celebrated that the plague was receding and that his family had safely increased by one. "I have increased as well, a daughter is born. And the pestilence, which surrounded us all in the fear of death, has by God's mercy ceased."[4] Elisabeth, however, never truly thrived. She died in August 1528. Luther was devastated, "My baby daughter, Elisabeth, has died. It is amazing what a sick, almost woman-like heart she has left me with, so much has grief for her overcome me. Never before would I have believed a father's heart could have such tender feelings for this child. Pray for me."[5]

In her 2005 article, "'Lustful Luther': Male Libido in the Writings of the Reformer," Merry Wiesner-Hanks laments that gender history has almost exclusively focused on women and ought to be expanded to examine in more depth men *qua* men. She notes also that because Luther wrote so much and because so many of his letters and even transcripts of his conversations exist, he represents an ideal figure through which to examine the question of masculinity in the Early Modern Era. She notes that such inquires have largely never taken place.[6] This essay seeks to answer that call by examining whether or not his life as a husband and father changed Luther, not just on a personal level, but on a professional, spiritual, and doctrinal level. At the personal level, he noted that before Hans and Elisabeth, he would never have believed the tender feelings of a father for a child. Did these tender feelings have an effect beyond life in the home, and if so, how? It would seem they did. Shortly after Hans was born, Luther remarked in class his amazement that women could calm a fussy child with just one finger, while men cannot do it with both hands.[7] But this example is largely conjecture. It fits both the timeframe and reflects a fairly common mystification among new parents—both fathers and mothers—at their own inability at times to quiet a newborn, and amazement at someone else's facility to do so. Whether Luther here was speaking more generally, or of his wife—or perhaps even his mother—is entirely unknown. It is less difficult to measure whether his new parental role actually affected his lectures, however. In order to assess that, it is necessary to look at similar topics, themes, or biblical figures before marriage and children and then again after he was married and became a father. Did his new roles as a husband and a father change his views on women, motherhood, parenting, or sex, for example?

Martin Luther married Katherina von Bora on 13 June 1525. Hans Luther was born in June 1526, Elisabeth in December 1527. Luther wrote a great deal before 1526. Indeed, many of his most famous treatises were written before either his marriage or fatherhood. And yet, while he did write on some of these themes—on marriage, for example—there are not a lot of places where one can compare exact themes before and after his marriage and fatherhood. Happily, one biblical persona touches on all these themes—sex, marriage, childbirth, and womanhood—and can be directly compared. This persona is Eve: first wife; first mother; commanded by God to be fruitful and multiply; cursed by God to painful childbirth. Genesis is also ideal because of the etiological freight it carries. It explains creation, procreation, and the relationships between men and women, parents and children. But also, because each etiology is rather short, they function as what I have called texts of opportunity.[8] Their relative brevity compared to what they seek to explain has historically meant that biblical exegetes have taken these pericopes and shaped them in different ways as they have sought to explain and discuss the natures of men and women, marriage, sex, and childbirth. Luther did this as well. Thus, Eve presents the perfect figure by which to measure any changes in his thought on these topics. Ideal for the purpose of comparison, Luther preached a series of sermons in 1523 on Genesis.[9] In 1535, he returned to Genesis, this time in the classroom. In 1523, Luther was living in the Wittenberg black friary and even though it was two years after being excommunicated, he was still wearing the cassock and cowl of an Augustinian Friar. Meanwhile in Grimma (about 60 miles south of Wittenberg), Katherina von Bora was plotting her escape from the Cistercian cloister where she had lived for nearly 15 years. By 1535, they had been married a decade. They had welcomed six children into their home, and buried Elisabeth.[10] In what follows, I shall compare Luther's Eve in 1523 to the Eve of 1535. The change is dramatic and demonstrates beyond any shadow of a doubt that when Luther looked at Eve through a husband and father's eyes, he saw a much different woman than he had seen as a celibate monk.

Be fruitful and multiply: Genesis 1:27–28

Genesis 1 offers the first telling of the seven days of creation. On the sixth day, God created humankind, stating in Gen 1:25: "Let us make man in our image and likeness."[11] In the next two verses, God makes them: "And God created man to his own image: to the image of God he created him: male and female he created them. And God blessed them, saying: Increase and multiply, and fill the earth."[12] There are two aspects of these verses that play important roles in the history of exegesis surrounding Eve. First, her ontological nature. Second, the command to be fruitful and multiply.

Adam and Eve, as the first humans, raised many ontological questions for Jewish and Christian exegetes because of the statement from God that humans would be formed "in his own image." What did or does it mean to be created in the image of God? Perhaps the most dominant view in West—certainly from Augustine forward—was to view the nature of the *Imago Dei* in trinitarian terms, that is to say: memory, intellect, and will.[13] Only human beings have all three—many animals have memory and will, but lack intellect. Because, reasoned Augustine, women shared these traits as much as men, women too shared in the *Imago Dei*. While only a few within the tradition, most notably Ambrosiaster, argued that women did not share in the *Imago Dei* at all, it was very common to argue that men participated in the Image of God more fully.

Women partially or derivatively participated in the *Imago Dei* because Eve was created from Adam's rib.[14]

When exegetes turned to the command from God to "be fruitful and multiply," they took the opportunity to discuss all manner of subjects related to procreation. For example, some asked hypothetically if the Fall had not happened whether children born in the Garden might have been born fully grown with complete rationality, rather than as helpless infants. However, far more common were questions around sex. Many queried whether or not sex, as it is known now after the Fall, would have been necessary for procreation at all. Gregory of Nyssa (ca. 335–ca. 394), for example, stated that had the Fall not happened, Adam and Eve would still have procreated but would have done so in some mystical fashion as angels do.[15] He allowed that sexual organs did exist before the Fall, but they were merely a provision of God who foreknew the Fall and graciously provided for post-lapsarian procreation. St. Jerome took a slightly different tack and noted that virginity was the natural and pre-lapsarian ideal for all of humanity. With Nyssa, he agreed that wedlock and sexual union were the result of sin and the Fall.[16]

It was Augustine who largely shaped the discussion of procreation in the West. Contra both Gregory and Jerome, Augustine states in *The City of God* that sexual union would have happened without the Fall. According to Augustine, God had a plan for the number of elect. However, it would have been without the lust that mars and marks sexual unions after the Fall. Instead, one's sexual members would be controlled not by passion, but like a hand—by the power of the will.[17] After the Fall, lust dominates many aspects of life—one can have a lust for fine food or wine or many other things—but most especially as it regards sexuality:

> Such lust does not merely invade the whole body and outward members; it takes such complete and passionate possession of the whole man, both physically and emotionally, that what results is the keenest of all pleasures on the level of sensation; and at the crisis of excitement, it practically paralyzes all power of deliberate thought.[18]

Such a powerful drive required a remedy, and for Augustine, marriage was the remedy to lust and sin. It provided a needed outlet for sexual desire—which for Augustine always had some sinful stain even within the confines of marriage, most especially if it was for pleasure. Marriage also had positive, non-rehabilitative aspects such as procreation, companionship, and fidelity. After Augustine, almost everyone who wrote on the command to "be fruitful and multiply" followed his lead at least in the topics discussed: the necessity of the procreative act, the role of each sex in procreation, the power of lust, and the relative sinfulness of the conjugal act.

By the high Middle Ages, the sinfulness of sex had all but overwhelmed the command to "be fruitful and multiply." In some ways, Jerome's view began to overwhelm Augustine in that sex was always sinful, always based in lust, and was always inferior to virginity. The *Glossa Ordinaria* is typical in lifting up the superiority of virginity even while seeming to praise marriage: "To multiply is completed through the union of a man and woman. Thus, marriage is not to be condemned. It was instituted with a blessing from above for the propagation [of humanity]; but virginity is to be preferred."[19] An interlinear gloss for the pericope states, "*nuptie replent terram; virginitas celum.*"—Marriage replenishes the earth; virginity heaven.

When Luther began to preach on Genesis 1 in 1523, the Reformation was already five years old. He had been excommunicated by Rome for two years. It is rather common-place to speak of the Luther of the 1520s as the "young Luther," but in 1523, he turned 40 and had been teaching in Wittenberg for almost a decade. He was neither a young man nor a novice teacher. He had also been preaching at St. Mary's—the city church—for nearly a decade and there he regularly interacted with men, women, and children. This is important because his thoughts on Eve, sex, and marriage are not the musings of a young, cloistered monk who had had little interaction with women beyond his own mother and ladies who may have worked in either his school or monastery. While in 1523, he still wore a cassock and cowl and still tonsured his hair, he had daily interactions with women. By 1523, Luther's close associate and protégé, Philip Melanchthon, had been married for nearly three years and had an infant daughter.[20] So if Luther changed his views on any aspects of Eve, it was not because after 1525 he began to interact with women or children generally or even familiarly. Rather, by 1523, he had had time to think considerably about cloistered life and marriage. He had written a treatise on marriage and against monastic life.[21] The imprint of those works can be seen in his sermon on Genesis 1, but a more intimate, familial knowledge of women seems largely absent.

Luther began to preach on Genesis in March 1523 and continued preaching through chapter 34 until September 1524.[22] The sermon on Genesis 1 is rather traditional in some regards and a striking renunciation of medieval exegetical and theological opinion in others. He begins by acknowledging Augustine's trinitarian notion of human nature but sets it aside in favor of Paul's dichotomy between the old fallen Adam and the restored *Imago Dei* of Christ. According to Luther, Adam may have had Augustine's three-fold nature, but all goodness has been lost and replaced with lust for honors, pleasures, and gains. Sounding a Reformation-like call, he then pronounces that it is only in Christ that one finds mercy, charity, and righteousness.[23] But, in the very next moment, he returns to a more traditional line of exegesis. Eve, he declares, "would have conceived without carnal pleasure," had Adam not fallen.[24] Likewise, he continues a very hierarchical understanding of men and women. People do not choose, according to Luther, their sex. It is determined by God, and men are thus chosen by God to be superior to women—as the sun is superior to the moon.[25] But then he makes a sudden turn from Eve's natural inferiority to launch into an outright attack on the superiority of virginity and clerical celibacy, calling celibacy a demonic doctrine.[26]

Procreation should not be undermined by such a "pernicious plague." Indeed, Luther argues that procreation is a work of God (*se est opus Dei*).[27]

Thus, in 1523, Luther had definitively rejected monastic celibacy and struck a rather Evangelical chord by contrasting Adam to Christ and reinforcing the idea that Christians are restored from their fallen condition only through the cross of Christ. Regarding Eve, however, he was entirely traditional. She was created second and therefore subordinate. He does not really even speak of her human nature at all, save that she is the weaker vessel. Had she procreated before the Fall, it would have been without passion—so even while he denigrates celibacy, he still maintains that sexuality, as we know it, is a result of the Fall. In fact, a bit later, in another sermon, he also continued the medieval trope that Eve was the more lustful of the two, noting that "lusts of the flesh (*cupiditates carnis*) are stronger in women."[28] In keeping with medieval tradition, Luther also made this carnality largely responsible for Eve's susceptibility to the Devil's temptations. Now, because of her, lust for a whole host of things must be checked by parents, the sword, and secular authorities. Eve, in 1523, was lustful and disobedient.

By 1535, Luther paints a different portrait. The context is different; from 1523 we have sermons preached in the Wittenberg city church to the laity. In 1535, we have lectures. The lectures tend to be longer and more in-depth. They were meant to instruct future pastors—and so give us a good sense of what Luther hoped would be preached in the pulpits of Germany.[29] He opens his discussion of the creation of humanity by noting that Adam and Eve would still have had all the normal biological functions that people after the Fall have—a need for food, sleep, even procreation. Procreation would have been accomplished in such a way as to not be embarrassing, however. Such procreation would have been pleasing to God. After the Fall, however, "we all know how great a passion (*furor*) is in the flesh, which is not only passionate in its desiring (*concupiscendo*) but also in its disgust after it has acquired what it wants."[30] As he began his 1535 treatment, then, he does not sound much different from either 1523 or the medieval tradition.

There are small differences that change the emphasis and that seem at first sight to be interesting but not particularly significant. By the end of the Adam and Eve story, however, their significance will be apparent and, I would argue, arise as a result of his role as husband and father. The first difference is apparent immediately. In 1535, he begins his discussion not with Eve, but with Adam. He also uses *omnes* throughout. Lust and concupiscence are now something all people feel. Gone is the language that Eve and women are more carnal. All people burn with it. It also seems both more powerful and more visceral in 1535. In 1523, in a public sermon he stuck to theological terms for lust that were nearly ubiquitous in medieval theology—*cupiditas* and *concupiscentia*. While they can both be translated lust or passion, they are also rather technical, even antiseptic. In 1535, however, while he continues to use those terms, he adopted far more evocative words. In 1535, lust is a sickness (a leprosy) that seeps into every pore and sense. In 1535, lust rages; lust burns furiously. He uses *furor* and its various forms again and again in the lecture.[31]

In his writings on marriage, he repeated the Augustinian idea that marriage provides an outlet to lust. He also used leprosy as a metaphor for lust in those sermons. But he did not use *furor*. He did use that language another time, however. While at the Wartburg in 1521, he wrote to friends and noted that he was struggling mightily with lust—it burned and raged in him. Timothy Orr has posited that this might well have been the result of being seen for the first time in his life as an eligible suitor and mate—hiding as a knight, no longer a monk.[32] The monk who wrote that sex within marriage would quench lust has by the Genesis lectures perhaps discovered, even ten years into marriage, that it could still rage. Concupiscence no longer feels theological in 1535, it feels embodied.

The second change that one notes in the text is that Luther now has a different, fuller understanding of the command to "be fruitful and multiply." As noted earlier, the normal discourse on this verse discussed only the sinfulness of sexual congress. Luther touches on this, as just noted, but also adds in a new discussion of the dangers of pregnancy and childbirth. While the dangers of childbirth were well-known, medieval exegetes almost never used this verse to discuss them. The more normal verse is Genesis 3:16, where God curses Eve and all women to painful childbirth. Also, for most medieval exegetes, the focus was only on the dangers of the delivery of a child; the pain and travail of childbirth are a recompense for Eve bringing Adam and all humanity to doom by eating the fruit and convincing Adam to do likewise.[33] Discussing childbirth difficulties in Genesis 1 is thus in itself very unusual. What is more unusual is that Luther expands beyond just the delivery. For Luther, it is not only the birth that is dangerous and difficult, but "the perils of pregnancy, and of birth, the difficulty of feeding the offspring, and endless other problems."[34] Here we see an echo of that earlier lecture when he expressed mystification that mothers seem to be able to quiet a child with a single finger.[35] A few years and a few children later, Luther the father remained impressed by how difficult it can be to get some babies to nurse and how many parents weep in frustration at those moments. I have been unable to find a single medieval exegete who discusses the difficulties of feeding or quieting a child when discussing the command to be fruitful and multiply. Luther the celibate monk certainly did not. Luther the husband and father has thus deepened and expanded the exegetical scope of this command through the expansion of his own life and experience of the vocation to fatherhood. Those expansions will only continue when Genesis returns to the Adam and Eve story in Genesis 3. For the purposes of this essay, it is the curse pronounced upon Eve in Genesis 3 that is important, because it is here where we see the most definitive evidence that Luther's exegesis has been directly affected by life as a husband and a father.

The malediction of Eve: Genesis 3:16

Genesis 2 is a recapitulation of the days of creation, and so the Adam and Eve story picks up again in chapter 3 where Eve is tempted by the serpent, eats the fruit, and gives it to Adam, who likewise eats. Then in the chapter's climax, God finds them in the Garden and discovers what they have done. God curses the serpent first, then turns to Eve and says, "I will multiplie thy travailes, and thy child bearings: in travaile shalt thou bring forth children, and thou shalt be under thy husbands power, and he shall have dominion over thee."[36] As noted earlier, the exegetical focus for most medieval theologians was on the pain of childbirth and then its dangers. In the late medieval era, especially in sermon exempla and penitential manuals, the focus shifted slightly away from its pain to the dangers of delivery. John Mirk, an English Augustinian Friar who flourished in the early fifteenth century, is rather typical of this tradition. In both his exempla collection, *Festial*, and his pastoral instruction manual, he noted the curse of painful childbirth, but he focused more attention on the dangers facing the mother and her child. He encouraged pastors to be sure that soon-to-deliver mothers were completely shriven, "for the dread peril that may be-fall in their travailing that shall come."[37]

Despite the fact that Luther was preaching to the Wittenberg community in the city church in 1523, there is no mention of the need for mothers to be completely shriven before giving birth. While Luther continued to maintain the pastoral importance of confession, it did not have the same immediate, salvific weight or importance for the post-Reformation Luther that it would have had for Mirk. But, what that left him, then, was only the painful childbirth. And in 1523, the painful nature of childbirth seems to be his sole focus, "you shall give birth to your children in sorrow and pain."[38] He goes on to note that birth will always be painful because of Eve's sin, adding that the curse falls not just on Eve, but all women: "*non dictum est ad unam mulierum, sed omnes.*" But just in case any in the congregation might get the wrong idea and somehow believe men were likewise cursed to such pains and travails, he adds, "*viro non est impositum ferre dolores in pariendo.*"[39]

One of the first things one notices in 1535 is the change in tone and tenor. Even though these are more formal lectures, Luther is not as formal. Indeed, the opening line is one of the paradoxes that Luther loved to play with, "This punishment is inflicted on the woman, but it is a happy and joyful punishment."[40] Why is it a happy punishment? It is happy because, according to Luther, her punishment to childbirth is linked to the ultimate defeat of Satan—her offspring will crush the head of the serpent. Her body may die, but in the curse pronounced upon Satan, she also hears the surety of the resurrection, Luther says. Yes, she must be punished with death—but faith will enliven her soul to the sure hope of the resurrection.

When he turns to the specifics of Eve's punishment, the differences between 1523 and 1535 become even more apparent and, I argue, reflect the experiences of a father and husband. Pain is still there, of course, but his understanding of childbirth has expanded incredibly,

> This means that Eve's sorrows, which she would not have had if she had not fallen into sin, are to be great, numerous, and also of various kinds. The threat is directed particularly at birth and conception. But conception

designates the entire time during which the fetus, after being conceived, is carried in the womb, a time beset with severe and sundry ailments. From the beginning of that time a woman suffers very painful headaches, dizziness, nausea, an amazing loathing of food and drink, frequent and difficult vomiting, toothache, and a stomach disorder which produces a craving, called pica, for such foods from which nature normally shrinks. Moreover, when the fetus has matured and birth is imminent, there follows the most awful distress, because only with utmost peril and almost at the cost of her life does she give birth to her offspring.[41]

Luther the husband now understands the pain of the curse differently than Luther the celibate. He has lived with Katherina through six pregnancies. He seems intimately aware now of the pains and distress that begin almost immediately—headaches and morning sickness, odd food cravings, and the sudden—sometimes immediate—revulsion to specific foods or all food. Though certainly not exhaustive, I examined nearly fifty different medieval commentaries, sermon series, and exempla representations of Eve, none of them exhibits such details.[42] Most of those authors were celibate monks, some were priests—but even if the rare non-celibate priest was in that mix, they did not express their own experiences in their exegesis.[43] But Luther, proudly—and largely happily, I think—married, has brought his experiences in the home into his lecture hall. His early mystification at a mother's ability to calm an infant also continued into this lecture where he called mothers, "Masters at bearing and feeding and nurturing their children."[44]

Conclusion

Luther the father and husband has done more than just learn new information about pregnancy. Something more than just mystification at the brilliance of mothers has happened to him. He has been changed on an existential level, and that change has bled over into his work as a professor and exegete. Nowhere is this more evident than in his final thoughts on Eve's curse. In 1523, Luther went out of his way to note that men do not participate in the curse of a painful childbirth at all—the curse fell only upon Eve and her daughters. In 1535, he asks his students, "For what is there of such things that a man suffers in his own body?" The 1523 Luther would have said nothing. In 1535, however, he knows differently. He immediately answers his own question, "Through marriage the husband transfers, as it were, a part of those penalties (*poenarum*) upon himself (for he cannot without pain (*dolore*) see those things in his wife)."[45] Luther the husband heard his wife scream in childbirth and felt her pain. It changed him.[46]

The birth of a child is life's most pedestrian miracle. It happens day in and day out, all over the globe. Yet to the parents, it is miraculous and mystifying, awe-inspiring and exhausting, overwhelming and life-changing. We see such feelings in the letters Luther wrote to friends soon after Hans was born, when Hans was ill with the plague, and his terror when then-pregnant Katherina became ill with the plague as well. Those experiences overwhelmed centuries of theological and exegetical constructs of Eve and womanhood and changed how he understood Eve's curse. This was not a change wrought by his new Reformation theology.[47] This was not a change brought about even by ordinary encounters with women. This change is only attributable to the deeply personal experiences of being a father and husband.

Notes

1. *D. Martin Luthers Werke: Kritische Gesamtausgabe*. 120+ volumes. Weimar: Bohlaus, 1883 -. (Hereafter, *WA* for the writings, *WADB* for the Luther Bible, *WABR* for the letters, *WATr* for the Table Talks). "To Spalatin," End of June 1526, no. 1025; *WABr* 4:97.
2. Perhaps one of the most familiar to nearly all parents is the letter of 19 June 1530 to the three-year-old Hanschen in which Luther, away for the 1530 Diet of Augsburg, writes directly to the toddler, praising him for learning new letters and behaving well. Luther then promises, "keep this up, dear son, and I will bring you a nice present from the fair." *WABr* 5:377-378.
3. "To Justus Jonas," 10 November 1527, no. 1168; *WABr* 4:279-280; *LW* 49:173. Translation slightly altered.
4. "To Jakob Probst," 31 December 1527, no. 1193; *WABr* 4:313.
5. "To Nicholas Hausmann," 5 August 1528, no. 1303. *WABR* 4: 511; LW 49: 203.
6. "'Lustful Luther': Male Libido in the Writings of the Reformer," in Scott H. Hendrix and Susan C. Karant-Nunn, eds., *Masculinity in the Reformation Era* (Kirksville, MO: Trumann State University Press, 2008), 190–212.
7. Lecture on Ecclesiastes 7:35; *WA* 20:149.
8. David M. Whitford, *The Curse of Ham and the Early Modern Era: The Bible and the Justifications for Slavery* (Farnham, England: Ashgate, 2009), 4.
9. There was one earlier set of sermons, from 1519–1520. These sermons do cover Genesis 1–3 but are very brief snippets taken down by Johannes Poliander and thus are insufficient for sake of comparison. See, *WA* 9.
10. Hans, 7 June 1526; Elisabeth 10 December 1527–3 August 1528; Magdelena 4 May 1529; Martin 9 November 1531; Paul 28 January 1533; Margareta 17 December 1534. Magdelena died at 13 on 20 September 1542. Her death sent Luther into a deep depression.
11. All English translation of the Bible are from the Douay-Rheims edition of the early seventeenth century, as it is a near literal translation of the Latin Vulgate. Despite the fact that Luther had already translated Genesis into German by 1523, he continued to use the Vulgate in his teaching. The Latin reads, "*et ait faciamus hominem ad imaginem et similitudinem nostrum.*" Luther's 1523 German version reads, "und Got sprach, last uns menschen machen, eyn bild das uns gleych sey." Both the Latin and German use the word—human (homo/Mensch)—not man (vir/Mann).
12. Vulgate: "*et creavit Deus hominem ad imaginem suam ad imaginem Dei creavit illum masculum et feminam creavit eos benedixitque illis Deus et ait crescite et multiplicamini.*" 1523 German: "Und God schuff den menschen yhm zum bild, zum bild Gottis schuff er yhn/und er schuff sie eyn menlin und frewlin. Und Got segenet sei und sprach zu ynh, seyt fruchtbar und mehret euch."
13. Augustine, *On the Trinity*, X.12.19.
14. Kari Elisabeth Børresen, "Imago Dei, privilège masculin? Interprétation augustinienne et pseudo-augustinienne de Gen 1,27 et 1 Cor 11,7," *Augustinianum* 25 (1985): 213–34. Børresen notes that Ambrosiaster's denial of the *Imago Dei* also survived in Canon Law.

15 Gregory of Nyssa, "On the Nature of Man," XVII.2: "but whatever the mode of increase in the angelic nature is (unspeakable and inconceivable by human conjectures, except that it assuredly exists), it would have operated also in the case of men, 'who were made a little lower than the angels,' to increase mankind to the measure determined by its Maker."
16 Jerome, Letter 22, "To Eustochium."
17 Augustine, *City of God*, 14.24.
18 Augustine, *City of God*, 14.16.
19 *Glossa Ordinaria*, Genesis 1:27 – marginal gloss – wrongly attributed to Augustine. The quote is from Bede. See Karlfried Froehlich, et al, editors, *Biblia Latina cum glossa ordinaria: Introduction to the facsimile reprint of the edition princeps, Adolph Rusch of Strassburg 1480/81*, (Turnholt: Brepols, 1991), Genesis 1:27.
20 Melanchthon married Katharina Krapp in November 1520. Their daughter Anna was born in August 1522.
21 He wrote *On Monastic Vows* in 1521. He preached a sermon on marriage in 1519 and discussed marriage extensively in *On the Babylonian Captivity of the Church*, and again in another sermon on married life in 1522.
22 For more information on the sermons in general and their complicated and somewhat convoluted printing history, please see the introduction in *WA* 24 and Mickey Leland Mattox, *"Defender of the Most Holy Matriarchs": Martin Luther's Interpretation of the Women of Genesis in the Enarrationes in Genesin, 1535–45* (Leiden; Boston: Brill, 2003), 51. Much more extensively in his "Martin Luther's Interpretation of the Women of Genesis in the Context of the Christian Exegetical Tradition" (Duke University, 1997), 11ff. On the Genesis sermons and lectures relative to women and gender more generally, see Sabine Hiebsch, *Figura Ecclesiae: Lea und Rachel in Luthers Genesispredigten*, Arbeiten zur historischen und systematischen Theologie (Münster: Lit, 2002); John Lee Thompson, *John Calvin and the Daughters of Sarah: Women in Regular and Exceptional Roles in the Exegesis of Calvin, His Predecessors, and His Contemporaries*, Travaux D'humanisme et Renaissance (Geneva: Librairie Droz, 1992).
23 *WA* 24:50.
24 *WA* 24:51.
25 *WA* 24:53.
26 For Luther's very complex understanding of virginity and celibacy, please see Amy Leonard's chapter in this volume.
27 *WA* 24:53.
28 *WA* 24:89.
29 For a discussion of the ways in which Luther used these lectures to form Evangelical identity, see John A. Maxfield, *Luther's Lectures on Genesis and the Formation of Evangelical Identity* (Kirksville, MO: Truman State University Press, 2008).
30 *WA* 42:46; *LW* 1:62. Translation altered.
31 *WA* 42:46ff.
32 Timothy J. Orr, "Junker Jörg on Patmos," *Church History and Religious Culture* 95, no. 4 (2015): 435–456.
33 Bede is normative of this tradition.
34 *WA* 42:54. This perspective, like some others of his, will become normative later in exegesis (both Protestant and Catholic), but was not then. The significance of this change in emphasis will become even more apparent when Luther turned to discuss Genesis 3:16 directly.
35 Indeed, he seems even more impressed than he had been earlier. Fathers are reduced in his mind to the clumsiness of camels: "As for the mothers themselves, how deftly they move whenever the whimpering baby either has to be quieted or is to be placed into its cradle! Get a man to do the same things, and you will say that a camel is dancing, so clumsily will he do the simplest tasks around the baby!" *WA* 42:151; *LW* 1:202.
36 Douay-Rheims translation.

37 John Mirk, *Instructions for Parish Priests: By John Myrc [I.E. Mirk]*, ed. from Cotton Ms. Claudius A. II., by Edward Peacock (Millwood, NY: Kraus, 1975).
38 *WA* 24:101. This focus on the painfulness of birth itself seems to also be present in his translation of Genesis, which was also done in 1523, "Ich will dyr veil kummer schaffen wenn du schwanger wirst/du solt deyn kinder mit kummer gepern." 1523 Genesis, a2^v.
39 *WA* 14:141.
40 *WA* 42:148; *LW* 1:198.
41 *WA* 42:149-50; *LW* 1:199.
42 Medieval commentaries included Augustine's *Litera Genesis*, Gregory the Great's *Moralia*, Bede's *On Genesis*, Hugh of St. Cher, Bonaventure, Chrysostom, Alan of Lille, and others. Exempla and sermon series included, *Speculum Ecclesiae*, Vincent of Beauvais' *Speculum historiale*, the *Golden Legend*, Jacques de Vitry's *Sermones Feriales et Communes*, John Mirk, the anonymous *Vita Adae et Evae* (including Latin editions and Lutwin's High Middle German translation), Old English Homilies, and the *Repetorium of Middle English Sermons*. I did not limit myself to only German sources purposefully, since I was not interested in discovering Luther's possible sources, but the general ecclesiastical consensus on the text.
43 For a discussion of the precarious life of a non-celibate priest (and therefore why such a priest would be disinclined to use any life experiences in exempla or exegesis), see Marjorie Elizabeth Plummer, *From Priest's Whore to Pastor's Wife: Clerical Marriage and the Process of Reform in the Early German Reformation* (Farnham, England; Burlington, VT: Ashgate, 2012).
44 *WA* 42:150: "*Procreandae, alendae, et fovendae sobolis magistrae sunt.*"
45 *WA* 42:150; *LW* 1:200f. Translation altered.
46 Though it lies beyond the scope of this study, there is certainly a degree to which this was an emotional reaction for Luther. He was a man prone to strong emotions—in both good and ill measure. Susan Karant-Nunn has examined the ways in which different Reformation traditions (Lutheran, Calvinist, Roman Catholic) created or manifested different emotional timbres in their respective congregations via sermons on the Passion of Christ. This essay points out the need to examine the emotions of the reformers and preachers themselves and the roles those emotions played in their theological and ecclesiastical work. See Susan C. Karant-Nunn, *The Reformation of Feeling: Shaping the Religious Emotions in Early Modern Germany*, (Oxford: Oxford University Press, 2010). See also, Merry Wiesner-Hanks, "Overlaps and Intersections in New Scholarship on Empires, Beliefs, and Emotions," *Cromohs* 20 (2017): 1–24; Birgit Stolt, *Martin Luthers Rhetorik des Herzens* (Tübingen: Mohr Siebeck, 2000). Stolt has a brief discussion of Luther's emotional relationship with his children and the ways in which that reframed his understanding of God the Father. See pp. 177–180.
47 Again, it lies beyond the scope of this essay, but a larger study must examine the degree to which his new theological understandings of marriage, of the vocation of parenthood, and a generally more positive view of sexuality and children can also be attributed to his own life experiences as a parent and husband.

4

A "PRODIGAL SON" REMEMBERS JOHN OF THE CROSS[1]

Jodi Bilinkoff

Early in 1587, a young man of 19 entered the Discalced Carmelite friary in the Castilian city of Segovia, taking the religious name Alonso de la Madre de Dios. That April, John of the Cross, the cofounder of this new monastic order, stopped by for a visit. A brief encounter with this friar, noted for his deep spirituality and asceticism, would change Alonso's life. Many years later he would vividly recall the event and John's words:

> This occasion ... was the first and last time that I saw our holy Father and received his blessing and I had the great favor that in the morning, just before he left, coming to the door of the choir he asked that they call me. And after I left [the choir] he told me some things about Our Lord and the obligations that I had to be a good friar, since His Majesty had brought me to such a good religious order and because I had a brother of great worth and virtue in the same order then living in Genoa, called Fray Ferdinando de Santa María, for whom he had much love, this also obligated me to be good. With this he embraced me and gave me his blessing and left. A similar favor I desire that he grant to this his prodigal son at the hour of my death.[2]

In studying the life and writings of Alonso de la Madre de Dios, the twentieth-century Discalced Carmelite Fortunato Antolín cited this poignant testimony on at least two occasions. He quoted this passage but, intriguingly, left out the last sentence, Alonso's prayer.[3] This editorial decision raises several questions. Did Alonso identify with the young man of the parable in Luke 15:11-32 because he too had been guilty of misbehavior? Had he been wasteful with expenses? Anxious to preserve the reputation of a respected foundational figure and avoid retroactive scandal, did Antolín and others simply expunge Alonso's allusion to the scriptural text? In this essay, I examine the monastic career of Alonso de la Madre de Dios and his intense dedication to John of the Cross. As organizer of beatification hearings, witness, biographer, and guardian of John's tomb and relics, Alonso played a pivotal role in constructing his order's early history. Beyond this single example of identity-formation, moreover, his life suggests ways to consider the emotions, the senses, social relationships, and family dynamics in the making of male religious experience in early modern Catholic Europe. I offer, as well, my suggestions as to why Alonso equated himself with the problematic figure of the prodigal son.

Alonso Martínez Fernández was born in 1568 to a large family in a small town in the province of Zamora, in northwestern Spain. He had eleven siblings, but only one would play a significant role in his life. This was his brother Fernando. Ten years Alonso's senior, he entered the Discalced Carmelite order in 1577, only 15 years after its foundation by the future St. Teresa of Avila. In 1581, thirteen-year old Alonso was sent by his parents to meet his older brother at his friary in Alcalá and accompany him back for a home visit. Fernando's example and encouraging conversation during that long journey must have deeply influenced his younger brother, just then coming into maturity. Six years later, after completing his basic education, Alonso, too, became a Discalced Carmelite. He and Fernando would now share both the bonds of blood and of spiritual affiliation within a new "family," the Order of Our Lady of Mount Carmel.[4]

As his "holy father" had exhorted, Alonso de la Madre became a virtuous friar. During a nearly fifty-year monastic career he earned respect for his sage advice, embrace of monastic poverty, and writings on Carmelite history and liturgy. He found his true vocation, however, in preserving and promoting the memory of John of the Cross. John died on 14 December 1591, less than five years after his meeting with the young novice. During those years, Alonso had become a devotee. His esteem undoubtedly stemmed from several sources, including his brother Fernando, who had met John by 1583, and his own preferences for the ascetic and eremitic aspects of Carmelite spiritualty. As stories spread of John's final sufferings, his exemplary death, and of individuals miraculously cured by contact with his relics, many religious and laypeople began to regard him as a saint. Among them was Alonso de la Madre de Dios. From the first years of the seventeenth century until his death in 1636, Alonso committed himself to recording John's life and expediting his canonization. In the process, he told and molded the story of his own life.[5]

John of the Cross died in Ubeda, a small city in southern Spain. Alonso received the news at his friary in Segovia. He felt a strong need to see where the holy man had ended his life, talk to eye-witnesses, and place himself near John's entombed body. He would spend a year and a half in Ubeda "because of the devotion that [he] had for this Saint."[6] Before long, Alonso became deeply involved in the fortunes of John's body, its final resting place, proper commemoration, and thaumaturgic properties. Over the years, he deftly deployed the saint's physical relics and attendant material objects: engravings, altar cloths, tomb sculpture, and the like to promote John's cult.

Neither Alonso de la Madre de Dios nor John of the Cross was a native of Segovia. But Ana de Peñalosa and her brother Luis de Mercado were. These wealthy members of the urban elite, John's long-time devotees, had founded the Discalced Carmelite friary there in 1586. Doña Ana stipulated as part of her endowment that the saintly friar be buried in this house. The members of the Ubeda community, however, were determined to keep their precious relic. In April 1593, employees of don Luis journeyed from Segovia to Ubeda and made off with John's body in the dead of night. Alonso, living at the southern friary at the time, may well have witnessed this stunning episode of "holy theft."[7]

After more than a decade of recriminations between the two communities and a threatened lawsuit by the Ubeda friars, monastic officials finally brokered a compromise in 1606. The Segovia friars would keep (most of) John's remains but offer some significant body parts as relics for the Ubeda house. They assigned the task of post-mortem surgery to the prior of the Segovia friary. This was none other than Alonso de la Madre de Dios, elected to the post two years earlier. Two decades later, he would recall this moment, so important for his religious community, but also fraught with personal meaning:

> I had the grating that was in front of the sepulcher taken off and, after the precious coffer with the holy body had been lowered, **with my own hands I cut** from it one leg, from the knee below and one arm, from the elbow to the hand, judging that it would not be decent to cut anything else from a body that was still intact. With that, after all of us who were present had venerated the holy body, it was returned to its proper place, behind the strong grating. It was a marvelous thing that **when I cut these relics** everyone there sensed a most delicate fragrance and odor coming from the holy body, which lasted there for many days.[8]

Alonso thus carefully highlighted his own role in this sacred drama and the very tangible experience of handling and cutting flesh and bone.[9]

In subsequent years, Alonso continued to promote the cult of John of the Cross. He was, for example, among the most vociferous petitioners for permission to construct a new and much more elaborate sepulcher for John's remains at the Segovia friary. The current tomb was decent enough, he acknowledged, but lacked the grandeur required by the holy man's "many miracles, the saintliness of his life and the universal acclaim and devotion, and, finally, the manifestation of his sanctity that God, through various ways has made to the world." Alonso triumphantly described the inauguration of a large new sepulcher and chapel on 18 April 1618, meticulously cataloging the "diverse ex-votos and wax votive offerings donated by the faithful who had received favors from the Saint," as well as "images, hangings, altar cloths, carpets, and other such items with which to adorn the cult of the Saint."[10]

Over time Alonso took upon himself the role of guardian and manager of John's relics. He recalled many instances in which he brought pieces of the holy man's clothing or body to suppliants for thaumaturgic healing. Once in Ubeda, for example, a woman suffered from such a severe fever that doctors despaired of her life. "I took the relic [of John's foot] at nightfall," he recounted, "and I carried it over and put in on the sick woman who was paralyzed. And as it was placed upon her face, suddenly she returned to her former self ... with such vigor and strength that she was amazed, for she had been totally deprived of strength"[11] By 1627, Alonso could claim that relics and printed portraits of John had been distributed far and wide, even beyond Spain's borders. "From the Indies, people have sent urgent petitions to [me] for relics of the Saint and when [I] sent them items of the Saint, [the relics] were very esteemed out there; and not only was his flesh or bones esteemed, but any other object that had belonged to the Saint."[12] In relating these episodes, Alonso underscored John's intercessory powers, but also called attention to his own contribution to the cult-making process.

In 1614, Alonso de la Madre de Dios, now 46 years old, accepted a position that would give him official status as promoter of John's cult. His superiors appointed him to a three-year term as *procurador,* the person responsible for collecting and transcribing testimonies during the first of two sets of beatification hearings. Between November 1614 and April 1617, Alonso threw himself into this enterprise. He traveled widely, helped to compose the required formal questionnaire, and arranged for dozens of people, religious and lay, to testify as to John's holy life, exemplary death, and numerous post-mortem miracles. He would now utilize written and oral sources with the same enthusiasm he had shown for relics and other material objects.

Alonso's work as *procurador,* in many ways, resembled that of a modern-day oral historian or ethnographer. His own testimony, given during the second phase of beatification hearings in 1627, provides insights into his earlier activities. We learn, for example, that he consulted a variety of documents: private letters, directives from ecclesiastical authorities, and records of his order's chapter meetings.[13] Asked if he had read any of John's books, Alonso replied that he had indeed seen them in both manuscript form, including some originals "in the Saint's own handwriting," and later, as printed books. He added that because of the great demand for John's writings he had prudently kept the manuscripts to prevent any more copies from being made before publication.[14]

Alonso also tried to learn all he could about John of the Cross by way of the spoken word. He interviewed people who had personally known the holy man, identifying some of his order's "elderly fathers and aged nuns." Alonso reported that he had visited locations in Andalusia, "where the Saint lived and served as a monastic superior for many years." He claimed that in these communities "the memory of his paternal governance has endured twenty-eight years after his death, and that his pronouncements and words were still considered oracles, and as such they are still cited and followed today by the most observant friars."[15] At his own house in Segovia, he asked his older monastic brethren to recall their emotions upon learning of John's demise, and spent time in Ubeda, "making inquiries among the friars and laypeople who had been there at [the time of] his death"[16]

For Alonso, this work proved integral to his very identity as a Discalced Carmelite. In a brief draft of John's life composed around 1627, the author explained that this account was "taken from beatification hearings by Father Friar Alonso de la Madre de Dios, their *procurador*."[17] The prologue to the full-length book featured an even longer presentation of credentials: "I have collected [information] from that which I saw and knew while the Saint was living and which after his death I ascertained from the hearings into his life, sanctity and miracles ... at which I, appointed *procurador* by my order ... was present."[18]

Others highlighted the association between Alonso and this office as well. A Latin document from the Segovia friary lists a *"Frater Ildephonsus a Matre Dei, Procurator beatificationis."*[19] Upon his death on 28 August, 1636, his friend Diego de Colmenares, chronicler of the city of Segovia, remembered Alonso's efforts on behalf of "the beatification of his great founder and master Friar John of the Cross."[20] A generation later, Francisco de Santa María, then official historian of the Discalced Carmelite order, would likewise praise Alonso for his work as *procurador*, which "added great esteem to the authority and sanctity of Our Venerable Father."[21] These people well understood the connection between the man and his role in the saint-making process.

After so many years of collecting written documents, material objects, and oral testimonies, Alonso de la Madre de Dios was eminently prepared for his final task, writing the life of John of the Cross. He spent his last 15 years in his first monastic home, the Segovia friary. Here Alonso devoted himself to the biographer's craft. He composed the first of three accounts, a concise *Summary of the Life and Miracles of the Venerable Father Friar John of the Cross* around 1623; this text was printed in Antwerp in 1625.[22] About two years later, he sketched out a *Brief Compendium of the Life of the Blessed Father Friar John of the Cross*, which would serve as a draft or outline for a longer work.[23] Finally, around 1630, Alonso completed an extensive biography he titled the *Life, Virtues, and Miracles of the Holy Father Friar John of the Cross, Master and Father of the Reform of the Order of Discalced Friars of Our Lady of Mount Carmel*. While the modern edition of this text well exceeds six hundred printed pages, the author left numerous spaces and blank pages in the manuscript. Failing health may have prevented him from adding even more material, as he had intended.[24]

The portrait of John of the Cross fashioned by Alonso de la Madre de Dios may come as a surprise to today's scholars and admirers. In his accounts, Alonso repeatedly stressed two features of his subject: his life as suffering victim and his afterlife as worker of miracles, especially thaumaturgic healing. The author said very little about John's work as a theologian or biblical exegete and made no comments about his poetry. From these Baroque beginnings one could never have guessed that in the twentieth century John of the Cross would be honored as a Doctor of the Church and declared the patron saint of poets in the Spanish language.[25]

While Alonso's *Life, Virtues, and Miracles* remained unpublished, Discalced Carmelite officials ordered the manuscript to be kept for reference in the archive of the Segovia friary. Consequently, his *magnum opus* became well-known among his monastic brothers and sons and was frequently cited by the order's chroniclers. In his 1655 history, for example, Francisco de Santa María acknowledged that he had consulted Alonso's written volumes in preparing his own and praised his predecessor's "great fidelity [to the truth]."[26] The life-writings of Alonso de la Madre de Dios thus played a key role in the formation of a hagiographical profile of John of the Cross. The long process of constructing and promoting his sanctity would finally bear fruit at John's beatification, in 1675, and canonization, in 1726.

When Alonso de la Madre de Dios died in 1636, members of his monastic community eulogized him as a man "of great qualities and holiness, on whom Our Lord bestowed grand gifts and favors."[27] Why then, would he identify himself with the prodigal son? The word that seems to stand out here is "prodigal," a person who is wasteful or extravagant. The first part of the parable, after all, relates how the younger of two sons "went abroad into a far country and there wasted his substance, living riotously." His older brother bitterly criticized him for "devour[ing] his substance with harlots ...."[28] This extremely negative characterization hardly seems to fit the conscientious and devout Alonso. His comment must have puzzled and possibly scandalized his Discalced Carmelite readers.

Let us return, then, to Alonso's account of his meeting with John of the Cross in 1587. John called the novice away from his choir duties for a fatherly exhortation. He reminded Alonso of the "obligations" he had to be "a good friar," reinforcing this sentiment by referring to his older brother Fernando, a friar "he much loved." The presence of the exemplary Fernando in the order further "obligated" Alonso "to be good," John instructed.

That Alonso would make the association between his own family circumstances and the biblical story of the prodigal son now seems entirely comprehensible, even inevitable. The parable is nothing if not a tale of two brothers. Some translators, in fact, render its title "The Prodigal (or Lost) Son and the Dutiful Son." Like commentators before him and since, Alonso de la Madre de Dios read this scripture in his own, somewhat idiosyncratic way.[29]

What if he understood John's exhortation to mean that he should be a good friar, just like his brother? This would have set a virtually impossible standard for him, because, in at least one, crucial respect, Alonso and Fernando were very different. Beyond contrasting personalities, their divergent paths reflect a paradox faced by male religious throughout the Christian centuries. As R. N. Swanson has persuasively argued, the medieval construct of clerics as "unworldly celibates" resulted in a deep ambivalence about their status and a "constant tension between the wish that priests be angels, and their urge to be men."[30] In the case of the Discalced Carmelites, friars were expected to embrace lives of ascetic humility, but also hold offices and exercise public authority in the service of their order.

Fernando de Santa María exhibited strong administrative and leadership abilities from early in his monastic career. Born in 1558, he professed as a Discalced Carmelite at the age of 20. Only five years later, in 1583, he was chosen to represent his friary at the chapter meeting held in the town of Almodóvar, where he met John of the Cross and other leaders of the reform. In 1585 he was among a small group sent to establish the first friary outside Spain, in Genoa. The following year Fernando's monastic brothers elected him assistant prior, then, in 1591, prior. He left Genoa for Rome in 1598, where he became involved in the foundation of Discalced Carmelite friaries throughout Italy and, eventually, other parts of western Europe as well. In 1605, Ferdinando di Santa Maria (as he was now known) was elected general of the Italian Congregation and reelected in 1614 and 1629. He died in 1631, at the age of 73, remembered for his nearly fifty years of service to his order and climb up its chain of command.[31]

Alonso de la Madre de Dios, in contrast, harbored a deep aversion to positions of authority. Around 1601, at the age of 21, he was called into temporary service upon the sudden death of the prior of his friary in Toro. Having first tried to excuse himself from this duty, he wrote hastily to his brother, who advised that he strengthen his resolve by reading the Psalms.[32] Alonso was elected to a three-year term as prior of Segovia in 1604. His tenure included the resolution of the conflict with the Ubeda friars when he cut and distributed the bodily remains of John of the Cross, arguably a significant achievement. Nevertheless, he turned down the offer of a second term and refused to accept the even more prestigious position of regional supervisor (*provincial*) of Castile. In September 1607, Alonso complained in a letter to a friend that he lacked both the health and fortitude required of superiors and expressed his desire to remain "un común religioso."[33] By 1619 his language had grown even more insistent. He wrote to Fernando in Rome that he experienced "bouts of melancholy that have made all [his] hair turn grey." Adding that he now possessed "so little bodily and spiritual strength," he begged his influential brother to intercede with his superiors to grant his request for exemption from office-holding.[34] Alonso spent a year at one of his order's remote hermitages, then returned to the Segovia friary. There he lived until his death, at the age of 68, praying every day at the tomb containing the body of John of the Cross that he had touched with his own hands.[35]

Ironically, Alonso's preference for solitude and contemplation and marked indifference to authority closely resembled the spiritual style of his revered role model, John of the Cross, who, famously, in a mystical dialogue with Christ, had asked to die as a humble friar, without office.[36] It differentiated him, however, from the older brother he believed John wanted him to emulate. Alonso's perceived failure to measure up to Fernando and merit the same love from their common spiritual father made him feel like the prodigal son and compelled him to beseech John for his forgiveness and blessing.

There may have been another reason why this parable resonated so deeply with Alonso. For him, the crucial passage could be found in the middle of the story, when the younger son decides to make the journey home: "And when he was yet a great way off, his father saw him and was moved with compassion and running to him fell upon his neck and kissed him." Recall that the friar was remembering the time many years before when John sought him out, offered words of advice, and then "embraced [him] and gave [him] his blessing." Experiencing that embrace, the physical touch of the man he believed to be a saint, may have been the single most significant moment in his emotional life. As the cultural historian Constance Classen has noted, the "most highly valued form of religious touch was that which brought one in direct physical contact with holiness ...."[37] Little wonder, then, that Alonso would fervently pray that at his death, John, like the compassionate father of the parable, would offer again his embrace.[38] It was this privileged status as recipient of John's remarkable touch that made Alonso his prodigal son, not any profligate spending or loose moral behavior.

Examining the texts produced by Alonso de la Madre de Dios reveals a valuable, even unique perspective on the early history of the Discalced Carmelites and the myriad efforts to construct their complicated first friar as a saint. Alonso dedicated himself to glorifying and preserving the memory of John of the Cross, an enterprise that required his mind, his spirit, and his body with its sensory faculties.[39] His case reminds us of the need to take seriously the issues such as affective bonds, family relations, the meanings assigned to material objects, and the emotional power of touch in the formation of male monastic identities in early modern Catholic Europe.

Notes

1 I offer my sincere thanks to Jessica Boon, David Boruchoff, William A. Christian Jr, Ignacio López Alemany, Katrina Olds, Rebeca San Martín Bastida, Carole Slade, Alison Weber, and David Whitford for reading earlier drafts of this essay and offering their help and support.
2 Alonso de la Madre de Dios, *Vida, virtudes y milagros del santo padre Fray Juan de la Cruz, maestro y padre de la Reforma de la Orden de los Descalzos de Nuestra Señora del Monte Carmelo*, ed. Fortunato Antolín (Madrid: Editorial de Espiritualidad, 1989, orig. c. 1630), 448.
3 Fortunato Antolín, "El P. Alonso de la Madre de Dios, Asturicense," *Astorica* 4 (1986): 125–166 (here, 128); Fortunato Antolín, "Vida inédita de San Juan de la Cruz del Padre Alfonso de la Madre de Dios 'El Asturicense'," *Astorica* 8 (1989): 107–142 (here, 110). In neither article did Antolín include ellipses to indicate that he had truncated this passage.
4 Antolín, "El P. Alonso," 126–132.
5 Antolín refers to Alonso as "un enamorado de S. Juan de la Cruz," and comments, "Se puede decir que toda su vida desde que le conoció no cesó de gravitar en torno al Santo, de una manera o de otra." "El P. Alonso," 155, 164.
6 "Procesos de Beatificación y Canonización," in *Obras de San Juan de la Cruz*, ed. Silverio de Santa Teresa (Burgos: El Monte Carmelo, 1929–1931), 5:397–398.
7 For the foundation and early history of the Segovia friary see Fortunato Antolín, *San Juan de la Cruz en Segovia: Apuntes históricos* (Segovia: Caja de Ahorros y Monte de Piedad, 1984), ch.1; Teófanes Egido López, "San Juan de la Cruz: Reflexión histórica desde Segovia," *Estudios Segovianos* 36 (1995): 257–277; *God Speaks in the Night: The Life, Times, and Teaching of St. John of the Cross*, trans. Kieran Kavanaugh (Washington, DC: Institute of Carmelite Studies, 1991), 317–341. Alonso offered a detailed account of the "translation" of John's body from Ubeda to Segovia but was vague about his own role. *Vida*, 586–591. See also Tomás Alvarez, "S. Juan de la Cruz—De Ubeda a Segovia: Relato del traslado de sus restos mortales, 1593," *El Monte Carmelo* 99 (1991): 273–317.

8 "…[H]ice arrancar la reja que estaba ante el sepulcro y, bajada la preciosa arca con el santo cuerpo, con mis manos corté de él la una pierna de la rodilla abajo y el un brazo, del codo a la mano, juzgando a menos decencia cortar otra cosa a un cuerpo que aún entero. Con esto, después de haber todos los presentes venerado el santo cuerpo, se volvió a su lugar decente, debajo de su fuerte reja. Fue cosa maravillosa que cuando corté estas reliquias sentimos todos los presentes salir del santo cuerpo una fragrancia y olor suavísimo, el cual duró allí por muchos días." *Vida*, 623 [emphasis mine]. See also "Procesos," 402.

9 For the theology and practice of venerating the bodily relics of saints, see Caroline Walker Bynum, *Christian Materiality: An Essay on Religion in Late Medieval Europe* (New York: Zone Books, 2011), 19–31, 131–139, 177–186.

10 "… sus muchos milagros, su santidad de vida y aplauso y devoción universal y, finalmente, la manifestación que Dios, por diversos caminos hacía al mundo de su santidad … diversos votos y presentallas de cera que los fieles por mercedes que han recibido del Santo le han ofrecido … imágenes, frontales, manteles, alfombras y otras cosas tales para adorno del culto del Santo." *Vida*, 626–631; "Procesos," 402. Antolín, *San Juan de la Cruz en Segovia*, 37–43; María Luisa Herrera García, "La capilla y los sepulcros que acogieron el cuerpo de San Juan de la Cruz en el convento de Carmelitas Descalzos en Segovia," in *Segovia 1088–1988: Actas del Congreso de Historia de la Ciudad* (Segovia: Junta de Castilla y León, 1991), 673–686. Ten years later Alonso's brother, Fernando, now general of the order's Italian Congregation, sent more gifts for the sepulcher. *Vida*, 631, no. 8.

11 *Vida*, 649–650.

12 "Procesos," 410.

13 "Procesos," 372, 385, 392–393, 402.

14 "… los ha visto manuscritos, y después impresos, y algunos de ellos originales de letra del Santo … y que todos han sido muy procurados de muchas personas y traslados a mano; y tan buscados, que tiene este testigo para sí que no ha habido libro alguno de que se hayan hecho más traslados manuscritos antes que se imprimiesen." "Procesos," 397. Interestingly, out of some thirty questions posed to witnesses during the beatification hearings, only one (#21) inquired about John of the Cross as a writer.

15 "Vió asimismo este testigo que en Andalucía, donde vivió el Santo prelado muchos años, duraba la memoria de su govierno paternal veinte y ocho años después de muerto, y que permanecían sus sentencias y palabras como oráculos, y por tales se citan y siguen hoy por los religiosos más observantes." "Procesos, "375. John lived in southern Spain, serving in various supervisory positions, between 1578 and 1588. I have suggested that opinions regarding his leadership were more complex and divided than Alonso indicated. Jodi Bilinkoff, "First Friar, Problematic Founder: John of the Cross in His Earliest Biographies," in *Reforming Reformation*, ed. Thomas F. Mayer (Burlington, VT: Ashgate, 2012), 103–118.

16 "Procesos," 397–398.

17 "Vida inedita," 122.

18 *Vida*, 39.

19 Transcribed in *Vida*, 630.

20 "Fue el primer novicio que aquí recibió hábito nuestro venerable amigo Frai Alonso de la Madre de Dios … procurador general en las informaciones … de la beatificación de su gran fundador y maestro Frai Juan de la Cruz …" Diego de Colmenares, *Historia de la Insigne Ciudad de Segovia y Compendio de las Historias de Castilla* (Valladolid: Ediciones Maxtor, 2005, orig. 1637–1640), 3:202.

21 "… a la autoridad, i santidad de N.V.P. Fray Iuan de la Cruz añadir grande estima, con las informaciones, que para su Beatificación hizo …" Francisco de Santa María, *Reforma de los Descalzos de N.S. del Carmen* (Madrid, 1655), 2:297. Antolin comments, "La causa de San Juan de la Cruz iba a ocupar la vida de Alonso durante unos años, y se iba a dedicar como ninguno al proceso de Beatificación." "El P. Alonso," 140.

22 *Summa de la Vida y Milagros del Venerable Padre Fray Juan de la Cruz Primer Descalzo de la Reforma de Nuestra Señora del Carmen* (Antwerp: En casa de Pedro y Iuan Belleres, 1625). This text is included in *Primeras Biografías y Apologías de San Juan de la Cruz*, ed. Fortunato Antolín (Salamanca: Junta de Castilla y León, 1991), 51–79. I have also consulted a copy of the original printed edition in the National Library of Spain, Madrid.

23 Antolín, "Vida inédita," 122–142.

24 See note 2 above. This critical edition of 1989 represents the first time Alonso's book was published. I also consulted the autograph manuscript copy in the National Library of Spain. For composition and publication histories of these early biographies, see José Vicente Rodríguez, "Historiografía sanjuanista: Inercias y revisiones," in *Aspectos históricos de San Juan de la Cruz*, ed. Comisión Provincial del IV Centenario de la muerte de San Juan de la Cruz (Avila: Institución "Gran Duque de Alba," 1990), 7–24.

25 Pope Pius XI declared John a Doctor of the Church on 24 August 1926. In 1952, the Spanish Ministry of National Education named him the patron of Spanish poets. On 8 March 1993, Pope John Paul II pronounced him patron saint of all poets writing in the Spanish language. *God Speaks in the Night*, v–xii; 374–379; José Vicente Rodríguez, *San Juan de la Cruz: La biografía* (Madrid: San Pablo, 2012), 867, 906–908.

26 "Pudo con esto dexamos algunos tomos que oy nos aprovechan a los que trabajamos ... con escribir despues de su vida con grande legaldad." Francisco de Santa María, *Reforma*, 2:297.

27 "Hombre de grandes prendas y santidad, a quien nuestro Señor comunió grandes dones y Mercedes." Antolín, "El P. Alonso," 145, quoting from the "Libro de Difuntos de Segovia."

28 I quote here from the 1582 Douay-Rheims English translation of the Vulgate that Alonso would have read.

29 "The parable of the prodigal son, since it arguably has been referenced and interpreted more than any other parable of Jesus, provides almost countless examples of the directions further explorations could take." David B. Gowler, *The Parables after Jesus: Their Imaginative Receptions across Two Millennia* (Grand Rapids, MI: Baker, 2017), 9.

30 R.N. Swanson, "Angels Incarnate: Clergy and Masculinity from Gregorian Reform to Reformation," in *Masculinity in Medieval Europe*, ed. D.M. Hadley (New York: Longman, 1999), 160–177 (here, 161). Jacqueline Murray makes similar points in "Masculinizing the Religious Life: Sexual Prowess, the Battle for Chastity and Monastic Identity," in *Holiness and Masculinity in the Middle Ages*, ed. P.H. Cullum and Katherine J. Lewis (Cardiff: University of Wales Press, 2004), 24–42.

31 Anastasio Roggero, *Genova e gli inizi della Riforma Teresiana in Italia (1584–1597)* (Genoa: Sagep, 1984), 34–36, 65–66, 140–141. Alonso digressed in his life of John of the Cross to brag about his brother's accomplishments, "En esta ocasion se despachó a Génova al padre fray Ferdinando de Santa María, mi hermano *secundum carnem* ... en cuyos brazos nació y se ha criado y propagado por el orbe la Congregación de Descalzos Carmelitas *extra Hispaniam,* de la cual ha sido general tres veces ... venerado de todos ..." *Vida,* 412. According to Antolín, Pope Paul V chose Fernando as his personal confessor. *Vida,* 412, n. 3.

32 Antolín quotes Fernando's reply from a history of the Discalced Carmelite reform published in 1706, "Si quiere V.R., acertar en un gobierno, ya que no ha podido excusarlo, traiga muy presente el verso 5 del salmo 44 de David ..." [in modern editions, 45:4]. "El Padre Alonso," 133, n. 44.

33 "Yo me veo no tengo fuerzas para más que un común religioso y no para añiduras. Estoy muy quebrado de fuerzas y salud y no ya para valentías de perlado." Antolín, "El Padre Alonso," 154.

34 "He llevado después acá tantas melancolías que me han encanecido del todo ... estoy tan desvencijado y quebrado y con tan pocas fuerzas corporales y espirituales que no estoy para ello." Antolín, "El P. Alonso," 143, 154. Francisco de Santa María commented in

his mid-seventeenth century history of the order, "Estos dos oficios últimos renunció con tanta esfuerzo, que consiguio, i añadió a sus grandes méritos este mayor que todos." *Reforma*, 2:297. Melancholy, its manifold definitions, causes, and treatment, has recently attracted much attention from scholars of early modern Europe. While there has been some treatment of individual nuns and convent communities, its incidence among male religious awaits sustained examination. For an introduction to the topic in Spain generally see Elena Carrera, "Madness and Melancholy in Sixteenth and Seventeenth-Century Spain: New Evidence, New Approaches," *Bulletin of Spanish Studies* 87–8 (2010): 1–15, and other articles in this special issue.

35 "Y asimismo, dijo este testigo que habrá tres años, poco mas or menos, que entrando un día a boca de noche, como tiene de costumbre todos los días, a visitar el sepulcro del santo padre fray Juan …" "Procesos," 407.

36 I discuss this episode in "First Friar," 117–118.

37 Classen adds that "the way in which the power of relics was accessed was, above all, through touch. If the relic could not be touched directly, then its container, whether a tomb or a reliquary, was touched." *The Deepest Sense: A Cultural History of Touch* (Urbana, IL: University of Illinois Press, 2012), 35–40. See also Pablo Acosta-García, "A Clash of Theories: Discussing Late Medieval Devotional Perception," in *Touching, Devotional Practices, and Visionary Experience in the Late Middle Ages*, ed. David Carrillo-Rangel, Delfi Nieto-Isabel, and Pablo Acosta-García (London: Palgrave Macmillan, 2019), 1–17.

38 Alonso's emotional and sensory responses may also have been influenced by his reading of John's poetry. Considering the first stanza of "Dark Night" (*Noche oscura*), Christopher Hinkle writes, "This urgent longing leads John into erotic raptures as he describes the search for his divine Lover and then to a point where words fail altogether as he receives the touch of divine union." "Love's Urgent Longings: St John of the Cross," in *Queer Theology: Rethinking the Western Body*, ed. Gerald Loughlin (New York: Blackwell, 2007), 188–199 (here, 188).

39 Here I show my indebtedness to the work of Merry Wiesner-Hanks, in particular, her brilliant organization of human experience according to the categories of body, mind, and spirit in *Women and Gender in Early Modern Europe*.

5

WOMEN, CONFLICT, AND PEACEMAKING IN GERMAN VILLAGES

Marc R. Forster

In the seventeenth century, women were a regular presence in the lower courts and village courts of Southwest Germany, as they were across Europe.[1] They appeared as plaintiffs and defendants, independently or alongside husbands or other family members. They pursued legal action against other women, and against men, and defended themselves against a range of charges. Just as men, they used the local courts to defend their property rights, negotiate inheritances, seek payment of debts or relief from creditors, often in search of arbitration leading to a compromise agreement. Also, like men, women defended their honor against slander and accusations of moral failing. In this realm, however, women faced the routine slander of "witch and whore," which had rather different implications than the standard insult of "rogue and thief" (*Schelm und Dieb*) faced by men.[2] The final set of issues that brought women into courts were those around marriage and family. Women came to court to try to enforce promises of marriage, to explain the "too early" birth of a child, and to ask for protection from abusive husbands.[3]

Taken together, the experience of women in these courts reflects tensions at the heart of gender relations in rural society. Women were clearly important to the success of the family economy and they played an active role in the management of farms, shops, mills, or taverns. They brought property into marriages which they continued to control and they understood and defended their rights. Women often stood by their husbands in court, testifying in defense of their family's rights and honor. Women were in important ways powerful and their voices were respected and often feared, and, although minimized as *Weibergeschwätz*, men and women often used the courts to try to suppress female voices. Women's status and honor, indeed their very place in their family and community, was publicly defined primarily by their sexuality, their virginity as unmarried girls and women and their sexual behavior as wives and widows. As Laura Gowing puts it: "… the word 'whore' stood for a whole way of defining women."[4] This tension, between the

TABLE 5.1 Involvement of women in the minutes (*Verhörprotokolle*) of the lower court of the Deutschordenskommende Mainau

Year	Total entries/cases	Women in entries	Percentage	Source
1661–1663	63	21	33%	GLAK 61/7599
1672	130	33	25%	GLAK 61/7600
1673	52	16	30%	GLAK 61/7600
1684	47	17	36%	GLAK 61/7602
1710	161	39	24%	GLAK 61/7606

Entries = an entry in the *Protokolle* (minutes). Some cases have multiple entries.
Women in entries = as plaintiff, defendant, or witness.

value and power of women and their vulnerability to sexual insult, which I might characterize as that between the practical realities of daily life and the demands of a patriarchal gender ideology, is continually reflected in the court records.[5]

The Niedergericht in Mainau in action

Some of this tension around the role of women in courts can be seen if we look at the routine activities of one of these courts in two different months, January 1672 and April 1684. The *Niedergericht* (lower court) at the headquarters of the Teutonic Knights on the island of Mainau adjudicated 13 different cases over 5 meeting days in January of 1672. The busiest of these days was January 23. On that day, the court first dealt with a dispute over damage done to a fishing net, a conflict that required finding an impartial observer to inspect the damage and report to the court.[6] Two of the entries record the appointment and swearing of oaths by two midwives and their two "helpers."[7]

On the same day, January 23, several women appeared before the court to defend their families. A fight between two boys led to injuries, and the mother of the injured boy demanded *Schmerzensgeld* (damages) for her son, as well as the barber costs (i.e. medical costs). Although the mother of the other boy defended her son, saying he had not started the fight, the court ordered her to pay damages and costs. In a second case, Elizabeth Golterin sued her brother for back wages and a pair of shoes he owed her. The court sided with Golterin. Finally, Barbara Bauchlin, supported by her father, brought suit against Jerg Mengin for getting her pregnant. It is unclear why Mengin's mother was a codefendant. Perhaps she was accused of abetting the crime, or perhaps because Mengin was a minor. The court asked for more evidence and the case disappeared from the records. Perhaps the parties had come to an agreement, as frequently happened in such cases?[8]

This same court heard seven cases in April 1684.[9] Several of the cases are typical of agricultural communities. A man was fined for stealing grapes, several others for stealing wood, and a group of four men were fined for illegally selling manure. A husband and wife sued their neighbors in a dispute over the boundary between an orchard and a vineyard. Two men disputed ownership of a field. Jacob Mayer

Hebraer, a Jewish horse trader, brought six different complaints in one hearing, all against men, seeking to collect debts from the sale of horses. In these cases, the court worked to arrange agreements between the parties, since many of the debtors clearly had few resources.

The court also recorded the resolution of a dispute over a marriage, in which the young couple had agreed to marry. The record explicitly states that the bride, Anna Maria Mergin, agreed to marry "... with well-thought-out reason, without being forced or pressured."[10] Here the court was not only concerned to make sure that Anna Mergin's promise of marriage was legitimate, but also defended her right to make such a promise on her own.

Finally, the court heard the complaint of Mathias Waldpardt against his sister-in-law, Ursula Bonauerin. Waldpardt sought redress because Bonauerin had accused him "... of being responsible for the blows that she [Ursula] gets from her husband, Georg Merckhen, [which Georg gives her] for her insufferable mouth" (*unerleidenlichen Mauls*)." He also accused Bonauerin of trying to break up his marriage by calling him *ein Ehe vertrenner* ("a marriage divider"). Bonauerin did not deny her words and "did not want to understand or back away [and refused to say] that the complainant was not guilty of this [i.e. encouraging the beatings]." The court ruled that, since she could not prove Waldpardt's guilt, and that her husband had suffered from her "evil mouth," Bonauerin would be punished by being displayed in the stocks before the church on the following Sunday. Furthermore, she was to stay away from Waldpardt and not enter his house, which was of course also her sister's house.[11] The court in this case was digging deeply into the domestic and family relations in these two families and, as happened fairly often, finding a woman guilty of a sharp tongue. As also happened often, Bonauerin was punished for faults that were not part of the original charge, in this case verbally abusing her husband.

These examples reflect general patterns in how people used the lower court in Mainau from the 1660s until the 1720s and probably beyond. Women were active in the wide range of cases involving property and the regulation of agricultural life. Yes, certain kinds of conflicts were male domains, for example the buying of livestock and the illegal cutting of wood (*Holzfrevel*). But women could be involved in illegal pasturing cases, in the stealing of fruit and other crops, and in boundary disputes as well. These cases reflect the gender division of work in this region, but we see that women could, and often did, testify in court alongside their husbands, sons, and fathers in property disputes.

Other disputes that came to court were even more likely to have female protagonists. Women brought suit against men who had reneged on promises of marriage and they sued for child support from men who had fathered their illegitimate children. In 1672, for example, about 40% of the cases involving women revolved around issues of marriage, family, and sexuality. Four of the 33 the cases were about marriage promises, two were paternity suits, and four were cases of men and women being fined together for pregnancy before marriage (*frühzeitige Beischlaf*).[12] Women were also parties to inheritance disputes, whether within families or in cases where families tried to retain rights—such as the right to keep a land lease—against lords or landlords. Finally, as we saw in the Ursula Bonauerin case above, women were frequently implicated in slander cases. And, although these slander cases often derived from other disputes, or came to replace the original issues in that conflict, in doing so women came to be judged almost exclusively on two issues—their "foul mouths" and thus the concern with publicity, usually framed as "women's gossip" (*Weibergeschwätz*), and, above all, their sexuality.[13]

The fate of Johanna Silberin, Wirtin in Mimmenhausen

In the early 1690s, Johanna Silberin was the *Wirtin*, that is the wife of the innkeeper, in the large village of Mimmenhausen, near the monastery of Salem. Between 1696 and 1698, Silberin appeared at least six times before one of the two courts at Salem.[14] In all these cases, Silberin and her husband came into conflict with their neighbors (and with each other). Furthermore, it is clear that these neighbors, men and women, considered Silberin a difficult woman of questionable moral character. In her case one can see clearly the significance placed on the twin issues—publicity and sexuality—that came to the forefront in all cases of slander involving women.

Silberin first appears in the records of the *Oberamtsgericht* at Salem on 22 February 1696 as the complainant.[15] She accused another woman, Catherina Messmerin, of slander, saying Messmerin had publicly called her a *Luoder*, a wicked or debauched person. Messmerin admitted using this word "stating, if she (Silberin) were an honorable person, she would not have a camisole made for her [purchased for her?] by the soldiers in the camp." Furthermore, she said, the *Wirtin* has called her a whore. Silberin testified that this latter accusation was true, since Messmerin, a servant, had arrived in Mimmenhausen pregnant. Messmerin admitted this as well but testified "she had only said that she was pregnant so that she could get a husband, it was not true, she had done nothing with the fellow" (*sie habe auch nichts mit dem Kerl gehabt*). Pressed by the court, which was not convinced by this story, Messmerin (apparently successfully) hit a different emotional register. "She responded very mournfully and with tears in her eyes, that she is an ignorant girl and had not thought through what she was saying. Despite what she had said, she is innocent and a virgin."[16] The court ruled in favor of Silberin, requiring Messmerin to apologize and telling both women, under threat of more serious punishment, "to use such words more carefully in the future."

This case involved a dispute between women. Silberin, the wife of the innkeeper, was using the court to defend her honor, with some success. This was, as we will see, a risky strategy, as testimony in these local courts was fairly freewheeling and the behavior and reputation of the complainant was always fair game. What stands out about these cases is that two issues, women's sexuality and issues of publicity, were central to both the way people used courts and the way courts thought about their work. Almost every dispute involving women, and certainly every dispute involving slander, referenced sexuality. At the same time, women's words were powerful, especially if delivered in a public setting. Furthermore, it is worth noting that it was not uncommon for women to bring complaints against other women; they too were invested in notions of "proper" sexual behavior and gender norms.[17]

In May 1696, Silberin again appeared in court, this time as the defendant.[18] Early one morning, she had confronted Catherina Hagenbacherin, the servant (*Dienstmädel*) and cousin of Valentin Hagenbach. "Who said you, Hagenbacherin, could cut grass there, to which she answered her employer told to do this, to which the *Wirtin* said further, your cousin is doing this to me, he wants to take the field from me, come here I want to mess you up. At this point, she [Silberin] began to hit her hard." The maid fled, but she admitted in court to calling Silberin a "soldier's whore" one time, although Silberin testified that Hagenbacherin had called her a *Stutten* (a bawd) at least twelve times, while Hagenbacherin said Silberin had called her a whore. The court ruled against Silberin this time, fining her 1 *Gülden*, a substantial fine. In the final decision, the court stated that in the future Silberin should "contain her unnecessary slander and fighting and should seek to maintain peaceful behavior, if she should ever seek help from the lordship when her honor or good name are injured."

A year later, in June 1697, Silberin came into conflict in a similar way with another woman, this time Barbara Steüerin, not a maid but a person of some status in the village.[19] Silberin brought a charge of slander against Steüerin in a dispute that began with a conflict between their husbands over a debt. While the husbands appear in the records as co-complaint and co-defendant, they neither testified nor appear in the records after that. Although Silberin was the complainant, the case came to revolve around her sexual honor. Steüerin's initial insult echoed earlier slander—"[Silberin] had a whore's child (*hueren Khind*) from a Corporal …" and, furthermore, Steüerin said Silberin had confided in her that she was passing the child off as her husband's. Steüerin also reported that Silberin had heard that she was going regularly to a chapel to pray and has said "she wished that the thunder (sic) would strike Barbara in the chapel." Silberin denied all of this, but the court was now interested in learning more about her behavior and, what was dangerous for her, about her reputation in the village. Her attempt to use the court to quash gossip about her seems to have backfired.

Several other women were called to testify about Silberin's relationship with the soldiers. One, Magdalena Huerzen, gave a virtuoso performance of how to slander someone without explicitly doing so.

> The corporal was often at the *Wirtin's* [tavern], by day and night, and drank and ate. Whether he paid, she did not know. People say that she [Silberin] often went to Bermatingen because of the corporal (*dem Corporal zu lieb*) and that the Corporal had taken her to and from Markdorf on a horse. Now if this is true, she does not know. This much she knows, that the *Wirtin* often went to Markdorf. She has actually not seen anything improper (*unrechts*)

from the *Wirtin*, but she has been seen walking together with the corporal (*aber sye seye dem corporal zu Steeg undt weg zu lieb geloffen*), the Wirtin has not shared with her with all she [shared] with Barbara Steüerin, so she does not know what they [the Corporal and Silberin] had with each other ... [20]

Then the court investigated a purported exchange of letters between Silberin and the Corporal. Magdalena Knechtin admitted that she had written one or two letters for Silberin to send to the Corporal. She claimed that she could not remember the content, since this had happened three years earlier. Still, under questioning she was quite specific "... this much she knows, that Johanna reported to the Corporal, that the Mimmenhausener were opening their snouts (*Mäuler*) as if [there were a relationship] between her and the Corporal, [and] he should come and shut people's snouts." Knechtin also pointed out that Silberin had come regularly to her house to learn to read and write, and this had led to the rumor that she was writing all the time to the Corporal, which was not true.[21] The court did not come to a decision, but rather asked for more information in order to find out if the rumors about Silberin's adultery, which had spread to the whole *Herrschaft*, were true.

One is tempted to look behind the testimony about Silberin's relationship with the soldiers for something we might call the "real" issues. After all, there were property disputes here over the use of fields and the payment of debts. There is an implication of family conflicts and the idea that Silberin might be doing a poor job managing the tavern by giving free food and drink to the soldiers. These issues are there in the record, and we know that courts adjudicated such issues when the parties were men. But the testimony of the parties, most of them women, led the court to focus on Silberin's sexual behavior, not property issues. Silberin was herself adept at deploying the language of sexual honor and dishonor to attack her enemies, but this language was also hard to control.

In March 1698, Silberin was again in front of the Salem *Gericht*, this time as the defendant, along with her husband, Simon Strigel.[22] The plaintiff, Barbara Bommerin, accused Strigel of slander, for calling her an adulterer (*eine Ehevertrännerin*) for having taken money from a Swiss soldier. Bommerin, in a classic fashion, stated that she was not an adulterer, but "the defendant's wife certainly was," an accusation she followed with details of Silberin's relations with the soldiers stationed in nearby Öwingen. Bommerin listed in detail clothing items, a ring, and a book she said Silberin had received as gifts. In a seemingly random aside, Bommerin testified that Strigel had accused her of ruining a tree and stealing some ducks. Perhaps this was the issue that triggered the clashing charges of moral turpitude?

Strigel did not appear to answer the charges, but Silberin did. She claimed that it was Bommerin who had tried to lead her astray and had encouraged her to leave her husband, whom Bommerin regularly badmouthed as a heretic and a scoundrel (*Schurken*). Silberin admitted to taking clothes from the soldiers one time, at Bommerin's house, encouraged by Bommerin. Bommerin denied these charges and said that Silberin had borrowed 9 *Gülden*, which she took to Bergetreute (a local shrine) "to have prayers said for her husband's death (*Ihren Mann todt betten lassen*)."[23] The court responded to all of this with skepticism:

> It appears from the complaint and answers, that both sides are not worth much, with each one helping and encouraging the other to do bad, and also trying to scare the other, both should be "stretched." Then they should be turned over to the *Herrschaft* for further punishment.

Barbara Bommerin and Johanna Silberin seemed to have known each other well. Bommerin's critical comments about Silberin's husband may have referred to a court case from several years earlier (November–December 1696).[24] In that case, the complainant had been Silberin's husband, Simon Strigel, who had gotten into a fight with two men on the road from Markdorf to Mimmenhausen. The two men, Michael Brunner and David Hausen, had intervened when Strigel, "because of a quarrel, was disciplining [his wife] with blows." Hausen testified that Silberin had called to them for help and that Strigel had called the men "whore's boys" (*hueren bueben*). Hausen also commented that Silberin's "wicked life is known," implying perhaps that she deserved the blows from her husband.

> Silberin's testimony took a different tack. When the two men came to defend her, … her husband told them it was no one else's business if he is hitting his wife. Then the two men had asked her what the reason was for the blows, she said she does not know what goes on in the man's head. [However], he had reproached her that she surely knows other whore's birds she would like to go with. The men asked if he meant them, but Simon said he had not named them. To this the men said that she should not go with the man, he is a rogue, a scoundrel, a puker (*Kotzer*), and a s.v. dog's etc., [and] he could kill her.

Strigel fled from the two men, injuring himself in the process. Brunner and Hausen, Silberin's erstwhile defenders, were sentenced to 8 and 6 hours in the stocks and Silberin to 3 hours, although her punishment was converted to a money fine.

Johanna Silberin then became, in a sense, the victim of a more efficient and activist court system in the territory of Salem.[25] In April 1698, referencing all the cases discussed above, the court convicted Silberin, along with two other women involved in court cases with Silberin, Barbara Bommerin, and Anna Lieberin, of solicitation and public scandal. The court focused on Silberin, citing her stealing of a book, her exchange of gifts with the soldiers, and her keeping company with the soldiers in a way that was inappropriate for a respectable wife, as clear evidence of her "debauched life." Bommerin and Lieberin were given light sentences of three hours each in the stocks. Silberin was considered the ringleader and deserving of an exemplary punishment. She received a sentence of six years exile from the territory.

This was a major and severe punishment and very unusual for a person of property and status. It is impossible to determine if this punishment was enforced, or if it was perhaps converted to a money fine.[26]

A straightforward analysis of these court cases might suggest that Johanna Silberin was a combative woman who made enemies among the other women in Mimmenhausen and even in the wider region. As the wife of a tavern keeper, she helped run the tavern, which gave her the power that came from access to gossip and stories exchanged in the tavern. It also brought her into contact with travelers and other strangers, particularly the soldiers stationed nearby. Just like all women who worked in taverns, her sexual morality was always suspect. Even her husband came to suspect her of adultery or of running a prostitution ring, or at least that is what he is reported to have said. So, in this interpretation Johanna was guilty of violating gender norms and was punished.

But, the story is not that simple. Did Simon Strigel really think his wife was a whore? Or did he resort to the standard language of sexual insult as well as physical violence when angry with his wife? And, as we have seen in this case, and as was true in all slander cases involving women, the accusation of whore (and often witch) was quite literally ubiquitous.[27] And, attacks on a woman's sexual honor were powerful in multiple ways. They reverberated on the whole family, calling into question a family's ability to function within a community, to buy and sell property, to exchange favors, and to live cooperatively with neighbors.

Johanna Silberin, and the women she engaged with in court, knew that these words—whore and witch—had power and they hurled them at each other, in the streets and in court. Silberin also believed that the court at Salem could be used to defend her honor and to denigrate others. And, the court basically agreed, seeing its role as one of regulating and controlling gossip and attacks on honor, as one way of protecting order in the lordship.[28] Silberin, however, used the court too often and exposed herself to counter charges too frequently.[29] It is an indication of the willingness of this court to regulate local society (and the growing professionalization of its staff), that court officials went back into their records to investigate Silberin and eventually punish her severely. Here we have a court operating in an administrative fashion that was becoming the norm even in tiny German states.

The Johanna Silberin case highlights several interconnected aspects of the social experience of village women. Most of all, men, women, and the law defined women by their sexuality. But there are other lessons from Silberin's story. The willingness and ability of women to use courts demonstrates that women were far from powerless in this world, despite their considerable legal and political disadvantages. A further aspect of women's agency was the power of publicity, the fear that everyone had of women's words, their networks of communication, and their ability to criticize and attack others' honor, what David Sabean calls the village "circuits of discourse" that ranged from gossip, to rumor, to outcry (*Geschrei*), legend (*Sage*), or simply talk (*Rede*).[30] Of course, the *Wirtin*, with privileged access to the rumor mill of the tavern, was especially powerful and dangerous. Johanna Silberin personifies this combination of female sexuality, women's legal activity, and women's powerful role in local "circuits of discourse."

Taken together, these aspects of Silberin's experience also illustrate a central tension about gender relations in the countryside. As Martin Ingram has written about English country women:

> A variety of sources testify that, in practice, the balance of authority between husbands and wives in marriage varied considerably. Equally it is plain that strong, active, able wives were often prized, despite the fact that the behaviour of such wives was unlikely to conform exactly to the stereotype of female virtue.[31]

Merry Wiesner-Hanks puts the same issue in a slightly different frame. "A woman's labor, rather than her father's occupation or wealth, determined her value as a marriage partner, giving her more power within the family and in the community at large."[32]

By all accounts, Joanna Silberin worked hard and exercised power in her community. She was a strong, active wife. Perhaps she was also able, although her misjudgments about how and when to go to court may call that into question. Was the beating she took from her husband an effort on his part to assert his authority when his wife questioned it? Were her dealings with the nearby soldiers part of an effort to make money off of them, leading to jealousy from other women and perhaps suspicion from her husband? The people of Mimmenhausen did not say this in court or in the public conversations they testified about. Unfortunately, we cannot know what they "really thought." For here we come up again against the way in which women were attacked. Silberin's enemies, no matter what their dispute with her might have been, could only call her a whore. The use of the language of sexual honor then created a community-wide reputation that was spread and reinforced by further gossip. Silberin's often heavy-handed efforts to change that reputation failed, perhaps because her counterattacks could only be couched in the same terms.

So, we will probably never know what "really happened" and if Johanna Silberin had an affair with one or more of the soldiers, or if she and the other women ran a prostitution ring to serve the soldiers. The language of sexual honor so pervaded this society that it both created gender relations and reinforced them in ways that clashed with, and perhaps distorted, the realities of a world where "strong, active, able wives were prized."

Notes

1 Laura Gowing, *Domestic Dangers: Women, Words, and Sex in Early Modern London* (Oxford: Clarendon Press, 1996); Tommaso Astarita, *Village Justice: Community, Family, and Popular Culture in Early Modern Italy* (Baltimore, MD: Johns Hopkins University Press, 1999); Rainer Walz, "Schimpfende Weiber, Frauen in lippischen Beleidigungsprzessen des 17. Jahrhunderts," in *Weiber, Menscher, Frauenzimmer. Frauen*

in der ländlichen Gesellschaft, 1500–1800, ed. Heide Wunder and Christina Vanja (Göttingen: Vandenhoeck & Ruprecht,1996); Ulinka Rublack, *The Crimes of Women in Early Modern Germany* (Oxford: Clarendon Press, 2001); Martin Dinges, "Ehre und Geschlecht in der Frühen Neuzeit," in *Ehrkonzepte in der Frühen Neuzeit: Identitäten und Abgrenzungen,* eds. Sibylle Backmann et al. (Berlin: Akademie Verlag, 1998), esp. 133–144.

2 Gowing, *Domestic Dangers* has a lot of comparable material on this issue.
3 *Frühzeitige Beischlaf* was the term used to describe sexual relations between a couple that intended to marry but had not yet done so.
4 Gowing, *Domestic Dangers*, 138.
5 Courts themselves functioned at a comparable intersection, between the pragmatic desire to resolve disputes and the (more) theoretical demands of laws and regulations.
6 GLAK 61/7600, 1672, 9 Jan., 23 Jan., 2 April, 9 April. (GLAK=*Generallandesarchiv Karlsruhe*)
7 GLAK 61/7600, 1672, 23 Jan.
8 GLAK 61/7600, 1672, 23 Jan.
9 GLAK 61/7602, 10^r-15^v.
10 GLAK 61/7602, 11^r.
11 GLAK 61/7602, 15^r-15^v.
12 GLAK 61/7600.
13 André Holenstein and Norbert Schindler, "Geschwätzgeschichte(n)." in *Dynamik der Tradition: Studien zur historischen Kulturforschung,* ed. van Dülmen (Frankfurt am Main: Fischer-Taschenbuch-Verl., 1992), esp. 79–88.
14 GLAK 61/13337, pp. 169, 245 (and more). It is not clear how long Silberin's husband, Simon Strigel, kept the inn. Valentin Hagenbach, one of Silberin's opponents in court in 1696, was the innkeeper, *Amtmann,* and *Stabhalter* (an administrative position) in Mimmenhausen from about 1700 through the 1730s. GLAK 62/19821, GLAK 98/3142.
15 GLAK 61/13337, 169–171.
16 "welche daß vorige ganz betrübt, und mit weinenden augen widerholt, sie seie ein unverstendiges Madl, habe ihre reden nicht uberlegt, sie seie einmahl wider ihr angeben unschuldig und ein jungfraw gewesen." GLAK 61/13337, 171.
17 Compare Gowing, *Domestic Dangers*; Martin Ingram, "Ridings, Rough Music, and the Reform of Popular Culture in Early Modern England" *Past and Present* 105 (1984): 79–113; and Merry Wiesner Hanks, *Women and Gender in Early Modern Europe*, 3rd Edition (New York: Cambridge University Press, 2008).
18 GLAK 61/13337, 245–250. "ich will die schon Zech machen."
19 GLAK 61/13340, 71–74, 81–84, 89. I believe Steüerin was married to the *Amtmann*.
20 GLAK 61/13340, 82.
21 GLAK 61/13340, 83.
22 GLAK 61/13340, 172–177. In March 1698, Silberin was also charged in a similar case by another woman, Anna Lieberin. GLAK 61/13340, 177–178.
23 GLAK 61/13340, 176. *streckhen* = stretched, but are we talking stocks or real torture on the rack?
24 GLAK 61/13337, 395–399, 408–411, 417–418.
25 GLAK 61/13340, 193–195.
26 Servants and vagrants were expelled from the territory at times, but Silberin was a person of status and her husband was a citizen, so her expulsion was unusual. See Jason Coy, *Strangers and Misfits: Banishment, Social Control, and Authority in Early Modern Europe* (Leiden: Brill, 2008).
27 The use of the insult "witch" could be, of course, especially dangerous. See Gudrun Gersmann, "Gehe hin und vertheidige dich! Injurieklagen als Mittel der Abwehr von Hexerei Verdächtigungen—ein Fallbeispiel aus dem Fürstbistum Münster," in *Ehrkonzepte in der Frühen Neuzeit*, 237–266.

28 See for example, André Holenstein, *"Gute Policey" und lokale Gesellschaft im Staat des Ancien Régime. Das Fallbeispiel der Markgrafschaft Baden(-Durlach)* (*Frühneuzeit-Forschungen*, Bd. 9/1, 2) (Tübingen: Bibliotheca-Academica-Verl., 2003).
29 Slander cases often resulted in punishments to all parties involved, since courts general understood these cases to be the result of an exchange of insults.
30 David Warren Sabean, "Village Court Protocolls and Memory," in *Gemeinde, Reformation und Widerstand: Festschrift für Peter Blickle zum 60. Geburtstag*, eds. Heinrich Richard Schmidt, André Holenstein, and Andreas Würgler (Tübingen: Bibliotheca-Academica-Verlag, 1998), 3–23.
31 Ingram, "Ridings, Rough Music, and the Reform of Popular Culture in Early Modern England," 97.
32 Wiesner-Hanks, *Women and Gender in Early Modern Europe*, 112.

6
JAMES I AND UNRULY WOMEN

Carole Levin

When Elizabeth died and James VI of Scotland became James I of England not only did it end a woman's rule, but it also heralded a strong shift about attitudes toward women, especially those, who, for better or worse, moved beyond their expected realms of behavior. James disliked and feared women who moved out of their accepted roles and encouraged the same attitudes in court and country. There are many cases that demonstrate James' fear and dislike of women, but one that James described as being a second garden of Eden was the scandal around the Thomas Lake family, where Mary Lake was cast in the role of the serpent. This case came to a head in 1619 but James' ambivalent attitudes toward powerful women was strong throughout his reign. As Merry Wiesner-Hanks has described in much of her scholarship, male concerns about women, their unruliness, and their ability to use their bodies to entice men, were a large concern in early modern Europe.

In the early summer of 1603 Henri IV of France sent Maximillian de Bethune, Duke of Sully, to England as ambassador extraordinaire to James I to express his condolences for the death of Elizabeth and his congratulations upon becoming king. Henri told Sully that to show his respect he should make sure that he and his suite went to the new king wearing mourning garments. When Sully arrived, however, he was informed "no one, whether ambassador, foreigner, or English, was admitted into the presence of the new King in black." James found it highly insulting if anyone came into his presence wearing mourning for his predecessor. Sully learned so "strong an affection prevailed to obliterate the memory of that great princess, that she was never spoke of, and even the mention of her name industriously avoided." The whole court assured Sully that James was deeply offended that he and his retinue planned to come to him in black, so the Duke decided that it was more important for there to be good feelings between the two kings than to follow his master's order, and told his men to find the best clothing they could, though the first meeting with James was still strained. By June 29 James was more at ease with the French ambassador, and Sully reported back to his king that "the opportunity offering for the King to speak of the late Queen of England, he did it, and to my great regret, with some sort of contempt." James even bragged that while he was still in Scotland, long before the queen's death, it was he who directed her Council and governed all her ministers, that they were far more eager to obey him than Elizabeth herself. After finishing this surprising statement, "he then called for some wine, his custom being never to mix water with it."[1] The contempt that he expressed toward Elizabeth continued through his reign and was aimed at a range of women, especially those who moved out of accepted roles. To give another example, Bathsua Reginald Makin, daughter of the schoolteacher Henry Reginald, was from a young age a very fine scholar. Bathsua was only about sixteen when her father published *Musa virginea* (1616), which was a collection of Bathsua's poems and epigraphs praising James I and his family. Bathsua did this in six different languages: Latin, Greek, Hebrew, Spanish, French, and German. When Bathsua was presented to the king and described as an "English rarity" since she could "speake and rite pure Latine, Greeke, and Hebrew," James responded with a joke that would put her in her place: "but can she spin?"[2] Makin was not the only woman James wanted put in a closed, humiliating place.

About the same time was a pamphlet war on the subject of women's capabilities that contained some terrible reflections about women. In 1615 Joseph Swetnam published *The Araignment of Lewd, Idle, Froward and Unconstant Women*, originally under the pseudonym Thomas Tell-Troth, but soon reissued in his own name. The book had two further editions in 1616 and 1617, and was reprinted twelve times during the seventeenth century. Swetnam described women as greedy, lusty, dishonest, and cruel. He wrote, "a woman that hath a faire face, it is ever matched with a cruell heart, and her heavenly lookes with hellish thoughts; their modest countenance with mercilesse minds." These were very similar views to the women at the Jacobean court. Swetnam also warned men that "When a woman wanteth any thing, shee will flatter and speake faire, not much vnlike the flattering Butcher, who gently claweth the Oxe, when hee intendeth to knock him on the head."[3] Swetnam's text sparked many heated responses.

In January 1619 John Chamberlain wrote to Dudley Carleton in the Hague that James was so upset by the "insolencie of our women, and theyre wearing of brode brined hats, pointed dublets, theyre hair cut short or shorne" that he commanded John King, the bishop of London, to order the clergy to preach against this. Two weeks later Chamberlain updated Carleton: "Our pulpits ring continually of the insolencie and impudencie of women." But it was not only preachers whom the king wanted to take up this cause. "To help the matter forward the players have likewise taken them to taske; and so too the ballades and ballad-singers, so that [the women] can come no where but theyre eares tingle." Chamberlain added that if this campaign was ineffective, "the King threatens to fall upon their husbands, parents, or frends that have or shold have powre over them and make them pay for it."[4] In Jacobean England it was not only concern about women's behavior that was central but also the worry that men in charge could not control unruly women, a worry that this would upend the underpinnings of society.

But though James may have had the same attitudes toward many different women, the women under discussion in this paper were no Bathsua Makins nor did they parade about in London in male clothing. But they did behave in ways that showed strong will. In the second decade of the seventeenth century, James I's court was rife with scandal, and a number of these scandals led to legal cases that had to do with women who were perceived as women behaving badly, and men not being in sufficient control to keep the women in their households in line. The most famous case was the charge that Frances Howard, first the Countess of Essex and then Countess of Somerset, had had Thomas Overbury, former close friend of her second husband, murdered in 1613, the same year she had had her marriage to Robert Devereux, third Earl of Essex, annulled, and celebrated her marriage to the king's favorite Robert Carr, Earl of Somerset. In 1616 the Earl and the Countess were put on trial for Overbury's murder and convicted. While only those of their circle of lower status, such as Frances's maid and confidant Anne Norton, were executed, Carr and Frances spent years in the Tower, not released until January 1622 when they were then exiled from court.

The same year as the Somerset case women of much lower status were also found guilty of murder and were publically executed. In July 1616 Chamberlain noted in a letter to Carleton that recently in the "morning early, there was a joiner's wife burnt in Smithfield for killing her husband … Her husband having brawled and beaten her, she took up a chisel, or some such other instrument, and flung [it] at him, which cut him into the belly, whereof he died." Another woman executed was also a husband-killer, but this time the method was poison. Chamberlain concluded, "such like foul facts are committed daily, which are ill signs of a very depraved age," and the implication is that the age was depraved because of women's behavior.[5]

Later that July Chamberlain wrote to Carleton about another incident. Though she was to remain in the Tower for some more years, rumors spread that King James had issued a pardon to Frances, Countess of Somerset. Some of the Londoners assumed that she had thus been released and were upset. "On Saturday last the queen, with the Countess of Derby, the Lady Ruthin, and the Lord Carew, coming privately in coach …, there grew a whispering, that it was the Lady Somerset and her mother; whereupon people flocked together and followed the coach in great numbers, railing, and reviling, and abusing the footman, and putting them all in fear. Neither would they be otherwise persuaded till they saw them enter into Whitehall."[6]

In 1619 Frances' parents, Katherine and Thomas Howard, the Earl and Countess of Suffolk, were on trial in Star Chamber, the highest court in the realm, for the bribes taken when the earl was Lord Treasurer, a post he had had since 1614. But it was Lady Suffolk who had used her position to extort kickbacks before people were paid. People at the time expressed their sympathy to the Earl, but their contempt and condemnation were for his wife. The earl was "more pitied than condemned," while the countess was "more condemned than pitied."[7]

This was another family scandal. There were charges and countercharges between the Thomas Lake family and the Countess of Exeter, leading to the Star Chamber. The case not only tells us about conflicts between the gentry and the aristocracy but even more about the king's own beliefs about women's nature, going all the way back to Adam, Eve, and the serpent.

In Elizabeth's reign Lake read Latin to the queen, even doing so while she was on her deathbed.[8] Soon after Elizabeth was dead the Council sent Lake to Scotland to tell James about what was going on in England. Lake made such a good impression on the new king that in May 1603 James knighted him and frequently invited Lake to go hunting with him. In June 1604 the Spanish count of Villa Medina, who was in England on a special embassy, noted that King James thought very highly of Lake; "he trusts him the most and gives him many duties to perform."[9] There was quite a bit of tension between Robert Cecil, Earl of Salisbury, James I's Principal Secretary, and Lake in Cecil's last years at court. Cecil attempted to keep Lake from gaining too much influence, but James thought well enough of Lake that in December 1609 James appointed Lake as his Latin secretary. The Earl of Salisbury died in 1612. James ordered that now all official communications should be sent to Lake, but the king refused to give him the title along with the work. Though James clearly felt good about Lake, there were some doubts. Chamberlain suggested there were worries over the soundness of Lake's religious beliefs—just how sympathetic was he to Catholics? Was he one himself? Despite the fact that his younger brother Arthur was a committed Anglican, who was to become bishop of Bath and Wells in 1616, many suspected that Thomas was a covert Catholic. Living next door to the Venetian ambassador, Lake and his family were able to go through a secret door and participate in the Catholic services held in the embassy chapel. But Chamberlain was sure that there was another reason as well—that Thomas Lake's wife Mary was so known for her arrogance and ill-temper that, though her husband was no Socrates, she was often compared to Xantippe, who was known in the Renaissance as a shrew who abused her husband.[10]

Yet one might wonder if Mary Lake completely deserved this reputation. Mary Lake was a strong woman who supported her family, though in some unethical ways. Lake had married Mary Rider in 1591 when she was 16. Mary's father had been a merchant and local politician who had done very well for himself. The Lakes had three sons and four daughters. The oldest three were Thomas (b. 1595), Arthur (b. 1598), and a daughter Ann, (b. 1600) who was said to take after her mother.

Though Thomas Howard, Earl of Suffolk, had convinced James to appoint Lake as principal secretary in 1614, he changed his mind when committed Protestants assured the King that members of the Parliament, who would meet soon, would find the appointment unacceptable. In an effort to have an easier time with Parliament, James instead appointed the clearly Protestant Sir Ralph Winwood, and Lake had to be satisfied with becoming a member of the Privy Council. Perhaps the annual pension of £500 awarded to him by the Spanish king also comforted Lake. Even with pulling back on the Lake appointment, the 1614 Parliament, known as the addled Parliament, had not been a success for the king, and by 1616 James was more interested in good relations with Spain. Lake's pro-Spanish leanings finally convinced James to give him an appointment of Secretary of State, though he was still considered second to Winwood, whose area was foreign relations. As well as being within Suffolk's circle, by 1616 Lake had become powerful enough to arrange a marriage between his daughter Anne and William Cecil, Lord Roos, grandson of Thomas Cecil, first Earl of Exeter. Exeter was the eldest son of Elizabeth's principal secretary William Cecil, Lord Burghley, by his first wife, Mary Cheke. At the time of the marriage the Earl was not in the best health and had pretty much retired and was enjoying his life with his second wife. In 1610, a year after the death of his first wife, Dorothy, the Earl at the age of sixty-eight had married the thirty-year-old widow Frances Brydges Smith.

At the time of the Lake-Cecil marriage Lord Roos had only been back in England for less than a year, having spent the last decade wandering the continent. It was not necessarily a propitious match, as neither Ann nor William had a good reputation. The Venetian ambassador, for example, described him as "very light brained."[11] Chamberlain stated that many people at court described Lady Roos as a "very pert lady," who was able "to domineer as much over her mother as her mother doth over some others."[12]

The couple were married February 12, 1616. But the marriage went badly right from the start. In April James named Lord Roos as ambassador-extraordinary to Spain to congratulate Philip III on his marriage treaty. As he was preparing for his embassy Thomas Lake and his wife Mary were pressuring him to sign over to Ann the valuable manor of Walthamstow. Ann and her family attempted to blackmail her husband into agreeing to do this by threatening to reveal that he was sexually impotent, which would have led to a humiliating annulment, similar to the humiliation suffered by Robert Devereux, third earl of Essex. Lord Roos was willing, but his grandfather, wanting to protect family financial interests, refused to allow him, and he went on his embassy that October with the matter unresolved. People began to remark that Lord Roos was much closer to Sir Ralph Winwood than he was to his father-in-law, Thomas Lake. As Lord Roos was leaving England he sent Winwood a diamond worth £40. By this time Ann had gone back to living with her family. The summer of 1616 both Ann's mother and William's step-grandmother gave birth to daughters.[13]

Lord Roos returned in the spring of 1617, deeply in debt from the expenses of the embassy, and James was not particularly impressed by what he had—or had not—accomplished while in Spain. Lady Roos, living at her parents' home, sent her husband a message asking to see him about a possible reconciliation. But it was a trick arranged by Ann's brother Arthur. When he arrived Arthur and his servants attacked him and his retinue. George Gerard wrote to Dudley Carleton that Lord Roos was furious and planning to "indict his wife's family for riot." Because of the attack, he was "mortified and insulted, [and] forced to return alone." But Gerard added that he had heard that Lord Roos "has settled £800 a year on [his wife], that she may conceal from his grandfather some former misconduct of his."[14]

Yet a few weeks later Lord and Lady Roos were living at the Earl of Exeter's house at Wimbledon, one of the finest houses of the day. Lord Roos knew if he could not get his grandfather to agree to give his wife Walthamstow, she and her family would publicly humiliate him. It was all too much for him. By the end of the summer he had secretly fled to Italy and Ann was again back with her parents. Many at court were watching the actions of Lord and Lady Roos and her family, and wondered how much Lord Roos' mother-in-law and brother-in-law had to do it with his flight. Chamberlain wrote to Carleton in August that "Lord Roos has suddenly gone away, writing that he is driven to it by Lady Lake's dealings." Winwood noted that "Lord Roos has suddenly left England." Lord Roos himself sent a letter to Winwood explaining that the diabolical dealings of the Lady Lake have driven him to absent himself, and he hoped that Winwood would forgive him for leaving without notifying him.[15]

The Lakes responded by starting rumors that the reason Lord Roos could not consummate his marriage was that he was a one-woman man—and that woman was his step-grandmother. Also, they whispered the Countess had attempted to poison the young Lady Roos during the time of their attempted reconciliation that July and early August of 1617. Since Frances was almost forty years younger than her husband and only ten years older than his grandson, this was not an impossible scenario, and worse, once their rumors really started circulating, some questioned whether Frances' daughter Georgi-Anna, baptized 1616, was the Earl's daughter or Lord Roos's. The Lakes told a few friends about their claims and they then went to the Countess letting her know that the world would learn about these charges unless Lady Roos got the settlement she wanted. The Lakes claimed that the Exeters' servant Luke Hatton had signed a statement that the Countess had discussed with him how she had considered poisoning Lady Roos and her father.

But instead of crumbling and giving the Lakes what they wanted, the Earl of Exeter was furious and became intent on forcing the Lakes to publicly retract what they had said. The body of his wife had been slandered and he would not put up with it. He wrote frequently to the king on this topic. The Earl appealed to James and brought suit against the Lakes. The Lakes and the Exeters filed charges and counter-charges. The fact that Lord Roos was not in England to answer questions disturbed many. King James and his Council demanded that Lord Roos return and speak to the matter, and both his father and his grandfather, the Earl, strenuously requested he return. But, as Chamberlain wrote to Carleton, Lord Roos kept moving, never staying in one place very long. He also mentioned that Lord was "further indebted than I thought his credit could stretch."[16] Finally Lord Roos, now in Italy, wrote to James apologizing for fleeing England, explaining he had done so only because he was in such despair, but vehemently defending the

Countess's honor. He promised he would eventually return home. But this was not to be.

In July Thomas Lorkin wrote to Sir Thomas Puckering that "News arrived yesternight to my Lord Burghley that my Lord Roos is dead, which, whether it be certain or no, I know not."[17] It was certain. In late June Lord Roos suddenly became ill and died in Naples at the age of 28. It appears to have been a natural death; at the time rumors swirled that it was poison.

In the meantime, the Lakes claimed they had proof of the Countess's perfidy, producing a paper they claimed had been written by the Countess admitting her guilt. They also had a witness to the Countess confessing to Lady Roos that she and Lord Roos were lovers and that she had attempted to poison both Lady Roos and her father. While this was going on more and more people with connections to the court were gossiping about the case and spreading rumors. As early as April 1616 Chamberlain had written to Carleton saying there was some scandal about Lord Roos but not being exactly sure what it was.

But the Lake's evidence was highly problematic, demonstrating the difficulties they were in because of these charges. Chamberlain wrote to Carleton that the Lakes had "fallen into a labyrinth, whence they know not how to get out."[18] Even though Thomas Lake was a man in a powerful position and the head of his household, some at court were convinced he was not the one to blame. John Castle wrote to William Trumbull, "I am inclined to believe that the whole business has been contrived by mother and daughter out of sheer malice. I would be glad, if it were possible, to exonerate her husband from the ugly affair." Castle was convinced that Lake "never knew the bottom of their doeings," and that he allowed it to happen because of his "over much uxoriousnes to his wife."[19]

As the charges and counter charges grew, the number of pages kept growing as well, but it took a long time before King James was ready to hear the case in Star Chamber. Chamberlain wrote that "The Lady Roos's business with the Lady of Exeter hath been heard twice or thrice; and the whole process sealed up and sent to the king. I hear the Lord of Exeter hath sent to crave leave to prosecute the contrivers of this scandal against his wife in the Star Chamber."[20]

In 1618 Lake's position was even more problematic because of the troubles that his patron Suffolk was in. There were accusations that Lady Suffolk was receiving bribes. She had temporarily taken refuge in the country, but was bored and decided to return to London. James was furious when he learned of her return, threatening to have her forcibly removed, and Lake too was in more trouble with his monarch.

At about the same time that the Suffolks were to be brought before the Star Chamber, so too was the case of the Lakes and the Exeters. It was clear to many that King James favored the Earl and Countess of Exeter. William Camden recorded in his diary that "The King was peeved at Secretary Thomas Lake because of Lady Roos' slanders against the Countess of Exeter." Later he wrote, "There is a dispute over the form of proceeding in the Star Chamber in the cause between the Countess of Exeter and Secretary Thomas Lake."[21] Thomas Wallis wrote to Dr. Ward on January 23, 1618/19: "You hear also of my Lord of Suffolk and his Countess, that they are to appear in the Star Chamber on Wednesday next, (which is the first Star Chamber day,) whereupon it is expected that they shall be censured for matters of high consequence. Also, it certainly reported that his Majesty will be in person at Star Chamber three or four days this term, upon occasion of the Countess of Exeter's case and Sir Thomas Lake's."[22] Edward Sherburn wrote that "the matter is so foul that an open law proceeding will be needed."[23]

For some at court, despite the roles of Thomas Lake and the Earl, this case was all about women. Adam Newton wrote to Sir Thomas Puckering that James and his Council "are troubled with no business so much at the foul matter betwixt … the Countess of Exeter and the Lady Roos and her mother."[24] Certainly the efforts that Lady Roos made, with or without the encouragement and connivance of her mother and the complicity of her father, only made the Lakes fall deeper. Lady Roos stated publicly that her husband and his step-grandmother were having an affair, and that Lady Exeter had attempted to poison her in an effort to keep the affair secret. Lady Exeter and her husband had counter sued for slander. In the trial before King James in Star Chamber Lady Roos produced her evidence. She stated that by threatening to disclose what she knew, she had gotten Frances, Lady Exeter to acknowledge her guilt to her and even put it in writing which she then gave to the court. She also produced another paper that she claimed had been signed by Luke Hatton, one of the Cecil servants, in which he confirmed that not only did Lady Exeter attempt to poison Lady Roos but also her father, Thomas Lake. Then Lady Roos brought a witness, her servant maid Sarah Swarton. Sarah swore that that she had been hidden behind the tapestry hangings in the room at Wimbledon where the two women had had their confrontation, and she had witnessed Lady Exeter admitting her guilt to Lady Roos without the Countess knowing she was there.

But then it all began to unravel. Luke Hatton swore that the one paper was a forgery, as did Lady Exeter of her "confession." Lady Exeter's servant George Williams testified that Thomas Lake had offered him a bribe to accuse his mistress, and when he had refused Thomas Lake had ordered that he be imprisoned. Luke Hatton had also been imprisoned when he had refused to join in the accusations. King James was very proud of his skill as an investigator, and insisted that they all go to Wimbledon and the room where Sarah Swarton supposedly hid and listened. The Earl and Countess of Exeter had lavishly entertained James at Wimbledon in July 1616 so he may well have remembered the room where the conversation had supposedly taken place. The king told Sarah to go where she hid, but when Sarah did the hangings barely reached her knees, so that had she attempted to conceal herself there she would have immediately been noticed, as King James pointed out with triumph. Her woman's body had betrayed her. Sarah was sent to the Fleet, with the order that she would then be led through the streets to Westminster being whipped along the way, and from there to Cheapside, where she would be branded. On one cheek would be the letter F and the other the letter A, for false accusation. She would then be sent to Bridewell, "there to spend and end her days."[25] But when a few months later Sarah Swarton confessed all her crimes, she was released.

On 13 February 1619 King James found against the Lake family in all particulars. Camden found the timing ironic. "It should be noted that this sentence was passed on the 13th of February, while on February 12, 1616, the marriage of Baron Roos with Lake's daughter was celebrated with great joy."[26] The only one of the Lakes not fined and/or imprisoned was the son Arthur, though he "was reputed generally in the conscience of the court guilty, but for want of direct proof not censured." His older brother Thomas had gotten involved somehow and was fined but not imprisoned as his parents and sister were. Thomas Lake was fined £5200, his wife Mary £5000, his daughter Anne 10,000 marks and his son Thomas 500 marks. The younger Thomas also had to pay the Countess of Exeter £1000, her chambermaid Elizabeth Gresham £100, and her servant George Williams £200. Thomas Lake the father had to pay Luke Hatton £50 and the Countess £3000. Sir Thomas, his wife, and his daughter were also to be imprisoned in the Tower "upon their own charges" at the king's pleasure.

But as well as these punishments, King James had something else to say to the Lake family. To restore the Countess of Exeter's honor there had to be a public recognition of the Lakes' offense. The King went on to describe the event as the second fall of man, and placed the most blame on Mary Lake, seeing her as the old serpent who beguiled her daughter who stood in for Eve; and she seduced her father, a second Adam, into the conspiracy, and now the world would know it. Eve gave the apple to Adam, leading them to be expelled from the Garden of Eden. But though it was Eve who was the active one, she would not have done this without the urging of the serpent. In the same way, while it was Ann, Lady Roos who had caused the most trouble, the King blamed her mother, Lady Lake, believing her to be the instigator. But though this was how James stated it, not all heard it correctly. John Chamberlain wrote: "The King spake long and excellently to every point, comparing this to the first judgment, Sir Thomas Lake to Adam, his Lady to Eve, and the Lady Roos to the serpent."[27]

James was far from unique in thinking of the serpent as female. In the later Middle Ages into the seventeenth century there were many portrayals of Adam, Eve, and serpent with the snake as a female head and sometimes part of a female body as well. And often the face of the serpent and the face of Eve look like the same person, or possibly a mother and daughter. And yet despite what the Lakes had tried to do, and how culpable they might be, we might wonder how much of this description has to do with the Lakes and how much with the King's attitudes and beliefs about women. Despite the fact that as a man Thomas Lake had far more power than the women in his family, James put far more blame on Lake's daughter and especially his wife, and those who wrote and gossiped about the case agreed.

On 15 February Lady Anne Clifford recorded in her diary that the situation between the Lakes and the Exeters "was one of the foulest matters that fallen out in our time." She had heard that many believed that instead of an incestuous relationship between Lord Roos and his step-grandmother, "reports went that among others [Anne] lay with her own brother." She concluded that Anne was "counted a most odious woman."[28] When the Lakes were taken to the

Tower crowds cursed Ann as they passed. While some might put more blame on Lady Lake and others on Lady Roos, Thomas was mostly blamed and pitied for allowing the women in his household to rule.

Yet though the Lakes knew they had to confess to be freed, Lady Lake refused and spent far more time in the Tower than the rest of her family. By June, Lady Roos "confessed that those slanders about incest ... [and] poisoning" were invented and begged for forgiveness, though she claimed the "crimes were inventions written by Arthur Lake ... with her father and mother accomplices."[29] Despite the conditions of her first marriage, in November 1621 Ann married George Rodney, the second son of Sir John Rodney. The two moved to Somerset, where the Rodney family had land. While we know nothing about what passed between Ann and her second husband, we may infer that it was a more successful marriage than her first. At the age of 30, Ann died in 1630, the same year as her father, and her husband put a memorial that listed her as the daughter of Thomas Lake and the widow of Lord Roos as well as the wife of George Rodney, "who by this Stone doth acknowledge her deserts toward him & desireth to perpetuate the Memory [of a] Good Wife & Most Penitent Christian ... & now hopes for a Joyfull Resurrection."[30]

Ann's parents did not have such a positive view as their lives continued. In the summer of 1619 Thomas Lake was ill and briefly released. For a while he kept protesting his innocence. After he returned to the Tower he bargained for his release and in January 1620 he publicly "read out an acknowledgement of the slanders by which he had done damage to the Countess of Exeter ... He acknowledged that the sentence handed down against him on the preceding February 13th, was just, because his fault was disgraceful, hateful, and scandalous to the said Countess. But he was misled by his great credulity, indulgence, and ignorance ... and professed that it grieved him to his heart to have defended such a disgraceful, hateful, and scandalous case."[31] In March 1620 Mary Lake was also conditionally released because of ill-health. By May Thomas Lake was allowed to kiss James' royal hand, but his wife was remanded back to the Tower "because she stubbornly refuses to make her submission."[32] In September Lake was struck by a carriage and broke his arm. This bad luck continued for him; he was never able to regain the king's favor.

James was furious when instead of making her submission, admitting her guilt, and begging pardon, Lady Lake wrote to the Countess in a letter dated 9 November suggesting that "after all this business in which you have had too much glory," the Countess might want to cast her eyes on Psalm 136 and examine her heart. Neither James nor the Countess would have found this psalm soothing since it said in part

> for his mercy endureth for ever.
> To him which smote great kings:
>   .....
> for his mercy endureth for ever.
> Who remembered us in our low estate

Lady Lake added, "I wish my submission could make you an innocent woman, and wish you as white as a swan; but it must be your own submission unto God." Lady Lake was convinced that "truth lives, and God's glory will appear in his good time," and that eventually "all the world" would see "I die God's servant. To whose justice I commend myself."[33]

The week after she wrote the letter Lady Lake was brought to the Star Chamber since her letter to the Countess had been "derogatory to the kingdom's justice ... [and] summoned the Countess to Divine Judgement." [Camden] After being reprimanded, she was returned to the Tower. But by the end of the year, James was apparently tired of the whole business, even of the one he considered the serpent in the Garden. A month later, on 14 December, Camden noted that "Mistress Lake is freed from prison, under I know not what conditions."[34] Ann, Lady Roos and her father Thomas Lake, the Adam and Eve as named by James, had figured out that their best way to gain back a modicum of their status was through confession and public repentance. Lady Lake, the king's serpent, like her original counterpart, would never admit her fault. She stands clearly as a Jacobean example of how dangerous women could be.

Notes

1 *Memoirs of Maximilian de Bethune, Duke of Sully, Prime Minister of Henry the Great*, newly translated from the French edition of M. de l'Ecluse; to which is annexed the Trial of Francis Ravaillac, for the murder of Henry the Great (Edinburgh: Printed by Alex. Lawrie and Co., for Bell and Bradfute [et al.], 1805), III:126, 158–159.
2 Frances Teague, *Bathsua Makin* (Lewisburg: Buckness University Press, 1998), 43.
3 Joseph Swetnam, *The arraignment of lewd, idle, forward, and uncostant women or the vanitie of them* (London: printed for Thomas Archer, 1615), 4, 11.
4 Chamberlain to Carleton, *The Letters of John Chamberlain*, edited with an introduction by Norman Egbert McClure, 2 vols. (Philadelphia: American Philosophical Society, 1939), II:286–287, 289.
5 Thomas Birch, *The Court and Times of James the First: Containing a Series of Historical and Confidential Letters, in which Will be Found a Detail of the Public Transactions and Events in Great Britain During that Period, with a Variety of Particulars Not Mentioned by Our Historians; Transcribed from the Originals in the British Museum, State Paper Office, and Private Collections* (London: H. Colburn, 1849), 418.
6 https://archive.org/stream/greatoyerofpoiso1846amos/greatoyerofpoiso1846amos_djvu.txt.
7 *Calendar of State Papers: Domestic series of the reign of James I, 1619–1623*, ed. Mary Anne Everett Green (London: Longman, Brown, Green, Longmans & Roberts, 1858), 93.
8 Anthony Weldon, *The Court and Character of King James whereunto is now added the Court of King Charles, continued unto the beginning of these unhappy times* (London: Printed by R.I., 1651), 189.
9 Albert Joseph Loomie, *Toleration and Diplomacy: The religious Issue in Anglo-Spanish Relations, 1603–1605* (American Philosophical Society, 1963), 54.
10 *Letters of John Chamberlain*, I:367.
11 *Calendar of State Papers and Manuscripts, Relating to English affairs, existing in the archives and collections of Venice and in the other libraries of Northern Italy, 1613–1615*, ed. Rawdon Brown (London: H.M.S.O., 1907), 328.

12 *The Letters of John Chamberlain*, II:145.
13 *The Letters of John Chamberlain*, II:148.
14 *Calendar of State Papers, Domestic, James I, 1611-18*, ed. Mary Anne Everett Green (London: Longman, Brown, Green, Longmans & Roberts, 1858), 472.
15 *Calendar of State Papers, James*, 480.
16 Birch, *The Court and Times of James the First*, II:37.
17 Birch, *The Court and Times of James the First*, II:83.
18 *The Letters of John Chamberlain*, II:145.
19 William Sanderson, *Aulicus conquinariae: or, A vindication in answer to a pamphlet, entituled The Court and Character of King James* (London, 1650), 513.
20 Thomas Birch, *The Court and Times of James the First*, II:62.
21 http://www.philological.bham.ac.uk/diary/.
22 Godfrey Goodman, *The Court of King James the First: To which are Added, Letters Illustrative of the Personal History of the Most Distinguished Characters in the Court of that Monarch and His Predecessors: in Two Volumes* (London: Bentley, 1839), II:176.
23 *Calendar of State Papers, James*, 523.
24 Birch, *The Court and Times of James the First*, II:68.
25 Birch, *The Court and Times of James the First*, II:139.
26 http://www.philological.bham.ac.uk/diary/.
27 Birch, *The Court and Times of James the First*, II, 136; *CSP, James*, 1619–1623, 14; *The Chamberlain Letters*, ed Elizabeth McClure Thomson (London: John Murray, 1965), 239.
28 Anne Clifford, *The Memoir of 1603 and the Diary of 1616–1619*, Katherine O. Acheson, ed. (Peterborough, Ontario: Broadview Press, 2006), 158, 159.
29 http://www.philological.bham.ac.uk/diary/.
30 Le Neve, *Monumenta Anglicana: Being Inscriptions on the monuments of several eminent persons deceased, deduced into a series of time by way of annals* (London: Printed by Will. Bowyer, 1717–1719), I:128.
31 http://www.philological.bham.ac.uk/diary/.
32 http://www.philological.bham.ac.uk/diary/.
33 Goodman, *The Court of King James the First*, 196–197.
34 http://www.philological.bham.ac.uk/diary/.

PART II
Women between reform, subversion, and self-determination

7

PROTESTANT AND CATHOLIC NUNS CONFRONTING THE REFORMATION

Marjorie Elizabeth Plummer

When asked in 1533 whether she would follow the new evangelical convent order, Margarethe von Zedwitz, a nun living in Saalburg, answered the visitors that she was quite willing to accept "God's word" because she understood the dangers of the "shameful, irksome monastic life." By asking for more time to consider what she would do in response to this knowledge, however, she qualified her decisions about what this meant for her future as a nun by stating that she needed to consider God's will and whether the other nuns would bother her before taking action.[1] In her 1544 petition for financial assistance after her husband's stroke had left the family penniless, the now widowed Margarethe (Zedwitz) Leupold was less circumspect about her decision-making process. She pinpointed the moment of her 1533 resolve to leave the convent and enter the "honorable estate" of marriage to the visitors' promise of a dowry for any nuns electing to leave the convent to marry. In describing how she implemented her decision, she noted that she first asked the local ducal official for permission to leave and only after her honorable departure, did she marry. After this assertion, she then complained that those who remained in the convent were provided with all their necessities, but that she was poor despite her accepting the true religion.[2] The abbess of Saalburg confirmed the outline of Zedwitz's testimony, reporting that the former nun had left the convent sometime after the visitation and that she soon thereafter married a tailor.[3] After considering the evidence, Elector John Frederick recommended giving Zedwitz an annuity based on her "timely acknowledgment" that her monastic life was "against God's word." In doing so, he linked his decision to Zedwitz's 1544 recitation of the 1533 events.[4]

At the outset of the chapter on religion in her *Women and Gender in Early Modern Europe*, Merry Wiesner-Hanks described how women's religious lives were seldom private, and that most women found themselves confronting several layers of authorities—husband/father, clergy and theologians, ruler and officials, and texts—when determining how they wished to display their faith.[5] Decisions made by these women to leave or stay in the convent often became part of a public discourse over reform when retold in printed pamphlets where women are shown conforming to reform ideals. What is seldom shown for these and other women is what happened after such decisions or when women did not make a decision in keeping with the expectations of those authorities. In addition, when women changed their minds, that decision did not usually get printed as an addendum to the previous work by the original author.

During the early reform movement between 1523 and 1534, at least 304 nuns in 22 convents in Ernestine Saxony confronted distinct moments when they faced deciding whether or not to leave their convent. Less than half, around 135, ultimately left.[6] The irreparable damage and closure of some of the convents, such as Petersberg near Eisenberg or St. Katharina's in Eisenach, during the Peasants' War (1524–1525) certainly influenced why the women left due to the closure of their houses. But, the significant financial and physical attacks on at least 17 of the Ernestine convents did not cause most of the convents to close. Most of the convents still housed nuns decades after the official ending of monastic life in 1525; most of the convents were still open in 1527 and 1530, and a third were still open in 1540. The continuation of so many female houses led Elector John Frederick to ask visitors in 1532 to figure out how to manage the spiritual lives of the approximately 122 nuns still living in convents, but they found that the women did not always behave as promised or expected, and many kept their decisions to themselves. Even among the women that left, some merely moved to another convent in nearby Albertine Saxony.[7]

The erasure of such private decisions from local records and the concentration on a seemingly single moment of decision-making has meant that later historians often miss the indecision or change of mind after publicly embracing the reform movement and departing the convent. For at least two iconic examples of the public rejection of convent life—Ursula von Münsterberg and Martha Elizabeth Zitter—the decision to leave the convent described in pamphlets was temporary and each sought to enter another convent. Münsterberg certainly tried and may have entered Gernrode, an evangelical-leaning house of canonesses.[8] Zitter succeeded in returning to Catholicism in an Ursuline convent in Kitzingen less than a year after her conversion to Lutheranism and after leaving her Ursuline convent in Erfurt.[9] Thus, their moment of deciding to leave or stay did not define their whole religious experience.

In addition, expectations changed over time. Although Luther and his clerical and political supporters accepted decisions made by nuns like Zedwitz as spiritually necessary, leaving the convent remained controversial even among followers of the evangelical movement.[10] In some cases, sudden individual actions undertaken by nuns later became problematic in hindsight. Concerns emerged after 1525 about why and in what circumstances a woman left a convent and ultimately led to new questions: Was it honorable for a woman to leave the convent without permission or in the middle of the night? What if she decided to return to the convent?

Could a woman decide to stay in the convent if she accepted the Saxon Church Ordinance and followed the Augsburg Confession?

Many former nuns presented their past decision as motivated by scriptural and spiritual reasons to avoid any association with potential interpretations of their actions as immoral and to improve chances of gaining financial support. Thus, their self-reported memories followed a particular narrative structure to accommodate the new expectations. Evidence—including printed pamphlets, recorded testimony, reports, and petitions—from three distinct moments—around 1525, 1533/34, and between 1540 and 1560—provide a unique record from these women about their decisions. The later material particularly detailed how these women remembered, or at least presented, how they made their decisions to stay or leave. In some cases, such as Zedwitz, an evolving explanation of the moment of decision for the same woman exists. This essay will explore how the complex, individual experiences and decisions of nuns during the Reformation led to the creation of religious hybridity in convents. It will also look at how nuns used the external interest in their devotional lives to make institutional and devotional changes, which led to the creation of Protestant and pluriconfessional convents, something authorities did not anticipate, but eventually had to accept. Some women even found that temporarily conforming to authority or demurring in answering questions provided an effective strategy to achieve effective freedom of religious practice and belief.

Early reform propaganda and the norming of departure

Making a decision and the construction of an appropriate decision-making process for nuns and those that helped them leave the convent began almost immediately after the first group of nuns from Nimbschen and Sitzenroda left convents in early 1523. The difference between the two concepts and the stress on whose decision is being emphasized becomes evident in the way that Martin Luther presented how nuns left Nimbschen in private and in public. In letters to Spalatin, Linck, and Amsdorf, Luther praised Leonhard Koppe, Wolf von Dommitzsch, and their relatives for helping nine (or maybe 12) Nimbschen nuns escape the oath for "impure celibacy." His emphasis to his fellow theologians was on the decision of family members to help nuns out of the convent because of their new awareness and understanding of the spiritual danger of monastic life to their female relatives. He did suggest one path for the nuns to decide for themselves when he promised to help any nun unable to return to her family to justify her decision to marry.[11]

As his work with convents grew, Luther emphasized the individual religious decision of the women to leave the convent, in part to protect those that helped them and to counter growing reports of women being forced to leave the convent against their will.[12] In the revised version of this letter in the polemical pamphlet, *Ursach und antwort*, Luther summarized the common accusation that he had incited the nuns and had sent Koppe to kidnap them. He responded that God's will and Word alone motivated the women and that the nuns, once they knew the truth about their convent life, asked for Koppe's help after their parents and friends ignored their pleas for help.[13] In this way, Luther emphasized the individual decision of the women to leave the convent for spiritual reasons. His call was thus two-fold: the laity were obliged to help nuns leave the convent and the nuns should make and execute the decision themselves.

After 1524, Luther's emphasis on the women making their own decisions appeared frequently in pamphlets purportedly written by nuns, perhaps not surprisingly given Luther's forwards to the works. Florentina von Oberweimar and Ursula von Münsterberg each outlined the process by which she decided to leave her convents: First, she underwent a gradual discovery of the sinfulness of the convent life as she moved from childhood to full majority in the convent. Second, she realized that she must leave the convent to enter into the true Christian estate outside of the convent after reading and/or hearing God's Word and through God's mercy. Third, she faced opposition from the abbess or others in the convent, which she finally overcame and escaped from her prison, often in secret or at night. These works leave the women at the moment when their struggles are resolved by their departure from the convent.

Published narratives certainly influenced other women's accounts of how they left the convent in their petitions for assistance from the elector of Saxony. In 1527, Dorothea Merzsch, a former nun from Sitzenroda, described how she entered the convent because her father knew no better way for her salvation than this "special service to God." She came to understand, through God's illumination, that this human understanding made the convent a "prison" where "poor children unwittingly" were bound. Now that she knew better, she wanted the elector's permission to leave and his financial assistance before doing so.[14] Thus, although many nuns demonstrated an awareness of the discussions over theology, scripture, and regional religious politics, the decisions they made were not always motivated by those reasons.

In Ernestine Saxony, the largest percentage of the 135 women leaving the convent did so during and just after the Peasants' War when departure could be due as much to the imminent threat to the women's well-being as to theological and political arguments. Many nuns remained cautious about making any decisions and did so in less than perfect circumstances since the process of exit was far from secure. Many of those nuns sought to return to their convent once the conflict was over and for many years after. Following the destruction of their convent in 1525, the abbess and nuns of Allendorf petitioned the elector numerous times to allow them to return to the convent, citing poverty forcing them to beg for food and their unprotected situation outside the convent.[15] As they represented their situation, their departure and their desire to return were based on hunger and physical danger rather than on religious matters.

In other cases, the desire to return to convent life was the primary concern. In 1529, according to Saxon visitors, two nuns from a convent in Gotha asked that they be allowed to return to their convent, promising to give up their severance in return for the right to live out their days in the convent.[16] In such cases, asking to return to the convent necessitated demonstrating a reason not motivated by a desire to return to their traditional rituals and monastic life, lest authorities suspect the women of lapsing into "the Roman Superstition" as electoral officials called it. In 1533, after being suspected of wanting to return to the convent to practice the "old evil traditions," Katharina Sanders responded that she and her sister had been nuns in Oberweimar for "a long time" and that she had held the office of bursar until forced to leave the convent in 1525, thus giving evidence of her virtuous and stable life as a nun.[17] She explained that she decided to return to the convent because the death of her sister, her own illness, and crushing poverty meant that she could no longer care for herself.[18] She avoided discussion of religion and presented her decision to return as based on pragmatic reasons alone.

Even the exemplary women praised by Luther and other Lutheran pastors in pamphlets rethought their decision once they left the convent. The attempt to return to a convent life by Ursula von Münsterberg and Martha Elisabeth Zittern shows that the decision made even in the pamphlet was not final. For Münsterberg, the death of her sister and her inability to find a stable home led her to seek a return to the convent. Zittern's testimony a few months after her departure from the Ursuline convent in Erfurt showed that she had been trying for months to get a transfer to Kitzingen, closer to her family, and had little contact with Lutheran ideas. Thus, because many understood the discussions over theology, scripture, and regional religious politics, the presentation of their reasons to leave, stay, or return remained complicated, multifaceted, and changeable for most nuns and were often dependent on a narrative designed to achieve their goal.

Visitations

During the decade between the Peasants' War and when the second visitation held in convents concluded in 1534, nuns continued to leave and reenter convents without any formal process. It was only during the 1533–1534 visitations that officials in Ernestine Saxony addressed this lack of procedure with a rule designed to create ritual compliance inside the convent while also convincing women to decide to leave. The reason for this approach was that, increasingly, legal decisions on property and religion before the Imperial Chamber Court had upheld that the convents not be dissolved without the nuns' consent and that nuns could not be forced on religion. This workaround—that officials could influence the behavior and decisions of the women using regulations—proved more difficult than anticipated.

The intent of the visitations of gaining compliance and assuring that the women were following the local church ordinances is evident in how officials stated their goals and how they approached the nuns. In a 1533 letter to the sequesters of Thuringia, Elector John wrote that he expected that giving the regulation on clothing to the nuns of Heusdorf would lead them to "turn away from the mischief and contempt among them" without external interference.[19] During the 1533–1534 visitations in five convents (Altenburg, Cronschwitz, Nimbschen,

Remse, and Saalburg), the visitors arrived at surviving convents and handed each abbess a document with specific instructions about how spiritual and devotional life was to be conducted in each convent until its final closure. They interviewed 71 of the 77 remaining nuns (six were sick) and required a verbal statement from each woman about whether intended to stay in the convent. They then questioned the women to see if they would set aside "papist ceremonies," accept "God's will," and abide by the regulations outlined in the territorial church order. They then asked for a verbal confirmation of their acceptance of several devotional rituals and marking signs of laicization, most notably giving up wearing habits and donning lay clothing.[20] The visitors expected that giving the women these requirements in order to remain in the convent and receive financial assistance would break down resistance to their church ordinances and get them to choose to leave the convent or at least to accept the new rituals and liturgy.

The nuns' responses were mixed: eighteen adamantly refused to comply; eight stated they would pray to God for guidance; nine promised to give up their habits or ask family members for advice; fourteen had already given up their habits but gave no other promises; sixteen expressed acceptance of specific aspects of the convent order such as willingness to listen to the gospel, accept communion in both kinds, or even leave the convents; and four avoided answering any questions at all. This diversity of responses indicates a certain level of confessional fluidity and individual decision-making about compliance to the visitor's demands. The nuns were also presented a process by which they could leave with an annuity, dowry, and/or severance payment if they asked the permission of the elector, visitor, or abbess. Yet, only 12 of the 77 women left the convent, while the vast majority remained firm on their earlier decision to stay in the convent, regardless of their stated degree of willingness to follow the church ordinance.

Some of the differences in the answers probably stemmed from local convent cultures. In 1534, the visitors praised the nuns in the convent of Nimbschen as "entirely Christian" (*ganz christlich*) for diligently attending sermons and taking communion in both kinds.[21] In 1533, visitors to Cronschwitz focused on whether the nuns would put aside their habits or not as an indication of their willingness to accept reform: 13 had done so and 14 had not. After the pastor was replaced, another five set aside habits by 1534.[22] The greater success occurred shortly after this visit when four nuns from Cronschwitz wrote to the sequesters that they had been rescued from the "unfemale burden" in the convent for the "benefit of their soul" and "conscience," "with the permission and previous knowledge" of the elector to enter "god-ordained, Christian" marriage. All statements echoed the words of Luther in 1523 and followed the new expected progress of decisions.[23]

Although perhaps not as compliant as visitors might have hoped, the nuns of Remse and Brehna showed more diversity and discord about religious reform than their neighboring convents. The nine women interviewed at Remse, for instance, gave diverse responses to the visitors' questions. Abbess Veronica Grüner was openly hostile to changes and willing to use "all means to hinder the other nuns from hearing God's word," and Elisabeth Holeuffer stated that she was not willing to give up her habit for secular clothing. Margarethe Wolframsdorf, in contrast, stated that she would follow the church order and would gladly leave the convent. None of the remaining nuns expressed any particular opinion one way or another, other than their intent to ask for "God's mercy."[24] In 1537, Conrad Glischen, pastor of Brehna, described how some of the uncompliant nuns in the convent prevented the others from worshipping according to the new rituals by continuing their "malicious" (*mutwillig*) rituals.[25] Most responses showed that the women still made decisions within the context of the convent congregation and that most women remained unwilling to state their confessional position to the visitors and/or their fellow nuns.

This internal process of institutional decision-making is clearest in the growing consensus among the nuns of Altenburg between their first and second visitations. In 1534, the 11 nuns interviewed gave diverse, individual responses: six adamantly refused to accept the ordinance, with the visitors describing several as "stubborn" (*halsstarrig*). One nun, Anna Bresen, answered that she thought that communion in both kinds was fine, but otherwise was unwilling to follow the church order. The four remaining nuns expressed willingness to consider communion in both kinds, but only if God, or, in one case, her parents approved.[26] In 1538, visitors once again questioned the nuns of Altenburg. This time their responses were unequivocal. Barbara Reich stated she would be "ashamed" to wear anything other than her habit and that she had no intention of taking communion in any way "other than the way she had been instructed from her childhood up." Barbara Stein said that "she wanted to remain with God's word," and would not give up her habit or her convent vows. Elisabeth Gross declared that communion in both kinds was "against her belief and conscience" and that she would "stick to her Gospel." Even Anna Bresen said that she could not do anything "against her heart," including taking communion in both kinds in, a change from her equivocation in 1534.[27] Most denied the efficacy of communion in both kinds and asserted forcefully their unwillingness to give up their monastic lives. These responses indicate how community dynamics dominated in what were now effectively multiconfessional convents, containing some religiously hybrid nuns exhibiting intermixed confessional markers or conforming to rituals even while believing something else.

Once nuns made the decision to stay in the convent, they insisted that their decision be respected and that they receive the financial support that they were due as owner. They were aided in this in part because of legal decisions on convent property that uniformly upheld the women's right to their property. These changes aided in their willingness to challenge local officials, including contacting the elector, and secured their means to continue living in the convent.

The creation of memory

The creation of memory occurred as the events of the past were reorganized and elaborated to fit the presently accepted model of choice to leave. At the same time, however, the establishment of a formal procedure for deciding to stay or leave in

1533 had left *former* nuns in a precarious position when petitioning for funding. Their resolve to leave their convent before any official legalization of the evangelical movement or establishment of an official protocol for departure left them vulnerable once the movement was legalized and such a protocol to leave did exist. The actions of women heralded as heroic during the early Reformation suddenly could be viewed as having acted against the current expectations of state, family, and church officials. This change in the expected process to leave led to a shift during the 1530s to 1550s when former nuns carefully crafted narrative explanations of how and when they left the convents in previous decades. They presented their past decision as motivated solely by religious concerns to avoid any association with potential interpretations of their actions as immoral.

Many petitioners emphasized an early departure from the convent as evidence of religious conviction. In 1537, Catharina (Schöpperitz) Reichman, formerly a nun in Cronschwitz, began her request for an increase in her annuity with an explanation of how she had left the convent around 1534 after the visitation helped her understand what an unchristian life she lived in the convent. She described how she went on to marry as "ordered by God."[28] She also noted the social cost of that decision to laicize and views of clerical marriage. In 1544, Elisabeth Steinbrecher of Arnstadt described her decision to leave the convent of Oberweimar in Weimar as beginning with God's "opening of his heavenly treasure of the divine Word" where she learned that the "falsely named religious, monkish and nunnish, estate was godless" and decided with her pastor and the Elector's support to leave to marry in 1525. She stated that during the intervening years of poverty, she had never doubted God even as the "godless papists heeded married priests, monks, and nuns as motivated by impertinence and lust."[29] Many also highlighted their early decision to leave the convent as a sign of their commitment. In 1538, Ave von Grosse, one of the nuns to leave the Nimbschen convent with Katharina von Bora in 1523, reminded the Elector that she was among the "first nine nuns out" and had left everything behind when she fled. She also mentioned that she waited to marry, underscoring that this had not been the purpose of her flight.[30] These narratives of the decision-making process emphasized a woman's honor and Christian behavior before and after her departure from the convent. Scriptural justification, permission from the authorities, and the considered decision to marry with parent's involvement were used by many to demonstrate these women's earlier actions as motivated by personal morality and deference to textual and spiritual authority, as was the recounting of a continued Christian life as a wife and mother after departure.

Similar attempts at crafting the narrative of their decisions to defend against moral or religious accusations are seen in nuns, particularly those returning to the convent. These women highlighted their non-religious reasons for leaving the convent to counter any suspicion that they had religious reasons for being there. In 1538, numerous reports reached the elector that Elisabeth and Margarethe Meckler, two former nuns from Oberweimar, had put back on their habits, first in Freiburg and then in Beuditz, so that they were could freely to "do papist works" as they pleased.[31] In 1539, Elisabeth responded that she and her sister had been forced to leave the convent during the Peasants' War and that their poverty drove them to wander around "like pilgrims" until they were taken in as guests in a convent in "Duke George's land."[32] In explaining their decision to leave, she emphasized her leadership position as abbess in Oberweimar to show her morality and, for both women, she described their experience during the rebellion as the reason why they left. She placed implicit responsibility for their decision to return to the convent on the elector for failing to provide them with necessary financial support. Some returning nuns stated that their religious belief remained in line with the church ordinance, even as they noted their physical necessities drove them back into the convent. In 1567, for instance, Elisabeth Breul stated that during the Peasants' War, that Elector John permitted her and her fellow nuns to return to their convent in Eisenach after they agreed to give up "papacy and accept the teaching of the pure Gospel."[33]

What is interesting is to see the transition in these presentations of choice over time. During the events in 1525, the nuns reported that the storming of the convent of Ichtershausen was particularly brutal with their guardian, Jörg von Volkstädt, being tied up after trying to defend the convent, an event that led to their seeking refuge in the community. When the nuns found themselves homeless, Abbess Catharine Frenckl wrote to Count Günther of Schwarzburg for permission for herself and four other nuns to settle in Arnstadt and provide for themselves by handicrafts.[34] Their arguments and petitions in 1525 were matter of fact and pragmatic as were those written seven years later. In 1532, the surviving nuns from Ichtershausen asked for additional compensation from what they had received in 1525, stating that some were "old, weak, and poor," while others were "married, and so burdened with children that they suffered need."[35] In 1534, the brother of Dorothea Spättler, another of those nuns, wrote to the sequesters to complain that he had attempted to retrieve the remainder of his sisters' inheritance for her, but that each time the provost did not have her money.[36] In all three cases, the request was neither tied to memory of why the women left or to their spiritual state, although the mention of marriage for some does hint at concern to meet the expected course of laicization.

By the 1540s, the memory of how these nuns came to leave the convent emerged as a vital part of the petition. In 1540, Volkstädt stated that when Katharine Gebhardt, one of the Ichtershausen nuns, left the convent during the Peasants' War, she did not do so "secretly or silently" but with the permission of her parents, with whom she then resided until she married honorably. He elaborated that she and her husband had raised their children as Christians.[37] Gebhardt thus took the time to make her decision, consult her parents, and then live an honorable, Christian life as a dutiful daughter and then wife, a far cry from the sense of confusion and privation in the earlier petitions. The narrative of the decision-making process after the creation of a formal process of petitioning funds led women, and those writing to support their petitions, to emphasize a woman's honor, decision-making process, and Christian behavior after their departure.

Conclusion

The desire of authorities and later confessional historians for a clear choice made by the nuns to stay or leave was grafted on top of the reality of what amounted to micro-decisions or, in some cases, public dissimulations. What becomes clear upon closer examination of the petitions and testimony of these women is that they did not make simple yes or no choices to embrace or resist the reform movement. In addition, factors other than religious belief or affiliation often went into these decisions, especially in 1525 and beyond. Faced with a myriad of options about specific religious rituals, external practices, and internal beliefs, most nuns underwent an ongoing process of confronting aspects of the reform movement based on their personal and collective social and financial circumstances. Their decisions made during this first decade, as seen in letters to reformers and in testimony to visitors, and then how they remembered, or at least presented, their decision-making process years, even decades, later in petitions to the elector of Saxony and to the convent provosts and the sequesters charged with managing convent property provide a unique window into exploring how women, particularly those in convents, confronted the Reformation and how they came chose to present how they made their decisions to embrace or reject the new religious rituals and practices.

Although authorities and later historians accepted specific markers as defining confession, a closer look at the context indicates the women may not have viewed such moments in that way. For many, a public avowal of the decision-making process was divorced from their private belief. Thus, nominal conformity to expected religious norms from nuns often masked confessional fluidity at the local level. In addition, several layers of memory and justification obscured the decision-making process throughout the sixteenth century. Beginning with the first groups of nuns leaving the convent, scriptural justifications were given to protect them and their helpers from legal consequences of their actions. Many nuns remaining in the convent, regardless of religious inclination, sought ways to continue to do so without risking financial support from the elector and so acted or said enough to deflect closer inspection of their beliefs. Later recounted memories of leaving the convent constructed a past that fit the current expectation by evangelical leaders and community members. A final layer was added by historians in presenting or not presenting some actions of women during the early Reformation. The erasure of the decision of nuns such as Münsterberg or Zitter to return to the convent or the continuation of convents beyond when we would have expected them to close shows a great deal about how historians selectively deal with complicated response of nuns to the reform movement. Doubt, second-guessing, lack of enthusiasm, or even hybridity did not fit a heroic ideal of religious conviction. While some women certainly did leave for reasons of religious conviction, more women remembered that they had done so than perhaps had.

Notes

1 Landesarchiv Thüringen—Hauptstaatsarchiv Weimar, Ernestinisches Gesamtarchiv (Hereafter as ThHStAW, EGA), Reg. Ii 9, 63^r (11 February 1533).
2 ThHStAW, EGA, Reg. Kk 1282, 1^{r-v} (17 June 1544).
3 ThHStAW, EGA, Reg. Kk 1282, 2^{r-v} (10 July 1544).
4 ThHStAW EGA, Reg. Kk 1282, 3^{r-v} (24 November 1544).
5 Merry Wiesner-Hanks, *Women and Gender in Early Modern* Europe, 3rd ed. (Cambridge: Cambridge University Press, 2008), 207–208.
6 57 nuns in these convents left by 1525/1526, 22 between 1527 and 1532, 19 between 1533 and 1539, and 37 at an unknown date. The fate of 38 of the nuns remains unclear, although some may have died in the convent.
7 For a study on the convents of Albertine Saxony, see Sabine Zinsmeyer, *Frauenklöster in der Reformationszeit: Lebensformen von Nonnen in Sachsen zwischen Reform und landesherrlicher Aufhebung* (Stuttgart: Franz Steiner, 2016).
8 ThHStAW, EGA Reg. Kk 561 (14 August 1530); Hubert Ermisch, "Herzogin Ursula von Münsterberg: Ein Beitrag zur Geschichte der Reformation in Sachsen," *Neues Archiv für Sächsiche Geschichte und Alterthumskunde* 3 (1882): 290–333, esp. 321.
9 Staatsarchiv Bamberg, Hochstift Bamberg, Geistliche Regierung, Nr. 31 (1678); Johann Eliae Höffling, *Gründliche Vorstellung der Heiligen Römisch-Catholischen Lehr von den Geistlichen Stand, und dessen Gelübden; ... oder Aufferwachtes Gewissen und Wahrhaffte Ursachen Welche mich Schwester Marthen Elisabeth von JESU bewogen von dem Lutherthum und Hof-Leben zu der H. Catholischen Kirchen under die Clösterliche Zucht widerumb zuruck zu treten* (Bamberg: Johann Jacob Immel, 1678). Höffling's work is just one of the many books published surrounding Zittern's conversion and reconversion.
10 Marjorie Elizabeth Plummer, "'Nothing More than Common Whores and Knaves': Married Monks and Nuns in the Early German Reformation," in *Mixed Matches: Transgressive Unions in Germany from the Reformation to the Enlightenment*, ed. David M. Luebke and Mary Lindemann (Oxford: Berghahn Books, 2014), 45–62.
11 ThHStAW, EGA, Reg. N 161, 1^{r-v} (10 April 1523); 2^{r-v} (11 April 1523); Anne-Katrin Köhler, *Geschichte des Klosters Nimbschen: Von der Gründung 1243 bis zu seinem Ende 1536/1542* (Leipzig: Evangelische Verlagsanstalt, 2003), 117–118. The changing numbers shows the degree to which even Luther was confused about the evolving situation.
12 Amy Leonard, *Nails in the Wall: Catholic Nuns in Reformation Germany* (Chicago: University of Chicago Press, 2005), 40–41; Antje Rüttgardt, "Die Diskussion um das Klosterleben von Frauen in Flugschriften der Frühen Reformationszeit (1523–1528)," in *"In Christo ist weder man noch weib": Frauen in der Zeit der Reformation und der katholischen Reform*, ed. Anne Conrad (Münster: Aschendorff, 1999), 69–94, here 91–92.
13 Martin Luther, *Ursach und antwort, das Junckfrawen klöster götlich verlassen mögen* (Augsburg: Sigmund Grimm, 1523), A4a, cf. *WA* 11.
14 ThHStAW EGA, Reg. Kk 1277 (15 December 1527); ThHStAW EGA, Reg. Kk 1279 (25 December 1527).
15 ThHStAW, EGA, Reg. Kk 80, 2^r–3^r (6 October 1525).
16 ThHStAW, EGA, Reg. Kk 529, 1^r.
17 ThHStAW, EGA, Reg. Oo 792, 641 (15 May 1533).
18 ThHStAW, EGA, Reg. Oo 792, 641, #3 (1533).
19 ThHStAW, EGA, Reg. Oo 792, 446 (4 May 1533).
20 See, for instance, ThHStAW, EGA, Reg. Ii. 9, 96^r–97^v (Saalburg,11 September 1533); ThHStAW, EGA, Reg. Ii 7, 203^v–205^v (Cronschwitz, 26 September 1533); ThHStAW, EGA, Reg. Ii 6, 10^v–13^v (Remse, 30 November 1533); 160^r–162^v (Nimbschen, 6 March 1534); 40^v–43^r (Altenburg, 22 April 1534).ThHStAW, EGA, Reg. Oo 792, 446 (4 May 1533).
21 ThHStAW, EGA, Reg. Ii 6, 158^r (6 March 1534).
22 ThHStAW, EGA, Reg. Ii 7, 200^r–201^r.

23 ThHStAW, EGA, Reg. Aaa 331 (27 July 1533).
24 ThHStAW, EGA, Reg. Ii 583, 25^r–26^r (Remse, 1 December 1533).
25 ThHStAW EGA, Reg. Ii 1061 (16 October 1537).
26 ThHStAW, EGA, Reg. Ii 583, 59^v–60^r (Altenberg, 22 April 1534).
27 ThHStAW EGA, Reg. Kk, Nr. 70, 2^r–3^r (7 September 1538).
28 ThHStAW, EGA, Reg. Oo 792, 164 (5 July 1537).
29 ThHStAW, EGA, Reg. Oo 792, 660b (1 October 1544).
30 ThHStAW, EGA, Reg. Oo 792, 626 (19 October 1538).
31 ThHStAW, EGA, Reg. Oo 792, 651 (7 January 1538); ThHStAW, EGA, Reg. Oo 792, 651 (2 September 1538).
32 ThHStAW, EGA, Reg. Oo 792, 651 (16 October 1539; 20 October 1539)
33 ThHStAW, EGA, Reg. Kk 433 24 March 1567).
34 Wilhem Rein, ed., *Kloster Ichtershausen. Urkundenbuch, Geschichte und bauliche Beschreibung* (Weimar: Herman Böhlau, 1863), 204 (9 May 1525).
35 Rein, *Kloster Ichtershausen*, 188–189 (4 December 1532). For a follow-up to this request, see ThHStAW, EGA, Reg. Oo 792, 463 (20 March 1533).
36 ThHStAW, EGA, Reg. Kk, 1679 (6 February 1534).
37 ThHStAW, EGA, Reg. Oo pag. 792, 484 (18 October 1540).

8

FEMALE RELIGIOUS COMMUNITIES DURING THE THIRTY YEARS' WAR

Sigrun Haude

The Thirty Years' War did not stop at the doors of female religious communities. Like their contemporaries, they faced violence, disruption, and often dislocation, but their status also set them apart from the rest of society and influenced how they encountered the war. Several of them wrote about their experiences in diary-style testimonies, which give us some insight into their lives. A selection of these works forms the focus of this study that seeks to explore how these women forged their lives in response to the challenges of war.

Considering that female perspectives are rare for the early modern period, the study of convent women offers some rich resources. Besides institutional records of their convents, the leaders of these houses or someone in an administrative position generally wrote an account of her life and that of her community. These varied in character depending on the author and the circumstances. The Thirty Years' War elicited especially vivid testimonies, which take us into these women's world. The following analysis focuses on a particular set of experiences, namely temporary exile, homelessness, separation, and disruption of monastic life because of the war. In tracing the women's responses to these realities, one intriguing feature stands out in particular, namely the ingenious ways in which these women appropriated the male construct of enclosure. Moreover, their strategies were not uniform but reflect the diverse situations of the nuns.

While the chronological context is the Thirty Years' War, the geographic foci rest on the territories in and around modern-day Bavaria, which represented a region hit hard by the war. During the 1620s, troops regularly passed through its northern parts (Franconia) and took up quarters there. For Franconia, the conflict began in earnest in 1631 when the Swedish King, Gustavus Adolphus (r. 1611–1632), led his army south to aid Augsburg's Protestants. After beating the troops of the Catholic League, the Swedes marched through Erfurt, Würzburg, and Bamberg to winter in Eichstätt's diocese. Bavaria's elector, Maximilian (r. 1598/1623–1651), sided with Emperor

Ferdinand II (r. 1619–1637), which gave Gustavus Adolphus the justification to invade Bavaria. In April 1632, the Swedes conquered Weißenburg, Donauwörth, and Rain am Lech, and Augsburg's starving Protestants received him enthusiastically. Since Gustavus Adolphus' repeated attempts to subdue Maximilian's heavily fortified university town, Ingolstadt, remained unsuccessful, the king instead headed for the more vulnerable court city Munich, from where the elector had already fled to Austria.

As a consequence of these military battles and troop movements, the degree of devastation in Franconia and Bavaria was immense. When one reads the many descriptions by contemporaries and later historians, one wonders who and what was left. It is widely understood that, overall, the repercussions of war—such as the quartering of troops, contributions, plunder, famine, inflation, pest, and disease—took a far greater human toll than the military actions themselves. Certain regions that functioned as corridors of troop movement were more prone to destruction than others. The route from Nuremberg through Eichstätt to Munich was one such zone that was particularly affected during the Swedish Intervention in the first half of the 1630s. For these reasons, the Thirty Years' War tends to evoke rather uniform and one-dimensional images of ruin and devastation. On the local level, however, the encounter with the war proved to be remarkably diverse. Other important factors—such as networks and one's personal situation—influenced how people responded to the reality of war as well.

As mentioned, in certain ways nuns were set apart from other women in their experience of the war. Their status as members of a religious order afforded nuns advantages and disadvantages. They formed a community that could sustain them and in which they could find companionship. Typically, these communities were linked to a wider network of convents and monastic houses, to which they could flee or to whom they could appeal for help. Many of them had resources and were the recipients of alms. And often women religious were under the "protection" of a male guardian (whatever that might mean). On the other hand, the religious, male and female (indeed the clergy in general), were frequently the target of violence. In some cases, they were suspected of being more affluent; in others, they were taken hostage to extract money from cities and communities. Confessional animosities added to the antagonism toward them. To avoid harassment, monks and nuns on their flights regularly disguised themselves and traveled in secular clothes, which highlights their exposed status and their sense of threat connected with it.

The analysis centers on several convents in what is today Bavaria and the autobiographical accounts their inhabitants left behind. Some of these narratives have been published; others come from Munich's and Augsburg's archives. Among them are the well-known diaries of Clara Staiger, prioress of the Augustinian convent Mariastein by Eichstätt in Franconia,[1] and Maria Anna Junius, stewardess of the Dominican convent Heiliggrab (sometimes: Heiligengrab) by Bamberg;[2] but also, lesser-known testimonies by the Dominican nuns of St. Katharina in Augsburg[3] and the Poor Clares of Munich's Angerkloster.[4]

These diary-style narratives tell us about the religious women in their communities. Scholars have debated intensely both the subject of "experience" and the terminology of sources that might provide access to it. Is it possible to recover or know anything about how early modern people experienced certain events or situations?[5] No matter what we call these narratives—autobiographical accounts, testimonies about or to oneself (*Selbstzeugnisse*), ego-documents, or self-narratives—the most important development in this discussion has been the spotlight on the collective dimension of the experience expressed in personal accounts.[6] To quote Kaspar von Greyerz: "personal narratives, both in reproducing and in creating discourse, are deeply embedded in a collective context."[7]

The women reacted to the perceived and real dangers of war in several ways. Flight constituted one of the most common responses to an approaching army. Like other contemporaries, nuns were faced with the decision whether they should stay or flee, but, for them, many variables came into play with regard to this decision. Some had the option to flee, while others did not. For some the choice lay largely within their power to make; others were bound by the verdict of their male superior. If the community fled, some of the women typically had to stay behind to look after the convent, which led to the group's separation.

The Augustinian nuns by Eichstätt belonged to those who had a place to withdraw to. Indeed, they had several options, but they were dependent on the say-so of their male guardian of the nearby Augustinian canons (Rebdorf). Every time soldiers were sighted in Eichstätt's vicinity, their guardian ordered Prioress Clara Staiger and her sisters to take their belongings and flee—first to Eichstätt, then to St. Willibald's Castle high above the city, and eventually to Ingolstadt. Still, the degree of protection that could be offered through this guardianship was not only limited but doubtful. Safety could not be guaranteed at either one of these places. The enemy conquered both Eichstätt and its castle while the nuns resided there. Nor did Staiger always welcome their guardian's patronage because their flights were not of their own choosing. At times, she would have liked to have held out a little longer in her cloister, but a delay of their departure only earned them their guardian's displeasure.[8]

The Poor Clares of Munich's Angerkloster also had a place of refuge—in the Tyrol, but once the danger approached there, they were out of options. They, too, were beholden to their male superior (Commissarius Pater Ambrosius de Albabata), who determined when they would flee. The Commissarius ordered them to be ready for the convoy and had them wait for four days packed and in the same clothes. He also decided on the speed of their journey, which at times tested their patience. Instead of moving swiftly to their destination, they had to hang about at Tölz castle for over a week.[9]

Others hardly had an alternative to staying in their cloister. The Dominican nuns, whose convent lay just outside Bamberg's city walls, had no direct male guardian. Thus, when the Swedes approached in 1632, the sisters turned to Bamberg's prince-bishop, Johann Georg Fuchs of Dornheim (r. 1623–1633), for advice.[10]

Slow to answer, the bishop counseled them in case of need to disperse throughout Bamberg—a city he had just left for the nearby fortress of Forchheim.[11] Besides suggesting a break-up of the convent's community and holding out the dubious safety of a city he had just fled, he offered no concrete suggestion, no house where they might find refuge. In desperation, the nuns wrote to the Protestant margravine of Bayreuth, whose husband then pleaded their case with the Protestant military leader, Gustavus Adolphus. The margravine begged the sisters to stay in their convent and to make sure that no secular people would be quartered in their cloister.[12]

In contrast, the Dominican nuns of St. Katharina in Augsburg represent a convent with options and the power to make its own decisions. This is certainly not unrelated to the fact that many of its members had ties to influential families in the city.[13] It is fascinating to see Prioress Maria Magdalena Kurz at work in negotiating the best possible solution for her cloister. In the back and forth between Prioress Kurz and a wide range of secular and religious authorities, we also get a close-up of the confusion, disbelief, shock, and uncertainty among the Catholic leaders when confronted with the Swedish offensive in the early 1630s, and of their reluctant realization that their fortune was about to change. Exchanges range from convictions that all was still well to the slow recognition of potentially very bad outcomes, and the prioress was caught up in the leaders' attempts to find their way in the thicket of war. First, the nuns were urged as a group to go to the Tyrol (no breakup of the convent!); then Munich seemed the best destination since Elector Maximilian would not let anyone take his court city or Bavaria. But soon it dawned on the men that no place in Bavaria was safe. Instead, they held on to their hope that "contracts" with the occupiers would ensure their protection. In the end, the advice of the nuns' spiritual fathers was to stay in Augsburg since it would also be a heavy burden on the prioress to sustain her very large convent in exile for a potentially long time. At this point, the convent counted 42 women—31 nuns and 11 lay sisters, with another 6 nuns from the convent St. Marx in Würzburg who had fled to them. In addition, several of the sisters had relatives in Augsburg and could stay with them.[14]

When the Swedes threatened to take Augsburg later that month, the question was once again whether they should flee or remain. Besides obtaining advice from a broad range of leaders (both male and female, namely the mothers of the councilors) and acquiring as much information about the military situation as possible, Prioress Kurz placed the decision in the hands of her sisters. Significantly, when she presented the options before her charges, her touch points were rooted in the history of this particular convent:

> Although she could not hold back anyone, she nevertheless advised us out of motherly love that we should stay steadfast and think about the example of our most honorable mothers and sisters, who lived in this cloister at the time of the Lutheran heresy (*Lutherey*), and who had preserved the entire cloister

with their steadfastness, despite the fact that all spirituals had been expelled from the city so that they did not have any confessors and had been robbed for many years of all their holy sacraments.[15]

Back then, they had to listen to Lutheran sermonizing and proselytizing, but "God preserved them."[16] After the prioress' address, 29 of the 42 women agreed to remain (a mix of older women including Prioress Kurz, 12 nuns, and all 11 lay sisters). The prioress also declared that anyone who would want to stay with her kin could do so without incurring sin.[17] In the end, the entire convent decided to remain in Augsburg.

Given these varied realities from forced movement to staying put, how did the nuns experience homelessness and separation, and, at the other end of the spectrum, staying home? For most of the religious communities under discussion, their flights led to temporary exile, not permanent emigration.[18] While this was certainly the hope of those in exile, there was no certainty of the outcome, or any knowledge of how many more times they would have to flee. The nuns described their experience as "going into misery" (*ins Elend gehen*). This standard phrase found throughout narratives of secular and spiritual men and women implied having to leave one's place for a region that was not home. This strange land could be a distant county or a foreign country, but it could also be as close as the nearby forest, the next city, or, in the case of the nuns, another convent.[19]

Flights typically led to separation of the community, since a contingent stayed behind to look after the convent and only fled when the enemy was all but upon them. Some communities were split up among other convents that still seemed safe—either because no other refuge was available or because the group was too large to be sustained abroad. Exile, then, not only separated one from the space one regarded as home, but also disrupted the community that shaped one's life. Flights, however, also fostered new associations of fate. The Augustinian prioress, Clara Staiger, noted that, in Ingolstadt, they received many alms, "but more from the Neuburgers and foreigners than from the Ingolstädters, who did not greatly respect strangers. The (natives) had neither experienced our grief nor did they understand it."[20] The experience of exile fused people together, but it also separated them from those who had little conception of what the refugees had suffered.

Yet, for the sisters who remained home, life was not easy either. The remaining nuns also faced disruption in their familiar spaces since they often had to take in women from other convents and orders, which led to friction over religious lifestyle. The split of their own group weighed heavily on them, and some felt abandoned and exposed. In her correspondence, Sister Anastasia of Munich's Angerkloster (Poor Clares) referred to herself as "orphan": "with regard to us poor orphans, I cannot express in words what fear and sorrow are among us. We are simply without protection (*vogelfrei*)… We need nothing more than to prepare for the blessed end."[21] While the nuns were anxious for the safety and comfort of those who had fled and had to sleep roughly, the smaller group that operated the convent at home felt overburdened with running its economy all by itself. It meant hard work and chores that many were unused to or not trained to do. Keys and vital documents could not be found because suddenly a crucial layer of their operation was gone.[22] While some had no regrets about having stayed behind, others became heavy at heart. Sister Anastasia, with six other nuns, had not gone all the way to the Tyrol and had instead returned (from Tölz) to the Angerkloster, but she eventually regretted having done so. For her, being a nun meant being quiet in her cell with God: "O my dear heart, it is a pleasure above all pleasure for the one who can serve God in her cell in silence."[23] Instead, she had to take on tasks she never wanted to and be involved in the business of running the economy. If the experience of exile led to a form of disequilibrium (*Gleichgewichtsstörung* in the words of the twentieth-century exile, Stefan Zweig), the experience of a reconfigured home also tested one's sense of identity.[24]

Space is an important dimension in these experiences.[25] Some nuns were carted off to new places,[26] but for those who stayed behind, the landscape of the place they called home changed as well, not only because of the potentially real destruction of their convent, but also due to the shifts in the home community once the better part of the sisters had left. "Home" needed to be constructed anew in accordance with the altered situation. Some adjusted and rallied; others become disoriented not so unlike their exiled sisters. To some extent, then, space eluded the nuns' control.

And, yet, there is ample evidence that, in this theater of war, nuns also used their space in ingenious ways and to their greatest advantage. I am referring to enclosure.[27] Augsburg's Dominican prioress once again provides fascinating insight into her shrewd negotiations for her convent's safety, and it centers on the nuns' enclosure. In the case of St. Katharina, enclosure became the most important bargaining chip to keep the occupiers out. Prioress Kurz insisted on honoring their enclosure and stood up to military men, who suspected great stores of ammunition behind the closed doors. She went so far as to refuse refuge to the abbess of the Benedictine convent Holz, who was looking for new quarters for herself and a few of her charges. Prioress Kurz argued that she had "highly important reasons" for rejecting the abbess' request, "especially regarding enclosure, which would have been broken had they admitted them, and we would have undoubtedly given cause to the Swedes as well as to the local evangelicals to enter the cloister."[28] While Maria Kurz incurred a lot of grief for maintaining this stern but painful position, even from relatives of her nuns, she received backing from one of her trusted male advisors (Buechler): "She should by all means turn down [the request] in consideration that at this time the barrier [*Spörr*, referring to enclosure] is our greatest treasure [*Klainot*], which has protected them this long from all danger."[29] The Dominican prioress thus capitalized on a male construct that often functioned to control female religious and employed it to keep the aggressor out and ensure safety for her convent.

Enclosure, however, could also be used in entirely opposite ways. Under the menace of war, Bamberg's Dominican nuns let the occupiers enter their space.

Their situation was very different from that of their sisters in Augsburg, who had powerful and supportive ties to the city. Indeed, during the course of the early 1630s, it became clear that the Dominican nuns had more to fear from their own authorities in Bamberg than from the Swedish enemy. Since the sisters stayed in their cloister, their foremost concern was to shield themselves from harm by establishing good relations with whoever governed their city.[30] In doing so, they showed themselves as expert negotiators with the occupying forces, the Swedes. At various times, the commanding officers made the wellbeing of the nuns their personal mission. The Swedish general, Wilhelm Georg von Lohausen (1584–1640), had the princely order to raze Bamberg's suburb, including the cloister Heiliggrab, for defensive purposes.[31] According to the convent's chronicler, Maria Anna Junius, the general responded instead:

> I cannot do such a thing without doing harm to the good maidens of Heiligengrab/also I am unable to let something evil happen to my spiritual daughters/I would rather suffer it myself. He also told us: you, my dear daughters, can say in truth that you preserved the suburb [of Bamberg]/ because if it had not been for you, nothing would be left of the suburb.[32]

Several high officers repeatedly made their rounds to the convent, including Duke Bernhard von Saxe-Weimar (1604–1639), the new governor of Franconia, who had given Lohausen the above order. Presumably, von Saxe-Weimar wanted to see for himself why the Dominican nuns attracted such fierce protection from his officers. This Swedish assistance to the nuns contrasted starkly with the "aid" they received from their own people. There was the earlier noted nonchalant and unhelpful response of Bamberg's bishop to the sisters' request for help. Moreover, the city fathers tried to rid themselves of the Swedish pressure by sending the enemy to the supposed bread baskets of the religious orders—and especially to the two female convents, Heiliggrab and St. Clara.[33] A couple days later, two Dominican friars came to Heiliggrab and told the sisters that their grain would be confiscated, but, luckily for the nuns, their neighbor, Junker (Knight) Hans Georg von Rothenhan, and another colonel happened to come by and reassured the sisters that not a single corn would be taken from them since they knew how poor the sisters were.[34] Instead, Colonel Rosta sent them six Reichstaler, thanked them for the homemade goods, with which the sisters had presented him and his wife upon their last visit, and showed again concern whether the nuns "had any complaint on account of our soldiers."[35]

In April 1634, the councilor once again set Bernhard von Saxe-Weimar's steward (*Hofmeister*) upon the nuns. This time they were to give a cow. When the women responded that they would write the duke soon to explain their poverty, but would at least send some of their homemade goods, the steward was so embarrassed that he apologized, explaining that he had come to them at the suggestion of the city council.[36] Junius' remarks, then, suggest that the Dominican nuns were in greater danger from their own city fathers, who may have been motivated by a desire for control over the convent, than from the Swedes who showed great concern and consideration for the sisters.

The consistently high regard and protection of the Swedes demonstrates that the sisters of Heiliggrab were skilled tacticians, who knew how to turn a dangerous and delicate situation to their advantage. Presumably, in an attempt to justify their breaking of enclosure, Junius explained that they at first resisted the visits to their cloister. According to her, it was the Swedes who "forced" their way into the cloister, and the nuns had to give in to them. Very quickly, however, any mention of coercion fell away. She recorded the comment of a colonel, who said that the sisters were right to allow the officers into their cloister since they would thus see for themselves how poor the sisters were and that they lived very simply.[37] In other words, giving the Swedes access to their convent and insight into their lifestyle was part of ensuring their own protection from plundering and extractions.

The story of the Dominican nuns of Heiliggrab is an intriguing one. Apparently, their cloister remained a home not only for the sisters living there, but also a refuge of sorts for the besiegers. Officers frequently trekked to the cloister to be with the sisters, to eat with them (they often sent provisions to the convent in the morning), to hear them sing, and to watch them go through their religious routine of vesper and compline. These men, who often brought their wives, may have regarded the convent not only as a welcome space to which they could bring their female companions, but also as a safe haven away from the turmoil of war, a civilized place where one could recover briefly from its brutishness and messiness. By protecting the sisters, the generals and colonels may have responded as much to the nuns' appeal to the besiegers' humanity as to their own need to preserve some place of sanity, peace, and gentleness in the midst of mayhem and destruction. Gender played a significant role in these patterns of behavior. The Dominican nuns' relationship with the Swedes was a gendered relationship, just as that of the sisters to Bamberg's councilmen and the Dominican friars, who attempted to control them. Junius and her fellow nuns exploited the ambiguity about defenseless, religious women by appealing to the besiegers' manliness and to their urge to protect this fragile female community.

In the first edition of her masterful *Women and Gender in Early Modern Europe* (1993), Merry Wiesner highlighted how convents, instead of restricting women, could afford them opportunities for action and expression.[38] The women discussed above are eloquent examples of this fact.[39] Merry Wiesner also underscored the need to look beyond the narrow roles and places assigned to women and to investigate how they forged their lives within and despite the realities of their times. Prescriptive and actual roles often diverged considerably. Our exploration of convent women's responses to the challenges of the Thirty Years' War amplifies these insights. Faced with violent threats and grave dangers, these women exhibited amazing initiative. Depending on their situation, nuns fled, stayed home, separated, endured exile, shouldered the economy at home under back breaking and dangerous circumstances, and used whatever assets they had to survive.

Consequently, the actions they took were quite diverse because they were largely shaped by local conditions and the convents' circumstances.

These diverse responses, however, were tied together by an important commonality: the women realistically and smartly assessed their situations and exploited every opportunity to advance their own agenda, which revolved around keeping their community safe. At crucial junctures, the women's actions defied the strictures placed upon them by their male superiors. Nowhere is this more evident than in the matter of enclosure. The war times gave them not only the license, but made it also necessary to employ enclosure for their own purposes and benefits, rather than blindly following the rules laid before them.

Notes

1 The Augustinian convent Mariastein lay about 40 miles south of Nuremberg outside Eichstätt's city walls. Situated on the Altmühl River in close proximity to the Augustinian canons of Rebdorf who functioned as the nuns' guardians, the convent was in good financial and disciplinary shape prior to the war. Both noble and bourgeois women belonged to the religious community. See Ida Wallner, *Clara Staiger. Ein Lebens- und Kulturbild aus dem 30 jährigen Krieg*, Kleine Allgemeine Schriften zur Philosophie, Theologie und Geschichte, Geschichtliche Reihe, 10 (Bamberg: C. C. Buchners Verlag, 1957), 9–10. The diary-style *Verzaichnus* of the prioress Clara Staiger (1588–1656) offers a minute record of the convent's day-to-day happenings with occasional comments and gives the reader insight into her personal experiences and reactions to the war, as well as the larger context of her convent and the monastic world in war times. *Klara Staigers Tagebuch. Aufzeichnungen während des Dreißigjährigen Krieges im Kloster Mariastein bei Eichstätt*, ed. Ortrun Fina (Regensburg: Friedrich Pustet, 1981) 326. Her entries start in earnest in 1632 with the attack of the Swedes. Her notes are interrupted from 1645 until August 1646, when she was gravely ill and could not continue her writing.

2 Junius (ca. 1605–1675) left behind a *Kurze verzeignuß* ("Short Account"), which provides fascinating insight into the experiences of the nuns during the years 1631 to 1634. Friedrich K. Hümmer, ed., "Bamberg im Schweden-Kriege. Nach einem Manuscripte (Mittheilungen über die Jahre 1622–1634)," in *Bericht über Bestand und Wirken des historischen Vereins zu Bamberg* 52 (1890): 1–168 (part 1); and 53 (1891): 169–224 (part 2). We do not know when she was born. She probably became stewardess (*Schaffnerin*) around 1630 and eventually prioress of the cloister, since she is listed as prioress when she died. See Uta Nolting, *Sprachgebrauch süddeutscher Klosterfrauen des 17. Jahrhunders*, Studien und Texte zum Mittelalter und zur frühen Neuzeit, 16 (Münster: Waxmann, 2010), 76–77. The daughter of Johannes Junius, burgomaster and councilor of Bamberg, she began her writing in 1631, even though her recordings go back to 1622, the year of her entrance into the cloister, and include brief notes on the city's preoccupation with witchcraft, which claimed the lives of both her parents in 1628. Her account follows the days and months of the years, but, unlike Clara Staiger, she rarely talks about the finances or the daily routines of the cloister. Rather, Junius captivates the reader with stories of the sisters' plight and how they managed to overcome the dangers of war, and as such her testimony is more consciously constructed than Staiger's.

3 Diözesanarchiv Augsburg, Handschrift (hereafter, HS) 97. *St. Katharina im Schwedenkriege: Kurtze Beschreibung Wie eß mit, vnd Jn vnnserm loblichen Closster, vnd Conuent Jn dem Schwedischen Krieg gestanden, und ergangen Jst.* This narrative was not written by the prioress Maria Magdalena Kurz, but by one of the nuns, most likely one in an administrative position.

4 Besides three reports/chronicles of the abbess and the convent recorder, we also have some of the correspondence between the exiled sisters and those who stayed or went home—a most rare and fortunate circumstance. Irmgard E. Zwingler's detailed study of the Angerkloster offers an extensive section of transcribed documents: *Das Klarissenkloster bei St. Jakob am Anger zu München. Das Angerkloster unter der Reform des Franziskanerordens im Zeitalter des Dreißigjährigen Krieges* (Munich: Verein für Diözesangeschichte von München und Freising, 2009). For the larger original correspondences, see Hauptstaatsarchiv München, Klosterliteralien (hereafter, KL) 393/1831. See also Hauptstaatsarchiv München, Dreißigjähriger Krieg, Akten 315 (Die Flucht der Klosterfrauen am Anger nach Tirol); KL 16, München Angerkloster.
5 Joan Scott, "The Evidence of Experience," *Critical Inquiry* 17 (1991): 773–797; Paul Münch, *"Erfahrung" als Kategorie der Frühneuzeitgeschichte* (Munich: R. Oldenbourg Verlag, 2001). Kaspar von Greyerz summarizes the debate on experience: while in the 1990s scholars with different agendas and approaches have warned against the dangers of essentialism and constructivism, most studies are now situated somewhere in the "middle ground between pure constructivism and the evidence of experience offered by their sources." Greyerz, "Ego-Documents: The Last Word?" *German History* 28 (2010): 273–282, here 276.
6 See the special issue of *German History* 28 (2010) that is dedicated to ego-documents.
7 Kaspar von Greyerz, "Ego-Documents: The Last Word?" *German History* 28 (2010): 273–282, here 276. Von Greyerz thus finds the term 'Ego-documents' inadequate in capturing the broader implications of such accounts. For this and a discussion of the history of the term 'Ego-document', see von Greyerz, "Ego-Documents." See also Mary Fulbrook and Ulinka Rublack's comment: "(o)ne does not have to follow down a post-modernist route to realize the significance of the fact that no account of the self can be produced which is not constructed in terms of social discourses: that the very concepts people use to describe themselves, the ways in which they choose to structure and to account for their past lives, the values, norms, and common-sense explanations to which they appeal in providing meaning to their narratives, are intrinsically products of the times through which they have lived." "In Relation: The 'Social Self' and Ego-Documents," *German History* 28 (2010): 263–272, here 267. Gabriele Jancke and Claudia Ulbrich underline furthermore that early modern autobiographical writing shows the authors in their various relationships, both horizontal and vertical. Idem, eds., *Vom Individuum zur Person. Neue Konzepte im Spannungsfeld von Autobiographietheorie und Selbstzeugnisforschung.* Querelles: Jahrbuch für Frauen- und Geschlechterforschung 2005 (Göttingen: Wallstein Verlag, 2005), 22.
8 *Klara Staigers Tagebuch*, 66, 62.
9 Zwingler, *Klarissenkloster*, 1063 (Nr. 16: Bericht der Äbtissin Catharina Bernardina Graff über die Flucht des Konventes, 1632).
10 Hümmer, *Bamberg im Schweden-Kriege,* 53 (1891), 224.
11 Hümmer, *Bamberg im Schweden-Kriege,* 52 (1890), 17.
12 Hümmer, *Bamberg im Schweden-Kriege,* 52 (1890), 20.
13 Bernd Roeck calls it a "Versorgungsinstitut für den Adel" ("a premium care facility for the nobility") in *Eine Stadt in Krieg und Frieden. Studien zur Geschichte der Reichsstadt Augsburg zwischen Kalenderstreit und Parität* (Göttingen: Vandenhoeck & Ruprecht, 1989), 1:91. The subsequent discussion will show that such labels are not helpful in understanding the women and their concerns in these institutions.
14 Diözesanarchiv Augsburg, HS 97, fol. 3^{r-v}.
15 Diözesanarchiv Augsburg, HS 97, fol. 10^r.
16 Diözesanarchiv Augsburg, HS 97, fol. 10^r.
17 Diözesanarchiv Augsburg, HS 97, fol. 5^r.
18 Among the burgeoning literature on exile and migration, see especially Matthias Asche et al., eds., *Krieg, Militär und Migration in der Frühen Neuzeit*, Herrschaft und Soziale Systeme in der Fühen Neuzeit 9 (Berlin: LIT Verlag, 2008); Joachim Bahlcke, ed.,

Glaubensflüchtlinge. Ursachen, Formen und Auswirkungen frühneuzeitlicher Konfessionsmigration in Europa, Religions- und Kulturgeschichte in Ostmittel- und Südosteuropa 4 (Berlin: Lit Verlag, 2008); Manfred Briegel and Wolfgang Frühwald, eds., *Die Erfahrung der Fremde. Kolloquium des Schwerpunktprogramms "Exilforschung" der Deutschen Forschungsgemeinschaft* (Weinheim: VCH Verlagsgesellschaft, 1988); Johannes F. Evelein, ed., *Exiles Traveling. Exploring Displacement, Crossing Boundaries in German Exile Arts and Writings, 1933–1945*, Amsterdamer Beiträge zur Neueren Germanistik 68 (Amsterdam: Rodopi, 2009); Helmut Koopmann, "Exil als geistige Lebensform," in *Exil: Transhistorische und transnationale Perspektiven* (Paderborn: Mentis Verlag, 2001), 1–19; Marita Krauss, "Heimat—Begriff und Erfahrung," in Herrmann Haarmann, ed., *Heimat, liebe Heimat. Exil und Innere Emigration (1933–1945)* (Berlin: Bostelmann & Siebenhaar, 2004), 11–27.

19 The expression has its roots in the middle high German word "ellende" (old high German: alilanti/elilenti) and connotes an alien country, Fremde, Verbannung, exile, as well as the notion of suffering and desolation. Early modern narratives continue the conceptual association between exile, misery, and hardship. Otto Eberhardt, "Exil im Mittelalter: Einige Streiflichter," in *Weltanschauliche Orientierungsversuche im Exil*, ed. Reinhard Andress, Amsterdamer Beiträge zur neueren Germanistik 76 (Amsterdam: Rodopi, 2010), 13–36, here 15. And Grimm, *Dt. Woerterbuch*.

20 *Klara Staigers Tagebuch*, 142. Catholic Ingolstadt was never taken by the Swedes.

21 Zwingler, *Klarissenkloster*, 983 (letter 2/3: from Sister Anastasia on 3 May 1632 to Sister Anna Catharina in Hall). Among the Poor Clares of Munich's Angerkloster, twelve stayed behind to keep the convent going, while forty-eight fled to the Tyrol.

22 Zwingler, *Klarissenkloster*, 988.

23 Zwingler, *Klarissenkloster*, 989 (letter 2/12) and 983, n. 58.

24 Stefan Zweig, "Die Welt von Gestern. Erinnerungen eines Europäers," in *Gesammelte Werke* 6 (1942), 468.

25 On the spacial turn, see Doris Bachmann-Medick, *Cultural Turns. New Orientations in the Study of Culture*, trans. Adam Blauhut (Berlin: De Gruyter, 2016); Jaimey Fisher and Barbara Mennel, "Introduction," in *Spacial Turns: Space, Place, and Mobility in German Literary and Visual Culture*, Amsterdamer Beiträge zur Neueren Germanistik 75 (Amsterdam: Rodopi, 2010), 9–23; Karl Schlögel, *Im Raum lesen wir die Zeit: über Zivilisationsgeschichte und Geopolitik* (Frankfurt am Main: Fischer Taschenbuchverlag, 2006).

26 A very important point here is also the hierarchy of space. Nuns often inhabited spaces that had just been vacated by monks. This reshuffling was plainly done in accordance with gender, position, and connections. Safety apparently could only be had in accordance with one's station and gender.

27 See Ulrike Strasser's pertinent discussion of the complex dimensions of enclosure in her *State of Virginity: Gender, Religion, and Politics in an Early Modern Catholic State* (Ann Arbor: University of Michigan Press, 2004). See also Francesca Medioli, "The Dimensions of the Cloister: Enclosure, Constraint, and Protection in Seventeenth-Century Italy," in *Time, Space, and Women's Lives in Early Modern Europe*, ed. Anne J. Schutte et al., Sixteenth Century Essays & Studies 57 (Kirksville, MO: Truman State University Press, 2005), 165–180.

28 Diözesanarchiv Augsburg, HS 97, fol. 61^v. Allowing someone in from a different order would have broken their enclosure.

29 Diözesanarchiv Augsburg, HS 97, fol. 61^v, 64^r

30 A Jesuit chronicle of the events in Bamberg mentions that the Dominican convent did flee briefly in 1643, but this later phase is not covered in Junius' account. The Jesuit Chronicle "Historia Collegii S. J. Bambergensis, Litterae Annue," translated and published in excerpts by Heinrich Weber, "Bamberg im dreiβigjährigen Krieg. Nach einer gleichzeitigen Chronik bearbeitet," in *Bericht des Historischen Vereins Bamberg* 48 (1886): 1–132, here 102.

31 Lohausen was not only a military man but also a humanist, who was a member of the *Fruchtbringende Gesellschaft*. On Lohausen, see Klaus Conermann, *Die Mitglieder der*

Fruchtbringenden Gesellschaft 1617–1650 (Weinheim: VCH Edition Leipzig, 1985), 3:173–175; Thomas Elsmann, "Humanismus, Schule, Buchdruck und Antikenrezeption. Anmerkungen zur Bremer Entwicklung bis 1648," in *Stadt und Literatur im deutschen Sprachraum der Frühen Neuzeit*, ed. Klaus Garber (Tübingen: Max Niemeyer Verlag, 1998), 1:203–238, here 229–230.

32 Hümmer, *Bamberg im Schweden-Kriege*, 52 (1890), 129 (24 March 1633).
33 Hümmer, *Bamberg im Schweden-Kriege*, 52 (1890), 112.
34 Hümmer, *Bamberg im Schweden-Kriege*, 52 (1890), 112.
35 Hümmer, *Bamberg im Schweden-Kriege*, 52 (1890), 113. A further example of the antagonistic behavior of Bamberg's councilors toward the sisters occurred in March 1634. First, Burgomaster Keim demanded that they send an ox to the colonel in Geyerswehr, but the nuns only responded that the colonel surely would not want them to do such a thing, since he himself had promised them an animal. Junius then commented disapprovingly on the councilmen's damaging conduct toward them and the citizenry: "This was just the intention of the pretty councilors that, if they could have gotten the Swedes to take much from us, they would have been overjoyed, as they also treated the poor citizens in this way." Rather than protecting its citizens, Junius charged, the councilors set the Swedes upon them and insinuated that the citizenry could pay all right. "Such a comfort was the government to its poor citizens. And the Swedes told us themselves that the councilors did the same to us and pointed [the Swedes] to us, saying we [the sisters] are rich, they could find with us what they wanted." Ibid., 174–175.
36 Hümmer, *Bamberg im Schweden-Kriege*, 53 (1891), 182.
37 Hümmer, *Bamberg im Schweden-Kriege*, 52 (1890), 118–119.
38 See also her *Convents Confront the Reformation: Catholic and Protestant Nuns in Germany*, ed. Merry Wiesner-Hanks, trans. Joan Skocier and Merry Wiesnery-Hanks (Milwaukee: Marquette University Press, 1996).
39 See also Amy Leonard, *Nails in the Wall. Catholic Nuns in Reformation Germany*, Women in Culture and Society (Chicago: The University of Chicago Press, 2005), for a poignant study of how religious women used their space and calling to their utmost religious, political, and economic advantage.

9

CONFLICTS BETWEEN MALE REFORMERS AND FEMALE MONASTICS

Elizabeth A. Lehfeldt

Early modern convents were largely self-contained households. Work and liturgy were structured in such a way as to make the nuns mostly self-sufficient. They did, however, have to rely on male personnel for certain services and were accustomed to receiving them within the cloister. Priests came regularly to provide sacramental services. Physicians cared for the sick. But these men were not strangers and they had a recognized and necessary role to play. Tensions rarely arose over the place of these men in the daily lives of convents.

But the nuns did not receive all visitors this neutrally. Ecclesiastical visitors sent to investigate convents and implement reform were often a profound source of tension and outright conflict. In 1494, for example, male ecclesiastical visitors arrived at the convent of Santa Clara of Barcelona. They told the nuns in no uncertain terms that they expected a series of changes. They mandated various alterations, such as covering, blocking, or putting grilles on windows in an attempt to limit the visual access the convent had to the outside world. They instructed the nuns to limit the access that secular women had to the cloister. The nuns refused to accept the visitors' instructions and claimed that they were acting in accordance with the "use, practice, and custom" of the convent.[1] Tensions escalated and ultimately the visitors removed the abbess from office and forced the community to elect a new leader.

Tensions could also arise over the source of male ecclesiastical authority more generally. In 1490, the nuns of Kington Priory were exposed for trying to free themselves from the jurisdiction of their bishop, the Bishop of Salisbury. The source of their dissatisfaction was not clear, but they were willing to go to great lengths to be outside of his authority. With the aid of a Franciscan friar, they forged a papal bull to transfer them to the oversight of the Abbot of Glastonbury. The ruse was quickly exposed, and the abbess was removed from office.[2]

These episodes illustrate the hostility that nuns could direct at the male ecclesiastical authorities who had the power to supervise and reform them, as well the price that they could pay if they resisted. Scholars of female monasticism have extensively documented these encounters between nuns and male authorities, but these studies are sometimes plagued by a particular narrative assumption. Modern accounts of these confrontations implicitly or explicitly characterize the nuns as recalcitrant and unwilling to give up bad behaviors or old practices. Thus, the story that emerges is one of misguided nuns being corrected by male supervisors. In some instances, this was undoubtedly true; nuns resisted the imposition of stricter standards of observing the common life at meals or chafed against reprimands about their excessive and elaborate styles of dress.[3] And that many of these confrontations resulted in the removal of the abbess or prioress from office privileges an interpretation that faults the nuns for bad behavior.

Yet scholars have also acknowledged in their analyses of these encounters some of the very real issues at stake that often made the nuns reluctant to accept change or reform. The imposition of enclosure, for example, might threaten financial stability since the nuns could no longer leave the cloister to seek alms. Reform could more generally be an affront to the autonomy of these communities that were accustomed to conducting their own affairs with minimal interference. Joining considerations of the validity of the nuns' resistance to male oversight with the portrayal of stubborn or even misbehaving nuns allows a more complete picture of these confrontations to emerge. Critical to an analysis of the reactions of the nuns, however, is a piece of this puzzle that has not typically been addressed: the men sent to impose these reforms. Without closer attention to their background, the role they played in the introduction and enforcement of reform, and their behavior, we lack a full understanding of these tense confrontations.

This essay will employ a comparative methodology to examine the role played by male agents in the overall reception of female monastic reform. In this instance, a comparison centered on late-fifteenth and early-sixteenth century England and Spain reveals important differences between the visitation campaigns and the male personnel entrusted with these visits in each country. Because most studies of female monasticism are bound by rigid geographies, they create a false sense of what is normative. An examination of the reform of convents in Spain, for example, could create the impression that only clerics did the work of visitation. A comparison to England, however, reveals that laypeople could participate and that this undoubtedly shaped the course of events. Differences such as these in the status and identity of male visitors had a significant impact on the reception, pace, and relative success of their visits to the cloister. This comparative approach, then, permits a more complete portrait of these male "outsiders" and thus, in turn, enhances our understanding of how and why convents resisted, modified, and even accepted monastic reform.

Convents appeared on the radar of religious reform for very different reasons in these two countries. In Spain, the royal couple, Isabel of Castile and Ferdinand of Aragon, included the reform of convents, and monasticism more generally, under the umbrella of a larger religious reform campaign that also included secular clergy. Yet their dissatisfaction with monasticism was clear; in a 1478 letter to the papacy, they wrote "in our realm there are monasteries, and houses of religion, of men and women, that are very dissolute and disordered in their life, the administration of their houses, and spiritual and temporal matters."[4] They probably intended this letter to lay the groundwork for the campaign. In 1493, they sought papal permission to receive reforming oversight of all monasteries and convents in their kingdoms. This letter to the papacy provides telling details of how they viewed the question of reform. To begin with, they asked for general permission to reform, but pleaded that if that was not possible that they at least be granted "una bulla para reformacion y encerramiento de los monesterios de monjas desta ciudat [Barcelona], en los quales ay tanta deshonestidad y profanacion" (a bull for the reformation and enclosure of the monasteries of nuns of this city, in which there is so much dishonesty and desecration).[5] Though it is unclear what had alerted the monarchs to the particular problems with convents in Barcelona, it is clear that they were especially interested in the reform of convents and that they saw enclosure as a means to remedy abuses.

Ultimately, the papacy provided two bulls, and both authorized the monarchs to appoint visitors who would be entrusted with reform. Significantly, one of the two addressed itself specifically to the reform of convents and gave the royally-appointed visitors the "authority to visit, correct abuses, and introduce into convents a set of rules by which to govern their everyday life."[6] The visitors' powers were not nearly as broad in the case of monasteries, and the language of the papal license did not include the power to dictate in matters of monastic standards. From the start, then, the campaign was gendered in such a way as to involve greater oversight of convents than monasteries. In many ways, then, the monarchs' concerns about the nuns of Barcelona would come to frame the campaign and would drive, as we will see, the insistence upon the decidedly gendered standard of claustration. Although they had already experimented with monastic reform in Galicia in northwest Spain, they would ultimately devote their initial, and in many ways, most forceful efforts in Ferdinand's homeland in Catalonia and Aragon, using this bull and the letter that prompted it as their blueprint. The prominence of the Catalonian campaign, in addition to the well-documented account of its progress, make it the focus of the Spanish side of this study.

The visitors arrived at these houses empowered with a clear set of royal instructions, which were quite specific and addressed ten areas. They were to investigate the observance of the common life, the observance of silence, the norms of visitation in the convent parlor, egress from the convent, the disposition of windows and doors, the service of sacristans, the care of sacred objects, disciplinary practices, and the accounts.[7] The final prescription was that the nuns were to observe faithfully all of the visitors' admonitions. In addition, the monarchs were very clear about the penalties the nuns would receive if these measures were resisted; they included fines and being banished from the convent for a period of time, depending upon the severity of the infraction. Anticipating the possible resistance of the nuns' local supporters, the monarchs even went so far as to specify that no one from outside the convent be allowed to enter during the period of the visit.[8]

The circumstances surrounding monastic reform in England were almost entirely different. To begin with, there is no evidence of a royal campaign. Before the mid-1530s, monastic reform lay entirely in the hands of local ecclesiastics, primarily bishops. In 1510 and 1511, for example, Archbishop William Warham visited monasteries and convents in Kent. He followed a fairly standard script for such visits, beginning with an assessment of the institution's property and an accounting of the number of residents. He then turned to individual interviews with the monks and nuns who were encouraged to comment upon daily affairs and the observance of monastic standards. Based on what was revealed in these interviews, he issued a series of injunctions meant to remedy any infractions or problems.[9]

When male ecclesiastics like Warham visited convents in the early sixteenth century, they encountered various problems. Between 1525 and 1532, Bishop Longland of Lincoln oversaw various visitations of monastic houses. At the convent of Elstow, he contended with violations of the observance of the common life, such as the abbess and other nuns enjoying a private table at meals where they entertained a privileged few.[10] The nuns were also cited for their too-colorful and fashionable styles of dress.[11] In addition, visitors enacted measures to block up various doors and windows. Other investigations of convents in the diocese in 1530 revealed minor problems with the style of dress, excessive expenditures, and concerns about the egress of nuns and the ingress of male secular visitors.[12] In a similar fashion, the bishop of York, Edward Lee, visited the convent of Nunburnholme in 1534. Here there were serious problems with secular visitors entering and even sleeping within the convent precinct, violations of the common life, and the possible transgression of active enclosure.[13] He found similar problems with claustration at the convents of Esholt and Sinningthwaite.[14]

In all of these campaigns, because the visits were performed as part of the archbishops' or bishops' standard duties, they visited both male and female houses and employed the standard methodology outlined in the case of Warham's visits in Kent noted above. It does not seem that there was much differentiation between monasteries and convents, and the inhabitants of both were disciplined according to the infractions revealed by the visit.

Yet in the 1530s, the landscape of monastic visitation in England shifted, largely due to broader shifts in national politics. The 1534 Act of Supremacy effectively severed ties with the papacy and declared Henry VIII "the only Supreme Head on Earth of the Church of England." Henry followed this declaration with a decision to tax the church properties and offices at a rate of ten percent. But before these sums could be collected, an assessment of the value of these properties would be necessary. Consequently, the first half of 1535 was devoted to visits to hospitals, monasteries, convents, and other religious institutions that resulted in the *Valor Ecclesiasticus*, a thorough, though sometimes flawed, accounting of the church's wealth. Henry's actions during this period are virtually inseparable from the initiatives and counsel of his chief advisor, Thomas Cromwell. In January of 1535, in fact, Henry named him Vicegerent for Spirituals. This new position afforded Cromwell the authority to oversee all ecclesiastical matters and function, essentially, as the king's vicar. This was, then, a broad mandate. One of Cromwell's first responsibilities was to secure the loyalty of all religious in the realm to Henry's newly-constituted authority by having them give their assent to the Act of Supremacy, which had established Henry's authority over the English church. He achieved this, in part, through a far-reaching visitation campaign that sent visitors he appointed to many of the monasteries and convents in the realm. This campaign appears to have been delayed by visits that resulted in the *Valor*, and thus did not begin in earnest until the second half of 1535. As we will see, the visitors were empowered to make a range of inquiries, based on an established questionnaire, about the physical state of the house, the number of inhabitants, and any additional concerns, including matters that touched on questions of reform.

Because these are the events and visitations that preceded the eventual suppression and dissolution of English religious houses, the scholarly interpretation of them is fraught. Most scholars have assumed, mostly with the benefit of hindsight, that reform was not a sincere objective of these visitations. Recent scholarship, however, has begun to challenge the notion that suppression was inevitable and that the reformers were simply sent out to discredit these institutions and their inhabitants.[15] The visitors were, in fact, supposed to document any evidence of wrongdoing or misbehavior. But in this, their work was identical to the formula for episcopal visitations: they had a scripted list of questions, they recorded what they discovered in the course of interviews, and they issued injunctions to remedy any problems or immorality. But here, too, as in the Spanish case, an examination of the male agents of reform also helps to create a more complete picture of the campaign. Such an analysis, in fact, provides further evidence of the sincerity of reform.

As in Spain, the visitors that would eventually undertake these visitations had a scripted set of questions to guide their inquiries. This list was circulating as early as 1534 and was remarkably comprehensive and included 86 items.[16] They included fairly obvious questions about the number of inhabitants, whether monastic ideals like chastity, silence, and obedience were observed, what habits were worn, the rule that was professed, any debts the house had, and the handling of novices. The last 11 were directed specifically at convents and, not surprisingly, addressed questions like whether nuns left the convent precinct with the permission of their superiors and whether the nuns held conversations with outsiders at grates or doors to the convent. Here, then, we have an instance of gendered reform that parallels the Spanish example. English convents were singled out for a type of scrutiny that did not apply to monasteries. By January of 1535, these questions had been joined by a set of general injunctions. These flowed from the questions of 1534 and instructed professed religious in matters of enclosure and the common life. Overall, the questions and injunctions point to a program of reform that was intended to be comprehensive: addressing everything from general monastic ideals to the management of monastic estates and finances.

In each country, then, although the impetus differed, a visitation campaign began to coalesce around a specified set of questions or instructions. The next step was to identify visitors. Who was chosen? How and why were they empowered to visit the convents in the first place? Turning to the men entrusted to implement these reforms, both in Spain and England, we find some significant differences. In Spain, Isabel and Ferdinand appointed the visitors by region, typically drawing upon local clerics, presumably because of their familiarity with the region and its ecclesiastical politics. In the case of Catalonia, however, the monarchs did not get their first choices. Of the five they originally selected, four declined to serve, claiming they already had demanding responsibilities. One remained: Juan Daza, the presiding canon at the cathedral of Jaén. The monarchs then appointed Miguel Fenals, an observant Franciscan from Mallorca. These two would visit the monasteries and convents of Catalonia.[17] Neither, then, was from the region. Daza, for his part, was a cleric, but not a monastic. Fenals was a friar, but curiously, he and Daza would be tasked with visiting not just Franciscan convents but also convents belonging to the Benedictine, Cistercian, Jeronimite, and other religious orders. In many ways, then, these men were not just strangers when they appeared at these institutions, they were also outsiders. Notably, however, they worked together, visiting each convent as a pair.

In the case of England, the selection process was quite different. Although the precise sequence of events has been debated,[18] Henry's assertion of supremacy over the church in England technically meant that his authority superseded, if not supplanted, episcopal visitations of religious houses. Once Cromwell was appointed Vice Regent in Spirituals, he became Henry's deputy in such matters. These developments occurred in 1534 with the result that by the end of the year, a visitation of the religious houses seemed likely, but the agents of this task had not yet been identified. Progress towards a visitation was interrupted by the inventory of church wealth that was not completed until May of 1535. But at that time, the visitations returned to the agenda.

Unlike the Spanish example of royal appointments, it appears that the eventual visitors of the English convents presented themselves to Cromwell as candidates, rather than being approached by him. In early June of 1535, perhaps sensing that the visitations were finally about to begin, Dr. Richard Layton wrote to Cromwell, suggesting that he and Thomas Legh would be ideal commissioners to send to the north country because of their familiarity with the region (Layton was from Cumberland and had served in the cathedral at York and Legh was also from Cumberland). Thus, he argued "no knaverie can be hyde from us in that contre."[19] Layton was no stranger to ecclesiastical reform. He had earlier worked in the service of Cardinal Wolsey at the same time as Cromwell. Cromwell had also assigned him to work on reforms at Syon in December 1533.[20] Legh was a minor diplomat who had been recommended to Cromwell for service by his cousin. Both Layton and Legh held the degree of Doctor of Civil Law, but only Layton had taken holy orders. Legh, then, was not a cleric. Thus, there is a striking difference from the Spanish case where both were clerics.

Layton and Legh may have volunteered themselves because of their past activity. Both had experience with introducing reform. In July of 1535, Layton had visited Oxford University where he had introduced disciplinary reforms and taken note of non-resident clergy. Legh, for his part, had previously conducted an inquiry at Rievaulx Abbey, which had resulted in the resignation of the abbot.[21] So neither man was a stranger to pursuing reform. In addition, Layton's own words suggested that he understood the objective of the campaign to be reform. In another part of the above-cited letter he referred Cromwell to a "booke of articles that I made for your visitacion" seven months previous (so around November of 1534). He argued that these would be instructive in allowing the visitors to detect abuses.[22] Further evidence of Layton's desire to truly reform these houses comes from another part of the letter where he cited the oft-mentioned dilemma of religious houses only being subject to their own orders. He complained that these "crafty meanys to be ther owne visiters" allowed them to avoid true reform.

Layton and Legh appear to have been persuasive; they became Cromwell's emissaries of reform. They were joined in these endeavors by John ap Rice and John Tregonwell—neither of them clerics—who served in mostly secondary roles as assistants at individual visitations. Ultimately, they would all traverse an ambitious itinerary that carried them not just to the north country but also to the south towards the diocese of Winchester and points in between. And significantly, they never visited a religious house together.[23] Overall, then, like the Spanish case, the English visitors were both strangers and outsiders. With the exception of Layton, they were not even ecclesiastics.

So how did things unfold when these outsiders appeared at the door of these convents? The surviving records provide a vivid insight into the reception of these men and their reforms. Interestingly, in both cases, the resulting correspondence suggests that the reform began to fray almost as soon as it was implemented. In Catalonia, the visitors encountered almost immediate resistance at some of the region's more powerful convents. At the convent of Las Puellas, the nuns immediately insisted that the visitors produce their credentials and refused to acknowledge the men until they did so.[24] At Valldoncella, the abbess asserted that the nuns conducted themselves according to high standards and that they did not need to heed the reforms proposed by the visitors.[25] Though each convent would ultimately voice concerns about particular parts of the reform program the visitors introduced at their specific institution, overall the convents questioned whether or not the visitors had authority over them.

Questions of authority were rooted in questions of jurisdiction. Fenals and Daza asserted male ecclesiastical authority over the nuns they visited, but the nuns pushed back against this, not in gendered terms but over other questions. The above-cited request by the nuns of Las Puellas that the visitors produce their credentials may have been an oblique reference to the convent's status as a Benedictine convent being asked to submit to the authority of someone outside their religious order (Fenals was a Franciscan). Similarly, the nuns of Valldoncella protested that Daza and Fenals were not their customary ecclesiastical visitors.[26] Isabel and Ferdinand were aware of this possible conflict of jurisdiction. They clearly intended this campaign to transcend the distinctions of religious orders. The convents, however, did not agree.

As a consequence of this early resistance, the monarchs intervened directly in other ways to bolster the campaign. Recognizing that imposing reform in the convents would cross multiple ecclesiastical jurisdictions, Ferdinand and Isabel requested that any disputes resulting from the visitation be heard by the papal court and no other.[27] This measure, they hoped, would streamline the process. In return, they promised that the visitors would conduct themselves appropriately and would not incur expenses for the monasteries and convents—something, that we will see, was a problem in England. Anticipating that local authorities and secular supporters might put up resistance, the monarchs also ran interference on this front. From 1493 onward, they sent numerous directives to the Governor of Catalonia, instructing him to support the visitors in any way possible and not to assist the nuns if they resisted directly or indirectly.[28] They did the same with the councilors of the city of Barcelona—a prestigious group of individuals who had the power to influence the course of reform. Royal correspondence also reveals that the monarchs frequently sought to shore up the enthusiasm of the visitors. In a letter to Juan Daza, written late in 1493, the monarchs assured him of their support and the value of his work.[29]

The path to reform in England was even bumpier. Here the problems were centered on both the reforms being introduced and the individuals responsible for introducing them. To begin with, a letter from Layton to Cromwell, dated July 28, 1535—so only about a month into the visitations—indicated his concerns about how to impose the injunctions. Layton asked Cromwell to temper the king's insistence that the injunctions be rigidly applied and to allow for some flexibility.[30] Though he did not provide details, Layton appeared to be suggesting that reform needed to be adapted to local circumstance. There were clearly discrepancies among the reformers when it came to imposing reform. Layton's counterpart, Thomas Legh, was much more rigid and unrelenting in his enforcement.

Unlike Layton, who had sought the tempering of the injunctions, Legh imposed them categorically, often with problematic consequences. On 20 August 1535, Legh wrote to Cromwell and said that he was enforcing enclosure at the houses he was visiting but that Layton was not.[31] He informed Cromwell that he was restraining "the heads and brethren of all the places to which he has been from leaving the precincts," to which many of them objected. Legh insisted that there needed to be "uniformity of action."[32] A letter dated the same day from ap Rice confirmed this discrepancy. According to ap Rice, Legh had restrained the heads of all houses, male and female, from leaving the cloister and allowed no women to visit male religious houses and vice versa. Ap Rice opined that in doing this Legh was being "over strict" and asked Cromwell to intervene.[33] The same problem arose again at the monastery of Bruton. In a letter to Cromwell, Legh indicated Layton had visited first and had not enforced enclosure on the abbot. Legh, when he arrived, sought to do so, as he believed this was part of his commission. This discrepancy troubled him since "Those, therefore, that I have visited think that I am too rigorous, and bind them harder than others do."[34] Again, he asked Cromwell to be sure that he and Layton were enforcing the same injunctions.

The heart of the disagreement between Layton and Legh over enclosure was an interesting one. It appears that both were insisting that ordinary monks and nuns observe enclosure, but Layton made exceptions for the heads of houses, leaving it to the individual discretion of abbots and abbesses, whether they observed it. Legh, however, believed that what was applied to the rank and file of monasteries and convents should hold for the heads as well.[35]

But such injunctions uniformly imposed could create problems, as the response of the abbess of Wilton reveals. Writing to Cromwell in September of 1535, she objected to Legh's insistence on rigid enclosure. As she explained, "the house is in great debt, and is not likely to improve without good husbandry, which cannot be exercised so well by any other as by myself, I beg you will allow me, in company with two or three of the said and discreet sisters of the house, to supervise such things abroad as shall be for its profit."[36] In addition, to the disagreement of the heads of houses, there could be other significant consequences to Legh's rigidity. Here, too, ap Rice expressed concerns. He wrote to Cromwell in September of 1535 because Legh had summarily dismissed 17 nuns at the convent of Wintney for not meeting the demands of the injunctions. Some of these women were under the age of 24, and ap Rice had cautioned him against doing this because he worried about the possible "slander" that could result from "the misconduct of one" if they were all released into the community without care for their well-being.[37]

Within a short time, a different set of problems arose. It became clear that not only the message of reform, but also the messenger could be problematic. Thomas Legh rankled the communities he visited for a variety of reasons. To begin with, he expected a certain kind of reception and recognition of his authority when he visited monastic houses. Despite the fact that many of his visits were unannounced, he expected a ceremonial reception when he arrived.[38] According to ap Rice, "Wherever he comes he handles the fathers very roughly, many times for small causes, as for not meeting him at the door, where they had warning of his coming."[39] He also put on airs. In October 1535, ap Rice reported that he traveled with a large retinue of men and that he had "twelve men waiting on him in livery, besides his own brother."[40] Housing and provisioning such a large group was more than smaller houses could bear, argued ap Rice. Further evidence of Legh's extravagant behavior comes from his own defense of his practices. In a letter to Cromwell dated at roughly the same time as ap Rice's indictment, he answered Cromwell's complaints about his "triumphant and sumptuous usage and gay apparel."[41] He insisted that he had not done anything extravagant and that his clothing was appropriate. It was clear that Legh expected a measure of extravagance and pomp—and even financial benefit—to accompany his appointment as visitor.

Legh's behavior reveals, in striking detail, the role that personality could play in the reception of reform. It also demonstrates the odd dilemma of having the two visitors travel separately and visit the houses independently. Unlike the Spanish example where the visitors always traveled as a pair, the organization of the English case was strikingly different, with the visitors arriving at different times. Had their message been consistent, such a structure might have been successful. As it was, however, the differences in their standards of reform produced disagreement, disruption, and often a lack of compliance. In addition, the various convents and monasteries had to contend with what appeared to be Legh's demanding personality. Coupling his desire for rigid reform standards with a contentious style undoubtedly ensured that the path of reform would be rocky.

We can also learn something about the character and reception of the visitations by examining their timetables and itineraries. The Spanish delegation visited 39 foundations over the better part of two years. Notably, the Spanish visitors do not seem to have followed a standard form for their visits. Analyzing the accounts of each visit suggests that while they had certain objectives in mind—the imposition of enclosure, for example—the ten questions previously identified in this essay were a guide, not a script. Unlike their English counterparts, they were not working from a set script of questions. This comparison, then, suggests that the Spanish visitors were adapting to the specific conditions and issues they encountered in individual houses.

Much has been made of the alacrity and geographic scope of the English visitors' work. In six months, the two men visited almost 300 foundations. This suggests visits that could only have been quick—and perhaps, as a consequence, cursory. Could they really have completed the list of questions that informed their mandate? Were they really at each house long enough to deal with complaints or issues that were particular to that setting? Could injunctions be modified in such a short span of time to suit the specific circumstances?

Knowles has argued that all of these things would have been impossible. He extrapolates from this, however, to argue that if the visitors were this rushed they could not have possibly been sincerely interested in reform.[42] This unnecessarily stretches the argument. The speed with which the visitors made their rounds undoubtedly shaped the character and nature of the visits, but it does not mean that their mandate was to do something other than reform. This interpretation is highly problematic because it has been used as "proof" that the visitors were not serious about reform and were simply gathering evidence of scandals to discredit monastic institutions.

Yet Knowles bases much of his contention on the contrast that he draws with less rushed and more customary visitations, such as those made by bishops as part of their regular duties. He argues, for example, that typically injunctions were issued at a later date after the visit had been completed, and presumably "processed" by the visitor. The records of the visitations of the Archbishop of Canterbury, William Warham, cited earlier in this paper (to give just one example), suggest otherwise. Warham issued most of his injunctions on site without the benefit of additional time.

The evidence surrounding the selection of and tasks entrusted to the male agents of reform prompts three significant observations. The first involves the flow of direction and information. In Spain, the monarchs took the lead and initiative in helping the visitors secure as smooth a path as possible towards reform. They sought to manage questions of ecclesiastical and secular jurisdiction and offered encouragement to the reformers themselves. By contrast, the English reform was less centralized. Though he possessed the imprimatur of the Crown, Cromwell did not direct affairs with as much foresight as the Spanish monarchs. Instead, he received reports from the visitors and their clerks and made adjustments and corrections as needed.

The second observation centers on the reception of reform. The scholarship on female monasticism of the past 20 years or so has focused closely on the battles between nuns and the reformers sent to visit them. But this same scholarship has sometimes assumed that nuns only resisted reform out of an unwillingness to accept stricter standards and regulations. And yet the evidence presented here suggests that the presentation of reform and who presented it could spark legitimate backlash. Someone like Thomas Legh, with his airs and presumptions and attempts to extract money from the convents, probably did little to advance the more lofty goals of reform. His actions and attitude guaranteed there would be resistance. Although with fewer fireworks, the resistance of the Catalonian nuns to visitors outside their religious order struck a similar note in its resistance to individuals with no previously established authority to provide oversight and correction.

A final observation is that an understanding of the ways in which the selection of personnel and their preparation and behavior shaped reform profits from a comparative approach. An analysis of Cromwell's role in the reforms of 1535/6 in England might foster the assumption that reform was administered with minimal foresight and was a mostly reactive process. Yet a comparison to Spain demonstrates that it was possible, under the right circumstances, to direct or even troubleshoot the path of reform. Breaking out of the narrowly defined geographies of the study of monasticism, and in this particular instance the experience of monastic reform, permits a broader understanding of the factors that shaped its reception and relative success.

Notes

1 *Acta visitationis*, Real Biblioteca del Monasterio de San Lorenzo de El Escorial, Ms. V.II. 14, 7^r.
2 Victoria County History, Wiltshire, accessed 17 February 2015, http://www.british-history.ac.uk/vch/wilts/vol3/pp259-262. Hereafter cited as VCH. Cited in Valerie Spear, *Leadership in Medieval English Nunneries* (Woodbridge: Boydell and Brewer, 2005), 53.
3 In 1508, for example, the nuns of the convent of Wix were chastised by the local bishop and forbidden to wear "silver or gilt hairpins and kirtles of fustian." VCH, Essex, accessed 28 December 2017, http://www.british-history.ac.uk/vch/essex/vol2/pp123-125.
4 *Colección de documentos inéditos para la historia de España*, 113 vols. (Madrid: Impr. de la viuda de Calero, 1842–1895), 7:554. All translations mine.

5 Garcia Oro, *La reforma de los religiosos españoles en el tiempo de los Reyes Católicos* (Valladolid: Instituto de Isabel la Católica de Historia Eclesiástica), 148.
6 Elizabeth A. Lehfeldt, *Religious Women in Golden Age Spain* (Aldershot: Ashgate, 2005), 141.
7 García Oro, *Reforma*, 66–67.
8 García Oro, *Reforma*, 65.
9 K. L. Wood-Legh, *Kentish Visitations of Archbishop William Warham and His Deputies, 1511–1512* (Maidstone, Kent: Kent Archaeological Society, 1984).
10 Roseanne Michalek Desilets, "The Nuns of Tudor England: Feminine Responses to the Dissolution of the Monasteries" (PhD thesis, University of California, Irvine, 1995), 167.
11 Desilets, "The Nuns of Tudor England," 168.
12 Desilets, "The Nuns of Tudor England," 169.
13 Desilets, "The Nuns of Tudor England," 170.
14 Desilets, "The Nuns of Tudor England," 171.
15 Anthony N. Shaw, "The *Compendium Compertorum* and the Making of the Suppression Act of 1536" (PhD thesis, University of Warwick, 2003).
16 Although all secondary sources reference these questions, there is no attribution for them. Even the manuscript that contains them does not indicate who authored them or called for their creation. They appear in British Library, Cotton, Cleo E IV. The sheer number of questions has led some scholars to suggest, in fact, that the visitors could not have investigated all of them thoroughly at each monastic house. This point will be explored later in the essay.
17 Garcia Oro, *Reforma*, 101–102.
18 F. Donald Logan, "The First Royal Visitation of the English Universities, 1535," *English Historical Review* 106 (October 1991): 861-888.
19 *Letters and Papers, Henry VIII* (hereafter cited as LP), vol. 8, #822. Full text in Thomas Wright, ed. *Three Chapters of Letters Relating to the Suppression of the Monasteries* (New York: AMS, 1968), 156–157.
20 *Dictionary of National Biography*, vol. 32, "Layton, Richard."
21 *Dictionary of National Biography*, vol. 32, "Legh, Thomas."
22 Shaw identifies these as the questions in Cotton, Cleo E iv. See note 15.
23 One might follow after another, but it appears that they were never present at the same time at an individual house.
24 *Acta visitationis*, 70^v.
25 *Acta visitationis*, 103^r.
26 *Acta visitationis*, 103^r.
27 Tarsicio de Azcona, "Reforma de benedictinas y cistercienses de Cataluña en tiempo de los Reyes Católicos," *Studia Monástica* (1967): 85.
28 Azcona, "Benedictinas," 87.
29 García Oro, *Reforma*, 256.
30 LP, vol. 8, #1127.
31 LP, vol. 9, #138.
32 LP, vol. 9, #138.
33 LP, vol. 9, #139.
34 LP, vol. 9, #167.
35 LP, vol. 9, #167.
36 LP, vol. 9, #280.
37 LP, vol. 9, #423. Although in a later letter, Legh said that he had never turned members out without care and had instead allowed them to stay at their houses if necessary: LP, vol. 9, #651.
38 LP, vol. 9, #622.

39 LP, vol. 9, #622.
40 LP, vol. 9, #622.
41 LP, vol. 9, #621.
42 Dom David Knowles, *The Religious Orders in England: The Tudor Age*, 3 vols. (Cambridge: Cambridge University Press, 1971), 3:287.

10

ANNA MARIA VAN SCHURMAN

Poetry as exegesis

John L. Thompson

Widely regarded as the most learned woman of her day, Anna Maria van Schurman was the object of an international admiration that was all the more wondrous for the diversity of achievements on which it was based. But if she seems at first glance to model a life dedicated to intellectual pursuits, a closer look quickly reveals how her stellar intellect was formed and guided by pious religious convictions as well as by a poignant spiritual quest that turned controversial late in her life. As we will see, Van Schurman's "complex and multifaceted self" cannot be reduced to merely the life of the mind, though that is how she was best known and mostly remembered.[1]

Born into a wealthy Reformed Protestant family that had settled in Cologne, Anna Maria van Schurman (1607–1678) was forced at a young age to flee from Catholic persecution with her extended family. Her precocious fluency in the Latin she was overhearing led her pious father to include her alongside two older brothers in a classical education in their home. She flourished beyond all expectation, even as she excelled in music and other arts, and her family's social connections brought only wider recognition. One of her earliest "public" compositions was a Latin ode composed for the opening of the University of Utrecht in 1636, but she also exchanged letters and poetry with well-known poets of the day, such as Jacob Cats and Jacob Revius. Van Schurman's linguistic interests and abilities extended to a mastery of all the biblical languages and many of their cognates, including Aramaic, Syriac, Arabic, and Ethiopic. She read extensively in classics and philosophy, but even more in theology and Bible, as well as in the Greek and Latin church fathers. She has rightly been identified as Europe's "first female university student" for having attended lectures by Gisbert Voetius and possibly those of other members of the faculty; on at least one occasion, her exegetical suggestions were incorporated into a formal disputation.[2] But few displays of learning brought her more international renown than the 1638 Latin treatise that explicitly addressed the question of "Whether a Christian Woman Should Be Educated"—a question she naturally answered in the affirmative.[3]

Van Schurman's achievements were widely heralded in her own day, even as they are increasingly noted in ours. What may be less well known, however, is that alongside her mastery of languages and letters, in addition to her painting and public poems, and besides her treatise defending women's education, Anna Maria van Schurman also produced a small body of vernacular Dutch poetry, including several poems never meant for publication—only for private circulation among her friends. Of eleven extant poems, nine were edited by Pieta van Beek in 1992.[4] Curiously, two of the eleven appeared in print in 1732, fifty years after Van Schuman's death.[5] Both are by turns pious and personal, theological and exegetical. Both were also rigidly metered in rhymed couplets.

The first of the two may have received the most attention, if only due to its length as a 944-line *Uitbreiding* (or "elaboration") of Genesis 1–3.[6] As I have described elsewhere, the *Uitbreiding* is not much concerned with the work of the six days of creation and thus is nothing like traditional hexameral literature. Indeed, only the first half of this didactic poem sticks all that closely to the themes of Genesis; the second half turns to consider Christology (reading Christ as the woman's seed that crushes the serpent, per Gen. 3:16, the so-called *protoevangelion*) and the Christian life (as a transforming union with Christ here and in the hereafter). Nonetheless, this poem makes ample display of Van Schurman's facility with major themes of Reformed Protestantism, and there are some fairly strong hints of her reading in traditional Christian exegesis as well as of the influences of some of her mentors, such as Voetius and André Rivet.[7]

Many of these traits are, therefore, also to be expected, at least, in the second of these two poems, which is the work that will occupy us here. The 1732 edition titled this work as *Gezang over het geestelyk huwelyk van Christus met de gelovige ziele*, that is, "Song (or Hymn) on Christ's Spiritual Marriage with the Believing Soul" (hereafter cited simply as the *Hymn*). Surviving in multiple versions, the *Hymn* has a more complicated textual history. Pieta van Beek has edited one version of the *Hymn*, which she dates around the year 1660.[8] But a different version of the poem was copied into the daybook of Jodocus van Lodenstein for the year 1659, suggesting that Van Schurman may have shared the poem with Van Lodenstein, a pastor and close friend.[9] The discrepancies between the handwritten copy in Van Lowenstein's daybook and the print edition corroborate what Van Beek's editorial notes aptly suggest, that the 1732 edition is marred by defects of transcription or compositing.[10] But the handwritten copy raises other questions, too, because several lines and even some whole stanzas differ significantly from the later publication. Most notably, the handwritten copy has two additional stanzas missing altogether from the print edition. Neither scribal nor printer's errors can account for all these variations; instead, there must have been two recensions of the *Hymn* in limited circulation. Which one was the rewrite of the other, however, will require further study.

Attempting to translate the *Hymn* uncovers complications of a different sort. Right below the title is an epigraph, "According to Psalm 77 or 86"—a clear indication that *Hymn*, unlike the *Uitbreiding*, was to be sung to the metrical tunes of the Genevan Psalter. It is not an easy thing to approximate rigidly-metered Dutch rhymes in English, but the second poem, because of its musical setting, demands even greater rigor in order to render its rhymed couplets in the strict 8.8.7.7 meter used by Psalms 77 and 86. Fortunately, the tune shared by these psalms has been stable over the centuries, as can be seen from the Dutch translation of the Genevan Psalter produced by Peter Dathenus as early as 1566. Closer to Van Schurman's day, a facing-page French and Dutch edition from 1635 likewise shows Psalms 77 and 86 with the musical notation used by versions of the Genevan Psalter even in our own day.[11]

All these factors place Van Schurman's *Hymn* at the intersection of half a dozen trajectories for research, including the textual criticism of a private manuscript; the expressions of women's piety and learning in the seventeenth century; Reformed liturgy, insofar as Van Schurman's poem demonstrates the importance of metrical psalms to her; the practical theology of the Dutch *Nadere Reformatie* (or "further reformation") as a pietistic expression of Reformed theology in its second century; the related question of the author's sources and influences; and additional issues that pertain to Van Schurman's life, including the question of how this poem may reflect her disposition later in her life but still prior to the controversial renunciation of her Reformed ecclesiastical commitments that was signaled by her affiliation with Jean de Labadie, beginning around 1666.

The balance of this essay will trace some of these historical trajectories through the *Hymn* in order to probe Van Schurman's theological and religious sensibilities and to consider the traces or influences of her predecessors and contemporaries. But first, let me offer some account of the character of the work along with its structure and content.

The text and character of the *Gesang*

Surprisingly, the poem's title and genre are open to debate. The 1732 edition gives the work different titles on three different pages, identifying it as a hymn (*gesang*) in one place but as a discourse (*vertoog*) in another. These seemingly trivial variations might bear on Van Beek's assertion that the *Hymn* is not really singable and is better characterized as *een vertoog*—a discourse or (better) a didactic poem. The latter is a form popularized by Jacob Cats, Van Schurman's contemporary and a notable Dutch poet; the genre was also favored by writers of the *Nadere Reformatie*. Van Beek, however, gauges Van Schurman's *Hymn* against the versified adaptation of the Song of Songs produced by another contemporary, Jacob Revius, and finds her work "less poetic" than his.[12]

Still, a cursory comparison of the two works suggests that Van Schurman's *Hymn* should not be dismissed as a genuine song. At the very least, she herself would surely have been singing the words as she composed and refined them, and again whenever she reread them, even if her performances were *sotto voce* or sheerly interior. Moreover, Revius's published adaptation of the *Canticles* could easily have offered her a precedent or even direct inspiration. That she knew this particular work is more than likely, for she was introduced to Revius as early as 1626, before she was twenty years old, and they would exchange letters and poems for some years to come. More salient still is the character of Revius's *Canticles*: seven of his eight compositions that set the eight chapters of the Song of Solomon to verse are scored with tunes from the Genevan Psalter. Matching Dutch verse to traditional Psalter tunes is precisely what Van Schurman did in her *Hymn*.[13] And while her work was not written for publication, one cannot assume that it was never performed. Its inclusion in Van Lodenstein's daybook not only argues that she shared a copy with him; it further suggests that her *Hymn* may have been read within the so-called "Utrecht Circle," a conventicle of pastors, students, and laity that met weekly "for the sharing of spiritual experiences and to sing hymns"—because hymns that did not draw their lyrics directly from Scripture were generally not sung in regular church services. Van Lodenstein himself wrote hymns for this conventicle, and the seven indications of "pause" in the handwritten copy of Van Schurman's *Hymn* strongly suggest that it, too, was sung.[14]

What all titles of the *Hymn* have in common is that the work is about Christ's spiritual marriage with the believing soul (or, once, with just "the believer"). The expectation, then, is that the poem will stand in the tradition of devotional poetry that employs nuptial imagery. Such imagery, traceable all the way back to the Song of Songs and corroborated, arguably, by St. Paul in Ephesians 5, was developed throughout the Christian mystical tradition, notably by Bernard of Clairvaux and Thomas à Kempis. All these sources, in turn, were mined by later medieval mystics as well as by Puritans, pietists, and the exponents of the Dutch *Nadere Reformatie*. Thus, a didactic poem on the spiritual marriage of Christ and the soul might be almost a set piece from the dominant emotive piety of the day.

The structure and content of the *Gesang*

In surveying the content of the *Hymn*, two warnings are in order. First, a poem written as a private exercise or devotional need not have been conceived in a systematic way. In fact, Van Schurman's *Hymn* has few markers that could be taken as subject headings.[15] Second, the *Hymn* is long: comprising at least 278 rhymed couplets, it was not composed in a day, and many of its details cannot be addressed here.

Six sections may be identified, the first of which is introductory (§§1–3). The poet begins with a perennial question: What is the meaning of life? Life is God's gift, she writes, God's first gift, and the gift of life is bestowed so that we might recognize and prize not lesser goods but the very highest good—which, traditionally, can only be God himself.[16] Life's meaning is realized only when we are joined to God and to Christ through the Holy Spirit as in marriage and—as emerges later on—transformed from desperate sinners into those who are purified and holy.

The next section (§§4–15) recaps salvation-history or the history of the covenant as understood by Reformed theology. The union between God and the soul thus is a manifestation of God's grace, eternally foreknown and directed toward God's elect, each of whom is to be a bride of the King. On their own, the elect have nothing to offer, but God's self-giving love nonetheless intends to save them, as revealed in God's promises—first of all, in the promise revealed after Adam broke God's covenant. Van Schurman alludes here to the covenant of works that was breached through disobedience, and "promise" has to mean the *protoevangelion*—God's declaration of war with the serpent in Gen. 3:15–16, in which God assures his people that their Head (§9.4) will emerge victorious over Satan. This promise anticipates the gospel and constitutes the covenant of grace. Though she doesn't quite label it as such, Van Schurman makes the traditional point that though this covenant was announced in various ways through history, it was fulfilled and ratified when God sent his Son Jesus Christ to us. But Christ arrives to find the human race obscenely disfigured, having traded the image of God for the image of Satan—and heaven, for hell. Van Schurman could not be more graphic at this point:

12.
What compelled him, then, to disown,
aye, he abdicated his throne,
   deprivations to abide
   in pursuit of such a bride?
Could her beauty rouse his favor?
Her love draw his heart to waver?
   Was her noble good adored?
   Did her honor please this Lord?

13.
No, she sprouts from that remiss race
that the Lord's crown tried to displace:
   she a traitor's heart has worn
   from the moment she was born.
Loathsome, she was misbegotten,
cast out and by all forgotten:
   premature, left in the field,
   welt'ring as her blood congealed.

Churchgoers today might well balk at singing the second of these stanzas: its closing lines are graphic, even grisly. But a comment is in order. What is on display here? To identify the bride of §12 not as genuinely beautiful or loving, much less good or honorable, but instead as a traitor and as horrifying as an exposed fetus—these images are deeply physical and embodied, as well as gendered. They could with some plausibility be read as a mark of the poet's self-loathing, but that would miss Van Schurman's theological point. What is really on display is far less the poet's subjective state than her creative and sophisticated exegesis, for the stanza simply juxtaposes some traditional themes in Genesis 3 with imagery from Ezekiel 16—itself an intentionally shocking rehearsal of religious "harlotry" that casts Israel, God's covenant people, in the role of the faithless wife over against God as the faithful husband.[17] It would be speculative to suppose we gain any other special insight into Van Schurman's state of mind, beyond her unhesitating willingness to reiterate and appropriate the severe indictment of sin and faithlessness proffered by one of the Bible's most visceral declamations of judgment. To be sure, that in itself speaks of her self-confidence as an interpreter of Scripture.

The third section (§§15–24) represents an excursus on the wonders of the Groom—Christ, the Son of God—and his benefits. Van Schurman alludes to his miracles, fame, divine identity, divine authority, his beauty, glory, renown (all of which are ineffable, she says), then singles out his faithfulness, love, light, and life, all of which starkly contrast with our own relative nothingness. Yet our emptiness casts in sharper relief the self-giving goodness of God, who draws life from death and light from darkness, restores the divine image, and brings glory from nothingness.

A fourth section (§§25–34) turns from Christ as the culmination of salvation history to something like the classic *ordo salutis,* the ordering of the events of salvation in the life of the individual Christian. She begins with an account of the atonement wrought by Christ, who became a curse for us and thus satisfied the Father's justice. Consequently, the sinner is clothed with the righteousness of Christ (imputed righteousness), but there is also an inward work of the Spirit that cleanses her heart and bestows "real" virtue. God the Father is now reconciled to her and loves her just as much as he loves his own Son. Curiously, though, she herself does not yet know it, even though the pledge of eternal life was granted while she was still in the cradle—surely an image of baptism, received in infancy. This is also the moment when her name is entered on the roll of those destined for eternal life, as well as when the marriage is "already enacted." That these lines denote *infant* baptism is confirmed by the account of how her *later* life will reveal Christ to her more and more as she grows up and begins to understand his words.[18] Then comes what she calls "a second seal," which has to be the Lord's Supper because it marks her as part of the covenant and is where she both "opens Jesus' wounds" and proclaims his death—an echo of Paul's words in 1 Cor. 11:26. *Seal*, of course, is a traditional Reformed designation for the two sacraments; the effects of this second seal include strengthening the bond of marriage with Jesus and renewing her life through the Holy Spirit.

At this point, halfway through, it becomes harder to discern the poem's structure. A fifth section (§§35–51) seems to constitute the poem's heart, which depicts the ebb and flow of the Christian life as a cycle of three phases. First, trials come to the Christian not so much through succumbing to sin and temptation but more as the stabbing realization of one's lingering sinful proclivities. Then, the stumbling Christian turns in despair to Jesus, recalling his benefits, his example, and his promise of marriage that is yet to be fully realized. That recollection then spurs the Christian toward greater humility and self-denial, and even to wifely submission (§46), all of which are forms of bearing the cross of Christ as well as means of acquiring Christian virtue. Significantly, while Van Schurman alludes to a husband's headship in passing, the *Hymn's* larger context makes clear that *all* Christians are enjoined to pursue this marriage with Christ by becoming an appropriately submissive and virtuous "bride."[19]

This fifth section subtly leads to a final section (§§52–end)[20] in which many of the same points about the dynamics of the Christian life are reiterated, albeit with greater exhortations to the poet's own self to exercise surrender, deny herself, walk in faith, nurture humility, be vigilant against sin, and—notably—learn to recognize the stirrings of the Holy Spirit so as to respond to them. These are all still Reformed themes, but even more are they themes that distinguish the piety of the *Nadere Reformatie*. The poem ends on an abrupt and possibly ironic note: having reiterated that the holy life of Jesus is her example, Van Schurman breaks off in mid-stanza to say she must now lay down her pen and get about the work of imitating Jesus.

Themes and influences in the *Gesang*

Turning to the main themes of the *Hymn*, it should be obvious that one theme is, in effect, a rehearsal of the basic tenets of the gospel as understood by Dutch Reformed theology, in both specific details and subtle allusions. Reformed doctrine forms the backbone of the first half of the *Hymn*, including accounts of covenant, divine election, the covenantal role of the Son of God, and the looser account of the order of salvation that terminates largely on the significance of the sacraments of (infant) baptism and the Lord's supper.

Undergirding this first half, however, and emerging into prominence in the second half, is the rhetoric of nuptial imagery that signals the poet's real quest: to grow more deeply into a relationship with the divine bridegroom, which goes hand-in-hand with a fuller renunciation of self, a fuller receptivity to the stirrings of the Holy Spirit, and a fuller acquisition of what Van Schurman repeatedly names as *deugd*—virtue. These are all key themes in the practical theology of the *Nadere Reformatie*, as expressed by the "father" of that movement, Willem Teellinck, but also by Van Schurman's more immediate teachers and friends, such as Gisbert Voetius and others who are mentioned in the autobiographical sections of *Euklaria*.[21] But to extract themes from Teellinck is necessarily to invoke also many classic motifs of mystical and devotional theology from Bernard of Clairvaux, John Tauler, and Thomas à Kempis—authors read and lauded not only by Teellinck but also by Labadie[22]—and thus to describe a mixture of pietism and bridal mysticism that almost defies source criticism. Still, three strands of the

Nadere Reformatie's quest for mystical, nuptial communion are distinctively appropriated in Van Schurman's *Hymn*.

First, while the *Hymn* is certainly about a spiritual marriage with Christ, it is hardly an erotic union or image, even by the guarded standards of the *Nadere Reformatie*. Despite the canonical precedent offered by the Song of Songs, marginal annotations on the Van Lodenstein ms. cite that book only three times, with no explicit affirmations of bodily expressions of love. There is a wedding and a banquet, to be sure, but the poet describes no kissing and precious little tasting; nor is there any admiration of the physique of bride or groom, aside from a lone reference to the bride's necklace of virtue that comes as one of heaven's treasures (§27.3–4).[23]

Second, one might ask at this point, what if anything makes the *Hymn* even mystical? Does speaking of a spiritual marriage necessarily make one a mystic?[24] It is well known that the devotional writing of the *Nadere Reformatie* avoided speaking of an "essential" union with God, wherein one's identity or consciousness dissolves into the undifferentiated divine essence. Such language characterized the writing of Meister Eckhart and his imitators; it also drew accusations of heresy. But even against the chastened mysticism of Bernard and à Kempis, who can still speak of rapture or ecstasy, Van Schurman's language here is sharply reserved.[25] And while her *Hymn* does speak of a marital union with Christ, the nuptial imagery often takes a back seat to the language of the battlefield, where the enemy confronts her in the traditional threefold form of the world, the flesh, and the devil. "The believing soul" is thus charged with the responsibility to live an active and assertive Christian life, even where such activity entails renunciation and self-denial. Despite the clear and repeated emphasis on prevenient grace and divine initiative, the believing soul is not really passive—or if she is, it is a fiercely active passivity. In any case, the bride in Van Schurman's *Hymn* is preoccupied far less with bliss than with learning and acquiring the virtues displayed by Christ, her groom.

A third strand could easily have been derived from Teellinck, but it entails a notion found earlier in Puritan writers, namely, the centrality of attending to the inner movements and promptings of the Holy Spirit. De Reuver reports this as an extremely important theme for Teellinck as both the source for and the result of fervent prayer and spiritual exercises.[26] As an epitome of the Christian life in both its passive and active aspects, it may well indicate the climax of Van Schurman's *Hymn*. As noted earlier, the final section of the poem begins at stanza 52 with a self-exhortation: "Well, my soul, be up and doing, | such a crown to be pursuing." But what lies at the heart of this "up and doing"? I think the nature of this "doing" is announced only four stanzas from the very end, where she obliquely refers to two powers or two strengths she wants her soul to learn or possess:

66.
Now my soul must learn for its own
how the Spirit's work can be known.

> Then my second strength will be
> to heed that work carefully.
> Spirit's stirrings I will discern,
> by its leading my soul may learn,
> and your powers I'll deploy
> to persist in your employ.

Though the poem does not actually enumerate the first strength or power, its identity is clear enough from her enunciation of the second. First, she seeks the ability to *recognize* the work of the Holy Spirit; then, the power to *attend* to the Spirit's inner stirrings. Is this the secret of the Christian life for Van Schurman at this point in her journey? De Reuver argues that for Willem Teellinck, discerning "the stirrings of the Spirit" was foundational to attaining to true practice, true discipleship, and true conversion.

Van Schurman's identification of this theme, late in the poem, may also explain the poem's unexpected ending. The stanzas that follow §66 are thick with active verbs voiced by the author, including "I will lift my mind up ... I will raise myself ... I will believe ... I'll strengthen myself ... I will perform all virtue," and finally, the last (truncated) stanza:

> 70.
> I will count up Jesus' steps now,
> his pace thus to intercept now.
>   And, that I may reach that end,
>   here I lay aside my pen.

The reason for ending the poem with half the psalter tune still unsung is enigmatic, and probably deliberately so. The abrupt ending may be ironic, or (better) disruptive: the work of the Christian life is not to write and rhyme, but to arise from one's desk and to do—to attend to those stirrings of the Holy Spirit. Breaking off in mid-stanza with a renunciation of writing forces the reader or singer to cope with a disrupted lyric and meter, provoking reflection on the call to action. One might also see this truncation as an expression of the poet's own self-denial, a way of recognizing that the highest good, the *summum bonum* of the Christian life, lies not in her own artistry but with Jesus, the faithful bridegroom whom she seeks to intercept.[27]

Anna Maria van Schurman's 1638 "dissertation" on whether a Christian woman should be educated was decidedly an early feminist overture (even granting what Merry Wiesner-Hanks has aptly called its socially and politically "conservative" character), rooted in the experience of freedom and personal enrichment brought by her own education. Thirty-five years later, convinced that Jean de Labadie was a more reliable guide to an authentic and transformed Christian life, she wrote *Eukleria*, a spiritual autobiography that repudiated her earlier writings and achievements as distractions and trifles rooted in vanity—her own, as well as that of even her former Christian companions and teachers. Yet both treatises are clearly shaped by her impressive learning and scholarship, as well as by a theological reflection that is academically astute yet no less existentially grounded.

The same may be said of her *Hymn* on "Christ's Spiritual Marriage with the Believing Soul," which furnishes the reader with a carefully-posed snapshot of a moment in time. To date the poem around 1660 puts it in the midst of her most important transitional decade, as her disillusionment with Utrecht, with Christendom, and even with the church of the *Nadere Reformatie* became progressively more explicit, but still well before Jean de Labadie was on the horizon. The *Hymn* is truly a manifesto of serious Christianity. But at this point in time, the target of Anna Maria's heart-rending protest is not the nominal and lax Christianity of her day but, rather, her own faltering faith and wandering mind.

In writing these semi-private verses, she could not but employ the same deep learning. The *Hymn* abundantly displays her mastery of Reformed theology, her incredibly detailed knowledge of the Bible, and her exquisite ability as also a vernacular poet. Yet she wielded these tools principally to give voice to her spiritual quest, to the longings of her heart. That she shared these poems with her closest friends—a circle that included both men and women, pastors and laity—suggests that she did not regard theological reflection as hermit's work. Indeed, the poem's multiple versions might suggest that she was open to sharing her work and her reflections with those friends while still in the process of settling on a final draft. More importantly, that she wrote the *Hymn* with an eye to its use in actual worship, on her own as well as within the conventicle of these friends, further suggests that she felt able to speak for these same men and women, offering her words and authorial voice to utter prayers, praise, and even lament on behalf of all.

During the main part of her lifetime, Van Schurman attained international fame for her learning and achievements; in her final decade, her fame turned to notoriety as she attempted to shed the life of the mind in order to draw still closer to Jesus in the life of the spirit. For this sharp turn in her religious allegiance, she was sharply faulted in ways she found unfair and unkind. She, however, was much more concerned over her real faults, which the piety of the *Nadere Reformatie* had been unable to mend. Yet even before her disillusionment with the Protestant church of her day, she had already learned enough from it to know that these faults would not have the last word: for "though my failings still bring travail, | Jesus' faithfulness will ne'er fail" (§68.1–2).

Notes

1 On the traditional tendency of men to reduce the significance of women's lives to but one dimension—whether body, mind, or spirit—see Merry E. Wiesner-Hanks, *Women and Gender in Early Modern Europe*, 3rd ed. (Cambridge: Cambridge University Press, 2008), 13–14.
2 The description frames the biography by Pieta van Beek, *The First Female University Student: Anna Maria van Schurman (1636)* (Utrecht: Igitur, 2010); see especially 87–88.

3 The authoritative text is the 1641 Leiden edition, which contains added correspondence: *Dissertatio de ingenii muliebris ad doctrinam et meliores literas aptitudine: Accedunt Quaedam epistolae eiusem argumenti.* Joyce L. Irwin translated this work in *Anna Maria van Schurman: Whether a Christian Woman Should Be Educated and Other Writings from Her Intellectual Circle* (Chicago: University of Chicago Press, 1998).
4 The definitive account of Anna Maria van Schurman's Dutch poetry is the introduction and edition by Pieta van Beek, *Verbastert Christendom: Nederlandse Gedichten van Anna Maria van Schurman (1607–1678)* (Houten: Den Hertog, 1992); see also idem, "'O Utreght, Lieve Stad…': Poems in Dutch by Anna Maria van Schurman," in *Choosing the Better Part: Anna Maria van Schurman (1607–1678)*, ed. Mirjam de Baar, Machteld Löwensteyn, Marit Monteiro, and A. Agnes Sneller (Dordrecht: Kluwer Academic, 1996), 68–85.
5 *Uitbreiding over de drie eerste capittels van Genesis. Beneffens een vertoog van het geestelyk huwelyk van Christus met de gelovigen. Beide in Zinrijke Digtmaat t' zamen gesteld, door wylen Juffer Anna Maria van Schuurman. Nu eerst na het Originele handschrift gedrukt.* (Groningen: Jacobus Sipkes, 1732). My essay here grows out of a larger project, in collaboration with Albert Gootjes, to edit and translate both of the poems that appeared in 1732.
6 The *Uitbreiding* is not included in Van Beek's edition; the only extant text is what was published in 1732. A summary of the poem with some analysis is provided by Joyce Irwin, "Anna Maria van Schurman," in *Handbook of Women Biblical Interpreters*, ed. Marion Ann Taylor (Grand Rapids: Baker, 2012), 440–441. Elisabeth Gössmann offers a longer treatment in the third chapter of *Das wohlgelahrte Frauenzimmer*, 2nd ed. (Munich: Iudicium, 1998), 1:103–112.
7 John L. Thompson, "Piety, Theology, Exegesis, and Tradition: Anna Maria van Schurman's 'Elaboration' of Genesis 1–3 and its Relationship to the Commentary Tradition," in *Church and School in Early Modern Protestantism*, ed. Jordan J. Ballor, David S. Sytsma, and Jason Zuidema (Leiden: Brill, 2013), 613–628.
8 In Van Beek, *Verbastert Christendom*, 93–121.
9 See J. H. van de Bank, "De overdenkingen van de heer Lodensteyn," *Theologia Reformata* 32 (1989): 37–60. Carl J. Schroeder observes that when Van Lodenstein composed his *Overdenkingen* in 1659—"a year of inner crisis" for him—he also developed a sudden interest in the Song of Solomon, which makes his interest in the subject-matter of Van Schurman's *Hymn* perfectly understandable; see *In Quest of Pentecost: Jodocus van Lodenstein and the Dutch Second Reformation* (Lanham, MD: University Press of America, 2001), 52–53.
10 Dr. Van Beek graciously shared information about this ms. with us, and we happily acknowledge her assistance in several other ways. The Van Lodenstein ms. came to Van Beek's attention after her *Verbastert Christendom* went to press; it is archived at the Free University of Amsterdam as *Dagboek van Ds Lodestein* XV.05092 (OCLC 801573561) and has been directly consulted in the course of this study.
11 See Peter Dathenus, *Alle de psalmen Davids, ende andere Lofsanghen* (N.p., 1566), sig. M.vii^r–M.vii^v, sig. O.ii^r–O.ii^v; and idem, *Les pseaumes de David mis en rime françoise: Psalmen Davids: m[i]t den francoyschen Dichte in nederlandschen obergeset* (Leiden: David Jansz van Ilpendam, 1635), sig. L.5^v–L.6^r, M.11^v–M.12^r.
12 Van Beek also demurs over the excessive length of Van Schurman's *Hymn* and its "withered" ending; see *Verbastert Christendom*, 93. For Revius's 1621 adaptation, see *Het Hoghe liedt Salomons*, ed. Jan Vinks (Moergestel: Van Kempen, 1997); the work has been reprinted erratically, but I have consulted *Het Hoghe Liedt Salomons* (repr.; Maestricht: Boosten & Stols, 1942). On Revius more generally, see Henrietta Ten Harmsel, "Jacobus Revius, Dutch Baroque Poet," in *Comparative Literature* 15, no. 3 (Summer 1963): 203–215; and idem, *Jacobus Revius: Dutch Metaphysical Poet* (Detroit: Wayne State University Press, 1968), 9–35.
13 Revius explicitly sets his songs to the tunes and meter of Psalms 5, 38, 45, 101, and 128, as well as two other tunes found in many versions of the Genevan Psalter, namely, those

used to sing the Ten Commandments and the Magnificat. Revius's first "song," though, was set to a fairly recent Lutheran hymn, "How lovely shines the morning star," which Philipp Nicolai published in 1599, drawing on the nuptial imagery of Psalm 45. Revius's eight songs comprise 818 lines, half again as much as Van Schurman's *Hymn*. For contacts between Van Schurman and Revius, see Van Beek, *First Female University Student,* 29–30, 54–55, 78. Most recently, Anne R. Larsen has suggested that Revius's first contact with Van Schurman occurred in 1630; see her *Anna Maria van Schurman, 'The Star of Utrecht': The Educational Vision and Reception of a Savante* (New York: Routledge, 2016), 45.

14 For more on the Utrecht Circle (aka the "Voetian Circle"), see Schroeder, *In Quest of Pentecost,* 53–56; on the "pauses" marked in Van Lodenstein's ms., see next note. In a later work, Pieta van Beek tells of at least one report of one of Van Schurman's Dutch poems being openly sung at a pastor's home, "in a circle of friends," which sounds very much like the activities of the Utrecht Circle. See Van Beek, *First Female University Student,* 215; and idem, "Poems in Dutch," 79.

15 The Van Lodenstein ms. may offer some such markers, to be sure: before stanzas 8, 15, 21, 28, 36, 44, and 52 (= groups of 7, 7, 6, 7, 8, 9, 7, and 21 stanzas), the word *pause* appears—on analogy with the Hebrew *selah*? But only two or three of these "pauses" correspond to the poem's apparent *thematic* breaks.

16 That Van Schurman would have identified God as the *summum bonum* can hardly be contested, but it emerges with special clarity in her *Euklaria,* as Bo Karen Lee has observed; see *Sacrifice and Delight in the Mystical Theologies of Anna Maria van Schurman and Madame Jeanne Guyon* (South Bend: University of Notre Dame Press, 2014), 29–35.

17 Both biblical texts, incidentally, are indicated by marginal annotations in the Van Lodenstein ms. The salient verses from Ezekiel 16 include vv. 4–6 ("As for your birth, on the day you were born your navel cord was not cut, nor were you washed with water to cleanse you, nor rubbed with salt, nor wrapped in cloths. No eye pitied you, to do any of these things for you out of compassion for you; but you were thrown out in the open field, for you were abhorred....") and perhaps v. 40 ("They shall bring up a mob against you, and they shall stone you and cut you to pieces with their swords."). The chapter concludes with God strongly insisting, nevertheless, that "I will establish my covenant with you."

18 Van Schurman's allusions to infant baptism thus display none of the scruples that would later lead Labadists to recommend deferring the baptism of children; see T. J. Saxby, *The Quest for the New Jerusalem: Jean de Labadie and the Labadists, 1610–1744* (Dordrecht: Martinus Nijhoff, 1987), 150, 181, 213, 248.

19 Van Schurman thus subverts the convention of male headship by identifying it as a pattern of submission to God that applies to all Christians in the *Hymn's* larger context. So §§45.6–46.4: "One with Jesus she must remain; | her desires she must restrain. | Two can't share a single throne | if it's God's Son's very own. || Earthly marriage works the same way: | woman's headship can't be retained. | Honor it does not afford | should her rule displace her Lord's." Gössmann makes a similar point in *Das wohlgelahrte Frauenzimmer,* 1:111–112.

20 There is little to distinguish the fifth section from the sixth except for the sudden shift in tone or address at §52.1, where the poet turns to herself to say, "Well, my soul, be up and doing..." However, one of the curiosities of the Van Lodenstein ms. at this point is that it marks both the final named "pause" in the text and the end of biblical citations in the margins. Instead, there is a final marginal note to the effect that "What follows can stand on its own"—meaning that it could be sung as a shorter version of the work? or that the biblical underpinnings are self-evident from here to the end? The remark remains obscure.

21 Teellinck stands as a kind of touchstone, even if his influence was less than that of others. Indeed, while it is likely that Van Schurman was familiar with Teellinck's writings, it is assured that she knew his reputation, as she later held up his leadership in

piety against "worldly and profane enemies" in Middelburg (Zeeland) as a type of what she hoped for from Labadie, from 1666 on; see her remark in *Euklaria, seu Melioris partis Electio* (Cornelius van der Meulen, 1673), 138; and also Saxby, *Quest for the New Jerusalem*, 128 and n.91. For Teellinck, see Arie de Reuver, *Sweet Communion: Trajectories of Spirituality from the Middle Ages through the Further Reformation* (Grand Rapids: Baker Academic, 2007), 105–160.

22 See De Reuver, *Sweet Communion*, 104, 111–113, 154–155; Saxby, *Quest for the New Jerusalem*, 146.

23 The restrained imagery in the *Hymn* is thus a sharp contrast to Van Schurman's account of being brought to the Bridegroom's wine cellar where he "intoxicates you with his delights." See Van Schurman, Letter 2 to Johann Jakob Schütz (12/22 August 1674); full text and translation in Lee, *Sacrifice and Delight*, 134–135.

24 The debate over Van Schurman's mysticism depends in crucial ways on one's definition of mysticism, as has recently been considered by Bo Karen Lee; see *Sacrifice and Delight*, 15–56 and notes. Similarly, the allusions Gössmann draws between Van Schurmann's *Uitbreiding* and earlier mystics (including Hildegard of Bingen, Mechthild of Magdeburg, Beatrice of Nazareth, and Hadewijch of Brabant) need a closer analysis of the texts and themes involved; see *Das wohlgelahrte Frauenzimmer*, 1:106–110.

25 Lee thus sees *Euklaria* (1673) as marking "a striking turn" in Van Schurman's rhetoric of piety, wherein she increasingly appeals to extreme metaphors of self-abnegation, including some—such as "immersed in the measureless ocean of divinity"—that are highly suggestive of the dissolution of the self in the divine. Lee argues that Van Schurman stops short of the extreme, even in *Euklaria*, stating not that the self is to *become* nothing but that the self is to be *considered* as nothing (*Sacrifice and Delight*, 28, 34–35). It is telling, therefore, that her earlier language (in the *Hymn*) is not as either/or with respect to self-abnegation but is, instead, gradational, as seen in the comparative rhetoric of §44: "The more herself she can deny, | more to Jesus she will draw nigh; | when herself as naught she deems, | she'll see more of his esteem."

26 De Reuver, *Sweet Communion*, 119–125. The importance of the "stirrings of the Spirit" for Teellinck is also noted by Joel R. Beeke, "Evangelicalism and the Dutch Further Reformation," in *The Advent of Evangelicalism: Exploring Historical Continuities*, ed. Michael A. G. Haykin and Kenneth J. Stewart (Nashville: B&H Academic, 2008), 161.

27 None of these observations is seriously challenged by the fact that the Dathenus psalter includes two metrical psalms that similarly break off at the halfway point (Psalms 17 and 79), insofar as neither of those psalms has any thematic indication for the truncation (except, perhaps, for the sake of musical variation); nor does either psalm seem to have any thematic or stylistic connection with Van Schurman's own composition.

11
SACRAL SYSTEMS
The challenge of change

Raymond A. Mentzer

Women in western Christianity and the French Reformed community in particular had long and substantial involvement in the sacral realm. They valued and sustained in various ways traditional medieval religious customs and the world of folk systems. In other respects, they adopted newly reformed official Christian belief systems and liturgical routines. Women were not passive recipients of the Reformation. They acted both as supporters of Protestantism and defenders of the old faith.[1] In accordance with their perceived responsibilities for maintaining the household and raising children, they acted as protectors as well as conveyers of religious traditions.[2] Some welcomed the religious developments associated with the Reformation. Others were fiercely loyal to existing belief structures and devotional practices and were stubbornly opposed to change. Women figured among those who challenged and occasionally subverted the sixteenth-century French Protestant transformation of belief and behavior, at least in the eyes of Reformed religious authorities. Later, during the late-seventeenth and eighteenth centuries, they were frequently the most stalwart defenders of the Reformed faith and its rituals. The two trajectories were not mutually exclusive. The situation prompts a number of basic questions. Chief among these queries is how effective were French Reformed women in defining and maintaining an autonomous, identifiable position in the sacred domain? Moreover, how successful were pastors and elders, generally regarded as advocates of a heavily patriarchal order, in restricting women's roles?[3]

The integration of women into the historical narrative of the Reformation is among the most significant developments of recent decades.[4] Scholars have paid increasing attention to a detailed and multifaceted exploration of the relationship between women and the many changes in the religious culture of the age. The Reformation in some ways expanded women's opportunities and diminished them in other respects.[5] A number of newer studies have focused on the substantial, but all too frequently underappreciated perspectives, experiences, and contributions of women to Reformation religious culture. The earliest investigations tended to emphasize the political achievements of prominent Protestant women. Historians have similarly drawn attention to the activities of celebrated, well-educated women in the theological and liturgical spheres. While the examples are numerous, let us focus on several of the more familiar and visible.[6]

Noble women were central to the advance of the Protestant movement in France. They possessed political power and social status, had access to financial resources, controlled patronage networks, and could influence immediate family members, above all children. Jeanne d'Albret (1528–1572), Queen of Navarre, is likely the best-known Reformed female political figure in the French orbit.[7] She was queen of the rump of the medieval kingdom of Navarre on the northern slopes of the Pyrenees. An important person in the political and religious activities of both Navarre and France, she announced her Reformed faith at Christmas 1560 by participating in a Reformed Lord's Supper. Jeanne protected Protestant preachers in her territories and, despite opposition from many of her subjects, promoted the Reformation in the kingdom of Navarre by outlawing Catholic processions, proclaiming liberty of conscience, and most importantly raising her son Henry of Navarre (the future King Henry IV of France) in the Reformed faith.

From the beginning of the Reformation, female authors and activists challenged male domination of the theological realm. Among the more remarkable was the noblewoman Marie Dentière (c. 1495–1561), a former Augustinian abbess from Tournai (in modern Belgium), whose arrival in Geneva with her second husband, the pastor Antoine Froment, predated that of John Calvin. She proved an indefatigable proselytizer, especially among Genevan nuns and other women. Still, Dentière ran afoul of the authorities when in 1539 she published a pamphlet entitled *Epistre tres utile*.[8] It was an open letter to Marguerite de Navarre, the sister of King Francis I, and the first explicit statement of Reformed theology by a woman to appear in French. While the *Epistre* affirmed Guillaume Farel and John Calvin's teachings on salvation through faith alone and attacked the Catholic mass, clergy, and papacy, it also defended women's equality before God and their right to preach, interpret scripture, and teach theology. Predictably, the Genevan city council took a dim view of Dentière's ideas regarding an enhanced role for women in religious practice and promptly banned the *Epistre*.

Although male Protestant authorities sought to restrain and suppress these and subsequent efforts, women continued to propose innovative theological perspectives. Thus, in the early eighteenth century, Marie Huber (1695–1753), who was born at Geneva, but later moved to Lyon, was one of the rare women who wrote and published theological works. Among her treatises was *Le sisteme des anciens et des modernes, concilié par l'exposition des sentimens différens de quelques théologiens, sur l'etat des ames separées des corps* (1731). In it, she posed a number of basic questions regarding the afterlife, hell, and eternal punishment. The issues were patently controversial.[9] Huber's rejection of traditional notions of hell and predestination entailed an unreserved questioning of the foundations of classical

Protestantism. At the same time, her denial of a vengeful God and strong advocacy of the search for happiness were wholly consonant with the transition from a traditional Christianity to an Enlightenment version. Her work, furthermore, influenced the thought of the philosophes and, in particular, Jean-Jacques Rousseau. Still, Huber and those who preceded her were exceptional by virtue of their political standing, social status, economic circumstances, and educational background.

As noteworthy and prominent women such as Dentière and Huber were in the development of Protestantism and advancing the goal of establishing women's position in the theological and devotional realms, many other women with voices far more muted were, in their own way, equally significant for comprehending the relationship between women and religious change in the early modern period. Past events are best appreciated when scholars take into account the full range of human participants. Even as historians increasingly drew attention to women's contributions in the political realm, their presence in intellectual endeavors, and their position in the religious and liturgical sphere, other avenues of inquiry remained. In her very first book, a study of working women in early modern Germany published in 1986, Merry Wiesner-Hanks reminded us of ordinary women's position and significance in everyday existence.[10] Clearly, the results of the study of women's place in the religious events that swirled about the early modern world have been impressive. Historians now appreciate that women as well as men were significant actors across a broad range of endeavors. We speak here of persons who have been in a sense doubly neglected: first as women, second as commonplace and unremarkable. What then was the place and role of women in the daily religious life of early modern Europeans? What activities did they pursue? How ought we to understand their relationship with the sacred?

Otherwise unexceptional, unlettered, and unschooled women were occasionally willing to challenge and, in some instances, undermine official theological views and liturgical practices. Some, how many is impossible to know, remained wary and ambivalent even as they accepted the new Reformed Christianity with its explicit promise of eternal salvation. They took a cautious approach, were not always completely persuaded of the value of the innovations, and sometimes continued to honor medieval Christian and non-Christian traditions. The staying power of older devotional habits as well as a continuing hesitancy regarding newer religious positions are striking. When people adopted fresh ideas or joined a different religious movement, they did not start with a blank slate. Even as they accepted the new, they retained something of the past. They kept remnants of the older views and practices that had become so much a part of their being that they did not always consciously realize their presence. Indeed, women (and men) developed hybrid religious theologies and practices that combined their folk traditions and medieval Christian beliefs with the innovations that characterized Reformed Protestantism. It is this element in the lives of French Protestant women—the persistence of traditional ways and, at the same time, the embrace of new ones—that merits special attention.

Women enjoyed a number of central sacral charges in late-medieval Christianity and were not always prepared to relinquish them with the advent of Protestantism. Chief among these responsibilities was the administration of emergency baptism to newborns. The midwife's task extended beyond providing for the physical well-being of mother and child. She, or a helpful neighbor woman, could also, if deemed necessary, afford the infant spiritual protection. Any Christian, male or female, could administer the sacrament according to medieval and later Catholic interpretation. Given the fragility of infants and the belief that a child who died without benefit of baptism would forever be confined to limbo and thus denied the eternal comfort of the beatific vision, parents were naturally anxious to have an infant baptized as soon as possible. Estimates are that in late-medieval Europe midwives baptized as many as one-half of all infants. Calvin and French Reformed authorities were adamant in their prohibition on the administration of emergency baptism, especially if administered by women. Baptism was a public ritual that took place in conjunction with the sermon service and performed by the pastor in the temple.[11] Church leaders strictly forbade private baptisms by laypersons.[12] Yet these ecclesiastical injunctions did not always dissuade people from time-honored practices.

Parental and, more specifically, maternal concern for a child's spiritual welfare could eclipse theological notions. The nurturing materfamilias was the protector of her children and she inevitably worried about their well-being in this world and the next. The risks were painfully apparent amid the high infant mortality of early modern Europe. Thus, in 1564, the elders of the Church of Saint-Gervais in rural southern France severely admonished a woman for baptizing a neighbor's infant daughter; they also chastised the child's parents. Several years earlier, the consistory of Nîmes summoned a widow and her daughter for having baptized a newborn.[13] The custom was so intricately woven into the fabric of everyday religious culture that a distraught mother, again from Nîmes, was able to persuade a deacon to baptize her frail baby. The infant in fact died the following day. The Nîmes consistory reprimanded the woman and summarily dismissed the deacon from office. Yet not even pastors were exempt from the pressures to administer the sacrament to dying newborns. As late as 1658, a couple at Blois persuaded the local pastor to come to their home to baptize triplets. They dared not wait until the Sunday sermon service "due to the frailty of the infants."[14]

Another key aspect of parental, again mostly maternal, obligation for children's spiritual welfare was to provide them elementary religious instruction and teach them their prayers. Here too, changes initiated by the Reformation challenged established routines. A central feature of the Reformed project, especially for ordinary, mostly illiterate members of the congregation whose knowledge of the theological transformation was limited, involved the abandonment of Latin prayers, which Calvin and others in the Reformed tradition regarded as more superstitious than pious. Relatively few among the faithful understood Latin, and Protestant authorities deemed a basic grasp of the meaning of the words crucial. Hence their insistence upon recitation in the vernacular of, for instance, the Lord's

Prayer and the Apostles' Creed. Still, learning to pray in new, unfamiliar ways could be difficult, and it was often adults, rather than children, who faced the greatest obstacles. The struggles associated with learning to pray in the vernacular is especially noticeable at the independent francophone city of Geneva. Witness the sheath-maker's wife who freely admitted to the pastors and elders seated in the Genevan consistory that her daughter "knows her faith better than she." The woman could recite her prayers in Latin, but not in French. She was far from the only Genevan, man or woman, for whom during the initial years of the city's Reformation, the linguistic transition presented a major problem.[15] Another woman pleaded that she did "not know how to pray to God except in the manner that her father and mother taught her."[16] More than a few people were puzzled and frustrated. Small wonder that a widow admitted that she said her prayers "in Latin and in the other tongue, French." Ironically, she also disclosed that sometimes she said, in the French vernacular, the Ave Maria, a prayer that the reformers vigorously discouraged. Equally telling was the perplexed mother who said her prayers in both Latin and French "for herself, her husband, and her children."[17] She appears to have instructed her children similarly as she sought to protect her family against all eventualities. Other Genevan women needed to remind themselves that they should no longer make the sign of the cross or kneel while praying. A midwife acknowledged that, when delivering infants, she still found herself, presumably out of habit, asking the Virgin Mary for assistance.[18] Pious routines acquired in childhood and practiced over a lifetime were not readily amendable to change.

On the other hand, some women had no intention of abandoning traditional Catholicism, stridently rejecting the introduction of Protestant Christianity. Perhaps the most famous case in the francophone world was Jeanne de Jussie, a nun of the Poor Clares convent of Geneva. Her *Short Chronicle*, likely written between 1535 and 1547, offers an impassioned account of opposition to the religious changes proposed by the early reformers Guillaume Farel and Pierre Viret.[19] Rather than submit, she and the other Poor Clares fled Geneva in 1535, settling in the nearby Catholic city of Annecy. While less celebrated, other women could be equally determined in their aversion to religious change. Thus, when an elderly woman from the small southern French town of Camarès balked at participating in the Lord's Supper, her son patiently explained to Reformed church authorities that "his mother was unable to understand anything, no matter how much they instructed her."[20] The woman defied the new order quietly yet effectively. Far more confrontational was the Genevan noblewoman who bluntly asserted that "sometimes she says her rosary ... believes in good works," and, furthermore, wondered whether Calvin thinks that he is God.[21]

If considerable maternal concern focused on the safety of infants—ensuring their immediate baptism and teaching them to pray properly—there was equal anxiety regarding the fecundity of a married couple and by extension the continuation of the family. Women and their spouses could be understandably distraught by the failure to conceive and accordingly appealed to established remedies involving sorcery and magical cures. According to a widely accepted southern French belief in the satanic ligature or *aiguillette*, a sorceress could "tie off" a couple and prevent them from having a family. As the pair stood before the pastor (or priest as Catholics were equally convinced of the satanic ligature) for the nuptial blessing, a witch presumably in the employ of an enemy or rival surreptitiously knotted a cord, symbolically binding the genitals, notably the male testicles, and rendered the union fruitless.[22] This is precisely what a young Protestant couple, living at Dieulefit in the foothills of the Alps during the first decade of the seventeenth century, believed had happened to them.[23] Someone had cursed their marriage and "impeded" the husband. When members of the local Reformed consistory later investigated, they discovered an intricate tangle of reproductive anxieties and magical therapies.

At the urging of several friends, the couple sought the advice of Damoiselle de Saint-Martin, an older widow who was familiar with these matters. The woman was clearly thought to be a sorceress; reputedly, she had been previously involved in similar "abominable affairs." She, in turn, put the young Protestant couple in contact with a Catholic priest who had the ability to "free" those who were "incapacitated" in their marriage. The three parties soon struck a bargain. The "sage and secret" priestly exorcist would remedy the young man's impotency in exchange for several sheep, and Damoiselle de Saint-Martin would receive a pair of pigeons for her invaluable mediation. The priest provided a pewter drinking cup on the bottom of which were inscribed several lines from Psalm 146:7-8 in the Vulgate version: *Dominus solvit compeditos, Dominus illuminat coecos*. The first part—the Lord releases the bound—seemed particularly apropos the man's dilemma. The curé directed that husband and wife drink "some wine" from the cup and he would be "freed." The pair did so and later reported that the priest's prediction was true (*veritable*). In addition, trusting in enchantments was hardly unique to this husband and wife. Troubled Protestant couples elsewhere in southern France continued to seek much the same remedy; belief in the "tying" and "untying" persisted well into the eighteenth century.[24]

The sorceress undoubtedly occupied powerful time-honored positions within early modern communities. She worked to resolve difficulties, which had vital individual and collective importance, yet required solutions that stood on the periphery of institutional religious systems. Skilled in the magical arts, she was a vital presence. Resort to her assistance seemed unamenable to facile eradication by the Reformed Church. For French Protestants, this often meant stealing away to a nearby Catholic town. Thus, Loys Martin traveled from Nîmes to Avignon in 1582 to consult a sorceress in hope of finding some coins that his deceased father had hidden. A few years earlier, a woman from Nîmes went to a nearby Catholic village to seek the advice of a "magician" and obtain a cure for her ailing husband. More desperate yet were the three women who towards the end of the sixteenth century brought a dying infant to a controversial healer at Ganges. Together, they engaged in what the local consistory termed "superstitions and idolatries" aimed at the child's recovery. They were not the only mothers to resort to healers. When her daughter fell ill after her eight-month-old son had already died, an anguished mother from late-sixteenth century Montauban hurried to a neighboring village to seek a curative from a local *divine*. As late as 1618, a Protestant woman from Layrac in Gascony enlisted the assistance of a *femme divineresse* to treat her sickly daughter.[25] Refashioning ancestral habits was no easy matter, especially in a society where experience and example were values in themselves. Not surprisingly, many women adopted a defensive role amid the religious turmoil of the age. It could prompt them to be wary of and resistant to change. They were reluctant to abandon late-medieval religious practices or, at a later date, Reformed Protestant forms.

Following the revocation of the Edict of Nantes in 1685 and the general proscription of Protestantism in France, women whose families had adhered to the Reformed tradition for well over a century were predictably unwilling to watch their daughters and sons fall prey to Catholicism, the religion of the anti-Christ. Protestant wives and mothers adopted a range of strategies in an effort to maintain the faith of their ancestors in the face of Catholic and royal pressure. Once again, women played a pivotal role in both the private and public spheres as they sought to preserve their children both physically and spiritually. The situation left Reformed families—mothers, fathers and children—with few and unpleasant choices. Landed Protestants had the option of hunkering down on their estates, outwardly conforming to Catholic liturgical demands while quietly maintaining Protestant beliefs and practices in the privacy of the household. Families whose fortunes were tied to royal office holding in the military, the judiciary, or the financial administration faced choices that were altogether more difficult. These male officials were typically required to make attestations of Catholicity. They found it difficult to avoid conversion, however half-hearted. Thus, all of the Protestant judges attached to the *chambre de l'Édit* of Castres, a special royal court for the adjudication of Protestant causes, were obliged to convert by 1685.[26]

Under the circumstances, many couples pursued a strategy common among early modern religious minorities throughout Europe. Husbands outwardly conformed, while wives quietly and privately guarded the family's religious traditions.[27] Pressure to convert was initially stronger for men than for women. Husbands tended to represent the family in the public sphere. Wives and mothers could, within the confines of the household, remain a discreet conduit for Reformed beliefs and practices. There are, moreover, examples outside the French Reformed community. Lutherans in Alsace, following the region's takeover by the French, appear to have pursued a similar approach when pressed by the Catholic crown. Men submitted to Catholicism while the women and children kept their distance. The tactic was consonant with the fundamental role assigned to women for the safeguard of the household and the religious upbringing of children. Indeed, women routinely displayed considerable confessional constancy. Husbands abjured to preserve the family's hard-won economic resources, while wives remained privately Protestant. Families thereby hoped to preserve cautiously and unobtrusively their Reformed religious commitment for themselves and for successive generations.[28]

Still, the desire to protect progeny occasionally ran in the opposite direction and propelled families to abandon their Protestantism for the relative security of the dominant faith. Some Protestants in seventeenth-century France, faced with increasing oppression by Catholic authorities, seem to have reacted by converting to Catholicism, ostensibly for the future welfare of their children. At least that was the perception of friends and relatives. Thus, a seventy-year-old Protestant man from the southwestern French hinterland reflected upon the relatively early religious fracture within his own family. Composing a family genealogy in 1630 after the disastrous failure of the Protestant rebellion directed against Louis XIII and Richelieu, he presumed that those of his kin who had abandoned the Reformed faith and "adopted the Roman religion" had done so in order to guard, keep, and protect their children.[29] The requirements of family well-being and a sense of parental obligation sanctioned, in this view, the decision to shift from Protestantism to Catholicism—and the stress on France's Protestants would increase dramatically by the end of the seventeenth century.

Some 150,000 to 200,000 French Reformed Protestants chose neither to resist quietly nor to buckle, however reluctantly, under the weight of Catholic royal coercion. Rather, they fled the realm in a movement known as the *Refuge*. Historians are only beginning to examine carefully the crucial position that women occupied in these developments.[30] To be sure, female willingness to emigrate rather than convert was evident already in the decades prior to the revocation of the Edict of Nantes. The prince de Tarente, whose mother had been a strong-willed supporter of the Reformed community, converted to Catholicism in 1670. His wife and daughter, however, chose not to follow his example. Instead, they sought refuge in Copenhagen.[31] Other women would make similar decisions.

The life of the noble woman Marie de La Rochefoucauld, though in some ways exceptional, is especially illustrative of the care that mothers and wives took to insure a safe and secure future for their children. Descended from a long line of Protestant matriarchs—for three generations the family had only daughters—Marie's determination and dedication, combined with careful planning and financial acumen, worked not simply to save, but in fact to advance her family amid the appalling circumstances of religious oppression associated with the *Refuge*. Marie and seven of her eight children fled France in 1687. Only an infant daughter, perhaps too frail for the journey, remained behind with Marie's husband. He joined them about a year later but died shortly afterwards. Thus, she quickly assumed full responsibility for the family's welfare. For three decades following her husband's death, Marie de La Rochefoucauld was head of the family. She had special responsibility for the management of financial affairs and demonstrated a remarkable independence in shifting the family's investments into movables and the financial markets. Marie's overriding purpose was to provide for her children. Indeed, they found suitable governmental and military offices, contracted advantageous marriages, and eventually settled across Western Europe in a pattern typical of the Huguenot noble "International." In all of this, the deep interweaving of maternal concern, family, and faith dominated.[32]

Even as a substantial number of Protestants fled the kingdom after 1685, the uncertainty and turmoil, maltreatment and disruption fostered the emergence of women's leadership and engagement among those who remained in France. Times of emergency and instability offered women opportunities to play public religious roles they would otherwise be denied.[33] Louis XIV's attempt to suppress Protestantism in the late seventeenth century was no exception. Early modern male authorities and even some modern scholars have woefully underestimated women's unhesitating willingness and ability to assume leadership roles in the public religious space long monopolized by men.

The flight of pastors and male authority figures created an immediate administrative and liturgical vacuum. The situation also offered an opportunity. The swift appearance of female preachers and prayer leaders following the revocation of the Edict of Nantes is not altogether surprising. The emergence of female preachers, especially during times of repression and transition was not new nor unique to the French Reformed community. During the Middle Ages, the Waldensians, another much-oppressed religious minority, also witnessed women step forward to shoulder the traditionally male task of preaching.[34] When in 1685 the crown forbade Protestant worship, the faithful soon began to assemble clandestinely and illicitly in the *Désert* or wilderness, a strong biblical image that accentuated Reformed determination. Rural artisans and others of lesser social and economic status dominated the earliest assemblies. Women, in particular, assumed a stronger, more conspicuous presence. No fewer than seven women are known to have taken on the role of preacher in southern France in the years directly following the Revocation.[35] Anne Montjoye offers a striking illustration. She traveled throughout Périgord for two years, conducting religious services in secluded woods and private homes. She directed the assembled faithful as they prayed, read passages from Holy Writ, and led in the singing of psalms. Royal authorities finally captured her and several dozen worshipers in 1688. Adamantly refusing to abjure, she went to the gallows. Over the next decade, assemblies in Poitou, to take another example, were occasionally led by returning pastors, equally often by unlettered farmers, artisans, and women. One woman, plainly held in high esteem for her preaching skills, was popularly known as the *prêcheuse*.[36]

The emergence of female preachers underscores the manner whereby the ordeal of the *Désert* suspended longstanding relationships and offered new and critical leadership roles to individuals whose activities Reformed ecclesiastical authorities had previously considered subordinate. Reformed women were certainly familiar with strong female figures from the Old Testament. In addition, they had long been the primary conveyers of religious traditions within the household, teaching their children to recite Scripture and vernacular prayers as well as taking them to sermon and catechism services. After the Revocation, they continued to guide and instruct their families in private and to take them quietly to secret worship services.

As a consequence of these activities, many women endured long and painful incarceration. Royal authorities sometimes dispatched women caught attending illegal religious assemblies or engaging in other dissenting and insubordinate acts to Catholic hospitals and nunneries. They were presumably force-fed Catholic doctrine and devotion. Yet most remained defiant, as evidenced by the confrontational words they inscribed on the walls and beams of their places of confinement. Thus, young women held at the convent of the Poor Clares at Montauban scratched their pleas for release into the plastered walls of the attic where they were held.[37] They wrote, for example: "La Bache anxiously awaits release from the Convent of Saint Claire"[38] and "Marianne de Pellet anxiously awaits release from the Convent of Saint Claire where she is dying from anguish."[39] Other women endured far harsher treatment, though it did not break them. The most famous defiant phrase is *"register"* (i.e. *résister* in the local dialect), which Marie Durand (1711–1776) and several dozen fellow female prisoners etched into the stone of their prison wall in the Tour de Constance at Aigues-Mortes. Durand, who was imprisoned in 1730 at the age of 19, became the very symbol of the courage and resistance that Protestant women demonstrated in the face of religious intolerance and persecution. She remained half-forgotten for 38 years, imprisoned in the tower at Aigues-Mortes, until her discharge in 1768. Other women died without the slightest expectation of release.[40]

Finally, while many French Protestants found consolation as they gathered to worship clandestinely, a much smaller group expressed its anguish through ecstatic visions and prophesying. A number of young women and eventually young men engaged passionately in a culture of divine inspiration as they protested religious persecution in less conventional though decidedly open and public fashion. The appearance of adolescent prophets was among the most stirring elements associated with reactions to the Revocation. Still, the movement ought not to have been completely surprising. Since the earliest centuries of Christianity, some women held authority because of their prophetic gifts, which in turn were a measure of rank and gave women access to community authority.[41] During the Reformation, prophetesses flourished in both Protestant and Catholic circles. The French prophetesses first surfaced in February 1688 when Isabeau Vincent, an ostensibly illiterate teenage shepherdess from the rural Dauphiné began to sing psalms and preach in her sleep. Her denunciation of "popery," call for repentance, and firm declaration that deliverance was at hand quickly attracted a large following. Other young women and men, also inspired by spiritual visions, followed her example. They shook violently, wept, and cried out for repentance in an increasing number of prophesying assemblies.[42] The prophetesses (and prophets) took psychological refuge in acting out biblical texts that they knew by heart. The women, who were very much in the forefront of this movement, gave special voice, accompanied by convulsive body language, to their torment over the disaster that had befallen their community of belief.

In all of these activities, whether it be a manifest tenacity to hold fast to familiar medieval religious forms or, a century and a half later, in the efforts to sustain Reformed beliefs and practices when confronted with royal Catholic intimidation and coercion, women acted within the framework of their central position in the family and the wider community of belief. They labored arduously to insure the survival of professed religious truths and practices as well as the transmission of religious dissent. Despite changes in confessional stance from medieval Christianity to Reformed Protestantism, women continued to engage in long-established protective and nurturing customs, many of which focused directly on their perceived roles as mothers, wives, and daughters. They could be hesitant to welcome certain elements of the Reformation's transformations and, later, resolutely resistant to the Revocation and its forced imposition of Catholicism.

Notes

1 Merry Wiesner-Hanks, *Gender, Church and State in Early Modern Germany. Essays by Merry E. Wiesner* (New York: Longman, 1998), 24, 34.
2 Martin Luther, for example, maintained that motherhood was women's only vocation. Merry Wiesner-Hanks, *Christianity and Sexuality in the Early Modern World: Regulating Desire, Reforming Practice*, 3rd ed. (New York: Routledge, 2010), 78.
3 The classic expression of the Reformation as the strengthening of patriarchy can be found in Lyndal Roper, *The Holy Household: Women and Morals in Reformation Augsburg* (Oxford: Oxford University Press, 1989), especially 1–5.
4 See the remarks of Merry Wiesner-Hanks, "Society and the Sexes Revisited," in *Reformation and Early Modern Europe: A Guide to Research*, ed. David Whitford (Kirksville, MO: Truman State University Press, 2008), 396–414.
5 Merry Wiesner-Hanks, *Women and Gender in Early Modern Europe*, 3rd ed. (Cambridge: Cambridge University Press, 2008), 214.
6 For a general assessment of women and the Reformation in France, see Amanda Eurich, "Women in the Huguenot Community," in *A Companion to the Huguenots*, eds. Raymond Mentzer and Bertrand Van Ruymbeke (Leiden: Brill, 2017), 118–48.
7 The classic study is Nancy Roelker, *Queen of Navarre, Jeanne d'Albret, 1528–1572* (Cambridge, MA: Harvard University Press, 1968).
8 Marie Dentière, *Epistle to Marguerite de Navarre and Preface to a Sermon by John Calvin*, ed. Mary B. McKinley (Chicago: University of Chicago Press, 2004).
9 Marie Huber, *Un purgatoire protestant: Essai sur l'état des âmes séparées de corps*, ed. Yves Krumenacker (Geneva: Labor et Fides, 2016).
10 Merry Wiesner-Hanks, *Working Women in Renaissance Germany* (New Brunswick, NJ: Rutgers University Press, 1986).
11 In the French Reformed tradition, the temple was the building in which the congregation worshiped, the church was the body of believers.
12 John Calvin, *Institutes of the Christian Religion*, ed. John T. McNeill, trans. Ford Lewis Battles, 2 vols. (Philadelphia: Westminster Press, 1960), 4.15.20-21, 4.16.26=2:1320-22, 1349; François Méjan, *Discipline de l'Église réformée de France annotée et précédée d'une introduction historique* (Paris: Editions 'Je Sers', 1947), 262-63; Karen E. Spierling, *Infant Baptism in Reformation Geneva: The Shaping of a Community, 1536-1564* (Aldeshot: Ashgate, 2005), 67-83.
13 The consistory was a disciplinary and administrative body composed of pastors, elders and, in France, deacons. The Genevan consistory is mostly commonly associated with strict morals control. French Reformed consistories bore broad responsibility for ecclesiastical administration, management of financial affairs, poor relief, and punishment of sinners. Raymond A. Mentzer, "Local Contexts and Regional Variations: Consistories," in *Judging Faith, Punishing Sin: Inquisitions and Consistories in the Early*

Modern World, eds. Charles H. Parker and Gretchen Starr-LeBeau (Cambridge: Cambridge University Press, 2017), 15-27.
14 Archives Nationales (Paris), TT 269, dossier 25, fol. 947^v. Bibliothèque nationale de France (hereafter BnF), ms fr 8666, fol. 57, 159, 162. Yves Guéneau, *Protestants du centre, 1598-1685* (Thèse de doctorat: Université François Rabelais de Tours, 1982), 262.
15 *Registres du consistoire de Genève au temps de Calvin*, vol. 1, *1542-1544*, eds. Thomas A. Lambert and Isabella M. Watt (Geneva: Librairie Droz, 1996), 1:25, 28, 36, 49, 58, 118–119, 134, 140, 147, 180.
16 *Registres du consistoire de Genève*, 1:138.
17 *Registres du consistoire de Genève*, 1:145.
18 *Registres du consistoire de Genève*, 1:121, 125, 136.
19 Jeanne de Jussie, *The Short Chronicle*, ed. and trans. Carrie F. Klaus (Chicago: University of Chicago Press, 2006).
20 Bibliothèque de l'Arsenal (Paris), ms 6563, fol. 82.
21 *Registres du consistoire de Genève*, 1:200.
22 Emmanuel Le Roy Ladurie, "L'aiguillette," *Europe: revue littéraire mensuelle* 52 (March 1974): 134–145.
23 Musée du Protestantisme Dauphinois (Le Poët Laval), ms A 1, Livre du consistoire de ceste Eglise reformée de Dieulefit, fol. 12ff.
24 In 1604, a couple from Castelmoron obtained a special powder. They added it to a soup, which they then consumed in anticipation of dissolving the ligature that had blocked their fertility. Bibliothèque de la Société du Protestantisme Français, ms 222/1, fol. 101^v-102^v; Michel Plénet, *Catholiques et protestants en Vivarais aux XVIIe et XVIIIe siècles: modes de vie, modes de croire* (Thèse de doctorat: Université Lumière Lyon 2, 2007), 134–135 notes an incident that occurred as late as 1726.
25 BnF, ms fr 8667, fol. 38^v, 51^v, 309, 321^v; Raymond A. Mentzer, "The Persistence of 'Superstition and Idolatry' among Rural French Calvinists," *Church History* 65 (1996): 220-233; Archives Départementales, Tarn-et-Garonne, I 1, fol. 213v. Archives Départementales, Gers, 23067, le 17 août 1618.
26 Raymond Mentzer, *Blood and Belief: Family Survival and Confessional Identity among the Provincial Huguenot Nobility* (West Lafayette: Purdue University Press, 1994), 168–169.
27 Barbara Diefendorf, "Houses Divided: Religious Schism in Sixteenth-Century Parisian Families, in, *Urban Life in the Renaissance,* eds. Susan Zimmerman and Ronald Weismann (Newark: University of Delaware Press, 1989), 84; Benjamin Kaplan, *Divided by Faith: Religious Conflict and the Practice of Toleration in Early Modern Europe* (Cambridge, MA: Harvard University Press, 2007), 141, points out that in England, husbands often conformed while wives lived as recusants and played leading roles in the preservation of Catholic life.
28 Wiesner-Hanks, *Women and Gender*, 231-32; Mentzer, *Blood and Belief*, 169-72; John McManners, *Church and Society in Eighteenth-Century France,* 2 vols. (Oxford: Clarendon Press, 1998), 2:627–628.
29 Camille Rabaud, *Histoire du protestantisme dans l'Albigeois et le Lauragais*, 2 vols. (Paris: Fischbacher, 1873 and 1898), 1:281–282.
30 See, in particular, the studies by Carolyn Chapelle Lougee, *Facing the Revocation: Huguenot Families, Faith, and the King's Will* (New York: Oxford University Press, 2017), and idem. "Huguenot Memoirs," in *A Companion to the Huguenots*, eds. Mentzer and Van Ruymbeke, 323–347.
31 Keith Luria, *Sacred Boundaries: Religious Coexistence and Conflict in Early-Modern France* (Washington, D.C.: The Catholic University of America Press, 2005), 174–179.
32 For the full detailed history of Marie de La Rochefoucauld's activities, see Lougee, *Facing the Revocation*.
33 Wiesner-Hanks, *Women and Gender,* 247.
34 Gabriel Audisio, *The Waldensian Dissent: Persecution and Survival, c. 1170-c. 1570* (Cambridge: Cambridge University Press, 1999), 15, 23, 112–113, 146.

35 Marianne Carbonnier-Burkard, "La Réforme en langue des femmes," in *La religion de ma mère,* ed. Jean Delumeau (Paris: Editions du Cerf, 1992), 188.
36 Samuel Mours and Daniel Robert, *Protestantisme du XVIIIe siècle à nos jours* (Paris: Librairie Protestant, 1972), 59, 80.
37 Now the Maison de Retraite protestante, 18 quai Montmurat, 82000 Montauban.
38 Il tarde si fort à La Bache de sortir de Sainte Clare.
39 Il tarde si fort à Mariane de Pellet de sortir de Saint Clare qui se meurt d'annuy.
40 Daniel Benoit, *Marie Durand. Prisonnière à la Tour de Constance 1730-1768. Sa famille et ses compagnes de captivité* (Toulouse: Société des Livres Religieux, 1884); Charles Bost, *Les martyrs d'Aigues-Mortes, 1686-1768* (Paris: La Cause, 1922); Anne Danclos, *Marie Durand et les prisonnières d'Aigues-Mortes* (Paris: P.-M. Favre, 1983); Étienne Gamonnet, *Lettres de Marie Durand* (Montpellier: Presses du Languedoc, 1986).
41 Joyce E. Salisbury, *Perpetua's Passion: The Death and Memory of a Young Roman Woman* (New York: Routledge, 1997), 66.
42 Georgia Cosmos, *Huguenot Prophecy and Clandestine Worship in the Eighteenth Century: "The Sacred Theatre of the Cévennes"* (Aldershot: Ashgate, 2005), especially 57–83; W. Gregory Monahan, *Let God Arise. The War and Rebellion of the Camisards* (Oxford: Oxford University Press, 2014), 36–49.

12

CATHOLIC WOMEN IN THE DUTCH GOLDEN AGE

Christine Kooi

Catholic women in the seventeenth-century Dutch Republic lived their lives within at least two constraints: the constraint of gender and the constraint of toleration. To be a woman in any early modern European society was, of course, to exist within the limits imposed by contemporary male constructions of gender. Women were expected by the predominating patriarchal culture to be chaste, pious, honorable, submissive, and largely confined to the domestic sphere.[1] The same patriarchal culture also deemed them to be afflicted by humors that made them quarrelsome, passionate, emotional, and irrational.[2] Because of this, ran the conventional wisdom, women had to be regulated and controlled. These notions, buttressed by cultural authorities such as the Christian churches and classical antiquity, led to laws, customs, and conventions that placed considerable constraints on the ability of women to own property, earn a living, obtain an education, marry a partner of their choice, or engage in public affairs. On the whole, women in the Dutch Republic appear to have enjoyed more personal and economic liberty and mobility than some of their contemporaries in other parts of Europe.[3] Nevertheless, gendered ideologies pertained there as well.

The second constraint, that of toleration, perhaps needs more explanation. Since 1581, the practice of Catholicism had been formally outlawed in the Dutch Republic, that is, it was illegal to celebrate any Catholic sacrament or rite anywhere within the country. This was the outcome of the sixteenth-century reformation and revolt in the Netherlands, which had resulted in the creation of a new Protestant state, the United Provinces or Dutch Republic. In this newly independent republic, all public worship of God could only take place within the Reformed Church, which was the only officially and legally sanctioned confession. At the same time, however, the urban oligarchs who ruled the Republic did not force anyone to join the Reformed or, as it was sometimes called, public church; freedom of conscience was legally guaranteed.[4] Memories of the severities of the harsh Habsburg inquisitorial regime of the sixteenth century may have left the regents of the new state with a reluctance to impose religious coercion. The decentralized, confederate nature of the Republic's polity also ensured that the management of religious affairs would remain in the hands of local authorities. The result was a new state that was at once Calvinist and pluralist, and one challenged with the task of managing confessional difference.[5] Thus, women and men who were Mennonite, Lutheran, or still faithful to the Catholic Church were free to believe as they wished. Women and men alike were at liberty to make their own religious choices or even to choose not to affiliate with any religion at all.[6] They were not, however, free to worship God as they wished. The Reformed Church held a monopoly on public worship. In practice, this meant that any non-Reformed worship had to take place within private spaces away from the public eye, mostly in homes. As long as this private worship did not disturb the common peace or impinge too much on Reformed sensibilities, local authorities mostly turned a blind eye to it, sometimes thanks to the payment of bribes known as "recognition money."[7] Indeed, the enforcement of the anti-Catholic laws, known as the placards, was lax and uneven enough to allow for the development of what became known as the Holland Mission, a network of ambulant priests who served Catholics across the Republic within a private realm of house churches and domestic spaces. In its early decades, when the likelihood of judicial persecution was greatest, the *Missio Hollandica* operated in subterfuge and clandestinity; tales of priests disguising themselves as women to escape law officers were not unheard of.[8] By providing pastoral and sacramental care, the Mission allowed Catholic communities within the Republic not only to survive the new Protestant regime but eventually to flourish within it.[9] Expelled from their churches and deprived of a large portion of their clergy, seventeenth-century Dutch Catholics in effect had to re-invent their confessional communities, and much of this happened through the work and efforts of lay Catholics, including women.[10]

The Dutch Republic's ecclesiastical settlement was, in effect, what the political theorist Michael Walzer has called a regime of toleration.[11] Political authorities tolerated non-Reformed confessions in the barest, most early-modern sense of the word: they were allowed to exist, gather, and worship within strictly observed limits.[12] Toleration is what the "winners" of the Reformation condescended to offer its "losers."[13] As such it could be taken away or altered as the Republic's various local governing bodies saw fit, which made it at best a precarious set of conditions for religious minorities. Dutch Catholics certainly did not see themselves as free Christians and experienced this state of affairs as both limiting and inconsistent. The tolerationist regime was how the Republic managed its highly variegated multiconfessional population. It accommodated religious difference by channeling it into distinct public and private realms.

The Dutch Republic's regime of toleration, however, treated different religious minorities in different ways. Mennonites and Lutherans tended to be seen more as competitors than enemies of the public church. But Catholic women and men, loyal to the old religious order that had been overturned, chafed most under the regime of toleration, for their religion was held in the deepest suspicion by both political and ecclesiastical authorities. The Catholic Church was the very one that Calvinist divines believed they had "re-formed," so the allowance of Catholic worship within a Protestant Republic was a source of continuing frustration to them. The Reformed Church complained, hectored, and lobbied local and provincial governments about the persistence of Catholic "idolatry" and "superstition" throughout most of the seventeenth century.[14] Accompanying this strong religious prejudice was a political one: until 1648, with the Peace of Westphalia, the Dutch Republic was at war with Europe's major Catholic power, the kingdom of Spain. Even if the civic regents who controlled the Republic might have borne little personal or confessional animosity towards Catholicism, the political climate, at least through the first half of the seventeenth century, could make them more inclined to be suspicious of Catholic activities within the population than they otherwise would be. A sharp official eye was always kept on Catholic communities across the Republic, where local law officers were free to enter private homes where they suspected conventicles to be taking place. Of all of the Republic's religious minorities, Catholics would bear the brunt of the Reformed regime most heavily.[15]

The regime of toleration, therefore, left Dutch Catholics, at least in terms of religion, as subaltern, second-class citizens. Hence the constraint of toleration for Catholic women. Not only were the parameters of their lives determined by gender, but they were still further affected by religious allegiance. To remain Catholic in a Protestant Republic meant that one's faith had to be exercised privately, sometimes irregularly, occasionally under threat of legal prosecution, and always under a veil of confessional animosity and political prejudice. As Judith Pollmann has pointed out, organized religion was one of the few venues for institutional sociability for early modern Dutch women, but in the case of the Catholic Church this still had to take place within constraints prescribed by the state.[16] That is, the sociability that their religion afforded to Catholic women in the Republic was still circumscribed by the regime of toleration. At the same time, the Republic's religiously pluralistic population meant that one often encountered neighbors, friends, and even relatives who were of a different religious persuasion. In such a complicated spiritual environment, one that was both Protestant and multiconfessional, Catholic women had to constantly navigate, negotiate, and maneuver in order to follow their religious inclinations.

Since the prevailing gendered ideology largely relegated their role to the domestic sphere, Catholic women, of course, spent much energy and time dealing with the religious dimension of family life, much like their non-Catholic counterparts. The life of Catholic families was inextricably bound up in the sacramental powers of the church—birth, marriage, and death were all milestones sanctified by the church for women and men alike. Catholic doctrine taught that the sacraments were essential to receiving God's grace, and therefore they were important markers in the life of the believer and her family. Sacramental care was provided by the ambulant priests of the Holland Mission; since Catholic worship was officially proscribed, it mostly took place in a private or domesticated sphere within house churches behind closed doors and away from public view. This sphere of family and kin was a world that Catholic women of course knew very well.

Marriage, for example, was one of the most intimate sacramental moments in the lives of Catholic women; indeed, it was arguably the sacrament that created and consecrated their families. Although there was an option for non-Reformed Christians in some of the provinces of the Republic to marry in the town hall before an alderman, the Catholic Church insisted that all marriages among its faithful, even under a Protestant regime, had to be conducted by a priest according to canonical rites. If both spouses were Catholic, this was not an obstacle, but it could present problems for Dutch Catholic women marrying a non-Catholic groom. Because of the heterogeneity of the Republic's religious make-up, mixed or interconfessional marriages were not an unusual occurrence, even though church authorities of all stripes strongly discouraged them.[17] Clergy of all churches had a stake in the maintenance of clear boundaries among the confessions; interfaith marriages muddied those boundaries considerably. The Reformed consistory of Delft, for example, spent years trying to discipline its church member Philips de Cuijper after he married a "papist" who was a "bitter enemy of the Reformed religion" in 1595. Although Philips initially promised the consistory that he would continue to attend Reformed services, by 1598 he was no longer coming to church, told the preachers and elders in no uncertain terms to leave him and his wife alone, and blithely ignored all threats of excommunication.[18] The clerical pressures brought to bear on the Catholic partner in such interfaith marriages could also be considerable. A Franciscan missionary in the town of Gouda, for example, told one Catholic wife in 1650 that she and her Calvinist husband, who had been married in the Reformed Church, needed to be married before him; otherwise they were living in sin, and the Catholic Church would condemn their offspring as "whore's children." In other words, the priest appealed to traditional notions of female sexual honor—the woman would not be considered chaste until she married properly—as a way to bring her to the sacrament. Her husband went so far as to seek the intervention of the local civic authorities to stop the priest's importuning of his increasingly distraught wife.[19] The competition for souls between Reformed and Catholic could occasionally take on such strident tones, including appeals to female honor and chastity.

The spousal relationship, therefore, because of its intimate power, was thought by ecclesiastical authorities, perhaps rightly in some cases, to have great influence over religious loyalty and conviction. A Catholic wife, in the eyes of Reformed preachers, was a potential cause for confessional backsliding. A Reformed Church member named Jan Willemsz in Amsterdam, for example, begged forgiveness in 1615 from the consistory there for having married a Catholic woman and swore that he would not allow her to "seduce" him into popery, a prospect the Reformed authorities clearly found altogether too possible.[20] Alternatively, some Catholic women adopted their spouses' faith in order to keep peace in the marriage. Such conversions may have been sincere, but they could also be expedient.

The widow of a recently deceased Reformed Church member in Dordrecht, for example, informed the dismayed consistory there in 1635 that in her heart she had always been a Catholic, had only attended Reformed services for her husband's sake, and now that he was dead she made it clear that she was returning to her childhood faith.[21] Widowhood had released her from allegiance to a church she had never really accepted. To deliberately choose to attend a church that they believed was wrong in order to keep a husband happy was one of the constraints within which Dutch Catholic women sometimes had to live.

Some Catholic wives did indeed confirm Reformed fears by seeking to convert their spouses. The opportunities for them to defend or even proselytize on behalf of their faith within mixed marriages could sometimes take remarkable forms. For some, the sickbed was a chance to bring their non-Catholic husbands to the faith; in 1668 the Gouda consistory learned that one its members, a skipper named Gabriel, while lying on his sickbed "weak and out of his senses," had been subjected to the pastoral ministrations of a priest called in by his Catholic wife.[22] Another wife was even more successful: an ailing Reformed man in the town of Oudewater asked for a preacher to come to his deathbed; a minister duly appeared, but the man's Catholic wife also brought in a Catholic neighbor who proceeded to argue theology with the preacher at the sickbed. The preacher became so flustered he left the house; thereafter the dying man asked for a priest, renounced his Protestant heresy, and after receiving last rites he died "at peace."[23] Other Catholic wives found even more drastic ways to remain faithful to the old church. During the Twelve Years Truce (1609–1621) that suspended fighting during the war with Spain, it was temporarily possible to cross the southern border into the Spanish Netherlands; in a handful of cases wives opted to move south into a comfortably Catholic land, effectively abandoning their husbands for their church.[24] Other Catholic women took advantage of the mobility allowed by the Truce to persuade their Reformed fiancés to marry them before a priest in the Catholic south.[25] Interfaith marriage, with all its emotional powers and possibilities, provided an arena for some intrepid Catholic women both to remain loyal to their church and to persuade their spouses to change their religious allegiance. It was hardly surprising therefore that Reformed divines looked askance at such confessional mixing and discouraged it as much as possible.

Another sacrament that intimately involved women was baptism, which for both Reformed and Catholic Churches signaled the child's entry into the community of Christ. Catholic practice dictated that this rite take place as soon as possible after birth, but the ambulant nature of the Holland Mission, where clergy were thinly spread out over a wide area, meant that a priest was not always easily or readily available. The Reformed Church, in fact, was willing to baptize all children regardless of confession, but priests often pressured Catholic parents to baptize their children according to the church's own rites. In the case of interfaith marriages, this sometimes meant that the offspring were baptized in different faiths, alternatingly Catholic or Reformed according to the order of birth.[26] Alternatively, a spouse would agree to have all the children baptized in the partner's church. Such complicated arrangements were often necessary for the sake of both marital harmony and confessional conformity.

The pressure from clergy on Catholic mothers to baptize and raise children from mixed marriages within the Catholic church was nevertheless great. Priests taught them that salvation for their offspring could only be received through the proper sacrament, and devout Catholic mothers, fearing for the souls of their infants, used a variety of means to see to it that this happened. Sometimes Catholic wives employed spousal pressure to make sure their children were baptized Catholic. Reformed church member Abram Danielsz of Delft told the Reformed consistory there that he had only acquiesced to his wife's demand that their child be baptized by a priest in order to keep the peace in their marriage.[27] He was certainly not the only husband to do so for the sake of domestic harmony; many such cases of Catholic mothers insisting that their babies be baptized in the old faith can be found in the minutes of Reformed consistories. Again, from the Reformed perspective, this could be a slippery slope. Not only did Reformed church member Gijsbert de Keyser of Leiden allow his wife to have their child be baptized by a priest in 1631, but worse still, in consistorial eyes, he went on to join the Catholic church himself.[28] Within the complicated psychology of the marital relationship, some Catholic women found room to maneuver and even manipulate in order to exercise their confessional loyalty. Sometimes, perhaps more rarely, Catholic wives resorted to subterfuge to have their children receive the proper sacrament: in 1604, for example, an Amsterdam Calvinist's Catholic wife instructed him to go wait at the Reformed church and she would arrange to have their newborn child baptized there. Instead, with the help of another Catholic woman, she had the child spirited away to a priestly baptism.[29] Such were the constraints which the regime of toleration sometimes imposed on faithful Catholic women in the Republic. Within the realm of the family, Catholic women found that the traditional sacramental devotion their faith required had to occur privately, yet at the same time they often found the fulfillment of those religious needs confronted or even hampered by the confessionally pluralist society in which they lived, especially if they were part of an interfaith marriage. Thus, the familial sphere which most Catholic women occupied had to operate within the constraints of toleration, and navigating those constraints often required intrepidity, resourcefulness, and occasional connivance.

There were, however, a few opportunities for Catholic women to exercise or even spread their faith outside the bounds of marriage; one of these was in the realm of public charity. Most Dutch towns had public almshouses, orphanages, and hospitals where, despite Reformed complaints, Catholic women sometimes worked. Within these municipal spaces, they sometimes found occasions to proselytize. One devout Catholic woman from Dordrecht, for example, recalled later in her life that she had first been exposed to Catholic teachings by a housemother in the orphanage in which she was raised.[30] Catholic devotional books were found inside the Haarlem municipal orphanage in 1648; apparently Catholic women had given them out to the children there.[31] Consternation arose among Reformed authorities in Gouda in 1657 when they learned that Catholic regentesses had taken children from the city almshouse to attend Mass in a private home several times.[32] Clearly, Catholic women took advantage of the sometimes lax oversight of magistracies over these public institutions in order to spread Catholic teaching. Reformed consistories complained frequently about this state of affairs but to little avail; magisterial supervision of these institutions remained uneven at best.

For some exceptionally devout Dutch Catholic women there was another option to exercise their faith outside marriage: they could choose to become what were known as "spiritual maidens," colloquially called *kloppen* or *klopjes*. Catholic religious orders had of course been outlawed by the Republic starting in the early 1570s, with religious houses shuttered and former monks and nuns either pensioned off or fleeing to the Catholic south.[33] There were no cloisters or convents under the new Protestant regime. Despite this, some Catholic women opted to live as if they were in a religious order as spiritual maidens, unmarried and devoted to Catholic service and piety. They sometimes lived together in communities, and they did not take vows, yet they lived as if in a religious order; in some respects they were an adaptation of the medieval tradition of beguines. Some 5000 *klopjes* lived in the Republic by the end of the seventeenth century (roughly ten times the number of priests), and they became an instrumental part of the work of the Holland Mission, raising money, bringing in converts, serving priests, visiting the sick, caring for the poor, maintaining worship spaces, and catechizing children.[34]

The spiritual maidens became indispensable to Catholic activity and worship in the Dutch Republic over the course of the Golden Age; the Holland Mission would have not functioned half so effectively or extensively without their labors. They served alongside the priests of the Mission with diligence and devotion. Most of them, though not all, came from Catholic families, and they often used those familial networks to full effect to further the practice of Catholic devotion. As women, they may have been particularly suited to function in the gendered world of domesticity and privacy within which most Dutch Catholic worship took place, moving discreetly within the extended and overlapping networks of neighborhood, family, and household that characterized the Republic's social environment. Given the ambulant nature of the Holland Mission priests' work, they were not always available to Catholic communities, and *klopjes* sometimes stepped in to fill the pastoral gap. In fact, the *klopjes* were a powerful tool in the Holland Mission's efforts both to serve the faithful and win new converts; one Jesuit priest in Leiden would frequently send spiritual maidens out into the surrounding countryside to find potential converts for him to instruct.[35] Indeed, the dedicated lives of chastity and service they lived gave them a kind of elite spiritual status within Catholic communities, and they were widely celebrated and lauded in priestly accounts of the Mission.[36]

The stories of the spiritual maidens' lives, collected and retold for the edification of pious Catholics, are full of examples at how adept they were at serving the church by proselytizing, especially among their kin.[37] One *klopje* in the town of Haarlem named Annetge Claes, for example, won back her mother, who had fallen under the spell of local Reformed preaching. Her mother, stool under her arm, had set out to the Reformed church to hear the sermon; Annetge, with many tears, implored her not to go to the gathering of heretics. Her mother, moved by her daughter's emotional pleadings, threw down the stool and declared she would not set foot in the public church again for the rest of her days. Another Haarlem *klopje* named Elysbeth Hendriks Verwer managed to convert her sister to Catholicism, even though the sister was married to a Reformed church elder, no less. Elysbeth then proceeded, with exceptional missionary heroism, to convert seven of her sister's children, one of whom became a priest and two of whom became *klopjes* themselves.[38] Such stories, all glowingly recounted of course, suggest that the presence of devout Catholic women such as the spiritual maidens within families of mixed confessional allegiance could be potent weapons in the competition for souls.

Spiritual maidens certainly were adept at operating within the private sphere of family, children, and household, a realm that allowed for a fairly generous degree of female agency. Reports of *kloppen* proselytizing within family circles were common, and their zeal raised occasional alarms in Reformed circles. In 1639, for example, a concerned Delft consistory learned that a local *klopje* had spirited away a Reformed church member's son off to Dordrecht to be raised in a Catholic household so that he would be converted to the "papist religion."[39] The Delft consistory alerted its Reformed brethren in Dordrecht, and a deputy sheriff from Delft came to that city to arrest the *klopje*.[40] In a far less coercive fashion, the spiritual maiden Aleida Gerretsz was able to persuade her father to convert to Catholicism with words of "such pious warmth … that all those who heard it were awed."[41] Likewise, an Amsterdam *klopje,* through "godly example and fervent prayer," convinced her Mennonite father to convert back to the Catholicism of his youth.[42] One maiden in Gouda became notorious in Reformed circles in the 1650s for her tendency to bring Reformed children into private homes where the Mass was being celebrated.[43] These kinds of instances occurred frequently across Dutch cities and towns. The private and intimate networks of kinship were a primary means by which the spiritual maidens sought both to exercise and to proselytize their faith.

In particular, the *kloppen* tended to focus their conversion efforts on members of their own sex. Female sociability proved to be a natural arena in which the spiritual maidens could persuade or pressure others about the rightness of the Catholic Church. Reformed consistory records frequently recounted complaints of *kloppen* pestering Calvinist women about their faith. In 1651, for example, *klopjes* in Delft told Margarita Jacobs, a Reformed church member and former nun, that she should return to the "true" church, uttering scandalous imprecations about the public church and even trying to prevent her physically from attending the sermons. Likewise a young woman who had recently converted to the Reformed church in the South-Holland village of Hoogmade in 1657 was openly jeered at by *klopjes* in the streets in order to stop her from attending services.[44] Reformed church member Josijn Carpentiers was admonished by the Gouda consistory in 1646 for allowing herself to be persuaded by an importuning spiritual maiden to attend a local Mass several times.[45] Ten years later, *klopjes* in the same town tried to lure Adriaentje Mosis from the Reformed church to attend Catholic conventicles, offering her financial support in exchange for conversion.[46]

Contemporary male stereotypes about women characterized them as prone to both devotion and superstition, and indeed the reports of Reformed consistories about the *klopjes* depicted these Catholic laywomen as both committed and pernicious. By the 1620s, male Reformed worthies were complaining about them frequently. The provincial synod of South-Holland in 1628 despaired that "the number of *klopjes* … is growing noticeably in various places … to the distress of many godly hearts, the vexation of the weak, the seduction of the simple and the increase of papist impudence."[47] Preachers warned darkly of "swarms" of *kloppen* running amok in the Republic's cities "like a nest of crawling ants."[48] A 1643 report on Catholic activities drafted by the Court of Holland openly conceded the power of these zealous Catholic women: "[they] do more damage to our land and religion than all the priests … among other things they say we Reformed are eternally damned, that all our churches were stolen, that our pulpits stand upon the devil's head … they give money to children to lure them into popery … they cause much unrest, even more than the priests themselves … they easily entice away the confused."[49] The spiritual maidens clearly struck a nerve with Reformed leaders, who saw them as a particularly sinister arm of the broader Catholic conspiracy threatening their Reformed commonwealth, perhaps precisely because of the *klopjes'* sex and anomalous status within the Catholic mission and community. They were women who acted like nuns in a place where nunneries were outlawed. Their conniving influence, especially within confessionally mixed families, was a matter of continual concern to Reformed authorities. Tales of *klopjes* worming their way into the chambers of the sick and the dying to insist on calling in a priest abound in consistorial records. One *klopje* in Delft managed to insinuate herself to the bedside of an ailing church member in 1651, invite in a priest to offer last rites, and even kept the official Reformed sick visitor out of the room while the sacrament was performed.[50] Two *klopjes* in Haarlem were accused of forcing a priest into the sickroom of a church member who was too weak to resist receiving extreme unction.[51] Private schools and lessons given by *klopjes* were also a matter of continuous and annoyed concern among Reformed consistories in towns across the Republic, and time and again preachers and elders lobbied local authorities to outlaw such schools.[52] The religious tasks of *klopjes* could assume a wide variety of forms, many of them domestic, such as sewing altar cloths and vestments for house chapels, baking the communion host, coloring and distributing devotional prints and images, or serving as guards or lookouts outside the spaces where sacraments were being celebrated.[53] These services, which ran from the practical to the spiritual, ensured the continuation of a lively Catholic presence in Dutch society. As women, they were perhaps better prepared to operate unobtrusively in domestic and familial spaces where Catholic worship was relegated. The privatization of Catholicism could sometimes give the spiritual maidens an unexpected advantage in their work.

What we can conclude from the Dutch Republic's religious settlement during the Golden Age is that for pious Catholic women it created both restriction and possibility. New religious arrangements and relationships became necessary. The regime of toleration had established boundaries between the public church and the private confessions. In effect, what the regime had done was to privatize all non-Reformed religions. The public sphere was Reformed while the private sphere was multiconfessional.[54] Catholicism, along with other minority religions, was relegated to a private, though not secret, realm of conscience, household, and family. This was a realm of female sociability, and Catholic women learned to negotiate the often amorphous and sometimes invisible boundaries between public church and private confession in order to exercise their faith. Indeed, the privatization of Catholicism allowed them to live out their faith precisely within the private realms with which they were already quite familiar. This domestication of Catholic worship allowed devout women, whether they were wives and mothers or spiritual maidens, an occasionally greater role to play in the maintenance and flourishing of early modern Dutch Catholicism. Over time, as the Republic's religious settlement grew more and more fixed, they were even quick to assert their rights of conscience when persecuted by the regime. In 1649, for example, an Utrecht Catholic named Grietje Janssen defiantly told the authorities who accused her of hosting a Mass in her home that "each one is free in his belief, also in his private exercise thereof."[55] Clearly, Grietje had gotten used to the privatization of her faith. The regime of toleration's establishment of a permanent private religious sphere over the long term gave rise to an expectation, at least for some, that activities in that sphere would go unmolested. Catholic laity, including dedicated women, understood that their religious liberties were circumscribed, but they nevertheless took an active role in their faith communities within the boundaries of those limitations. In doing so, devout women contributed to the evolution of a distinctive early modern Dutch Catholic identity, which emerged out of a domestic religious sphere, a world with which, as distinguished historians of gender such as Merry Wiesner-Hanks have shown, they were already well familiar and in which they could find agency. Thus, in a curious way, for Catholic women in the Dutch Golden Age the constraint of toleration could be exploited to loosen the constraint of gender.

Notes

1 Merry E. Wiesner-Hanks, *Women and Gender in Early Modern Europe* (Cambridge: Cambridge University Press, 2008), 17–51.
2 Els Kloek, "De vrouw," in *Gestalten van de Gouden Eeuw: een Hollands groepsportret*, ed. H.M. Beliën et al. (Amsterdam: Bert Bakker, 2005), 251.
3 Manon van der Heijden, *Women and Crime in Early Modern Holland* (Leiden: Brill, 2016), 13.

4 Joke Spaans, "Religious Policies in the Seventeenth-Century Dutch Republic," in *Calvinism and Religious Toleration in the Dutch Golden Age,* ed. R. Po-chia Hsia and H.F.K. van Nierop (Cambridge: Cambridge University Press, 2002), 72–86.
5 Jesse Spohnholz, "Confessional Coexistence in the Early Modern Low Countries," in *A Companion to Multiconfessionalism in the Early Modern World,* ed. Thomas Max Safely (Leiden: Brill, 2011), 47–73.
6 Judith Pollmann, "Women and Religion in the Dutch Golden Age," *Dutch Crossing* 24 (2000): 163.
7 Christine Kooi, *Calvinists and Catholics during Holland's Golden Age: Heretics and Idolaters* (Cambridge: Cambridge University Press, 2012), 90–129.
8 J.C. van der Loos, "De kleeding der priesters in het Hollandsche kerkdistrict," *Bijdragen Bisdom Haarlem* 58 (1940): 417.
9 Charles Parker, *Faith on the Margins: Catholics and Catholicism in the Dutch Golden Age* (Cambridge, MA: Harvard University Press, 2008), 24–68.
10 Parker, *Faith on the Margins,* 149–189. On the work of refashioning Dutch Catholic identity, see Carolina Lenarduzzi, *Katholiek in de Republiek: De belevingswereld van een religieuze minderheid 1570–1750* (Nijmegen: Van Tilt, 2019), 91–142.
11 Michael Walzer, *On Toleration* (New Haven, CT: Yale University Press, 1997), 14–36; Christine Kooi, "Religious Toleration," in *Cambridge Companion to the Dutch Golden Age,* eds. Helmer J. Helmers and Geert J. Janssen (Cambridge: Cambridge University Press, 2018), 213–215.
12 Benjamin J. Kaplan, *Divided by Faith: Religious Conflict and the Practice of Toleration in Early Modern Europe* (Cambridge, MA: Harvard University Press, 2007), 8–9.
13 Andrew Pettegree, "The Politics of Toleration in the Free Netherlands, 1572–1620," in *Tolerance and Intolerance in the European Reformation,* eds. Ole P. Grell and Bob Scribner (Cambridge: Cambridge University Press, 1996), 182–198.
14 Christine Kooi, "A Serpent in the Bosom of Our Dear Fatherland: Reformed Reactions to the Holland Mission in the Seventeenth Century," in *The Low Countries as a Crossroads of Religious Beliefs,* eds. Arie-Jan Gelderblom et al. (Leiden: Brill, 2004), 165–176.
15 Lenarduzzi, *Katholiek in de Republiek,* 15–49.
16 Pollmann, "Women and Religion," 173.
17 Parker, *Faith on the Margins,* 59–68.
18 Gemeentearchief Delft, Archief Nederlands-Hervormde Gemeente [hereafter ANHG], Consistorial acts, 26 June 1595, 20 April 1598.
19 Archief Hervormde Gemeente Gouda, Consistorial acts, 24 March 1650.
20 Stadsarchief Amsterdam, ANHG, Consistorial acts, 18 June 1615.
21 Stadsarchief Dordrecht, ANHG, Consistorial acts, 6 October 1615.
22 Archief Hervormde Gemeente Gouda, Consistorial acts, 28 June 1668.
23 R.R. Post, ed., "Zes verslagen over de werkzaamheden door de Jezuieten der Hollandsche Missie verricht," *Archief Aartsbisdom Utrecht* 58 (1934): 26–27.
24 Kooi, *Calvinists and Catholics,* 200; Judith Pollmann, *Catholic Identity and the Revolt of the Netherlands 1520–1635* (Oxford: Oxford University Press, 2011), 189–190.
25 Gemeentearchief Haarlem, ANHG, Consistorial acts, 26 March 1617.
26 Benjamin J. Kaplan, "'For They Will Turn Away Thy Sons': The Practice and Perils of Mixed Marriage in the Dutch Golden Age," in *Piety and Family in Early Modern Europe: Essays in Honor of Steven Ozment,* eds. Marc Forster et al. (Aldershot: Ashgate, 2005), 128.
27 Gemeentearchief Delft, AHNG, Censuurboek, no. 276, f. 117.
28 Archief Hervormde Gemeente Gouda, Consistorial acts, 15 March 1631.
29 Stadsarchief Amsterdam, ANHG, Consistorial acts, 13 May 1604.
30 J.J. Graaff, ed., "Uit de levens der 'Maechden van den Hoeck' te Haarlem," *Bijdragen Bisdom Haarlem* 17 (1891): 275–276.
31 Gemeentearchief Haarlem, ANHG, Consistorial acts, 15 July 1648.

32 Archief Hervormde Gemeente Gouda, Consistorial acts, 3 May 1657.
33 For a vivid example of this phenomenon in the northern town of Alkmaar, see Raymond Fagel and Joke Spaans, *Nonnen verdreven door geuzen: Cathalina del Spiritu Sancto's verhaal over de vlucht van Nederlandse clarissen naar Lissabon* (Hilversum: Verloren, 2019).
34 Marit Monteiro, *Geestelijke maagden: Leven tussen klooster en wereld in Noord-Nederland* (Hilversum: Verloren, 1994), 55.
35 Monteiro, *Geestelijke maagden*, 105.
36 Amanda Pipkin, *Rape in the Republic, 1609–1725: Formulating Dutch Identity* (Leiden: Brill, 2013), 143–145.
37 Joke Spaans, *De Leven der Maechden. Het verhaal van een religieuze vrouwengemeenschap in de eerste helft van de zeventiende eeuw* (Hilversum: Verloren, 2012), 99–117.
38 Catharina Jans Oly, "Leven van 'Maechden van den Hoeck,'" Bibliotheek, Museum Catharinaconvent, no. 92 B 13, vol. 3, f. 358^r.
39 Gemeentearchief Delft, ANHG, Consistorial acts, 19 September 1639.
40 Stadsarchief Dordrecht, ANHG, Consistorial acts, 29 September 1639.
41 Oly, vol. 1, f. 25^v.
42 Spaans, *Leven*, 48.
43 Archief Hervormde Gemeente Gouda, Consistorial acts, 8 March 1657.
44 Nationaal Archief, Oud-Synodaal Archief, Classis Leiden, 6 February 1657.
45 Archief Hervormde Gemeente Gouda, Consistorial acts, 11 October 1646.
46 Archief Hervormde Gemeente Gouda, Consistorial acts, 16 November 1656.
47 W.P.C. Knuttel, ed., *Acta der particuliere synoden van Zuid-Holland 1621–1700* (The Hague: Martinus Nijhoff, 1908), 1:277–278.
48 Samuel Ampzing, *Suppressie vande vermeynde vergaderinge der Jesuwytessen door Urbanus VIII by den gedoge Gods Paus van Romen* (Haarlem: Adriaen Roman, 1622), 3.
49 A. van Lommel, ed., "Bouwstoffen voor de kerkelijke geschiedenis van verschillende parochien thans behoordende tot het bisdom Haarlem," *Bijdragen Bisdom Haarlem* 7 (1880): 353.
50 Gemeentearchief Delft, ANHG, Consistorial acts, 20 August 1651.
51 Gemeentearchief Haarlem, ANHG, Consistorial acts, 4 February 1650.
52 Gemeentearchief Leiden, ANHG, Consistorial acts, 29 November 1659.
53 Spaans, *Leven,* 49–50.
54 On the notion of an early modern public sphere, see most famously Jürgen Habermas, *The Structural Transformation of the Public Sphere* (Cambridge: MIT Press, 1989). Also, Harold Mah, "Phantasies of the Public Sphere: Rethinking the Habermas of Historians," *Journal of Early Modern History* 72 (2000): 158–182.
55 Quoted in Bertrand Forclaz, *Catholiques au défi de la Réforme. La coexistence confessionnelle à Utrecht au XVIIe siècle* (Paris: Honoré Champion, 2014), 135.

13
WOMEN AND RELIGIOUS EXPRESSION IN CALVIN'S GENEVA

Jeffrey R. Watt

This study examines female religious expression in Reformation Geneva with special attention paid to the interaction of women with the Consistory, a type of morals court that was founded and dominated by John Calvin and served as a model for similar disciplinary institutions for Reformed Protestants elsewhere. Though it could not impose secular penalties, the Consistory nonetheless wielded considerable power through its ability to admit or exclude people from taking communion, or as Calvinists preferred to call it, the Holy Supper. This institution also regularly referred miscreants for sentencing to the Small Council, which had exclusive authority to pass judgment on criminal and civil cases in the Republic of Geneva.

The study of consistorial records can provide insight to the types of sins for which women and men were summoned. Throughout Calvin's ministry, men comprised the sizeable majority of those who were convoked by the Consistory. Among the most common reasons for which women and men were subpoenaed were illicit sexuality, domestic discord, and quarrels. The Consistory also summoned a not insignificant number of women and men for religious noncompliance, and one can learn much about popular piety by studying the registers of the Consistory. When the Consistory first started functioning, the registers indicate that women appeared more strongly attached to various forms of Catholic practices than men did. For the years 1542–1544, 137 women, as opposed to 67 men, were convoked for attending mass in neighboring states, saying prayers to the Virgin Mary, fasting for religious reasons, or observing other similar vestiges of "popery." Some of the discrepancies were quite remarkable. In those years, the Consistory convoked 24 women but only 2 men for possessing a rosary or Catholic literature and 23 women and 3 men for celebrating Catholic holidays. The unavoidable impression from the Consistory's earliest extant records is that women remained much more closely tied than men to Roman Catholic practices.[1]

Clearly one practice that resonated particularly among many women was praying to the Virgin Mary. Even years after the conversion to the Reformed faith, many women, especially those living in the surrounding countryside, resisted giving up saying prayers to the Virgin Mary. Jeanne, the wife of Jean Favre, and Claude, the wife of Pierre Voutier, both from the village of Chancy, appeared in August 1560, having been excluded from the Supper in part because of their prayers to the Madonna. In response to a question, Claude proclaimed that the Virgin Mary had been saved by her works and that she herself would likewise be saved by her own works, an opinion that of course would have been anathema to Calvin.[2] The Consistory was equally concerned when in February 1558, Pernette Baud of the village of Peissy reputedly said that a recently deceased woman had appeared to her in a dream and informed her that souls were being detained in purgatory—belief in which was of course rejected by all Protestants—because people were no longer reciting the Ave Maria. Though at first denying the charges, she relented and promised to confess her error to her pastor and to all those she had told about the dream.[3]

Far less docile was Clauda Blanc, summoned by the Consistory because of a conflict with her pastor in March 1562, 11 years after she was first accused of saying Catholic prayers. This latest encounter with the Consistory stemmed from a rebellion during a pastoral visitation. Starting in 1550, the pastors, usually accompanied by a lay official and perhaps by an elder, went to see all parishioners in their homes in the weeks preceding the Supper, especially that of Easter, in order to determine if they were spiritually in the proper frame of mind to take communion. In practice, this meant that they wanted to know if people knew the rudimentary tenets of the faith and were capable of reciting the Lord's Prayer and the Apostles' Creed. In the case at hand, the pastor Nicolas Colladon reported that when he asked Blanc if she still put her trust in the Virgin Mary, she angrily responded that she did indeed because the Virgin was her "advocate to her blessed son." Blanc conceded that she had responded thus in front of several other people, and the Consistory accordingly denied her access to the Supper and referred her to the Small Council, advising that she be sent to jail and obliged to do *réparation*, a public confession of her sin in church.[4] Genevan women were clearly more reluctant than men to give up the veneration of Mary. Although no one in sixteenth-century Geneva offered an explanation for the discrepancy in the numbers of men and women convoked for praying to Mary, we can speculate that many women drew comfort or inspiration from praying to a female figure, which was no longer an option under Protestantism.[5]

The records reveal examples of some grieving women, but no men, who sought solace in certain Catholic practices that were forbidden by Reformed leaders. Early in its existence, in November 1543, the Consistory convoked Tevene Peronet for having made a votive offering for her husband, Marquet, who had been seriously ill and had, in fact, since died. The bereaved widow told Calvin and his colleagues that she now realized that such rituals did no good and she begged mercy from God, the *seigneurie*, and the Company of Pastors. Convinced that she was repentant, the Consistory limited itself to admonitions and gave her two weeks to learn to recite the Lord's Prayer and the confession of faith.[6] In a similar manner, in November 1559, Antoine, the widow of Monet Pernin of the village of Onex, admitted that she said prayers for her late husband. Concluding that she was still a "papist," the Consistory ordered that she return before Christmas to show that she was better instructed.[7] In 1557 Jacquème Villet and her sister, Antoine Ballard, had to appear because they had gone to a riverbank outside of town where the plague hospital and cemetery were located, in order to pray for the deceased on 2 November, the Day of the Dead on the Catholic calendar. The two admitted that they had gone to this location but claimed that they had only said the Lord's Prayer and that they were not kneeling, as Catholics were wont to do, while they prayed. Concluding that the two had made this trip out of "superstition," the Consistory referred them to the Small Council and required them to meet with a pastor before the next Supper to show they had sufficient knowledge of their faith.[8] For these grieving women, prayers and votive offerings for the dead apparently provided some solace. Such examples were rather rare, however, which suggests that most Genevans had accepted the Reformed ban on these practices.

Occasionally the Consistory convoked women for more serious forms of nonconformity which even appeared heretical. An excellent example involved Marie, the widow of the goldsmith Louis de la Pierre, who claimed to receive divine revelations and to have the ability to prophesy. Facing Calvin and his associates in December 1560, Marie freely acknowledged that the Lord regularly answered her prayers and revealed to her everything that she wanted to know. God informed her in advance, for example, about how her husband Louis was going to die. Thus far, her testimony resembled cases of pretense of sanctity heard by the Inquisition in Italy and Spain. Scholars have found that most of those accused of false sanctity, which quite often included apparitions of saints or other visions that were supposedly divinely inspired, were women. Roman Catholic leaders since the later Middle Ages had expressed concern about pretense of holiness and visions, and in the 1520s the Inquisition in Spain started taking action for false sanctity against so-called *beatas*, "semi-religious" women who made informal vows of chastity and poverty without joining convents, many of whom claimed to have divine visions. Italian Inquisitions began prosecuting people, mostly women, for this alleged sin in the 1630s.[9] De la Pierre's testimony took a very odd turn when she further avowed that "the Spirit revealed to her that [John Calvin] was her husband."[10] According to witnesses, she warned Marguerite Gannerel, the wife of Simon Brouet, that she was among the reprobate (*reprouvee*). In spite of or perhaps because of that warning, Gannerel became a close associate of de la Pierre and began to experience similar visions and reputedly declared that the devils were in league with the Genevan ministers. Under interrogation, de la Pierre admitted that she had told others of a dream in which Calvin defecated in her mouth, though she now attributed that dream to an "assault by Satan." The Consistory asked the Small Council to arrest Marie and Marguerite lest they flee.[11] Gannerel was indeed incarcerated, but Marie de la Pierre somehow managed to avoid arrest by moving just outside Genevan territory. The Consistory thereupon advised the Council to release Gannerel with the expectation that upon learning of her release, de la Pierre would return to Geneva and that both could then be seized and questioned about their beliefs.[12]

This strategy apparently worked because the two women were interrogated on 2 January 1561. Gannerel was all too willing to discuss her visions with members of the Consistory. She related that one day while Calvin was preaching, she took a look at the second chapter of Revelation. Suddenly she felt a cold wind that enveloped her face and she found that her New Testament was open even though she had just closed it. Overwhelmed, she approached pastor Theodore Beza to ask what could have caused this, and he said that this was "a vision of Satan," whereupon she closed her book again. Gannerel reported that Marie, at whose abode she often stayed, told her that one day while in Saint-Pierre she saw the devil who was wearing "a cap with ear flaps with a beautiful feather and bouquet" and that the devil was Marie's master because she had abandoned herself to him. She further recalled that de la Pierre described a dream in which Calvin "put his milk in her mouth."[13] When questioned later that day, de la Pierre now insisted that she was not a "prophetess." The Consistory rebutted, however, that she had even claimed she had prayed to God to give her a husband and that He had granted this wish and that Calvin himself was her spouse. She denied making this and other claims, though Beza asserted that she once sought him out and announced that "she knew for a fact that Mister Calvin was her husband."[14] Marie and others avowed that Marguerite had once applied Jesus's words (John 14:6) to herself by saying that she herself was "the way, the truth, and the life." Marguerite confessed that she told others that Satan was living among them in the person of Calvin. For their scandalous and blasphemous bantering, the Consistory sent the two women back to prison and referred them again to the Small Council.[15] For the most part, Marie and Marguerite were not at all reluctant to discuss their visions and even took the initiative to describe them to Beza and others.

Later that day, civil authorities began a criminal investigation of the two, and both of them provided further details, much of which involved putting each other in a very bad light. Marguerite, for example, reported that Marie had proclaimed that Calvin was her husband and that he sometimes came to her at night wearing an overcoat and a hat and sometimes a nightcap with "a beautiful feather and a bouquet attached to it." Gannerel added that Marie confided that she had seen Calvin, her husband, in the pulpit in Saint-Pierre sporting the feather and bouquet in his hat, which would definitely have been a most unusual sight in Reformation Geneva. For her part, Marguerite asserted that Marie, not she herself, had said that all the devils were with the ministers, who devoured the goods (*la substance*) of the poor. When she was then questioned on the same issues, de la Pierre initially denied all accusations, apart from admitting to saying that Gannerel was among the damned because she had done Marie many wrongs. When confronted with Beza, de la Pierre backed down on whether she claimed that Calvin was her husband

and that she could prophesy. In the presence of Marie, Marguerite now admitted that she had claimed that the devils were allied with the ministers and said that this was because Monsieur Regné, who oversaw poor relief, had refused to provide her with any money for sustenance.[16]

Questioned again two days later, Marie de la Pierre admitted that she had prayed to God for the gift of prophecy but tried to shift attention away from herself onto Marguerite. She maintained, for example, that she told Gannerel she was damned only because of her claim to be the way, the truth, and the life. Moreover, Gannerel had related that she sometimes saw the stars, the sun, and the sky beating against and playing with each other above her bed. De la Pierre further averred that about three weeks ago, she encountered Marguerite who was returning from making complaints about Marie to pastor François d'Agnon. On that occasion, Marguerite reputedly told Marie that she must no longer be angry with her for bringing the devil one day and God the next because the devil was definitely allied with the ministers. Immediately after saying this, Marguerite supposedly picked up a Bible and read the following passage from the Book of Revelation: "Then a great and mysterious sight appeared in the sky. There was a woman, whose dress was the sun and who had the moon under her feet and a crown of twelve stars on her head" (Revelation 12:1). Marguerite purportedly explained to Marie: "Behold how I adhere to the word of God; the woman is me, the twelve stars are my children, and the sky is Jesus."[17] Interrogated again on 6 January, Marie referred to a complaint made by both women that the poor were not being treated well in Geneva; she admitted telling Marguerite that Calvin was not like a father because he gave nothing to some people while giving huge quantities of meat (*grosse viande*) to others. De la Pierre added that one day while heading toward the vineyards, Marguerite proclaimed that she saw the heavens opening up, whereupon Marie warned that she must be on guard because this was likely a diabolical illusion, though conceded that the faithful, when suffering persecution for the word of God, sometimes received consolation by seeing the heavens open up. When authorities questioned her three days later, Marie admitted that she had accused Marguerite of praying to Satan as her father. She also admitted telling Beza that Calvin was her husband and confessing to the Consistory that she could prophesy, but now claimed that she was so troubled when she appeared before the pastors and elders that she did not know what she was saying. De la Pierre emphatically denied all the other accusations.[18]

On 17 January 1561, magistrates passed sentence against these two would-be prophets. Marguerite Gannerel was condemned to be whipped in the presence of Marie de la Pierre. For her scandalous words, including her declaration that Calvin was her husband, de la Pierre was considered the guiltier of the two and was sentenced to be banished under pain of the whip.[19] The sentence did not specify how long this banishment was to last, but already on 6 February 1561, just three weeks after the verdict, the Council asked the Consistory for its opinion concerning de la Pierre's request to be allowed to return to Geneva. Calvin and the other members recommended that she stay away from Geneva a bit longer in light of the gravity of her offense and because she had been banished only quite recently.[20] In early April, however, the Consistory advised the Small Council to readmit de la Pierre, who appeared fully repentant for her "errors" and begged forgiveness from God and *Messieurs* of the Small Council; members the Consistory did warn her that she would be punished more severely if she fell back into her errors.[21] When Marie de la Pierre petitioned on 22 May 1561 to be readmitted to the Supper, the Consistory determined that she was truly repentant and granted her request.[22] In light of her claims of receiving divine revelations, her bizarre dreams, and her assertion that Calvin was her husband, the Consistory was surprisingly lenient, lifting her exclusion from the Supper less than five months after her expulsion. The key to this clemency was de la Pierre's admission of guilt and her repentance. Calvin and his colleagues routinely readmitted to communion those who were genuinely sorry for having strayed from the straight and narrow Reformed path.

Notwithstanding her renunciation of her previous ideas, Marie de la Pierre would again show an unusual interest in Calvin shortly after her return to Geneva. In July of 1561, she was arrested for having gone to Calvin's home in order to tell the reformer that she wanted to be either his wife or his chambermaid. Rebuffing her efforts to put her arms around him, the reformer bade Marie to follow him and proceeded to lead her to city hall to have her put under arrest. This time when questioned, de la Pierre freely described her first divine vision, which she claimed had taken place in September 1557. She asserted that the Lord showed Himself to her in all His glory and that she heard a voice enjoining her to pray for the faithful and that she "must pray with her brother, John Calvin." The voice told her further that she was being prepared for a mission, and the next day she discovered that she had received the "mark of the children of God so that her duty was to pray to God according to the doctrine of John Calvin." Marie added that she drew inspiration to announce the word of God not from men but directly from God, who spoke through her mouth, leaving her at times unable to eat or drink. Her direct spiritual union with God sometimes left her "surprised by joy" (*surprise de joye*), but she also experienced the torments of the devil who presented her with a "horrible vision," a vision from which God released her, however. For her scandalous words, Marie de la Pierre was to be whipped and then banished for the second time, with the threat of another whipping should she return.[23]

The experiences and treatment of de la Pierre and Gannerel can be viewed as both positive and negative for women as a whole. These women were not only literate but also had an impressive knowledge of scripture, though their interpretations of certain passages were unusual, to put it mildly. The two of them could easily have been accused of witchcraft, especially given their numerous references to the devil or devils. In particular, Marie de la Pierre's bizarre claims that Calvin was her husband or the devil might have resulted in her being tried and perhaps convicted and executed for witchcraft in other jurisdictions.[24] For their reputed visions, both de la Pierre and Gannerel might have been suspected of being possessed by demons. Alternatively, they might have been aggressively investigated for pretense of sanctity in Italy or Spain. Whenever a person reputedly experienced mystical visions, the Inquisitions virtually always raised the concern that the vision might be of diabolical rather than divine origin. The fact that Marie de la Pierre was readmitted to communion in Geneva just five months after being banished shows Calvin and the Consistory's strong interest in reintegrating into the community people who had gone astray.

Be that as it may, it must be noted that this lenience came at a price. Neither de la Pierre nor Gannerel was taken seriously by members of the Consistory. By contrast, in rare instances women called before the Inquisitions were able to persuade their interrogators that they had indeed received divine visions. Inquisitors' probing questions sometimes allowed female suspects to expound at length about their religious beliefs or practices, thereby serving as a means of hearing the voices of some early modern women. Teresa of Avila, for example, effectively used the Inquisition as a forum to defend her spirituality and female independence and eventually became a very significant actor in the Reformation. While inquisitions sought religious uniformity in word, deed, and thought, consistories were most concerned with the actions and practices of the laity and generally refrained from trying to probe their inner beliefs. Although consistories might convoke someone who, for example, openly rejected predestination, people who appeared were often asked to recite the Lord's Prayer and the credo but were virtually never subjected to lengthy interrogations concerning theological or spiritual non-conformity. In Geneva, as in all Reformed areas, women had no hope of ever being revered as mystics or even of pursuing a religious calling if they felt so inclined. Both de la Pierre and Gannerel were essentially laughed at and considered crazy. Indeed on the same day that both women admitted saying that Satan was in their midst in the form of Calvin, following the advice of the Consistory, authorities ordered that the two be returned to prison to be prosecuted as the Council deemed prudent since there were "many illusions in their brains."[25] Some of their claims, such as de la Pierre's dream that Calvin had defecated in her mouth, might seem to justify questioning their mental stability, and to be sure, for every Catholic woman, such as Teresa of Avila, who became widely revered, there were countless would-be mystics who were rejected, rebuked, and silenced by the Inquisitions. Nonetheless, Genevan authorities' casual dismissal of these women's "illusions" can be viewed as a mixed blessing.

It must further be noted that the registers of the Consistory provide more examples of women who conformed, often even enthusiastically, to Reformed mores than those who actively resisted them. Women, for example, generally appeared more interested than men in being readmitted to the Supper. In her work on Dutch Reformed churches, Judith Pollman found that being permitted to participate in the Supper affirmed a woman's moral good standing in the community. Dutch women were accordingly much more willing than men to submit to the discipline of the consistories; doing so amounted to restoration of their honor.[26] Similar attitudes may help explain why Genevan women seemed more willing to ask to be readmitted to communion than men did. Moreover, one can find many examples of women who were much more devout than their husbands. In June 1559, the baker Guillaume Rens and his wife, Philippa, were convoked for their domestic quarrels and insults. Guillaume was clearly more culpable than Philippa, whom he constantly berated and insulted. Many witnesses affirmed that Guillaume had told Philippa to go hang herself and regularly called her a "whore." Testimony further revealed that while Guillaume was chronically absent from the sermons, Philippa faithfully attended them, a habit that angered her husband. Apparently Philippa tried to recount to her husband the sermons she had heard, which provoked her husband to tell her derisively that she should go take the place of "Mister Colladon," a supposed reference to pastor Nicolas Colladon. When questioned by Calvin and his colleagues, however, Guillaume admitted having that conversation but insisted, not very convincingly, that he was referring to the attorney Germain Colladon, a cousin to the minister and close friend of Calvin, because his wife was acting as if she was arguing a case (*advocassoyt*) with him. Witnesses also indicated that Philippa recited Scripture to her husband when trying to persuade him to treat her better.[27]

Quite interesting was the probe into the actions of Jacquème Egipte in May 1557. When an unnamed woman questioned her about her faith and asked if she knew why God had created her, Egipte admitted that she crudely replied, "Eat shit" (*Mache merde*). Egipte regretted saying these words and now asked for mercy from God and the *seigneurie*. The Consistory referred her to the Council, which sentenced the repentant Egipte to one day in jail.[28] Significantly, the entry in the registers concerning Egipte comes right after inquiries about two other women who had shown disrespect toward pastors when they conducted visitations just before Easter. As noted above, the visitation involved a pastor and a lay official going to all the homes in each district to question everyone about their knowledge of the faith and their state of mind. Appearing where it does in the minutes, Egipte's case might mean that the unidentified woman was herself actively participating in the visitation alongside the pastor or perhaps that she took it upon herself to tutor Egipte (whether she wanted this assistance or not) in preparation for the upcoming pastoral visit. What is beyond dispute is that she wholeheartedly embraced the Reformed faith.

There were actually precedents for women openly proselytizing in Geneva to other women with the approval of reformers and secular authorities. In August 1535, Claudine Levet, married to an apothecary, entered the convent of the Poor Clares accompanied by several "prominent people." Writing years after the encounter, Jeanne de Jussie, the future abbess of that community, referred to Levet as "that devilish-tongued woman," who immediately began to preach to the nuns. To the nuns' horror, Levet cited numerous scriptural passages to praise matrimony and decry the state of virginity. According to de Jussie, when the vicaress asked that "this fool" be taken away, the men present defended Levet, proclaiming, "she is a holy creature enlightened by God and her holy sermons and divine teaching bear great fruit and convert poor, unenlightened people; she works very hard to save souls, and she would like for you to be among them."[29] De Jussie described similar efforts by another woman, Marie Dentière, a former nun from Flanders.

Married to the pastor Antoine Froment, Dentière resided in Geneva from 1535 until her death in 1561. In the same month that Levet visited the convent, Dentière, accompanied by the theologians Guillaume Farel and Pierre Viret, entered the convent to exhort the nuns to leave the monastic life and to reject celibacy. De Jussie complained about this false "nun ... named Marie Dentière ..., who meddled in preaching and in perverting pious people."[30]

Dentière also had the distinction of being the only woman to publish a work on theology in Reformation Geneva. In 1539, she wrote *A Very Useful Epistle*, dedicated to Marguerite of Navarre, sister of King Francis I of France, and this publication represented "the first explicit statement of reformed theology by a woman to appear in French."[31] Writing the *Epistle* after Calvin and Farel had been expelled from Geneva because of their rigid stand on discipline, the author, identified as "a Christian woman of Tournai" (Dentière's hometown), aggressively criticized Geneva's magistrates and pastors for their treatment of these reformers. She proclaimed to Marguerite, "though we are not permitted to preach in congregations and churches, we [women] are not forbidden to write and admonish one another in all charity .... I wish to write this letter ... to give courage to other women[,] ... principally for the poor little women [*femmelettes*] wanting to know and understand the truth, ... which is the Gospel of Jesus Christ."[32] Natalie Zemon Davis has aptly described Dentière's claim to want to teach the Gospel only to other women as "modest fiction."[33] Referring to numerous key female figures in the Bible, the ex-nun defended her right to expound on Scripture:

> Some might be upset because this is said by a woman, believing that this is not appropriate since woman is made for pleasure. But I pray you to be not offended .... I do this only to edify my neighbor, seeing him in such great, horrible darkness, more palpable than the darkness of Egypt. Nevertheless, if it please you to consult and diligently examine the texts cited here ..., comparing them to holy scripture, with good judgment, you will find even more than what I say here.[34]

Geneva's religious and political leaders clearly condoned the aggressive efforts of Dentière and Levet to convince the Poor Clares to leave the convent. At that very early phase of the Genevan Reformation, leaders were apparently quite willing to have women proselytize, at least to female religious. Moreover, Calvin no doubt appreciated Dentière's criticism of the Genevan leaders who were responsible for his expulsion.

That said, once the Reformed faith was well established in Geneva, Calvin clearly did not support an active role for women in the propagation of the faith and definitely disapproved of them proselytizing in public. In a letter to Farel, Calvin recounted a contentious encounter with Dentière in 1546. He told his fellow reformer, "I'm going to tell you a funny story, Froment's wife came here recently; in all the taverns, at almost all the street corners, she began to harangue against long garments." Laughing, she told Calvin himself that he and his fellow pastors "were dressed indecently, with great offense to the church," asserting that "false prophets could be recognized by their long garments," a reference to the scribes in Luke 20:45 "who want to walk about in long robes." According to Calvin, she "complained about our tyranny, that it was no longer permitted for just anyone to chatter on about anything at all. I treated the woman as I should have."[35] With this dismissive attitude, Calvin showed that while he and Jeanne de Jussie had virtually nothing in common, they agreed that by unabashedly speaking and preaching in public spaces, Dentière was not conforming to the norms imposed on her sex by contemporary society.[36]

All told, the evidence from Geneva on female religious expression is mixed. On the one hand, it is clear that women in Geneva were more reluctant than men to give up certain Catholic traditions such as saying prayers to the Virgin Mary; clearly many women regretted no longer being able to pray to a female figure. Some women resisted, either actively or passively, the efforts of the pastors and the Consistory to effect change in piety among Genevans. The Consistory of Geneva most certainly cannot be said to have championed the rights of women, but Calvin and other authorities did not appear overly concerned with female non-compliance. Moreover, their sexist attitudes—thanks to which they expected less from and were less threatened by female non-conformists—could result in more lenient treatment for women than men for the same infractions. Moreover, although Calvin and other authorities did not approve of women proselytizing in the streets of Geneva, the records of the Consistory provide evidence that many women strongly embraced the Reformed faith. The numerous requests to be readmitted to the Supper indicate that the large majority of women (and men) wanted to comply with Reformed mores.

This brief analysis is, in a modest way, testimony to the impact that Merry Wiesner-Hanks has had on many scholars of early modern Europe over the past few decades. Mentor, colleague, and friend to so many of us, she is especially esteemed for championing gender as a category of analysis in a wide range of historical research. For this particular contribution, I have drawn special inspiration from her provocative thoughts on the Reformation of the women—both the efforts of male authorities to reform women and the contributions of women to sixteenth-century religious movements.[37] I have fond memories of meeting Wiesner-Hanks when, fresh out of graduate school in 1987, I attended the Sixteenth Century Studies Conference for the first time. There, my very first experience at a scholarly conference involved participating in a lively roundtable discussion, deftly led by Merry Wiesner-Hanks, precisely on the subject of gender as a category of historical analysis. In the three decades plus that have passed since that moment, I have gotten to know Merry well and have the highest regard for her scholarship. My colleagues and I never cease to be in awe of her work and deeply appreciate her generosity in sharing ideas and offering encouragement to those of us who are less prolific than she is. All of us who are interested in the history of the Reformation are indebted to Wiesner-Hanks for encouraging us to consider the links between changes in religion, on the one hand, and in concepts of masculinity and femininity, on the other.

Notes

1 Jeffrey R. Watt, "Women and the Consistory in Calvin's Geneva," *Sixteenth Century Journal* 24 (1993): 433.
2 Archives d'Etat de Genève (hereafter AEG), Registres du Consistoire (hereafter R.Consist.) 17: 139^v. She remained suspended from the Supper until she was better instructed in religion.
3 AEG, R.Consist. 13: 7^r.
4 AEG, R.Consist. 19: 24^r. She had previously been accused of saying prayers to the Virgin Mary and for the dead in February 1551; *Registres du Consistoire de Genève au temps de Calvin*, 11 vols., ed. Isabella M. Watt et alii (hereafter *R.Consist.*; Geneva: Droz, 1996–2017), 5: 325.
5 Interestingly, there is no record in Calvin's Geneva of prayers being made to female saints.
6 *R.Consist.* 1: 277-8.
7 AEG, R.Consist. 16: 209^r.
8 AEG, R.Consist. 12: 124^r. For having prayed for the deceased, the Small Council gave them "grandes remonstrances"; Registres du Conseil (hereafter RC) 53: 446^r (6 December 1557).
9 Among the large number of publications on female mystics in Spain, be they "true" or "false," see Gillian T.W. Ahlgren, *Teresa of Avila and the Politics of Sanctity* (Ithaca: Cornell University Press, 1996); Alastair Hamilton, *Heresy and Mysticism in Sixteenth-Century Spain: The Alumbrados* (Toronto: University of Toronto Press, 1992); Richard Kagan, *Lucrecia's Dreams: Politics and Prophecy in Sixteenth-Century Spain* (Berkeley: University of California Press, 1990); Ronald E. Surtz, *The Guitar of God: Gender, Power, and Authority in the Visionary World of Mother Juana de la Cruz (1481–1534)* (Philadelphia: University of Pennsylvania Press, 1990). For cases of pretense of sanctity heard by the Roman Inquisition, see Anne Jacobson Schutte, *Aspiring Saints: Pretense of Holiness, Inquisition, and Gender in the Republic of Venice, 1618–1750* (Baltimore: Johns Hopkins University Press, 2001); Adelisa Malena, *L'Eresia dei perfetti: Inquisizione romana ed esperienze mistiche nel seicento italiano* (Rome: Edizioni di Storia e Letteratura, 2003); and various essays in Gabriella Zarri, ed., *Finzione e santità: Tra medioevo ed età moderna* (Turin: Rosenberg & Sellier, 1991).
10 AEG, R.Consist. 17: 193^v.
11 AEG, R.Consist. 17: 193^r-194^r.
12 AEG, R.Consist. 17: 204^r.
13 AEG, R.Consist. 17: 204^v.
14 AEG, R.Consist. 17: 205^r.
15 AEG, R.Consist. 17: 205^r-206^r.
16 AEG, Procès Criminels (hereafter PC) 2e Série 1222.
17 AEG, PC 2e Série 1222.
18 AEG PC 2e Série 1222.
19 AEG PC 2e Série 1222.
20 AEG, R.Consist. 17: 219^v.
21 AEG, R.Consist. 18: 27^r, 32^r.
22 AEG, R.Consist. 18: 55^r.
23 AEG PC 2e Série 1222.
24 As has been shown elsewhere, Calvin and the Consistory demonstrated an unusual degree of skepticism when considering accusations of witchcraft; Jeffrey R. Watt, "Calvin's Geneva Confronts Magic and Witchcraft: The Evidence from the Consistory," *Journal of Early Modern History* 17 (2013): 229-32. Moreover, William Monter found that Geneva's execution rate was exceptionally low and that the most intense hunts were associated with the reputed spreading of the plague; *Witchcraft in France and Switzerland: The Borderlands during the Reformation* (Ithaca: Cornell University Press, 1976), 45–49.

25 AEG, PC 2ᶜ Série 1222.
26 Judith Pollman, "Honor, Gender and Discipline in Dutch Reformed Churches," in *"Dire l'interdit": The Vocabulary of Censure and Exclusion in the Early Modern Reformed Tradition*, ed. Raymond A. Mentzer, Françoise Moreil, and Philippe Chareyre (Leiden: Brill, 2010), 29–42.
27 AEG, R.Consist. 15: 115ᵛ-116ᵛ.
28 AEG, R.Consist. 12: 42ʳ; RC 53: 129ʳ (10 May 1557).
29 Jeanne de Jussie, *The Short Chronicle: A Poor Clare's Account of the Reformation of Geneva*, ed. and trans. Carrie F. Klaus (Chicago: University of Chicago Press, 2006), 159-60.
30 De Jussie, *Short Chronicle*, ed. and trans. Carrie F. Klaus, 151–152.
31 Mary B. McKinley, Introduction to Marie Dentière, *Epistle to Marguerite de Navarre and Preface to a Sermon by John Calvin*, ed. and trans. Mary B. McKinley (Chicago: University of Chicago Press, 2004), 2.
32 Dentière, *Epistle*, ed. and trans. McKinley, 53.
33 Natalie Zemon Davis, "City Women and Religious Change," in *Society and Culture in Early Modern France* (Stanford: Stanford University Press, 1975), 82–83.
34 Dentière, *Epistle*, ed. and tr. McKinley, 76-7.
35 McKinley, Introduction to Dentière, *Epistle*, 19; citing *Ioannis Calvini Opera Quae Supersunt Omnia*, ed. Gulielmus Baum, Eduardus Cunitz, Eduardus Reuss (Brunswick, 1874), 12, cols. 377–378, Epistle, 824.
36 By contrast, in her preface to a sermon by Calvin in 1561, the ex-nun insisted upon the need for women to dress "with modesty and sobriety"; Dentière, *Epistle*, 91–94. For more on Dentière, see Irena Backus, "Marie Dentière: un cas de féminisme théologique à l'époque de la Réforme," *Bulletin de la Société de l'Histoire du Protestantisme Français* 137 (1991): 177-95; Isabelle Graesslé, "Vie et legends de Marie Dentières," *Bulletin du Centre Protestant d'Etudes* 55 (2003): 3–31; Cynthia Skenazi, "Marie Dentière et la prédication des femmes," *Renaissance and Reformation* 21 (1997): 5–18.
37 Merry E. Wiesner, "The Reformation of the Women," in *Gender, State, and Church in Early Modern Germany: Essays by Merry E. Wiesner* (London and New York: Longman, 1998), 63–78.

PART III
Gendered dynamics of displacement, migration, and conflict

14

WOMEN, GENDER, AND RELIGIOUS REFUGEES

Nicholas Terpstra

Sometimes the simplest questions are the most profound. With her earliest books and articles from the 1980s, Merry Wiesner-Hanks demonstrated that our view of an established field of inquiry like religious reform or of a period like the Reformation changes radically when we start to ask what difference gender made. When much of historiography took male experience as the default, the deceptively simple question of how women experienced reformation and *the* Reformation brought out fundamentally distinct interpretations of what particular actions like the elimination of convents, of saints' cults, or of purifying sacramental rituals meant for the broad mass of people. The questions continue. The Reformation witnessed a dramatic growth in the numbers of religious refugees of all creeds, and yet we have only begun to ask what difference gender made to the experience of expulsion, exile, and forced migration among Christians, Jews, and Muslims. One critical factor behind the exponential growth in the number of refugees over the course of the sixteenth and seventeenth centuries was the shift from exiling men alone to exiling women as well and by extension, exiling whole families. What lay behind this shift, and how did it shape familial and institutional structures within exile communities?[1]

In the case of research on refugees in the Reformation, asking about gender immediately underscores why this period marked a distinct turning point in attitude and approaches. The term *refugee* itself emerged far later in the context of Huguenots fleeing France after the revocation of the Edict of Nantes in 1685 and it spread more broadly only in the eighteenth century. The linguistic gap does not erase the phenomenon, but it does suggest that Europeans struggled for models for how to understand the practice and meaning of flight. Gender made a difference to that emerging conceptualization. Before the sixteenth century it was generally men who were expelled or banished while women remained to, quite literally, guard the home. It is when and as we see women being expelled, too, that we witness the very nature of community and of exile or exclusion shifting. This came as a greater shock to some of Europe's populations than to others. As this happened, we can see that within exile communities themselves, the role of women as preservers of communal religious identity within spaces of refuge became far more important, to the point where we might think of a household-based "cultural confessionalism" as reinforcing and perhaps even exceeding anything based on catechisms, creeds, and state power.[2]

The conventional model of the Reformation religious exile or refugee, passed down from the nineteenth and early twentieth centuries, was of the male intellectual fleeing for reasons of conscience. Michael Servetus, Giordano Bruno, Peter Martyr Vermigli, Sebastian Castellio, Sebastian Franck, Reginald Pole, David Joris, Lellio and Fausto Socino, Juan Luis Vives—the conventional list is both the product and source of a particularly individualist and masculine view of what the Reformation was; these were *minds* on the move in every way. The problem is a broader one within migration studies regardless of time and space—Raingard Esser notes that "the dominant image of a migrant in history is still male, young, and unconnected."[3]

The particular cast this gets in Reformation historiography of the past two centuries traces back to the largely biographical approach that emphasized theological ideas and those courageous men who had them.[4] In approaches ranging from Hegel's World Spirit to Carlyle's Great Men and spread more broadly by evangelical revivals across European Protestant denominations in the first half of the nineteenth century, reformers' intellectual courage was honed against the stone of ecclesiastical, and particularly Catholic, oppression. Historians who dealt more explicitly with exiles and refugees, like Roland Bainton, George H. Williams, and Delio Cantimori carried the torch of liberal modernity forward into the twentieth century with studies of tolerance and intolerance in the Reformation that emphasized the high cost of individual conscience. All gave prominence to refugees and exiles, above all from among Radicals and Anabaptists, and all wrote out of a deep and often personal connection to the people, the groups, or the ideas under study.[5] Cantimori's histories of Italian Protestantism, many written during the Fascist era, were largely a history of exiles and refugees being chased over the Alps by the Inquisition. While he began writing in the 1930s as a young advocate of the anti-clerical wing of fascism, by the end of the decade he had taken out membership in the Communist party.[6] George Williams, the son of a Unitarian minister who himself trained and taught in Unitarian schools, tracked radicals, spiritualists, and anti-Trinitarians across Europe and demonstrated an extraordinary determination to trace and categorize the fine differences between them.[7] Most of Cantimori's and Williams's subjects were men, and most were either explicitly single—because they were Catholic clerics—or implicitly single simply because little was known or said about their spouses. Their wives and families did not figure prominently as agents in the narrative and often were not even mentioned. Roland Bainton's effort to correct this with his three-volume series of biographies of *Women of the Reformation*

Women, gender, and religious refugees   **177**

published in the 1970s actually underscored the emphasis on heroic men, since many of the women he wrote about were the wives or mothers of male reformers—handmaids, helpmeets, and collateral damage.[8] That said, it is worth noting that Bainton believed that the Reformation's effect on family life was more profound than its effect on economics or politics.[9]

One early model for understanding the gendered nature of early modern exile came out of parallels to political exile from fifteenth-century cities and states. The usual practice of exile from Italian communes and republics, where it was perhaps most widespread and frequent, was that the males of a family were formally banned and sent out of the city while the females remained behind. This reflected the conviction that since the real threat posed by a banned family was political, then it was the family's political agents—that is, its males—who had to be removed from the urban polity and its governing assemblies.[10] One of the best-known examples was the Strozzi of Florence, who were critical agents behind the exile of Cosimo de Medici in 1433. On his return to Florence and to power in 1434, Cosimo and his allies sent hundreds of enemies into exile in order to secure their own grip on power. We know the most about the situation of the Strozzi because of the extensive correspondence of the family's matriarch, Alessandra Macinghi Strozzi.[11] Alessandra accompanied her husband into exile but returned to Florence after his death a year later in order to maintain the family's business and social interests there. For three decades, Alessandra worked through male legal guardians, including a son-in-law Marco Parenti, and through letters to her surviving sons in Naples in order to conserve and expand properties, arrange marriages, and convey political information and advice. This model of exile assumed that the male head of household would return and empowered the female spouse to preserve the family's interests during his temporary absence.

This model of political exile merges in traditional narratives with that of the wandering scholar, a male individual who is often treated as unmarried even when he has a spouse. The Iberian humanist Juan Luis Vives (1493–1540) moved to Paris for university studies at age 16 and then settled in a series of Flemish towns. A friend of Erasmus and Thomas More, he first traveled to England in 1523 but married a Bruges *conversa* Margarita Valdaura a year later and then shuttled back and forth six times to England until he was imprisoned and then exiled in 1528 for his support of Catherine of Aragon. While in England, he lived as a *de facto* bachelor at Corpus Christi College in Oxford. After being exiled from England, he resisted numerous appeals through the 1530s to take up a prestigious professorship at Alcalá, where he could have ended up teaching Ignatius Loyola. He refused because he knew that Spain simply was not safe for him as a *converso*, both of whose parents had been burned as Judaizing heretics. His father was burned in 1524, the year that Vives married. His mother's bones were dug up and burned posthumously four years later, the year he was expelled from England. Vives's parents had converted the year he was born, which was just a year after the expulsion of the Jews from Spain. With religious persecution marking so many key steps in Vives's life cycle, it is legitimate to think of this Catholic *converso* as an exile and a refugee *avant le letter*. More to the point, given his various identities as an Iberian humanist scholar of Jewish origin in a time of roiling social and religious ferment, he also marks a shift in the *nature* of the religious refugee. Not permanently on the road, but permanently on guard.

The new reality of religious exile in the early sixteenth century was that there were no non-combatants. In particular, the earlier model of political exile whereby women remained at home while men left the city became more difficult after the events in Münster during the religious reforms of the 1530s.[12] The early stages of Münster's reform followed a familiar model whereby evangelicals and guildsmen took charge of the city council in early 1532, helped by the preaching of the Luther-inspired Bernhard Rothmann. They eased out the Catholic bishop by a treaty of 14 February 1533 that owed a great deal to Philipp of Hesse's mediation. Rothmann's preaching became more radical over the course of that summer, and he came out against infant baptism by the fall of 1533. Within a few months, in January 1534, Rothman and 1400 other citizens—including the nuns of one of the city's convents—were rebaptized and took to wearing distinct clothing and publicly exchanging the kiss of peace. Apocalyptic expectations were high and events moved quickly as Dutch and German Anabaptists—many themselves refugees—began moving to this New Jerusalem, led by charismatic figures like the Harlem baker Jan Matthijs. As the bishop gathered troops, and as new elections of February 1534 entrenched a radical mayor and councilors, a large number of males began leaving town. This familiar pattern of self-protection gained additional urgency as believer's baptism became a test of civic belonging on the level of the former civic oath, and Jan Matthijs pushed for expulsion and even elimination of any who refused.

By the end of February 1534, roughly 2000 Münster Catholic and Lutheran males had followed the familiar pattern of exiting the town and leaving their spouses in charge of property, goods, and affairs. This traditional step was even more rational in the local context, since women in Münster already had unusually extensive property and legal rights. Yet it proved to be a critical miscalculation. Ongoing exits and arrivals through the winter of 1533–1534 skewed Münster's demographics and the city ended up with about 1500–2000 Anabaptist men and perhaps 6000–8000 women, many of them poor, single, working women. The city council's move to confiscate the properties of ecclesiastical institutions and institute a community of goods to help feed this flood of immigrants and local indigents was not out of keeping with conventions. Yet taking the possessions of married males who had temporarily abandoned the city was a property grab that entailed a serious curtailing of their spouses' rights, and indeed of women's legal rights generally. The move to polygamy a few months later in July 1534 triggered even sharper local opposition as a fundamental challenge to traditional understandings of blood, marital, and social kinship.[13] In the immediate showdown with Matthijs's successor, the tailor Jan of Leiden, 200 Münster men were killed and many women imprisoned. The greater slaughter came with the end of the eighteen-month-long Munster experiment when it was betrayed and seized in June 1535.

The Münster experiment horrified many across the confessions, and we should think of it as a cautionary tale for later refugees. The Münster men's departure from 1533 was the immediate social fact that opened the way for the reform regime to then declare their marriages invalid and the Münster women eligible for polygamous re-marriage. It was that enforced polygamy and the complete overturning of social and household norms that later propagandists put at the heart of their accounts of the Münster horror, with many opponents making much of the fact that at least some Radicals remained open to polygamy in theory for the next century or more.[14] As Ronnie Hsia notes, advocates saw it as "creating a fictive tribe, a chosen people, the 'New Israel,' a holy nation for a sacred city. It was the means by which the new social order was literally to be created ... comprehensive, not exclusive; communal, not private; sacred, not profane; eternal, not ephemeral; harmonious, not divisive; spiritual, not material."[15] Moreover, urban physical space was to be as open and shared as sexual space in a more fundamental rejection of privacy and intimacy—the Moravian radical communities built around *bruderhofen* certainly underscored this. Over a century later, English Anglicans would tar Baptists with the charge of sexual license on the basis of their presumed link to the Münster Anabaptists radicals.[16] Sexual deviance got all the rhetorical attention, but it was the dual threat of sexual and property expropriation obliterating lineages entirely in pursuit of holy republics that made artisanal, professional, and patrician refugees rethink their exit strategies. It is not coincidental that when we find mass movements of religious refugees developing in the decades that followed the collapse of the Münster experiment, it was more often whole families who hit the road and relocated to Geneva, Emden, Strasburg, Amsterdam, Norwich, or London. Geert Janssen has found that the traditional political model of a man leaving the city while his wife remained in charge of property and affairs until he returned still held for some Dutch Catholics in the 1570s and 1580s, but for many others that model was no longer reliably *safe*, even if the regime doing the expelling was not overtly millenarian or apocalyptic.[17]

A convergence of factors challenged the traditional political model, and Münster's example was just one of them. The larger reality was that definitions of religious community, of identity, and of purity were also shifting, and so too were responses to difference and dissent. This is why I believe that the example of the expulsion of the Jews from Iberia in the 1490s marks the beginning of a new era in which the religious refugee becomes a mass phenomenon and why I see Vives as an exemplary transitional example of the new religious refugee within Christendom. It is also why we need to look at the role of women in particular in order to fully understand the early modern refugee experience.

What the religious refugees to Geneva, Emden, and Strasbourg were experiencing was in fact nothing new. It was simply the transfer to Christians of what had been the Jewish experience of religious exile since at least the expulsion of 4000 Jews from England in 1290, and indeed since long before that. When Jewish communities were expelled from towns across France and Germany in the fifteenth century, or from Iberia in the 1490s, they did not have the option of leaving women behind to guard property and interests while men left the city. Cities were not just removing male political actors, as Florence had removed its anti-Medicans for reasons of political security. They were removing whole communities on the basis of concerns about identity, impurity and contagion in the *Corpus Christianorum*, even when, and indeed *especially* when, they forced them to move just outside the city walls.[18] Iberian Jews and Muslims were given the choice of conversion or expulsion, with forced baptism as a public sign (a sign which would have greater impact on women than on men, since neither of these communities had a parallel ritual for the inclusion of women). Not for nothing did the Münster radicals follow this same pattern when they gave residents the choice of rebaptism or exile in February 1534, with Jan Matthijs pushing for the execution of those who refused both. These radicals were early adopters of the same absolutist logic that drove the Iberian expulsions, that animated a good part of Observant lay and clerical reform, and that various states and polities followed when they implicitly treated their religious opponents as aliens and Jews.[19]

The Jewish experience of exile was *always* familial. Again, it's not co-incidental that the Jewish practice of faith was *also* always familial, framed as much around food, clothing, and domestic rituals as around doctrines. The latter was inconceivable without the former, and because of this Jewish women were always central to the practice of the faith and the survival of community traditions and identity; the household was more reliably present than a synagogue, particularly in areas with only a small number of Jews. It is why women could *not* be left behind, either in the eyes of those expelling or of those being expelled. Muslim identity was similarly framed around dietary restrictions and domestic rituals, although documents like the Oran fatwah of 1504 explicitly permitted the forcibly-converted to suspend these in order to avoid detection.[20] Diet, dress, and domestic rituals had long been the key markers that Inquisitors had interrogated when examining *conversos* and *moriscos* to determine whether conversions to Catholicism had been genuine, and these were largely the responsibility of women. "The Inquisitors realized the unusual importance of the home in crypto-Judaism and understood that women willingly became the carriers of the tradition they viewed as inimical."[21] Mary E. Perry similarly describes the home as a critical site of resistance in Spanish Islam's "retreat into domestic space," adding that it politicized *moriscas* as their choices around diet, washing, clothing, and language resonated both in and outside the homes; "while Inquisitors found the commonplace heretical, *Moriscas* made the ordinary subversive."[22] Forced conversion and exile reinforced the centrality of women in Jewish and Muslim communities, to the point of eroding some traditional gender ideology. It also strengthened those elements of domestic or cultural confessionalism that *they* in particular tended. When some *moriscas* hid their children to keep them out of Christian schools, they were using one confessionalism to resist another.[23]

Protestants did not have as full or established an array of domestic rituals to mark identity. Or did they? Merry Weisner-Hanks, Susan Karant-Nunn, and Lyndal Roper have shown both how *many* distinctly female-centered domestic practices and rituals around the life cycle or diet were suppressed by reformers, and how firmly women resisted.[24] The "Holy Household" ideology marginalized women, but was also contested and adapted by them, and as further research is showing, it was dominated but not entirely defined by males in its domestic details. The Cambridge-based research project "Domestic Devotions: The Place of Piety in the Italian Renaissance Home" explores the family and home as sites of spiritual formation shaped fundamentally by the gendered realities of household organization and expressed in physical spaces, material objects, textiles, and foods.[25] As we probe these dynamics of reform and resistance further, we should consider the extent to which the elevation of godly domesticity and the Holy Household in both Protestant and Catholic communions may have been influenced at least in part by the emphasis in these same years on the martyr and refugee identity.

What are the implications of exile or flight projecting a Jewish identity on to Christian refugees? The rhetoric of the flight from Egypt recurs in the letters, pamphlets, and sermons of Catholics and Protestants alike. It is a strong undercurrent in martyrologies like Foxe's *Actes and Monuments*, Crespin's *Book of Martyrs*, Verstegan's *Theatre of the Cruelties of the Heretics of our Age*, and Van Bracht's *Martyrs Mirror*.[26] These were among the key texts that families used to catechize and to pass on identity. Notably, the Exodus theme of the flight to the Promised Land is *not* about minds on the move but about the domestic, day-to-day struggle of finding food, water, and shelter for a large community traveling en masse through barren and hostile territory.

Early modern refugee women took a large role in these arrangements and also took a large role in training and socializing their children in religious faith. Esser notes that "in group and family migrants, which in the early modern period dominated the numerous waves of confessional migration within Europe and to the Americas, women participated to a larger extent than was initially suggested."[27] Martyrologies are full of stories of family persecutions, of the resistance of children and servant girls to oppressive authorities, and of women portrayed as exemplary because they hold with quiet, firm, but never prideful determination to the true faith. We are used to thinking of Jewish and Muslim dress and language and diet as being under the purview of women, but do we as readily recognize the same reality in the case of Radical, Protestant, and Catholic Christians who were drawn into the chain migration networks that characterized the religious refugee experience?

Domestic rituals and traditions gave women a critical role in socialization and identity formation within persecuted and exile communities. The Radical communities of Hutterites moved furthest from the nuclear family in their establishment of over 70 *bruderhofen* in Moravia from the mid-1520s until their expulsion in 1622, and emigration eastwards to the Ukraine. Yet holier households could hardly be found. Their communities, numbering up to 500 artisans, tradesmen, and agricultural workers, were firmly gendered. Those items of dress, language, and diet which remained identifying characteristics of the communities' religious and social values were very much the responsibility of the women of the community, and particularly those married women who were known as "marital sisters" since their primary relationship was to the community rather than to a husband or children.[28] The refugee context can also put a different light on some gendered distinctions within these communities. Radicals generally and Hutterites in particular held that men could remain married to those who had not converted or did not share the Hutterite faith, but women could not—they must abandon their unbelieving spouses. This patriarchal difference is certainly built on a deeply sexist view of women as subordinate and as property, but it also reflects a conviction that women must have full latitude to define and even lead the practice of faith in the domestic setting.[29]

Walloon exile communities in Frankfurt and Huguenot communities in Berlin and Den Haag worked hard to preserve French language and customs after the expulsions of the sixteenth and seventeenth centuries. Members of the Frankfurt Walloonian Strangers Church retained a distinct identity as the descendants of refugees and leveraged it as a source of local social capital while the Berlin French Stranger Church in Berlin spent significant amounts on French language instruction for almost a century after their arrival in 1702.[30] Both groups moved beyond catechisms to forms of collective identity rooted in household and familial practices and traditions. A good part of these were likely invented traditions, but Esser notes that this makes them more rather than less important as markers of identity. "Huguenot memoirs have demonstrated convincingly how refugees from seventeenth century France constructed a self-contained world turned inward on itself," with negative features of the native culture minimized or ignored, and positive values exaggerated.[31] This could carry on over generations in spite of intermarriage, as it did in Frankfurt, where those claiming a Huguenot or Walloonian identity often had more German than French branches in the family tree. We need more information about religiously-inflected familial and communal rituals, dialects, diet, naming practices, and calendars in order to reconstruct a picture of the role women played in preserving identity in an exile context over generations and what this meant for integration into surrounding civic and intellectual cultures. Do we read Vives's various prescriptive texts of Catholic Reform on education, on women's roles, on family relations, and on social welfare differently if we think that this *converso* took care to marry a *conversa*, and then decided to resist other offers and continue living in a place where he and Margarita Valdaura could *as a family* exercise their faith without fear of arrest or execution? How does this element of positionality shape Vives's thought?

We can also learn from Catholic recusant households in England how women worked to preserve religious identity when the threat was not foreign mobility but local scrutiny. While their husbands had to conform publicly at least on occasion in order to preserve political and social standing, Catholic wives and mothers maintained the domestic space that was the chief site for practice—hiding priests, securing supplies (including wax, wine, and wafers), disciplining servants, overseeing education and Catholic socialization of children.[32] This directly mirrors the experience of many Iberian *conversas* and *moriscas,* and also the experience of Jews and Muslims living in segregated neighborhoods and ghettos. Physical spaces, material objects, daily and weekly schedules, and consumer goods began to shape the collective piety of many of these clandestine or segregated groups, like the young Venetian Jews who developed domestic coffee-house spaces for late-night Torah study and sociability. The dynamics of reform (including responding to how others' reform impacted one's own community) fed a turn towards private devotion and mental prayer, which dovetailed with the need for discretion, privacy, and even secrecy. That in turn increased the importance of the household and those whose agency was expressed in and through it. The larger domestic spaces occupied by some of the Dutch clandestine house churches—at least 32 Catholic ones in Amsterdam from 1578–1853—complicated practical arrangements in ways that gave more prominence to the household and more work and status to the women who ran it. Around 1700, a network of 4800 Dutch Catholic single women, known as *kloppen*, worked from these churches and through covert confraternities to protect clandestine priests and educate children, and so they played a critical role in preserving Dutch Catholicism.[33]

This latter example underscores that adding gender and households to the religious refugee experience does not simply mean looking at married women. Single women also left their hometowns involuntarily, and some at least settled with stranger churches across borders. More single women than men joined the Lutheran stranger Church in Amsterdam in the seventeenth century, while over a fifth of the single householders in a 1568 census of the Dutch stranger Church in Norwich were women (41 of 193, with 17 of these being widows).[34] Not all of these migrants were involuntary, let alone religious exiles. Yet their sheer number warrants further investigation into their origins and motivations. We know that banishment was a common form of punishment for women charged but not successfully convicted of witchcraft, and that in some areas, beliefs commonly held by radicals, spiritualists, and Anabaptists (like a refusal to baptize infants) were taken as signs of heresy bordering on witchcraft. Moshe Sluhovsky, Anne Jacobson Schutte, and Gabriella Zarri have all shown how dangerously fluid the boundary between orthodoxy and deviance was for religiously charismatic women in particular, with social anxiety about independent women causing many to fall foul of church and civil courts alike. If forced on the road by political and ecclesiastical authorities, by social ostracization, or by shame from sexual exploitation, they would gravitate to larger cities like Amsterdam, London, and Hamburg and appear in contemporary records as servants, textile workers, or prostitutes rather than as religious refugees. If those who were banished or fled do not fit our expectations for religious refugees, that may say more about early modern anxieties and our categorizations than it does about their realities.

So, what difference do we find in our understanding of the Reformation of Refugees when we start our analysis by looking at gender? First, it wrenches us away from the old historiographical model of singling out individual men exiled for what they believed or wrote. Individual women and whole households fled to avoid persecution, to dodge accusations of heresy or deviance, and to practice their faith. Second, it underscores a new paradigm for understanding religious exile, in which the model for the early modern religious exile experience for Christians is no longer based on that of fifteenth century *political* exile, but rather on the much longer tradition of *religious* exile as experienced by Jews and later Muslims, including the triggering demand to either convert or leave. Third, this leads us to recognize the importance of what we might call a broader "cultural confessionalism" expressed mainly by women through rituals, foods, language, stories, and clothing in order to preserve and transmit religious identity when a community is under threat or in exile.

Catholics and Protestants alike drew on the Exodus motif of the people of Israel fleeing Egypt in order to give some symbolic meaning to their own flight as the move of a whole community fleeing an oppressive regime for reasons of *communal* religious identity. Ironically, while this was largely a literary or rhetorical trope, it came at a time when their own *actual* experience of exile was also coming to look more and more like the actual experience of their Jewish and Muslim contemporaries. It seems, unfortunately, that the parallels did not often make them much more tolerant of the Jews, Muslims, or other Christians they may have encountered on the road. The more that Christian exiles and refugees drew on historical and contemporary Jewish models in their creation of an identity and an imaginary, the more we should look for what they adapted from those same models in their actual practice of community and identity formation, including concepts like the Holy Household. Many of the expressions of cultural confessionalism that were disseminated by women through the home, including stories, songs, and catechisms that are in the exiles' *mother* tongue, and also food, clothing, and domestic space and ritual, share common forms and parallels across different religious traditions.

In short, then, to look at the Reformation of Refugees and ask what difference gender made is to become more aware how the dynamics of purity, contagion, and purgation as expressed in politics from the fifteenth through the seventeenth and even eighteenth centuries erased many of the cultural differences between Christians, Jews, and Muslims as they exited city gates or fled over borders. This was something new in European history, and it is something that bears further research and reflection.

Notes

1 Jesse Spohnholtz, "Instability & Insecurity: Dutch Women Refugees in Germany and England, 1550–1600," in *Exile and Religious Identity, 1500–1800,* ed. Jesse Spohnholtz and Gary K. Waite (London: Pickering & Chatto, 2014), 111–126.
2 Nicholas Terpstra, *Religious Refugees in the Early Modern World: An Alternative History of the Reformation* (Cambridge: Cambridge University Press, 2015), 241–308.
3 Raingard Esser, "'Out of Sight and On the Margins' Migrating Women in Early Modern Europe," in *Women on the Move: Refugees, Migration, and Exile,* ed. Fiona Reid and Katherine Holden (Newcastle upon Tyne: Cambridge Scholars Press, 2010), 9.

4 Arthur G. Dickens, John M. Tonkin and Kenneth Powell, *The Reformation in Historical Thought* (Cambridge: Harvard University Press, 1985).
5 They also maintained personal connections: *The Correspondence of Roland H. Bainton and Delio Cantimori, 1932–1966: An Enduring Transatlantic Friendship between Two Historians of Religious Toleration*, ed. John Tedeschi (Florence: Leo S. Olschki, 2002). See most recently: Mario Biagioni, *The Radical Reformation and the Making of Modern Europe* (Leiden: Brill, 2017), 1–17.
6 Delio Cantimori, *Eretici italiani del Cinquecento: Ricerche storiche* (Florence: Sansoni, 1939); Idem, *Italiani a Basilea e a Zurigo nel Cinquecento* (Rome: Cremonese Editore, 1947); Idem, *Per la Storia degli Eretici Italiani del Secolo XVI in Europa* (Rome: Studi e Documenti SED, 1937). Cantimori's own views are complex and controversial. See Stephanie H. Jed, *Wings for our Courage: Gender, Erudition, and Republican Thought* (Berkeley: University of California Press, 2011), 209–211.
7 George H. Williams, *The Radical Reformation*, 3rd ed. (Kirksville: Truman State University Press, 2000).
8 Roland H. Bainton, *Women of the Reformation*: Vol. 1 *In Germany and Italy*, Vol. 2 *In France and England*, Vol. 3 *From Spain to Scandinavia*. (Minneapolis: Augsburg Publishing House, 1971, 1973, and 1977).
9 Williams, *Radical Reformation*, 755 n. 1.
10 Randolph Starn, *Contrary Commonwealth: The Theme of Exile in Medieval and Renaissance Italy* (Berkeley: University of California Press, 1982); Christine Shaw, *The Politics of Exile in Renaissance Italy* (Cambridge: Cambridge University Press, 2000).
11 Alessandra Macinghi Strozzi, *Letters to her Sons (1447–1470)*, ed. and trans. Judith Bryce (Arizona: Center for Medieval and Renaissance Studies, 2016).
12 R. Po-Chia Hsia, *Society and Religion in Münster, 1535–1618* (New Haven: Yale University Press, 1984); James M. Stayer, *The German Peasants' War and Anabaptist Community of Goods* (Montreal & Kingston: McGill-Queen's University Press, 1991), 123–138.
13 Stayer, *German Peasants War*, 129–136; R. Po-Chia Hsia, "Münster and the Anabaptists," in *The German People and the Reformation*, ed. R. Po-Chia Hsia (Ithaca: Cornell University Press, 1988), 57–60.
14 In a letter of 5 June 1535 arguing for the prosecution of Anabaptists, Urbanus Rhegius noted that "blasphemy" about marriage was one of the chief sins of the "reprobates of Münster," in *Sources of South German/Austrian Anabaptism*, ed. William Klassen et al. (Scottdale: Herald Press, 2001), 224. Being "indecisively openminded on polygamy" was one factor in Bernardino Ochino's expulsion from Zurich in 1563. Williams, *Radical Reformation*, 785.
15 Hsia, "Munster and the Anabaptists," 60.
16 Anne Dunan-Page, "John Buyan's 'A Confession of My Faith' and Restoration Anabaptism," *Prose Studies* 28 (2006): 28–30; Lyndal Roper, "Sexual Utopianism in the German Reformation," *Journal of Ecclesiastical History* 42 (1991): 394–418.
17 Janssen credits this to the danger of travelling through war zones, the increasing limits on women's agency and mobility, and the fact that Delft, Den Haag, Utrecht, and other cities expropriated vacated Catholic properties and assigned them to protestant refugees. Geert Janssen, *The Dutch Revolt and Catholic Exile in Reformation Europe* (Cambridge: Cambridge University Press, 2014), 73–81.
18 Debra Kaplan, *Beyond Expulsion: Jews, Christians, and Reformation Strasbourg* (Stanford: Stanford University Press, 2011).
19 Bert Roest, "The Observance and the Confrontation with early Protestantism" and "From *Reconquista* to Mission in the Early Modern World," in *A Companion to Observant Reform in the Late Middle Ages and Beyond*, ed. James D. Mixson and Bert Roest (Leiden: Brill, 2015), 285–308; 331–362.
20 Leonard P. Harvey, *Muslims in Spain, 1500–1614* (Chicago: University of Chicago Press, 2005), 60–64.

21 René Levine-Melammed, *Heretics or Daughters of Israel? The Crypto-Jewish Women of Castile* (Oxford: Oxford University Press, 1999), 15; Richard L. Kagan and Abigail Dyer, *Inquisitorial Inquiries: Brief Lives of Secret Jews and Other Heretics* (Baltimore: Johns Hopkins University Press, 2004).
22 Mary E. Perry, "Space of Resistance, Site of Betrayal: Morisco Homes in Sixteenth Century Spain," in *Home and Homelessness in the Medieval and Renaissance World,* ed. Nicholas Howe (Notre Dame: Notre Dame University Press, 2004), 64–70.
23 Perry, "Space of Resistance," 71.
24 Susan Karant-Nunn, *The Reformation of Ritual: An Interpretation of Early Modern Germany* (London: Routledge, 1997), 5–42, 72–90; Lyndal Roper, *The Holy Household: Women and Morals in Reformation Augsburg* (Oxford: Oxford University Press, 1989).
25 *Madonnas and Miracles: The Holy Home in Renaissance Italy,* ed. Maya Corry, Deborah Howard, and Mary Laven (London: Philip Wilson Publishers, 2017). See also M. Laven, "Devotional Objects" and "At Home and On Display," in *Treasured Possessions from the Renaissance to the Enlightenment,* ed. Victoria Avery, Melissa Calaresu, and Mary Laven (London: Philip Wilson Publishers, 2015), 162–263.
26 Geert Janssen, *Dutch Revolt and Catholic Exile,* 37–44; Charles Parker, *Faith on the Margins: Catholics and Catholicism in the Dutch Golden Age* (Cambridge: Harvard University Press, 2008), 181–182; Brad Gregory, *Salvation at Stake: Christian Martyrdom in Early Modern Europe* (Cambridge: Harvard University Press, 1999), 274–314.
27 Esser, "Out of Sight," 12.
28 Stayer, *German Peasants' War,* 139-59; Williams, *Radical Reformation,* 777–779.
29 While Radicals had a reputation for being more open to women having a significant role in the community, Williams notes "one hears very little about the identities of Hutterite women." Williams, *Radical Reformation,* 657.
30 Francoise Moreil, "The Reformed of Orange: Community Identity and Exile," in *Exile and Religious Identity,* ed. Spohnholtz and Waite, 51–65.
31 Esser, "Out of Sight," 11.
32 Alison Shell, "'Furor juvenalis': Post-Reformation English Catholicism and Exemplary Youthful Behaviour," in *Catholics and the 'Protestant Nation': Religious Politics and Identity in Early Modern England,* ed. Ethan Shagan (Manchester: Manchester University Press, 2005), 194–199.
33 Janssen, *Dutch Revolt and Catholic Exile,* 173–179.
34 Esser, "Out of Sight", 12, 15. The census recorded 314 married persons, in households of various sizes, and 25 female servants and 19 adult female relatives: W.J. Charles Moens, *The Walloons and their Church at Norwich: Their History and Registers, 1565–1832,* 2 vols. (Lymington: Huguenot Society of London, 1887–88), 2:207–216.

15

REFUGEE WIVES, WIDOWS, AND MOTHERS

Timothy G. Fehler

By a fluke of mid-sixteenth-century recordkeeping and surviving sources that touch on the Dutch refugees who flooded Emden, Germany, in the early decades of the Dutch Revolt, we have far more named refugees from among the poorer echelons of Emden's society than from the middling or upper strata. Although we have usually directed our attention toward those refugees who rose in political, religious, intellectual, or economic prominence,[1] taking advantage of the extensive surviving account books of the poor relief administrators in Emden allows us to investigate the structure and perceptions of refugee families receiving charitable support from the community. Individual details about the lives, activities, and circumstances of particular women are rather curt in the poor relief ledgers, but a statistical analysis fostered by the sizable number of recipients in these account books highlights some general trends regarding apparent strategies and experiences of women from among the poorer members of the Reformed refugee community. As we will find, only a small number of women were identified without reference to their status as either a wife, widow, mother, or child.

The long-running Dutch Revolt against Spain, which began in the second half of the sixteenth century, created tremendous changes both for the Netherlands and for the many places of refuge that accepted large numbers of Dutch immigrants.[2] The north-western German port city of Emden, for example, became one of the premier refugee destinations: its population at least quadrupled between 1550 and 1570. Because of the religious issues that surrounded the Dutch Revolt, many of the refugees migrated to Emden on Reformed religious grounds. Most of the newcomers were religious and economic refugees fleeing the war; many, but by no means all, were poor.[3] Utilizing the poor relief rolls of the refugee deacons as well as the consistory minutes of the local Emden congregation into which the Dutch Reformed refugees were integrated, we can get a sense of the shape of refugee families—at least of those families receiving poor relief. This essay will begin with some of the quantitative evidence, largely from an analysis of the account books, before turning to some more detailed case studies of specific refugee women that can be reconstructed from the consistory records. Of course, studies typically show that there was often a preponderance of women among those receiving charity.[4] However, as immigration typically involved larger numbers of men,[5] we will find a reversal in the gender dominance in charity when looking at the refugee poor rather than the local poor.

Between 1559 and 1575, upwards of 8,000 poor relief recipients were listed in the account books of Emden's Dutch refugee deacons, this in a town whose population is estimated to have been between 3,000–5,000 in 1550.[6] Corresponding to the dramatic increase in the numbers of refugees after the explosion of the outbreak of the Dutch Revolt proper in 1566–1567, the refugee deacons began to be much more systematic in their organization, distribution, and recording of poor relief.[7] This more organized approach is clearly evident in a new account book which they began in 1569 with separate categories of "Regular" (or "Ordinary") rolls of those who received long-term or ongoing support from the deacons on a bi-weekly basis and running "Extraordinary" lists throughout each year of those who received one-off aid.[8] Because of the unsystematic lists of recipients who were seldom specifically identified in early years, it is far more difficult in the first account book to compare names or look for repeat recipients. Thus, for the statistics in this essay, I am using the more than 5,000 names in the second account book from 1569–1575, with occasional references to entries in the first book where they provide insights.

Of the total number of listed refugee poor relief recipients, almost three-quarters were men. Almost 20% of these men, however, were explicitly identified as being married (usually with phrases like "with wife" or "with wife & X children"), and a handful as widowers. In most of these cases, the wife's name was not provided. Thus, well over half, almost 60%, of the charity-receiving refugees were identified simply as single males, or at least were identified with no reference to wife or children.

Among the identified women listed as recipients, which is about 26% of the total for the account book, approximately one-third were widows. We also find an interesting dynamic among the female recipients: over 20% of them were also identified as married, usually identified as "wife of someone" rather than by her own name—yet the deacons chose to list the disbursement in these cases under her authority rather than the husband, who was still identified by name. More intriguing are the additional 8.5% of the female recipients who are identified with children but without a husband (these do not include the almost 14% of female recipients who were specifically identified as widows with children or as pregnant widows). In these particular cases, it is not clear from any other clues what the circumstances were that led to these women, despite having children (often multiple children), being recognized by their own names without reference to a husband. From the practice of Reformed church discipline, we know that sexually active unmarried women would not have been considered morally suitable for the church's relief. Did their husbands simply not come into Emden in exile with them? Or was this some indication of a husband who was not part of the Reformed congregation? Or simply bookkeeping oversight? A very small number of married women were specifically identified as being in Emden separated from their husbands. This fact was made clear when they received travel funds to visit their imprisoned husbands. For instance, in 1571, Tanneken, the wife of Hans van den Heede, received travel money to go to Dunkirk where he was imprisoned, while the wife of Job Dircksz received support for her husband in prison in Groningen.[9] However, in these cases, the husbands were explicitly named and their locations identified.

Thus, approximately 40% of the women (in other words 10% of the total recipients) were identified just under their own name without a description as wife, widow, or mother. Given Wiesner-Hanks's analysis of women's work identity,[10] we should not be surprised that for only 1.5% of the women in our account book is her occupation identified without reference to her husband's (or dead husband's) occupation. Moreover, over four-fifths of this tiny number of identified female occupations are servant or maid (the only others given are basket-maker, bobbin-maker, and spinner). Now, *most* recipients, male and female, were not identified by occupation, even some of the men who received support for being out of work. However, approximately one-third of the men (or the women's husbands) *were* identified by occupation compared to the tiny handful of women.

Emden's Dutch refugee deacons listed a specific need or reason for a disbursement in about half of the instances. The frequency of the various identified needs was largely the same for both women and men. The most common grounds were some acute crisis; the most frequent was sickness of someone in the family, which was followed closely in frequency by the general phrase "in her/his distress" and then by a pregnancy or childbirth. Although this latter cause is, of course, unique to women, a large number of men received charity because their wives were in the childbed. The next two most frequent reasons were for travel and rent. When separating these grounds by gender, the ranking of these top five reasons, as recorded by the bookkeeper, was the same for both men and women, with the exception that travel was a more common reason for men than distress.

One final quantitative finding offers implications about the role of women in the refugee community. The lists of Extraordinary expenditures make up almost 90% of the names in the account book, but only about 30% of the expenses of the refugee diaconate. This fact indicates both the somewhat chaotic nature of charitable need and perhaps the transience within the refugee community. Among the recipients of these Extraordinary disbursements, we basically find our 3-to-1 identified males-to-females ratio. However, on the Regular rolls, women made up closer to 40% of the identified recipients, over half of whom were widows.[11] And further, even among the male recipients on the Regular rolls, two-thirds were listed with wife and children (compared to only about 20% of males overall). Thus, the refugee deacons' Regular charity rolls, to which they devoted the bulk (over two-thirds) of their expenses, represented a much more stable portion of the poorer immigrant community settling in Emden, one in which women played a more prominent part. Though there were some extraordinary needs and crises on occasion even for those on the Regular lists (such as pregnancy, illness, travel, etc.), the annual Regular lists represent those whom the authorities recognized as having ongoing, legitimate claims to charity; 80% of these families included women.

Perhaps it is not surprising that when a Regular recipient (or family) did not receive several of the ordinary, bi-weekly disbursements, it was usually because there was a working man in the family. Most frequently, such periods without charity disbursements were in the middle of the year, and the refugee deacons' expenses would pick back up again toward the winter when employment was less readily available. The example of Jan Revels, a Flemish linen-weaver from Oudenarde, illustrates the occasional seasonality of poor relief. Jan Revels, with his wife and children, had received Extraordinary aid a handful of times in 1569 and even more in 1570. This ongoing need apparently made his family a candidate for the deacons' Regular rolls, as he and his five children received a place on the 1571 Regular list.[12] During 1571 and then each of the following years through 1575, Jan Revels with his wife and five or six children was on the Regular rolls; however, they received ongoing, bi-weekly aid only between November and the spring and lived without diaconal assistance after March–May, never receiving charitable support in the summer or early fall.[13] Such seasonal opportunities for external income to supplement diaconal support was more readily available to male than to female refugees.

The size of the Regular bi-weekly disbursements varied from family to family. Apparently, the deacons regularly evaluated the particular needs of individual families rather than simply providing a standard amount for all poor refugee recipients. More interestingly, there seems to have been no particular formula across the board (based on gender or even family size, number of children, etc.). Yet, when we follow specific Regular-roll families across years, we can see that a new child tended to increase the bi-weekly amount, while a death tended to reduce the disbursement (after sometimes a slight temporary increase). One intriguing example, however, seems to demonstrate that a wife's presence did provide an economic value to the household that was taken into account when the deacons calculated the need for charity, even if they did not record a woman's occupation. The Flemish shoemaker Gillis Stockman received extraordinary relief on a few occasions in 1569 and 1570 (for rent help, and for "his distress"). When his wife became ill in mid-1570, his distress increased, culminating with her death in November 1570. The now-widower Gillis with his three children was entered into the 1571 Regular rolls. Yet when he remarried the following year, the family's bi-weekly amount that they received actually decreased by a third. The presence and work of his wife apparently decreased the amount of charity that the family needed; indeed, even when their fourth child was born in 1573, the deacons' bi-weekly disbursement remained at the lower level. Unfortunately, we know nothing about her—even a name—except that she married Gillis and the following year had a child with him.[14]

The most explicitly gendered grouping within the refugee deacon accounts were those Reformed pastors who fled the crackdown on evangelical groups in the Netherlands. This exclusively male category was, in fact, recorded in their own section of the deacons' accounts. Beginning with the second *Fremdlingen* account book in 1569, the refugee deacons recorded annual expenditures under three categories, as the Regular and Extraordinary rolls were followed by a listing of the "service of the preachers" which typically included 10–20 pastors (and families) each year.[15] This particular group raises both gender questions as well as disputes over the nature of the use of congregational poor relief. The diaconate did not consider the refugee ministers to be in the same category of need as "common" poor refugees. Moreover, this was a group limited to men, although their wives and widows often received special recognition because of their husband's position.

The exiled pastors' status in the congregation required the support of them and their families, yet there was not a uniform approach due to the nature of their position; were they to be supported from the church's funds for pastoral salaries and church maintenance or from the deacons' charity? In the first such reference in January 1561, Emden's consistory decided that the refugee deacons should provide support for the wife of the Antwerp minister Adrian Haemstede.[16] Thus, a refugee pastor's wife qualified for alms. Within four months, however, the consistory decided that Adrian, too, should receive support while he was in exile, but because of his status as a pastor, they could not decide "out of what means."[17] The refugee deacons did not feel he was distinctly poor though they had provided for his wife, while the local deacons were reluctant to care for foreigners.

Although most of the refugee pastors (identified after the deacons had begun maintaining their separate list in the 1569 account books) had wives and children, single men in this religious category prompted discussions before the local consistory. Without wives who could potentially supplement the household, former monks who had left their orders to join with Protestants were particularly exposed. In September 1563, a prominent refugee deacon asked the consistory if the foreign deacons might be helped out of the fund that the local church had established for the care of Emden's "household of faith" because the Dutch deacons needed more resources to care "for the monks, who come here steadily."[18] As the influx of foreign pastors began to rise more significantly in late 1564, the Dutch deacons appealed to the East Frisian countess for funds from the territory's secularized monastic properties to finance the refugee pastors.[19]

Such institutional conflicts were exacerbated as the refugee population in Emden climbed dramatically in the late 1560s, and the refugee deacons' account books reveal that they were operating with large deficits. Some of these exiled pastors apparently maintained a position that was fully untenable for other impoverished men and women. Because of commitments to their churches back home in the Netherlands, many of the refugee pastors refused to accept available preaching posts during their time of exile in and around Emden as they waited for the revolt to be successful. In 1568–1569, Aggeus Hillenzoen, one of the Dutch pastors, lost his support because, in part, "he did not work actively enough."[20] This complaint was echoed more broadly by the refugee deacons in August 1571 as they demanded that Emden's pastors instruct several negligent Dutch pastors "who have been supported completely with alms now for some years, that they must make some plan in order to earn a living for their own person and wives and children, since people know that with the great difficulties of the congregation they henceforth cannot be so maintained solely [by the community]."[21] However, a comparison of the deacons' account books implies that the exhortation did not have great practical impact as the number of ministers with wives and children receiving poor relief remained relatively constant and began to decline significantly only several years later as success in the Dutch Revolt (in the northern Netherlands) brought a reduction in the overall number of refugees, allowing many of the pastors to return to the Netherlands. Not only were there only four entries of pastors in the final list of the Dutch deacons' accounts for 1575, but three of these were for surviving families of refugee pastors who had passed away in Emden exile (two widows and a nephew, who was subsequently placed into an apprenticeship).[22]

The minutes of Emden's weekly consistory meetings furnish the possibilities to move beyond the account books' quantitative picture for slightly fuller vignettes of some of these poorer refugee women in town. Of course, the women we encounter in these records are typically those who have come to the consistory's attention for some disciplinary question. In an opening example, the woman, in fact, does not appear, but the husband's disciplinary case sheds some interesting indirect light on the wife. Like records of Gillis Stockman's above-mentioned wives, the circumstances of Hermes de Grave present another almost anonymous wife; yet, this is an odd case in which, when we combine the consistory records and deacons' account books, she nevertheless seems to replace her husband as the head of the family. The schoolmaster, Hermes de Grave, was another poor refugee from Flanders. He, his wife, and two children had received poor relief from Emden's refugee deacons on a fairly regular basis for several years, since at least 1567.[23] He also received extraordinary relief when he was sick or when he and his wife had needed shoes, for example. We know that he had married a widow with a child in 1568, and the deacons recorded two more children being born. When his wife was pregnant with her third child in 1570, the deacons gave Hermes extraordinary alms on ten separate occasions, including help for a midwife in November. Hermes and his family were, therefore, no strangers to the Dutch refugee deacons.

Something, however, must have triggered a conflict between Hermes and the congregation. Perhaps the instigating event was the birth of the third child. Hermes was suddenly called before the consistory in June 1572 "because of his errors," as he had apparently "slandered" the congregation by calling it "devilish ... only because we baptize children."[24] His influence in the community as a schoolmaster heightened the consistory's concerns about these Anabaptist leanings. Over the next two months, the consistory publicly brought the case to the congregation. The consistory also encouraged the refugee deacons to cease providing charity; and on at least two more occasions they attempted to change his views before they declared him an apostate on 11 July.[25]

Though the case ends here in the consistory records, the deacons' account books provide further insights into the story of Hermes, raising questions about his wife's position relative to him. A number of surprising things occurred concerning Hermes' poor relief from the refugee deacons. First of all, it was not terminated as the consistory had wanted in the summer of 1572; the deacons actually continued his family's regular, bi-weekly alms disbursement for every period throughout 1572, 1573, and into 1574.[26] Moreover, the amount of the bi-weekly alms remained unchanged throughout the consistory dispute and its discipline. Though the consistory's desire for a complete withdrawal of alms did not result in even a reduction, there was one modification in the manner of relief provided them by the refugee deacons: the deacons changed their manner of recording the poor relief given to Hermes' family. In every one of the previous 16 references to Hermes in the account books (prior to the consistory controversy in June 1572), the identifications written by the deacons read "Hermes de Grave" or "Hermes de Grave with wife [and children]." Beginning immediately with Hermes' confrontation with the consistory, however, the deacons altered the heading in every one of their subsequent rolls to read "the wife of Hermes de Grave."

Hermes had clearly not died; in such cases the deacons immediately began to alter their lists to use the word "widow" rather than "wife." It is possible that he might have left town, but even the consistory had never suggested that. Yet, his family remained in Emden and continued to receive the same amount of relief that the entire family had been previously receiving. The deacons had neither withdrawn nor reduced the amount of poor relief to the de Grave family, but they appear to have punished Hermes by removing him as the recognized head of his family and identifying his wife as the one who handled the alms disbursement. Nevertheless, they still never named her; she continued to be recognized by his name only! Whether this symbolic move had any impact, psychologically or otherwise, on Hermes or on others who might have been tempted to follow his ideas, we cannot be sure. We do know that the "wife of Hermes de Grave with 3 children" continued to receive regular bi-weekly alms until 9 August 1574, with gradual reductions in the amount during the middle of 1574, when she left the Regular relief rolls of the refugee poor. With special approval, "the wife of Hermes" did receive two more extraordinary gifts to help with rent in October 1574 and April 1575. Hermes apparently died later in 1575 as "the widow of Hermes de Grave" received rent money in November.[27]

In a concluding extended vignette, a Flemish refugee woman finally is given a voice in Emden's consistory records. In this case, a long-running dispute over a married couple's beliefs lasting for six years with more than 20 appearances before the consistory, the woman is certainly not anonymous.[28] Whether she was actually the active one of the pair or not, this woman's voice in resistance to the consistory clearly caught their attention.

Jacob and Proene, refugees from Ypres, had received alms from the refugee deacons in Emden as early as 1559, and by 1560 they were involved in a consistory dispute.[29] The wife, Proene, seems to have been the instigator as the consistory claimed that she had written them a "slanderous letter."[30] When she was summoned in May 1560 to prove her charges, she appeared alone, and her only response to the consistory was, "Examine the scripture!" In August, both Proene and her husband, Jacob, were called before the consistory to account for the grave accusations which they had made against the pastors and the deacons. Jacob and Proene were clearly not happy with either the teachings or the poor relief that they found in Emden, and they came before the consistory at least another four times over the coming year.[31]

In the midst of this discontent, Proene and Jacob apparently found a local Anabaptist congregation appealing. A year and a half after their prior consistory appearance in August 1561, the couple again appeared before the consistory in February 1563 and were accused of having received alms from the Anabaptists.[32] The records of the consistory include no resolution to their earlier conflict, so perhaps the fact that they seem to have lost the consistory's attention might be explained by their having disappeared into an Anabaptist congregation. After a long disputation that day, the elders asked Jacob and Proene if they would leave the Anabaptists and thereafter receive no more alms from them. For a long time neither gave a clear response, but finally the wife, Proene, answered that she did not consider perishing a good option and would therefore continue receiving alms from "our adversaries," as the consistory's secretary called the Anabaptists in his notes. Proene went on to say that she and her husband had not left the Reformed congregation but rather the congregation had left them.

However, examination of the refugee deacons' account books indicates problems with Proene's claim of having been "left" by the Reformed congregation as a justification for her refusal to renounce the Anabaptists' alms. Indeed, comparing the sources reveals that Jacob, Proene, and their child had received aid from the refugee deacons for several years, as well as every month between August 1562 and their current consistory appearance in February 1563.[33] This discrepancy implies that Proene must have considered the amount of the alms offered by the refugee deacons to be inadequate for her child and her family. Proene had already demonstrated her strong voice during her May 1560 consistory confrontation, and she retained her active advocacy over the subsequent three years. Nevertheless, despite Jacob and Proene's harsh criticisms, the Emden consistory did not give up on them without a fight. The couple appeared—sometimes together, other times individually—before the consistory at least 17 more times through 1566, until Proene disappeared from the records.[34] The consistory did not let this allegedly belligerent refugee woman's voice bring an early end to their pastoral efforts regarding this family.

This brief quantitative and descriptive reconstruction of refugee women's experiences in the social welfare system in Emden will naturally not be entirely applicable for our understanding of the strategies, networks, and possibilities across the entire social spectrum. Nevertheless, this quick glance into the thousands of poor refugees in Emden at the height of immigration does reveal a few trends. First, there were more men than women among the recipients of relief in the Reformed immigrant community, but the percentage of women did increase significantly when focusing on those whom the poor relief administrators considered the "regular" or long-term poor. Second, there was an even higher percentage of men than women who were listed alone, without reference to family or dependents. Third moreover, women were relatively rarely identified by name, and even when they were, it was almost always accompanied by the reference "wife of," "widow of," or "daughter of." And even in circumstances when they had been given a key amount of authority—such as when the husband Hermes was excommunicated—the deacons identified her only in reference to her husband even as they appeared to be removing him from official symbolic headship. Fourth, women had a recognized value in helping to meet familial needs—reducing the need for charity, rather than being a drain on family resources—even if their occupations were rarely recorded in the sources. The appearance of women from time-to-time on the Extraordinary rolls indicates that some female refugees on the borders of poverty had the means to support themselves and families with only occasional assistance necessary in acute crises. Finally, it might have taken the bold personality of Proene, but women were, indeed, capable of gaining a recognized voice, openly criticizing authorities (while her husband was not recorded as speaking), and maneuvering the complicated religious and charitable boundaries in their new immigrant home to improve the circumstances for themselves and their families.

Notes

1 For instance, Ole Peter Grell has painstakingly reconstructed a refugee network among mercantile families that emerged through generations of persecution across Europe. See *Brethren in Christ: A Calvinist Network in Reformation Europe* (Cambridge: Cambridge University Press, 2011).
2 See Andrew Pettegree, *Emden and the Dutch Revolt* (Oxford: Oxford University Press, 1992); Jesse Spohnholz, *The Tactics of Toleration: A Refugee Community in the Age of Religious Wars* (Newark, DE: University of Delaware Press, 2011).
3 See Timothy Fehler, *Poor Relief and Protestantism: The Evolution of Social Welfare in Early Modern Emden* (Aldershot: Ashgate, 1999).
4 Merry Wiesner-Hanks, *Women and Gender in Early Modern Europe*, 3rd ed. (Cambridge: Cambridge University Press, 2008), 114.
5 Wiesner-Hanks, *Women and Gender*, 308; Nicholas Terpstra, *Religious Refugees in the Early Modern World: An Alternative History of the Reformation* (Cambridge: Cambridge University Press, 2015), 133.
6 Fehler, *Poor Relief and Protestantism*, 111. The two surviving sixteenth-century account books of Emden's Dutch Refugee (*Fremdlingen*) deacons are housed in the archive of Johannes a Lasco Bibliothek in Emden: *Fremdlingen Diakone Rechnungsbuch*, I (1558-68), II (1569-75). It is hereafter cited as *Fremdlingen*. The first volume has been burned and is badly damaged. It has been microfilmed, and attempts at preservation have halted the progressive damage.
7 Fehler, *Poor Relief and Protestantism,* 181–182, 190.

8 Sometimes a person might receive multiple, extraordinary disbursements over the course of several months and then appear in the following year's Regular roll.
9 *Fremdlingen* 2:237, 227.
10 Merry Wiesner, *Working Women in Renaissance Germany* (New Brunswick, NJ: Rutgers University Press, 1986), 4, 9, 195.
11 The Regular relief rolls were begun at the start of each year with the bookkeeper writing one recipient or family per half page with blank space allotted for the anticipated bi-weekly disbursements to be recorded throughout the year.
12 The omission of his wife here in the 1571 Regular roll entry —when Jan had been both previously and subsequently identified "with wife and children"—illustrates the caution that must be exercised when observing the particular phrasing utilized at any point in the sources.
13 *Fremdlingen* 2:188, 285, 366, 460, 536.
14 *Fremdlingen* 2:57, 59, 62, 129, 131, 132, 133, 135, 137, 138, 139, 140, 141, 143, 144, 146, 148(2), 193, 284, 365, 550.
15 *Fremdlingen* 2:32–45, 119–123, 217–222, 315–319, 395–398, 481–483, 545–546.
16 *Die Kirchenratsprotokolle der reformierten Gemeinde Emden 1557–1620*, 2 vols., ed. Heinz Schilling and Klaus-Dieter Schreiber (Cologne: Böhlau Verlag, 1989, 1992), 1:124 (21 January 1561). It is hereafter cited as *KRP*.
17 *KRP*, 1:127 (19 May 1561).
18 *KRP*, 1:173 (20 September 1563).
19 Their appeals were apparently unsuccessful. *KRP*, 1:191, 193 (29 December 1564, 8 & 12 January 1565).
20 *KRP*, 1:329, 355 (22 November 1568, 8 July 1569); here 355.
21 *KRP*, 1:420 (11 August 1571).
22 *Fremdlingen* 2:545–6.
23 For the records of the deacons' disbursements to Hermes and his family, see *Fremdlingen* 1:fols. 185^v, 211^r; *Fremdlingen* 2:22, 134, 135 (2), 138, 139, 140, 142, 143, 144 (2), 145, 147, 148, 169, 279, 362, 442, 480, 550, 554, 555.
24 *KRP*, 1:449, 450 (6, 16 June 1572).
25 The deacons had identified him as "schoolmaster" twice in 1570. *Fremdlingen* 2:134, 135; *KRP*, 1:449, 450, 452 (6 & 23 June, 11 July 1572).
26 *Fremdlingen* 2:279, 362, 442.
27 *Fremdlingen* 2:442, 550, 555.
28 The situation is recounted in Timothy Fehler, "Victims as Actors," in *Judging Faith, Punishing Sin: Inquisitions and Consistories in the Early Modern World*, ed. Charles H. Parker and Gretchen Starr-LeBeau (Cambridge: Cambridge University Press, 2017), 180–181.
29 *Fremdlingen* 1:fols. 9^v, 10^v, 13^v, 21^v, 47^v, 50^v, and 67^v.
30 *KRP*, 1:112 (27 May 1560).
31 *KRP*, 1:114, 119, 124, and 130–1.
32 *KRP*, 1:159 (22 February 1563).
33 *Fremdlingen* 1:fols. 50^v, 67^v.
34 *KRP*, 1:195, 197, 212–214, 220–222, 227, 233–234, 240, 244, and 250.

16

DID THE JESUITS INTRODUCE "GLOBAL STUDIES"?

Kathleen M. Comerford

In 1561, just two decades after the establishment of the Society of Jesus, founding member Jerome Nadal (1507–1580) famously stated, "the whole world is our home."[1] This vision was tied to empire-building, but not because the Society of Jesus attempted to create a new political order; that was left to the *conquistadores*. Jesuits worked for their superior general, the pope (an international, and soon to be global, monarch), and God, not for a government. However, many of the Society's activities were their own, and were developed based on experience rather than on centralized directives from Rome. The early modern Catholic Church, preoccupied with the unfolding Protestant Reformations and the European territorial and economic concerns that accompanied them, made relatively few official statements regarding the best manner of proceeding around the world even while Catholic kings were creating empires spanning that globe.

Beginning in the sixteenth century and continuing through the suppression of the Society (between 1759 and 1773), European empires made the Atlantic and Indian Oceans into conduits for raw materials, manufactured goods, and enslaved people, and the papacy and religious orders attempted to make the world Roman Catholic. Although Jesuits, empires, and popes each operated with definitions of "globalism" quite different from twenty-first century notions (displaying little respect for indigenous cultures or concern for environmental balance, and none for religious toleration), they all acted on a global stage. Scholars of the late twentieth and early twenty-first centuries have attempted to place the pre-suppression missions in more comparative contexts than those alive during that period would have appreciated, and more than some prior studies on Jesuit missions have embraced.[2] Takao Abé, Ana Carolina Hosne, and Shenwen Li, comparing the missions in Japan and China to those in New France and Peru, have identified major challenges in this revisionism.[3] The most pertinent to the current study are these: missionaries were engaged in a form of rhetorical persuasion, and adapted their message to their audiences; Jesuits were energetically opposed to all forms of non-Christian religion they encountered in the overseas missions, and condemned both worship practices and any art which celebrated them; this opposition sometimes led to deep misunderstandings of local beliefs and religious practices, and potentially to manipulative representations; and the failure of scholars to consider accounts of European activities in indigenous languages has helped obscure not only knowledge of local cultures, but the actions of the missionaries.[4]

The point of more comparative study is not the moment of introduction/encounter, or the development of the empire as a locus of power, but interactions, reciprocal influence, etc.: in other words, cultural exchange. As J. Michelle Molina has observed, the emergence of an "early modern self" occurred simultaneously in Europe and in Latin America, and was in many ways the product of activities and thought patterns associated with missions: defining Christianity and salvation, understanding the self and others, creating communities of like-minded believers in the midst of dissimilarity and opposition, etc. Members of the Society recognized these intellectual and philosophical activities on different continents as closely connected: "Jesuit spirituality needs to be understood in a transregional context because the Jesuits themselves envisioned their spiritual practices as key to shaping and expanding the early modern Christian world, one soul at a time."[5] Early modern Jesuits were criticized for adopting an approach in their missions which sought greater accommodation with local cultures than that taken by Franciscans or Dominicans; Alessandro Valignano (1539–1606), for example, insisted on this method for the Japanese mission.[6] Jesuit accommodation meant learning local languages, teaching catechism in those languages, engaging with the scholarly community of a region, etc., in the far-flung territories to which the Society traveled.[7]

This all raises a question: how prepared were early modern Jesuits for world-wide evangelism? Recent explorations of the means by which members of the Society requested to be sent on missions, the voluminous collection of sources known as *Litterae indípetae*, demonstrate that many young men submitted enthusiastic pleas, regardless of (or perhaps because of) the dangers involved.[8] Since the *Ratio studiorum* (the Jesuit curriculum finalized in 1599) required no classes dedicated to the culture, history, or languages of Africa, the Americas, or Asia, the knowledge these petitioners had would not have come from formal instruction. What, then, was its source? Using the contents of seven Jesuit libraries in Tuscany, the Papal State, the Holy Roman Empire, and the Low Countries, with particular attention to texts which concerned non-European territories, I shall suggest some answers to how global the pre-Suppression Jesuits in Europe, even those who never left that continent, were. The libraries of these Jesuits provided support for the spiritual and intellectual life of both teachers and students. Thus, a study of books they read, listened to, and wrote can help scholars understand what Baroque globalism really meant, and determine whether the Society of Jesus deserves the appellation "global."[9]

Briefly, the libraries under consideration were of two kinds. All but one are identified as college libraries, meaning that they were available for the use of lay and clerical students and staff alike, and in some way supported the educational endeavors of the Society. The remaining one was the library of the Professed House of Antwerp, and thus restricted to the use of those who were members of the Society. Several of the inventories have titles which suggest that they list only a portion of the collections. The 1660 Antwerp inventory, for example, is identified as "books on architecture, bequeathed by Willem Cornelis." This catalog of 39 titles in fact contains texts on multiple subjects, including cartography, casuistry, history, pastoral theology, optics, and rhetoric, along with architecture and related disciplines including geometry. The total number of books listed in inventories as belonging to the collections of Antwerp (1613 and 1660), Bagnacavallo (1774), Bologna (1690s), Florence (1578), Leuven (1635 and 1649), Livorno (1773–1775), and Siena (1565), is 2,878.[10] Among those, 217 (approximately 7.5%) are on subjects which might be considered of importance to missions, global issues, navigation, and/or travel.[11] Another 520 books (approximately 18%) were in the fields of rhetoric (religious and secular) and biblical commentaries, likely to be of equal importance in Europe as in the missions. The topics are unequally distributed among the institutions over the centuries. In this sampling, the smaller libraries of the Low Countries have a higher percentage of mission-related titles than the larger ones of the Italian states (9.7% vs. 7.6%). The sixteenth-century collections contain the smallest percentages (5.0%) and the seventeenth-century ones the largest (10.0%); the eighteenth-century inventories show a decline (8.0%).

Only 5.5% of the 217 books cover the history or geography of Africa, the Americas, and Asia combined. None of these, and only one book on missions, appear in the sixteenth-century inventories. The only language important to missions found among the listed titles was English.[12] The Society was aware that a lack of instruction in the languages spoken in their destinations was a problem. In the 1580s and 1590s, letters from the Province of New Spain referred to learning native tongues. The work of the Jesuit missionaries on this front was not always met with support from the provincial. For example, Visitor Diego de Avellaneda (d. 1598) wrote to Superior General Claudio Acquaviva (1543–1615) in March 1592 that Pedro Díaz (1546–1618), then Provincial of New Spain, did not emphasize this endeavor strongly enough. Such complaints did not produce quick results. In the early eighteenth century, lack of fluency in indigenous languages was still a significant concern. Joseph de Arjó (1663–1736, Provincial of New Spain 1722–1725), compiled instructions in 1725 for the permanent visitor of the northern missions in New Spain. They required that missionaries preach in Nahuatl (the dominant native language in the region) in the presence of the visitor and the rector of the Jesuit college, that future missionaries should not be accepted without demonstrating language skills, and that any priest moving on from a mission post should leave behind grammars, dictionaries, catechisms, and sermons in the "most common and generally understood" language of the region.[13]

Antonio Ruíz de Montoya's *Arte, y bocabulario de la lengua guarani* (Madrid: Juan Sánchez, 1640) is one example of an early European printed bilingual dictionary for learning South American languages, and one copy bearing the provenance markings of the Roman College survives.[14] Such books were rare. In New France, the Jesuits created manuscript dictionaries and grammars, but none of those were printed either in the colony or in France.[15] While one might expect a larger collection of, for example, Guarani-Spanish dictionaries or histories of central South America in Paraguayan and Argentinian Jesuit libraries, the online catalogs of national and university libraries in Latin America provide little provenance information to test this hypothesis.

Meanwhile, in the Asian colonies, the problem was partially addressed by sending people to Macau to learn Japanese or Chinese. Finding someone who could speak both a European and an Asian language was difficult, but finding someone to teach a European how to handle the thousands of characters in these written languages was harder still. Nonetheless, while the Jesuits struggled to understand, then speak, and then read, native languages, the Society did not open schools in Europe, or develop programs of study there, to help ease the transition.[16] For the most part, they would receive language instructions only on arrival. I have located only one copy of the Spanish-Japanese grammar by Dominican Diego Collado (1589–1641), with the provenance markings of the Paris Professed House, but no such aids for other Asian languages.[17]

In addition to problems with linguistic and cultural training, the average mission-bound Jesuit knew very little about the region to which he was sent. A mere 6.4% of the 217 books specifically address topics related to activity within the missions: the history of a particular foundation, accounts by individual Jesuits describing several years' presence there, etc. This includes a series of publications identified at least in part as "letters," referring to the mandate in the *Constitutions* for the on-site mission superiors to write to provincial superiors (at first monthly, but later biannually) and to the leadership of other provinces (initially quarterly, and later annually).[18] The circulation of these letters, in printed form, was intended to explain the Jesuit work on the missions to influential outsiders, such as sympathetic cardinals in Rome. They were also sent around to the different Jesuit residences to provide information on the workings of the Society and reportedly "aroused the imagination and awakened the enthusiasm of a great number of people."[19] They had an additional, more comprehensive goal: identity-building, via the construction of a pantheon of sorts, full of newer martyrs, some of whom were formally recognized as saints.[20]

This genre was based on European models. Reports from the colleges in Florence and Siena between the 1550s and 1620s, for example, provided descriptions of everyday business (numbers who attended classes, academic content of those classes, size of audience for Jesuit preachers in the community or at specific churches, size and disposition of the classroom and living space of the college, work of the resident priests in administering sacraments, etc.) and of extraordinary events (visits of local rulers, theatrical performances, conflicts between novices and their families, deaths of members, etc.). Their most dramatic prose was reserved for the discussion of conversion of heretics or the return of lapsed believers to the church. In the annual letters of 1607–1608 and 1612–1613, for instance, the authors reported great successes, not only in bringing in noble penitents to confession, but also in increasing the number of students, even convincing "some heretics, among whom were two very distinguished people," to return to the fold, despite their having heard dangerous ideas from some Genevan visitors to the city.[21] None of the library inventories in this study contained any such periodic letters from European Jesuit foundations.

Reports from the missions, which can be found in the inventory from Bagnacavallo (1774), were more exciting than their European counterparts. Francesco Giuseppe Bressani's 1653 *Breve relatione d'alcune missioni de' PP. della Compagnia di Giesù nella Nuova Francia* described the unfamiliar territory and its inhabitants.[22] His detailed discussion of the religion of the indigenous Wyandotte (Hurons) and their Algonquin neighbors contrasted certain beliefs (e.g. in the immortality of the soul) and practices (e.g. a native prayer "which one might translate as *miserere nobis*") with atheism as well as with Christianity.[23] The indigenous Americans found several theological concepts, in particular European concepts of sin, incomprehensible, as Peter Goddard's study of the New France mission to the Montagnais shows.[24] The missionaries in accounts such as Bressani's struggled against the dangers of a long voyage to North America from France, the devil, the "superstitions" of the natives, a lack of food, wet weather, difficult terrain, and the hostility between the Wyandotte and Iroquois. Bressani also remarked: "what a strange thing to find oneself in a country, where one had to learn without a teacher, without books, and without rules, while already an adult, a language that has no similarity to ours."[25] After several years with few converts, many of the Jesuits were captured, tortured and killed.

Alexandre de Rhodes's 1650 account of the Jesuit mission in Vietnam also began with geographical, agricultural, meteorological, and physical details of the region and its inhabitants, before progressing to a fairly lengthy discussion of the native religion, identified as "superstitious."[26] Here, the Portuguese Jesuits brought "great numbers of pagans to hear the proclamation of the Gospel," and many converted.[27] This put them at odds with Nguyễn Phúc Lan (1601–1648, r. 1635–1648), lord of Southern Vietnam, who practiced concubinage, kept eunuchs, and prohibited Christianity.[28] In this case, rather than facing the physical difficulties of starvation and war, the missionaries had to endure defeat and exile. A third example of such literature is Ludovico Antonio Muratori's 1748 account of the mission in Paraguay and Brazil.[29] Though not a member of the Society, Muratori, widely celebrated as the "father" of Italian historiography, studied with the Jesuits in Modena and believed their evangelical activities were beneficial to the indigenous peoples of South America. Muratori provided information on the people and the area in which they lived toward the end of the seventeenth century. The missionaries carried (or encountered) disease, argued the importance of monogamous marriages, and labored against the elements. They also met with a significant danger from "the slave-hunters of São Paulo, Christians by name, devils by work." This referred to Portuguese fortune hunters and slave traders called *bandeirantes* who raided the Reductions, sometimes disguised as Jesuits, during the seventeenth century. Muratori was critical of Spanish behavior as well, noting the cruelty of early settlers who behaved contrary to Christian morals: "men intent only on their own comfort and enrichment, and who might love for all the people of the West Indies to be Christians, but only if they could exploit them, as they do with beasts of burden, and to make them their own miserable slaves, and not faithful people subject to the Spanish Crown."[30]

Over 41% of the 217 mission-related texts concern hagiography and spiritual biography, often related to the missions. These accounts highlighted the heroic faith and acts of individuals. They ordinarily contained few details about the place in which said individuals were martyred. Notable examples of edifying literature either written as such or extracted from the periodic letters from the missionaries include biographies of the Jesuits Francis Xavier (1506–1552, missionary to Asia), Stanislaus Kostka (1550–1568, known for his austerity early in life), Peter Canisius (1521–1597, Catholic Reformation leader in the Holy Roman Empire), Alfonso Rodríguez (1532–1617, a lay brother of deep piety), Peter Claver (1580–1654, missionary to New Spain and patron saint of African slaves), and Jean François Régis (1597–1640, who labored among marginalized French communities, including orphans and prostitutes).[31] In addition, Giuseppe Patrignani's *Menologio di pie memorie d'alcuni religiosi della Compagnia di Gesù*, an account of several martyrs, was kept in Bagnacavallo.[32] These texts described the valiant activities of Jesuits faced with intellectual, spiritual, and physical challenges, and provided the readers with not only exciting narratives, but models of exemplary behavior in the face of dangers.

The question of what the audience would learn from these publications is a complex one. The mission letters and spiritual biographies provided information on the progress of the faith and the faithful. Such information was valuable, even if it descended into formulaic expression or exaggeration: readers wanted to know whether the endeavor was successful. They would also learn of (to them) exotic locations, strange animals and plants, and alien peoples. Studies of the *Litterae indípetae* suggest that reports from the various corners of the Jesuit world were successful in creating an appetite for such adventures, and Ulrike Strasser's contribution to this volume explores how this yearning was connected to a desire to emulate the masculine attributes of Xavier, the earliest Jesuit to engage in missions outside of Europe. Liam Brockey has observed that the accounts of martyrdom "incited emulation even when going to Nagasaki would be not only futile but suicidal. The cult of martyrs in early modern Catholicism evoked zeal potent enough to drive men around the world to certain death."[33]

The audiences therefore learned, in vivid detail, that missionary activity was exciting and dangerous. On the other hand, they encountered little information about the peoples they would seek to convert, or about the places where those people lived. What today are understood to be offensive portrayals of indigenous people were prized by the authors and audiences of the accounts. These narratives portrayed non-Christians as "pagan savages," perversely wedded to their idolatry, in order to spur on the young men studying to be Jesuits to become the conduits via which "primitive" peoples would be taught the truth and brought to God. As Camilla Russell and Brockey have noted, the stories of religious zeal in the face of danger led the petitioners to focus on the spiritual results of missionary journeys, rather than the time and place where these journeys occurred.[34] Texts like the six-volume *Nuovi avisi delle Indie di Portogallo* of 1565, at one time held by the Jesuit College in Florence,[35] included detailed stories of successful conversions among the peoples of the Portuguese Empire.[36] The authors emphasize the bravery, honor, and inquisitive nature of the Japanese people, and note that many converted to Christianity and were devout in their prayers and lessons, despite the occasional threat from some violent compatriots. In several instances, Christian settlements were destroyed, but the converts remained faithful.[37]

Some texts had a more nuanced approach than the largely formulaic good (Jesuits and those they converted) vs. evil (those who refused to convert or acted violently against the missions) which predominated in the mission letters and history. One example was the monumental *Thesaurus Indicus, seu, Generalis instructor pro regimine conscientiae, in iis quae ad Indias spectant* by the Jesuit Diego de Avendaño (1594/5–1688, provincial of Peru 1663–1666), at least a portion of which was once held by the college in Leuven.[38] This work discussed the indigenous peoples of Spanish America, arguing that they had been abused by the Europeans who colonized the area, and advocating a more ethical approach to governance there (and the severe punishment of the Spaniards who engaged in the abuses). Avendaño's probabilism was well known, so such a text likely served the dual purpose of teaching ethics and providing information about mission territory.[39] In Antwerp, the Jesuit college owned a copy of the 1642 *Litterae annuae provinciae Paraquariae Societatis Iesu*,[40] which included obituaries of members of the mission, emphasizing their piety and noting the successes of the endeavor: conversions among the locals, work in the city schools and on the remote Reductions, etc. to spread and maintain the faith despite geographical and political obstacles.

Russell has claimed that "Europe at the turn of the seventeenth century was awash with accounts from the Jesuit missions in the 'Indies,' while young Jesuits in colleges and novitiates eagerly sought a place on the missions, especially in the East."[41] These accounts were, however, not particularly informative about the locations to which the missionaries went, so their influence on the members of the Society is difficult to gauge. Copies of texts on topics of interest to the Jesuit missions were indeed printed and distributed to colleges as well as to potential donors, and subsequent to the suppression they have been scattered to libraries all over the world. From on-site research, I have compiled a data set of books with European Jesuit provenance currently held at Brown, Yale, and Georgetown Universities, the Universities of Maryland, Antwerp, Bologna, and Leuven, and at the Folger Shakespeare Library. In addition, I have conducted catalog searches of the collections of research libraries in England, Italy, and the US, and have used

Google, Hathitrust, the Internet Archive, and multiple auction catalogs. As of this writing, my data set consists of 4,359 books with known pre-suppression Jesuit provenance. Among these, approximately 8% can be classified as mission letters, stories of men martyred in the missions, histories of Africa, Asia, and the Americas, and geographical and cartographical studies. They have provenance information from different parts of the Low Countries, Spain, France, the Italian peninsula, the Holy Roman Empire, and Bohemia.[42] That is fairly consistent with the 7.5% identified from the inventories. Thus, signs point to a low level of preparation for Jesuit missionaries encountering the world. Even if every person at a given Jesuit college heard or read the stories of martyrdom and could speak of the risks of evangelization among non-Christians, they knew little of the places to which the martyrs had gone and to which they might be sent. They knew almost nothing of the languages, customs, or terrain of Africa, the Americas, or Asia. What they knew quite well was the possibility of great danger to their lives, and they embraced that danger with zeal—the "desire for the Indies" found throughout the *litterae indípetae*, even hoping for the martyrdom which claimed the heroes about which they read.

Merry Wiesner-Hanks has been a trailblazer in teaching Global Studies: via textbooks, sourcebooks, and the Advanced Placement Exams, her work has reached an enviably vast audience, ranging from high school students to university professors. This essay, inspired by that work, considers global education in early modern Europe by calling attention to the authors, teachers, and missionaries who engaged in world-spanning intellectual and spiritual activities—seeking to determine how global that education really was. The Jesuits, working alongside lay adventurers from all over Europe, created and maintained a trans-continental scholarly, religious, and administrative network based on cooperation not only with European elites, but also with individuals occupying different social and political strata within the local cultures where they evangelized. However, these early "globalists" were quite poorly equipped for their ultimate task. The job of missionaries was, at least in its purest sense, not martyrdom or adventure, but conversion. The Jesuits were not especially interested in the indigenous peoples except as converts, and their libraries' stronger emphases on rhetoric and biblical commentaries than on native languages and histories, combined with a healthy dose of heroic adventure stories, reflected this agenda. Jesuits were more accommodating toward indigenous peoples than other religious orders, but that was likely a function of experience; it was not the result of study.

Notes

1 Epistolae P. *Hieronymi Nadal Societatis Jesu, ab anno 1546 ad 1577*, vol. 5, *Comentarii de Instituto S.I.* (Rome: Monumenta Historica Societatis Iesu, 1962): 5:54, "totus mundus nostra fit habitatio," specifically referring to missions. For a recent collection of articles on Jesuits and globalization, see Thomas Banchoff and José Casanova, eds., *The Jesuits and Globalization: Historical Legacies and Contemporary Challenges* (Washington, DC: Georgetown University Press, 2016).

2 Cf., among many examples, Dauril Alden, *The Making of an Enterprise: The Society of Jesus in Portugal, Its Empire, and Beyond, 1540–1750* (Stanford, CA: Stanford University Press, 1996); Andrés I. Prieto, *Missionary Scientists: Jesuit Science in Spanish South America, 1570–1810* (Nashville, TN: Vanderbilt University Press, 2011); Florence C. Hsia, *Sojourners in a Strange Land: Jesuits and their Scientific Missions in Late Imperial China* (Chicago, IL: University of Chicago Press, 2009); and Victor M. Fernández, et al., *The Archaeology of the Jesuit Missions in Ethiopia 1557–1632* (Leiden: Brill, 2017).

3 Shenwen Li, *Stratégies missionnaires des jésuites français en Nouvelle-France et en Chine au XVIIe siècle* (Paris: L'Harmattan, 2001); Takao Abé, *The Jesuit Mission to New France: A New Interpretation in the Light of the Earlier Jesuit Experience in Japan* (Boston, MA: Brill, 2011); and Ana Carolina Hosne, *Jesuit Missions to China and Peru, 1570–1610: Expectations and Appraisals of Expansionism* (New York: Routledge, 2013). For an overview of recent historiographical trends, see Emanuele Colombo, "Gesuitomania: Studi recenti sulle missioni gesuitiche (1540–1773)," in *Evangelizzazione e globalizzazione. Le missioni gesuitiche nell'età moderna tra storia e storiografia*, ed. Michela Catto et al. (Rome: Dante Alighieri, 2010), 31–59.

4 Abé, *Jesuit Mission to New France*, 50–59; Li, *Stratégies*, 1–17. Hosne's discussion of these points is woven throughout her book, in what she calls selective biographies of her two protagonists (José de Acosta and Matteo Ricci), and her detailed discussion of the catechetical works they both wrote.

5 J. Michelle Molina, *To Overcome Oneself: The Jesuit Ethic and Spirit of Global Expansion, 1520–1767* (Berkeley: University of California Press, 2013), 5–6, here 6. For more on the domestic missions—"our Indies"—see e.g. Carlo Luongo, *Silvestro Landini e le "nostre Indie": Un pioniere delle missioni popolari gesuitiche nell'Italia del Cinquecento* (Scandicci: Firenze Atheneum, 2008) and Jennifer Selwyn, *A Paradise Inhabited by Devils: The Jesuits' Civilizing Mission in Early Modern Naples* (Rome: Institutum Historicum Societatis Iesu [IHSI], 2004).

6 See Josef Franz Schütte, *Valignano's Mission Principles for Japan*, trans. John J. Coyne, 2 vols. (St. Louis, MO: Institute of Jesuit Sources, 1980–1985). Takao Abé argues that the long-standing interpretation of cultural rigidity on the part of Franciscans vs. cultural relativism on the part of Jesuits, espoused by (among others) Bruce G. Trigger and Carole Blackburn in their work on North America, is an oversimplification: "Both the Jesuits and the Franciscans in Japan were clever diplomatists who were able to analyse their political situation in a foreign land and to figure out the best possible approach. The Franciscans in Japan carefully adopted a method based on the accumulated experience of the Jesuits and were in no way culturally more aggressive than the Jesuits …. No matter how Eurocentric from a cultural perspective the missionary strategy of the French Friars may have been, it was not because they were Franciscans but because they were the pioneer missionaries with little practical experience." Abé, *Jesuit Mission to New France*, 102.

7 For the special case of accommodating the "new" world of the Americas, see, e.g., Maria M. Portuondo, "America and the Hermeneutics of Nature in Renaissance Europe," in *Global Goods and the Spanish Empire, 1492–1824: Circulation, Resistance and Diversity*, ed. Bethany Atam and Bartolomé Yun-Casalilla (New York: Palgrave Macmillan, 2014), 78–99. On issues of translating Jesuit scholarship into China, see e.g. R. Po-Chia Hsia, *A Jesuit in the Forbidden City: Matteo Ricci 1552–1610* (Oxford: Oxford University Press, 2012). On catechesis, cf. Hosne, *Jesuit Missions to China and Peru, 1570–1610*.

8 For an introduction to the methods and contents of the *Litterae indípetae*, see Emanuele Colombo and Marco Rochini, "Four Hundred Years of Desire: Ongoing Research into the Nineteenth-Century Italian 'Indípetae' (1829–1856)," in *Representations of the Other and Intercultural Experiences in a Global Perspective*, ed. Niccolò Guasti (Milan: Mimesis International, 2017), 83–108, esp. 83–95. A lengthier exploration of the early *indípetae* written by Italian Jesuits is found in

Gian Carlo Roscioni, *Il desiderio delle Indie: storie, sogni e fughe di giovani gesuiti italiani* (Turin: Einaudi, 2001). Roscioni points out that Japan, which was understood to be a highly civilized nation, was particularly attractive to young Jesuits, in part because of the persecutions there, and in part because of the distance from Europe (110). Both reasons suggest an embrace of the more dangerous parts of the desire for adventure. A broader view of the *indípetae* can be found in the many studies in Pierre-Antoine Fabre and Bernard Vincent, eds., *Missions religieuses modernes: "Notre lieu est le monde"* (Rome: École française de Rome, 2007).

9 Residents and students learned some information about mission voyages at mealtimes, when spiritual texts were commonly read in Jesuit houses and colleges; however, it is difficult to determine which accounts were read where, and in what detail, and to what extent the audience attended to the stories. To understand the libraries of the missions, see, among others, Adrian Dudink, "The Inventories of the Jesuit House at Nanking Made Up During the Persecution of 1616–1617 (Shen Que, *Nangong shudu*, 1620)," in *Western Humanistic Culture Presented to China by Jesuit Missionaries (XVII–XVIII Centuries)*, ed. Federico Masini (Rome: IHSI, 1996), 119–157; the articles in "Jesuits and their Books around the World, 1541–2013," *Journal of Jesuit Studies* 2, no. 2 (2015), ed. Kathleen M. Comerford; Ines Županov, *Missionary Tropics: The Catholic Frontier in India (16th–17th centuries)* (Ann Arbor: University of Michigan Press, 2005); Noël Golvers, *Libraries of Western Learning for China*, 3 vols. (Leuven: Ferdinand Verbiest Institute, 2013–2015); and Sabine MacCormack, *On the Wings of Time: Rome, the Incas, Spain, and Peru* (Princeton, NJ: Princeton University Press, 2007).

10 The 1613 Antwerp inventory is from the college (Rijksarchief Antwerpen, Archief Nederduitse Jezuïetenprovincie [Flandro Belgica] 2045, fifth untitled document, 1613); the 1660 one, from the Professed House (Rijksarchief Antwerpen, Archief Nederduitse Jezuïetenprovincie [Flandro Belgica] 2046: Catalogus van de boeken over architectuur, achtergelaten door P. Guilielmus Cornelii, overleden te Leuven in 1660). For Leuven, Rikjsarchief Leuven, Jezuïeten College Leuven 20, Catalogus van de schenkingen aan de bibliotheek, 1635, includes a list headed "1649," with 20 titles. The Collegio di San Giovannino of Florence is represented by two MS archival inventories, one in 1565 and one in 1578. I have discussed the overlap between these two inventories in *Jesuit Foundations and Medici Power* (Leiden: Brill, 2017), Appendix 2, 300. For the sake of convenience, in this article, I have used only the 1578 inventory (Archivio di Stato di Firenze, Compagnie Religiose Soppresse dal Pietro Leopoldo 999, Filza 3, n. 104: Collegio S. Giovanni Evangelista, Firenze. Inventario di tutti i beni mobili di Casa fatto a 1º di X.bre di 1578 per ordine di'l P. Sebastiano Morales Visitatore della Provincia della Toscana). The remaining inventories are: Archivum Romanum Societatis Iesu Rom 124 I, ff. 235^r–236^v: Catalogo de libri Theologi del Collegio di Siena 1565; Archivio Arcivescovile di Bologna 244, Libreria, Missioni, Patronati; and Archivio Comunale di Ferrara, Ex Patrimonio Gesuitico 78: Descriptio Biblioteca Excollegi Societatis Iesu Balneocaballi [Bagnacavallo].

11 The subjects are: astronomy, cartography, cosmology, geography, history (Africa, Americas, Asia, Church, world), Jesuitica, missions, and travel.

12 The 1774–1775 inventory of Livorno contains the entry "Philosophical Transactions, e alcuni altri Libri Inglesi." In my tallies, I have counted this as a single entry for the sake of convenience because I know only the one title, but this clearly refers to an unspecified number larger than one. *Philosophical Transactions* is probably an edition of the publication by the Royal Society of London, which began printing its findings in 1665.

13 Antonio Astrain, *Historia de la Compañía de Jesús en la asistencia de España*, vol. 4, *Acquaviva (segunda parte) 1581–1615* (Madrid: Razón y Fe, 1913), 426–428; William Eugene Shiels, *Gonzalo de Tapia (1561–1594), Founder of the First Permanent Jesuit Mission in North America* (New York: United States Catholic Historical Society, 1934), 75, 89; Andrés Prieto, *Missionary Scientists: Jesuit Science in Spanish South America*,

1570–1810 (Nashville, TN: Vanderbilt University Press, 2011), 109–110; and Charles Polzer, *Rules and Precepts of the Jesuit Missions of Northwestern New Spain* (Tucson: University of Arizona Press, 1976).

14 This identification is from the online catalogue of the Biblioteca Nazionale Centrale di Roma, which provides provenance information for many of its early books. See http://bve.opac.almavivaitalia.it/opac2/BVE/ricercaSemplice (accessed June 18, 2020).

15 Micah True, *Masters and Students: Jesuit Mission Ethnography in Seventeenth-Century France* (Montreal: McGill-Queen's University Press, 2015), 58–60; Margaret J. Leahey, "'Comment peut un muet presche l'evangele?' Jesuit Missionaries and the Native Languages of New France," *French Historical Studies* 19 (1995): 105–131; and Johanne Biron, "Les livres que les missionnaires de la Compagnie de Jésus ont apportés avec eux un Nouvelle-France. Écrire l'histoire d'une bibliothèque jésuite," in *De l'orient à la Huronie: Du récit de pèlerinage au texte missionnaire*, ed. Guy Poirier, Marie-Christine Gomez-Géraud, and François Paré (Québec: Presses de l'Université Laval, 2011), 165–184, esp. 167 and nn. 6–7.

16 Cf. Liam Brockey, *Journey to the East: The Jesuit Mission to China, 1579–1724* (Cambridge, MA: Harvard University Press, 2007); Abé, *Jesuit Mission to New France*; and Qiong Zhang, *Making the New World Their Own: Chinese Encounters with Jesuit Science in the Age of Discovery* (Leiden: Brill, 2015). For the languages of India, also apparently not taught in Europe, see e.g. Inez Županov's work on Tamil Jesuit texts: "'I Am a Great Sinner': Jesuit Missionary Dialogues in Southern India (Sixteenth Century)," *Journal of the Economic and Social History of the Orient* 5 (2012): 415–446.

17 Printed in Rome for the Propaganda Fide, 1632; currently located at the Princeton University Library.

18 George E. Ganss, *The Constitutions of the Society of Jesus* (St. Louis: Institute of Jesuit Sources, 1970), Part VIII, 292–293, quote at 292, and Florence Hsia, *Sojourners in a Strange Land*, 14–15.

19 John Correia-Afonso, *Jesuit Letters and Indian History 1542–1773*, 2nd ed., with foreword by Valerian Gracias (Bombay: Oxford University Press, 1969), 33.

20 Florence Hsia, *Sojourners in a Strange Land*, 21. For a discussion on the revival of the importance of martyrdom in Catholic discourse, see Brad S. Gregory, *Salvation at Stake: Christian Martyrdom in Early Modern Europe* (Cambridge, MA: Harvard University Press, 1999), esp. ch. 7. Gregory focuses more on English martyrs than on non-European ones, but his observations are applicable to both contexts. Note that no early modern martyr was sanctified before 1700, though many were beatified in the seventeenth century. Cf. also Liam Brockey, "Books of Martyrs: Example and Imitation in Europe and Japan, 1597–1650," *Catholic Historical Review* 103, no. 2 (2017): 207–223, for the observation that the emphasis in the martyrological texts was on clerical deaths, despite the far larger number of lay casualties (210).

21 ARSI Rom. 129 fols. 375^v-376^r (1607–1608, the source of the quote) and ARSI Rom. 130/II: 1612–1614, ff. 503^r-505^v. I have discussed this at greater length in my *Jesuit Foundations and Medici Power 1532–1621* (Leiden: Brill, 2016), 224–226.

22 Bressani, *Breve relatione d'alcune missioni de' PP. della Compagnia di Giesù nella Nuova Francia* (Macerata: heredi d'Agostino Grisei, 1653), 7.

23 Bressani, *Breve relatione*, 19–20.

24 Peter Goddard, "Converting the 'Sauvage': Jesuit and Montagnais in Seventeenth-Century New France," *Catholic Historical Review* 84, no. 2 (1998): 219–239, here 229.

25 Bressani, *Breve relatione*, 6.

26 Rhodes, *Relazione de' felici successi della santa fede predicata da' padri della Compagnia di Giesù nel regno di Tunchino alla santità di n. s. pp. Innocenzio Decimo* (Rome: Luna, 1650).

27 Rhodes, *Relazione*, 2:1421–48.

28 Rhodes, *Relazione*, 2:186–221.

29 Muratori, *Il cristianesimo felice nelle missioni de' padri della Compagnia di Gesù nel Paraguai* (Venice: Giambattista Pasquali, 1743).
30 Muratori, *Il cristianesimo*, 30–31, 48, and 118. On the dangers of the *bandeirantes*, see, e.g., Massimo Livi-Bacci and Ernesto J. Maeder, "The Missions of Paraguay: The Demography of an Experiment," *Journal of Interdisciplinary History* 35, no. 2 (2004): 185–224. On Jesuit interpretations of their role in the disputes over Indian labor in seventeenth-century Portuguese America, see, e.g., Maria Beatriz Nizza da Silva, "Vieira e os conflitos com os colonos do Pará e Maranhão," *Luso-Brazilian Review* 40, no. 1 (2003): 79–87.
31 For example, the 1774 Bagnacavallo inventory lists Francesco Sacchini, *Vita b. Stanislai Kostkae* (Cologne: Kinchius, 1617); Arcangelo Arcangeli, *Vita del venerabil servo di Dio, Alfonso Rodriguez* (Rome: Rossi, 1761); Longaro degli Oddi, *Vita del venerabil servo di Dio, P. Pietro Claver* (Rome: Generoso Salomoni, 1748); and two copies of Antonio Francesco Mariani, *Considerazioni sopra le virtù e altri preggi de' santi Ignazio Lojola, Francesco Saverio, Francesco Borgia, Luigi Gonzaga, Stanislao Kostka, e b. Gianfrancesco Regis della Compagnia di Gesù [...]* (Venice: Occhi, 1740).
32 Venice: Niccolò Pezzana, 1730.
33 Brockey, "Books of Martyrs," 221.
34 Camilla Russell, "Imagining the 'Indies': Italian Jesuit Petitions for the Overseas Missions at the Turn of the Seventeenth Century," in *L'Europa divisa e i nuovi mondi*, ed. Massimo Donattini et al. (Pisa: Edizioni della Normale, 2011), 2:179–189, here 185; Brockey, "Books of Martyrs," 221.
35 Venice: Tramezzini, 1565. The copy held by the Folger Shakespeare Library (vol. 4) is inscribed "Societatis Jesu Collegii Florentini catal. inscrip" and, in a different hand, "Col: flor: Soc: Jesu Cubi: P. Jo: Angel de Benedictis." Neither inscription has a date, and the inventories I have for the Collegio Fiorentino do not include this book; hence, I cannot determine the date of ownership.
36 Ananya Chakravarti, "In the Language of the Land: Native Conversion in Jesuit Public Letters from Brazil and India," *Journal of Early Modern History* 17, no. 5–6 (2003): 505–524, here 516.
37 Cf. *Nuovi avisi* vol. 4, ff. 4^r, 8^r, 10^{r-v}, 17^v-20^v, 25^v-26^r, 29^r-29^v. See also Osami Takizawa, "El conocimiento que sobre el Japón tenían los europeos en los siglos XVI y XVII (I): Japón lugar de evangelización," *Cauriensa* 5 (2010): 23–33, here 28–33.
38 Brown University holds vols. 1 and 2, with the Leuven provenance marking in vol. 1 (Antwerp: Jacob Meursius, 1668). In total, there are six volumes, the last four of which were published as *Actuarium Indicum* (1675–1686). Cf. Angel Muñoz García, *Diego de Avendaño (1594–1698): filosofía, moralidad, derecho y política en el Perú colonial* (Lima: Universidad Nacional Mayor de San Marcos de Lima, 2003), 13–14. It is not listed among the books donated to the Leuven college library in 1635 or in a later list entitled "Anno 1649," included in the same inventory at Rikjsarchief Leuven, Jezuïeten College Leuven 20, so the exact date of ownership is unknown.
39 Francisco Cuena Boy, "El castigo de las injurias causados a los indios. Una página característica de Diego de Avendaño," *Cuadernos de Historia del Derecho* 19 (2012): 9–25, argues, "After all, Avendaño did not speak primarily as a jurist, but as a moralist" (25).
40 *Litterae annuae provinciae Paraquaraiae Societatis Iesu: ad admodùm R.P. Mutium Vitellescum ejusdem Societatis prepositum generalem missae à R.P. Jacobo de Beroa Paraquariae praeposito provinciali* (Lille: Tossani Le Clercq, 1642). The copy at Yale University is inscribed "Colegii Soc.tis Jesu Ant[werp] A[nn]o 1643," which places it in the College of Antwerp after the creation of RA ANJ 2045 in 1613.
41 Russell, "Imagining the 'Indies,'" 179. See also Elisa Frei, "The Many Faces of Ignazio Maria Romeo SJ (1676–1724?), Petitioner for the Indies: A Jesuit Seen through His *Litterae Indípetae* and the *Epistulae Generalium*," *Archivum Historicum Societatis Iesu* 85 (2016): 365–404, here 366–367.

42 I am currently working on a large project concerning the provenance of Jesuit texts, available as a data set and regularly updated: *The European Jesuit Libraries Provenance Project*, which can be found at www.jesuit-libraries.com. Images for which I hold copyright are housed at Georgia Southern University's Digital Commons archive, and the work to create and maintain that collection is being done by undergraduate and graduate student interns with interests in public history. For more information on the EJLPP, see "News and Notes: The European Jesuit Libraries Provenance Project," *Journal of Jesuit Studies* 7/2 (2020): 299–301 (doi:10.1163/22141332-00702009).

17
DEVOTION AT SEA
Ship voyages and Jesuit masculinity

Ulrike Strasser

One of the first global organizations of the early modern world, the Society of Jesus became a major transmission belt for the dissemination of European gender norms to different parts of the world. Jesuits not only brought new notions about masculinity and femininity to their mission territories, they also embodied and pioneered a new form of manhood in Europe and beyond.[1] Forged by Ignatius of Loyola amidst the religious fervor and confessional battles of sixteenth-century Europe, Jesuit manhood pivoted on missionary activity in the world, extreme geographical mobility, and—a first for a pre-modern religious order— the formal exclusion of women from the order.[2] To be a Jesuit meant to be a man. The emergence of this highly mobile, religious masculinity coincided with larger shifts in the gendered organization of the European Catholic Church. Not long after the society's founding, the decrees of the Council of Trent pushed women religious towards the confines of strict enclosure and severely curtailed their radius of action.[3] Trent's apostolic mandate in turn further underwrote the new brand of missionary manhood and Jesuit desires to seek salvation of self through the salvation of distant others.[4]

This essay highlights the importance of the sea journey to the making of Jesuit manhood.[5] It pays special attention to the ship as a space in which these men confronted fears, their own as well as those of others, and the ways in which experiences of fear during transoceanic travels served as occasions for performing missionary manhood in the world. Jesuit pedagogy and training valued the *passions animae* ("passions/emotions"), and especially fear, as a pathway towards God. As part of their formation, Jesuits learned how to convert unhelpful and debilitating fear into proper fear of God, a hallmark of true faith. To draw on a concept from the history of emotions, the early modern modulation of fear was constitutive of the Jesuits' "emotional community."[6] The ready embrace of fear as a moral guide shaped Jesuit homo-social bonds and emotional rules, setting it apart from modern and secular regimes and communities that associate masculinity with the control of fear and the ability to contain one's emotions.[7] Transoceanic vessels provided a crucial context for putting the Jesuit emotional regime and community members to the test, often the first in a series of tests in a missionary's formation. For Jesuits missionaries, the sea voyage was also an emotional journey in which they practiced and internalized the correct expression and experience of fear as stipulated by the Jesuit emotional regime.[8] Histories of Jesuit missions, however, have paid almost no attention to the transoceanic journey itself and focused instead on missionary activity on land.[9] When one looks at Jesuit accounts themselves, boat journeys, lengthy and challenging, take up considerable space. They mark not only a physical passage from one place to another, but also a rite of passage from one state of being to another. In the beginning, a religious man impelled to spread the gospel abroad excitedly boards a ship in Europe. At the journey's end, a true Jesuit missionary lands on foreign shores, his faith deepened by the sustained experience of pastoral work on board, his character seasoned by the experience of surviving the moral and physical perils of crossing seas, and his identity sharpened by having distinguished himself within the social microcosm of the ship.

The enormous ships that plied the oceans in the early modern era were male-dominated spaces. Although women were among the travelers on transoceanic vessels, they were few in number, forcing them to adapt to rather than set cultural and social norms on board.[10] Thus, men defined their brand of masculinity mostly vis-à-vis other men aboard, and a motley crew it was: seamen of all ranks rubbed shoulders with soldiers, merchants, nobles, regular clergy, and members of various religious orders. Among them were the colonial officials and authorities-to-be on whose political or financial patronage the Jesuits were going to depend upon reaching their destination.[11] How Jesuits presented themselves aboard ships mattered a great deal to the Society's fortunes.

Because Ignatius of Loyola was unable to travel beyond Europe, the task of representing Jesuits aboard transoceanic vessels fell to Francis Xavier, the first Jesuit to cross the high seas. The peripatetic Xavier left Goa in spring 1541 to die, many ocean journeys later in 1552, on the island of Shangchuan, just short of the Chinese mainland that he hoped to reach.[12] Canonized in 1622, the same year as Ignatius, Xavier became a towering figure within the Society, serving as an inspiration and guide for generations of missionaries in multiple respects.[13] This essay shows how Xavier, a century and a half after his own ocean journeys, still served as a masculine exemplar for conduct at sea for India-bound Jesuits. Section one reconstructs this exemplar through a reading of the vita of Xavier by Orazio Torsellini (1545–1599), the first printed biography of the saint and the most influential of its time. The second section analyzes Xaverian themes and tropes in the printed accounts of two French Jesuits, Joseph de Prémare (1666–1736) and Vincent de Tartre (1669–1724), who traveled to China at the turn of eighteenth century and whose reports were reprinted in German. Because Xavier's example was translated widely across languages, time, and space, the texts discussed here cross various boundaries as well.

Emotional self-governance emerges as the defining feature of missionary manhood in all of these stories. Even as the Jesuits displayed their religious manhood through various types of religious discipline and pastoral work on board, they showed their masculinity most clearly during the tensest moments of the ocean journey, when mast-breaking, sail-lacerating winds struck fear into the hearts of all men on board and other men succumbed to debilitating fear of death. To perform Jesuit manhood became tantamount to performing the transformation of sinful fears into correct fear of God. The circulation of these stories within the Society of Jesus can thus be understood as an attempt at normative speech, what William Reddy termed an "emotive" about both fear and manhood.[14]

"Whereas others cried a big mountain of tears out of fear, he cried one out of joy": Francis Xavier and the High Seas

The use of narrative exempla was foundational for Jesuit pedagogy and training in its pursuit of bringing the whole person into alignment with God's will. Jesuit teaching followed the triad of *praeceptum-exemplum-imitatio* ("precept-example-imitation") with the persuasive, instructive human example as the indispensable link between moral commands, on the one hand, and social practice, on the other.[15] A form of thought, the exemplum created new forms of action by working the human senses and passions. According to Jesuit understandings, original sin blocked "the direct intellectual path to God," at once confining human beings to the realm of the senses and passions yet also making humanity susceptible to the transformative power of exempla.[16]

The specific exemplum of Francis Xavier was marshaled to create an order of mobile missionaries. Although the "facts" of Xavier's life and especially the details of his journeys were (and have remained) elusive amidst contradictory sources and legends, his far-reaching travels quickly helped make his "hagiological identity of indefatigable Apostle."[17] Much of Xavier's early reputation was owed to the Jesuit grammarian and historian Orazio Torsellini. In 1596, Torsellini published not only the first edition of Xavier's letters,[18] which showcased Xavier as a successful missionary, but also the first biography of Xavier, which illuminated Xavier's own conversion and growth as a Jesuit.[19] Written in a complex humanist Latin that spoke largely to a Jesuit audience, Torsellini's vita soon appeared in a number of European languages to reach a wide audience and exert a profound influence on visual representations of Xavier as well.[20]

How then did Torsellino portray Xavier as an oceanic traveler? Torsellini's description of the very first leg of Xavier's sea journey from Lisbon to Mozambique already marked Xavier as standing out aboard a ship "that almost resembled a city, not only filled with shipmen, but also soldiers, the captain's servants, merchants, and slaves, in all some thousand people."[21] Unlike others, Xavier wasted no time taking in the sights but instead leapt right into pastoral action: "instructing the seamen and others in Christian doctrine, punishing the bad and evil vices, and admonishing everyone without difference to do penance and confess."[22] Notably, Torsellini linked Xavier's efficacy in instilling discipline to his emotional disposition of equanimity and friendliness, which drew others towards him, including those who were stuck "in horrible sins and vices, up to their ears, and shunned members of religious orders."[23] A subsequent outbreak of pestilential fever challenged Xavier's emotional equilibrium, but ultimately his Jesuit training served to restore it. Xavier distinguished himself by transforming fear into confident action. While everyone else who was healthy avoided and then altogether abandoned the sick and dying out of fear, Xavier stepped up. He recalled "what he had practiced during his first years of training… and turned his fear into compassion."[24] Torsellini concluded the longer description of the first ocean journey by noting Xavier's exemplarity: "Thus Xavier gave his companions who were going to travel just this way in the future a certain rule and direction for the Indian journey."[25]

Xavier's mastery of fear is a recurring and defining theme of other stories in the vita. Unusually attuned to the dangers of oceanic travels, the Jesuit reportedly made predictions on three separate occasions about the near shipwrecks of others followed by their miraculous recovery.[26] He himself had this very type of experience in transit from Malacca to India. Violent storms tossed his boat around for three days to the point where the sailors were all convinced that they were going to lose their life any minute. Yet Xavier, Torsellino relates, "remain[ed] entirely unafraid in those things that induce fear in others."[27] He prayed the litany and implored God and Mary, which transported him into another emotional state altogether, experiencing "a much greater joy in his heart in the midst of the dangerous storm than after he survived the danger. For whereas the others felt fear and shaking in the face of mortal danger, he felt and experienced the overflowing sweetness of God, … whereas others cried a big mountain of tears out of fear he cried one out of joy."[28] Fear is the pathway to God in this story. The intense emotional experience at sea indeed made Xavier wish and pray for more terrifying perils still.

Xavier had his wish on the 1552 voyage from Japan towards China. A defining event in the vita on account of its miraculous quality, the voyage was also featured in Andre Reinoso's cycle of twenty paintings dedicated to Xavier's life. Reinoso's large-scale cycle was the first of its kind and most likely assembled around the time of Xavier's beatification in 1619.[29] A week after departure, Torsellini's vita reports, the sky became covered with thick clouds, and darkness descended for days on end while fierce winds whipped the ocean into increasingly high waves and wild currents. To balance out the vessel, the captain ordered some passengers, two "Saracenes" among them, to board a smaller ship and had it tied to the larger boat with ropes.[30] But the ropes tore, pushing the men out onto the sea and thrusting the large vessel back into disequilibrium. Such wailing erupted on board that Xavier came out of his chamber where he had been praying peacefully. Sensing an opportunity, Xavier then asked God for a miracle so that everyone on board could recognize his power. He consoled the distressed shipmates with the prediction that the small ship would return to the mother vessel within three days. These were long days with more storms, and Xavier repeatedly had to assure the fearful and doubtful; one skeptical shipman was named Peter.[31] In the end, the boat not only returned, as predicted, but the two Muslims aboard asked to be instructed and baptized by Xavier. They reported that he had been physically present on the small boat and calmed their fears, a miraculous and comforting appearance that awakened the desire to convert in their heart. The story concludes with Xavier's ordering the captain to hoist the masts, which had been broken and repaired repeatedly during the storm, one more time. Calm settled on the sea and good winds returned.

On multiple levels, this is a story about controlling fears, of having or developing trust and true faith as opposed to fear and despair, a transformation epitomized by the conversion of the Muslims. In Reinoso's depiction, Xavier stands out for his calm presence and gaze towards the heavens amidst the agitated, frantic crew, the broken masts, and shreds of sail. In this respect, the image is reminiscent of another iconic, primal scene at sea: the biblical story of Jesus crossing the Sea of Galilee with his disciples, which was an integral part of the Jesuit imaginary. It was one of the biblical scenes into which Ignatius of Loyola's *Spiritual Exercises* invited exercitants to place themselves and converse with God to discern his will.[32] This primal scene further appeared in Jerome's meditative program *Adnotationes et Meditationes in Evangelia* as one of the vibrant visual prompts that like a biblical slide show ran parallel to and served to illuminate the readings of the liturgical calendar.[33] Aside from being reared on such images, Reinoso very consciously modeled the miraculous deeds depicted in his paintings of Xavier on the miracles associated with Christ.[34] Recall that Jesus was soundly asleep in the midst of a raging storm when his terrified disciples awoke him and charged him with not caring about their fate. Jesus first calmed the waves and then rebuked his disciples: "Why are you so fearful? How is it that ye have no faith?"[35] The disciples asked themselves in turn: "What manner of man is this, that even the winds and the sea obey him?"[36] In the biblical scene then, fear is also the central emotional quality. To be afraid of the storm means to lack faith in divine providence and fall short of true conversion. To believe means to display trust in God and equanimity in the presence of fear-inducing events.

In Catholic theology, fear was indeed a Janus-faced passion, perilous as well as productive. Augustine first distinguished between two types of fear, *timor servilis* (servile fear) on the one hand and *timor filialis* (filial fear) on the other, a binary that structured theological discourses about fear until the Enlightenment. *Timor servilis* was fear of the wrong things, such as fearing the punishment for a sin rather than the sin itself, or fearing the loss of life rather than eternal damnation, and as such it kept humanity in a state of servitude. It was considered a sad affect that, unless properly modulated, could veer all the way into despair. *Timor filialis*, on the other hand, was an uplifting fear; analogous to a child's primary fear of losing the parent's love, it centered on the possibility of losing God's love. It constituted a healthy form of fear, such as fear of sin or of undue attachment to one's life, and it was generative of pious action. A motivating and liberating affect, this type of fear freed one from false fear and led towards despair's opposite: security and confidence in divine providence. Proper fear and proper faith thus went hand in hand. It made fear a powerful instrument for gaining knowledge of self and God.[37]

Early modern Protestants and Catholics alike upheld the Augustinian binary between servile and filial fear, but there was disagreement over the role that servile fear, the lower half of the pairing, had in guiding humanity towards salvation. In the Protestant perspective, it was divine grace that instilled faith, and *timor filialis* helped conquer servile fear; the latter had a very narrow purpose in salvation, namely to direct human beings towards recognition of their inherent sinfulness. By contrast, Jesuits held a more positive and expansive view of servile fear, reflective of the valorization of free will and good works in Catholic theology. Fear, including servile fear, was a powerful educational tool for them.[38] Ignatius set the tone for this approach in his "Rules for thinking with the Church." In the Spanish original, Ignatius tellingly used the verb *sentire* whose meaning ranges from cognitive understanding to the states of feeling so central to Jesuit training. This double-ness corresponds to current theories of emotional life that reject the stark opposition between feeling and thinking and emphasize the cognitive dimension of emotions and the bodily dimension of cognition.[39] Ignatius notes of the state of fear in the culminating paragraph of his spiritual program:

> Through the zealous service of God, our Lord, out of pure love should be esteemed above all, we ought also to praise highly the fear of the Divine Majesty. **For not only filial fear but also servile fear is pious and very holy.** When nothing higher or more useful is attained, **it is very helpful for rising from mortal sin, and once this is accomplished, one may easily advance to filial fear,** which is wholly pleasing and agreeable to God, our Lord, since it is inseparably associated with the love of Him.[40] [Emphasis mine]

"The Difference Between Someone Who Faces Danger from Afar (…) and Someone Who is Actually in Such Danger": The Ocean Travels of Fathers de Prémare and de Tartre

To return to Xavier, his ocean journeys presented an occasion to apply the lessons of his training to himself and others on board. During terrifying storms, the Jesuit personified *timor filialis* while those around him were in the throes of *timor servilis*, which, if properly deployed in devotion, could still present a path towards the love of God and hence presented an opportunity for conversion. Like a truth serum, fear revealed the state of the soul and prepared the believer for the labor of evangelization. As an inevitable by-product of ocean travel, fear was thus high-stakes religious business for Xavier as well as the missionaries who followed in his footsteps.

By the time the French Jesuits Joseph de Prémare and Vincent de Tartre travelled to Asia on Xavier's route, it had become well known that the oceans along the way claimed the lives of many a missionary, a frustrating drainage of personnel that further exacerbated the chronic shortage of Jesuits in the Asia mission. Modern scholars have estimated that up to 50% of Jesuits drowned en route from Lisbon to East Asia while a considerable number of others perished from various illnesses aboard, often because they attended to the needs of other sick passengers.[41] Not surprisingly, tales of shipwrecks and survival of ocean travel became a staple of the period, with Jesuits as avid consumers of and contributors to the popular genre.[42] De Prémare and de Tartre travelled to China on the Amphitrite, the first French ship to traverse the route, in 1699 and 1700 respectively. They penned accounts of their ocean travails that appeared in the French *Lettres édifiantes et curieuses*, and then also in the *Neue Welt-Bott* ("New World Messenger"), the German counterpoint to the famous French collection, which likewise targeted both an internal audience of prospective missionaries and a broader educated public.[43]

Around the turn of the eighteenth century, Xavier's presence aboard manifested itself in a number of ways. His example of setting up a religious routine on board that mirrored pastoral activities on land had become the norm. The Society issued formal rules to be read aloud to the missionaries before departure and at various moments on the trip. They spelled out the rhythms of prayer and pastoral work and celebration of feast days that structured the journey, turning boats into floating spaces of devotion and ministry.[44] Xavier was further present as a special patron saint for ocean travelers. Boats were named after him, his image pinned to masts, and his help solicited in times of need, particularly when regular religious routine broke down and more ad hoc religious responses were needed.[45]

Although enemy ships and piracy posed threats, Jesuit letters speak most about adverse weather events. This usually meant one of two things: either a prolonged absence of winds leading to various diseases, starvation, and dehydration, or stormy winds and turbulent waves that threatened to destroy or topple the ship or drive it against rocks and cliffs, which sent everyone aboard into heightened states of fear. The order's founder, Ignatius of Loyola, was credited with special powers of propulsion. If they were in need of favorable winds, Jesuits carried out a special nine-day devotion to Ignatius. The breeze that allegedly always arose on the second day was termed the "Ignatius winds."[46] When the going got rough and frightening, however, Xavier was the go-to Jesuit saint.

Thus, Xavier was called upon repeatedly during de Prémare's travels. The Amphitrite followed a good part of the saint's route, and de Prémare had knowledge of some sights because, as he reveals, he had read Xavier's vita.[47] When the seamen miscalculated the route and detoured to Sumatra, de Prémare intervened and turned specifically to Xavier to get them back on track and to China by the end of the year. The Jesuits on board carried out special devotions on ten consecutive Fridays, because Xavier had preached the gospel abroad for ten years and had died on a Friday. They further took a vow to build a small chapel above Xavier's island grave and perform a mass inside.[48]

Although the ship found its way back on the course, it encountered a terrifying storm in the South China Sea. Soon everyone on board watched in "fear and shaking" as fierce winds pushed the boat towards rocky grounds, expecting it to splinter like glass.[49] De Prémare here offers a window into his own emotional state and, no doubt, that of many missionaries at sea: "On this occasion I indeed experienced what I had often heard and read, namely the difference between someone who faces danger from afar, say, kneeling in front of his crucifix on his prie-dieu and someone who is actually in such danger."[50] This was a far cry from the composure of Xavier in the Reinoso painting. Fear of God rather than fear of death was easily imagined at home but hard earned at sea.

A last-minute change of air currents averted catastrophe and in 1700 the Amphitrite reached Sangchuan. Convinced that Xavier led them there, the Jesuits paid their dues with a pilgrimage to his grave. They kissed the holy ground and shed tears on it, then built a tent structure using part of a torn sail and an altar on which they said mass after a night of almost constant devotion. Before they left, they pocketed soil from the gravesite for good luck.[51] When the Amphitrite arrived in Canton after eight months at sea, de Prémare credited Xavier for the safe passage.[52]

Pierre de Tartre's account of his voyage was more dramatic still, as it involved twenty near shipwrecks in only five months. On the ship, he noted from the outset, "we learned properly not only to disregard death together with all dangers to life, but also to place our entire trust, but with a complete acceptance, in God alone."[53] He recounted incident after incident of near disaster, fear of death, divine intervention, and deepened human faith. Since the other Jesuits suffered terrible seasickness, but de Tratre only once "paid his dues to the sea with a lunch,"[54] he had to be the ship's chaplain for the duration of the journey. This meant he was leading everyone on board in devotions, particularly when storms were rocking the boat. A first scare occurred around the Paracel Islands where the Amphitrite, on her first journey, almost shattered like glass had it not been, so de Tartre, for the oath to Xavier.[55] Although this time, the ship passed the islands without trouble, they were caught in awful weather in the South China Sea. Masts broke, sails tore, seamen hurt and thrown overboard, and the ship went adrift. The Jesuits pulled all registers to manage the panic on board. They pleaded with God for help and tried to lift everyone's spirit. They heard confessions and urged all aboard to surrender to God's will, whether it meant life or death, with equanimity. De Tartre himself ran around the boat to admonish the people on board to repent, which, as he put it, "did not require much encouragement, since having death before one's eyes was more persuasive than any kind of argument or conclusive speech."[56] Plain fear was more effective than the best rhetoric. Their rhetoric had failed the Jesuits earlier in the journey, when several crew members, recent converts, had gone into hiding to avoid the missionaries' Easter devotions.[57] The storms produced an eager audience.

As the situation deteriorated, de Tartre resorted to additional remedies. Interpreting the storm as the punishment of an angry God, he persuaded everyone on board take two vows: the first was a promise to Francis Xavier to say mass in his praise, confess, and take communion once they safely reached Canton with his help. The second was a promise to the Mother of God to set up a plaque in her honor at a shrine back in France. Within 24 hours, the storms vanished, and de Tarte saw the silver lining: everyone on board had been able to experience saintly intercession through "tangible miracle-work."[58]

Like de Prémare before him, de Tarte paid homage to Xavier at Shangchuan where the ship anchored for three weeks off the coast. Because violent storms once again rocked the boat, the captain dropped anchor and fired the cannons while the Jesuits prayed Xavier's Litany facing his burial place from the sea. When the waves calmed a bit, they boarded a small boat and traveled ashore to perform devotions at the site.[59] But the fiercest storm yet struck after their departure from Shangchuan Island. Unable to control the boat, the crew surrendered to the waves that pushed the boat towards cliffs in thick rain under a pitch-black sky. The dance between fear and faith started all over on board. Tartre reports: "Everyone believed themselves to be lost without hope, prepared themselves for death, everyone and each screamed to heaven for mercy. We listened to more confessions and urged the others towards a repentant exit from this world."[60] This time no one on board required persuasion to repent. Terrified sailors led more lukewarm shipmates to de Tartre to hear their confession. More notable still, fear of death delivered new believers to de Tartre, just as it had delivered the "Saracenes" to Xavier. A group of Huguenots appeared before the Jesuit ready to convert. The group included some men who had previously converted to Catholicism "only in outward appearance and who now in this utter danger converted sincerely."[61] Here too, the right fear was a most potent purgative of falsity, and an ocean storm a most potent producer of fear.

In the course of his turbulent journey, de Tartre wielded such fear repeatedly and productively, turning crew and passengers into his trusting flock. The boat became his most important mission territory rather than a means of getting to his final destination. In fact, his boat in some ways became more important than China, widely considered the jewel among the Jesuit mission territories. In a striking passage recorded towards the end of the journey, de Tartre recounted another storm or what he called "the longest day of my life."[62] What concerned him most that day was not the potential loss to the China mission if his boat sank, which he alluded to as an afterthought. What troubled him deeply was the potential loss of what he had accomplished in transit: "that my poor shipmates, who in ready repentance during so many dangers put their faith in God, now that they believed themselves out of danger and praised God from their hearts, should after all go down in a miserable shipwreck together with their trust."[63] It was as if his greatest feat had already been accomplished before he even set foot on Chinese shores by turning fearful doubters into trusting believers. In his account, de Tartre admitted that at that moment he would rather have stayed on board and fought his superior "with full force to remain and continue in my office" but, alas, in vain. When his feet touched the earth after eight months at sea during which he "suffered so much", the example of the apostles came to mind and how "they never produced so much fruit than where they received the most resistance and persecution."[64]

As de Tartre's transformation into an apostle illustrates, transoceanic journeys, while neglected in mission histories, marked an important stage in the making of missionary men. Boats not only made it possible to move physically from one part of the world to another to deliver the gospel, but also further transported one psychologically and spiritually in the course of the journey. Crowded quarters, colorful shipmates, and the threats of disease, wind, and waves truly put Jesuit manhood to the test. Francis Xavier, the true patron saint of Jesuit mobility, first modeled how to navigate this environment through action and attitude. As a seafaring forefather and imaginary guardian, he left his mark on the voyaging experiences of latter-day Jesuits. Like Xavier, they turned boats into spaces of devotion and ministry as if they were on land. When catastrophic events threatened the lives and salvation of those on board, they too stepped up and offered spiritual remedies, and seized the opportunity to make new converts.

Few phenomena struck fear into the hearts of men like a mast-breaking, sail-tearing ocean storm. Jesuits tried to show their own faith by facing such fear with equanimity. In others, however, they strove to turn this fear into deep and true faith in God. This ability to model and transform emotional states, an integral part of Jesuit formation, set them apart amidst the motley crew of men compared to whom the celibate missionaries may have looked less manly in other respects. It is important to note here that early modern thinking about human "passions" did not typecast women as the emotional and men as the rational gender. This polarization developed in the nineteenth century, first within bourgeois society. Men, just like women, were thought to be in the throes of big feelings like desire and fear and in need of regulating their passions.[65] These religious men showed themselves to be masters of self-regulation, which formed the basis of their claim to regulate others. What made ocean journeys so important for the Jesuits, aside from the practicalities of transportation, is that they accorded much opportunity for the repeated exercise of one's missionary mettle, as one experienced, in Father de Prémare's terms, the emotional difference between contemplating danger in one's chamber and being in danger at sea.

Notes

1 For an assessment and recent scholarship on Jesuits and gender, see the special edition *The Jesuits and Gender: Body, Sexuality and Emotions*, ed. by Mary Laven, *Journal of Jesuit Studies* 2, no. 4 (2015).

2 Ulrike Strasser, "'The First Form and Grace': Jesuits and the Reformation of European Masculinity," in *Masculinity in Reformation Europe*, ed. Scott Hendrix and Susan Karant-Nunn (Kirksville, MO: Truman State Press, 2008), 45–70; Ulrike Strasser, *Missionary Men in the Early Modern World: German Jesuits and Pacific Journeys* (Amsterdam University Press, scheduled release Fall 2020).

3 Silvia Evangelisti, *Nuns: A History of Convent Life, 1450–1700* (New York: Oxford University Press, 2007), esp. 41–54; Ulrike Strasser, *State of Virginity: Gender, Religion, and Politics in an Early Modern Catholic State* (Ann Arbor: University of Michigan Press,

2004), esp. 70–85; Elisabeth Makowski. *Canon Law and Cloistered Women: Periculoso and Its Commentators, 1298–1545* (Washington DC: Catholic University of America Press, 1997); Mary Laven, *Virgins of Venice: Enclosed Lives and Broken Vows in the Renaissance Convent* (London: Penguin, 2002); Elizabeth Lehfeldt,. *Religious Women in Golden Age Spain: The Permeable Cloister* (Burlington: Ashgate, 2005); Ulrike Strasser, *State of Virginity: Gender, Religion, and Politics in an Early Modern Catholic State* (Ann Arbor: University of Michigan Press, 2004), esp. 70–85.

4 Luke Clossey, *Salvation and Globalization in the Early Jesuit Missions* (Cambridge: Cambridge University Press, 2008), esp. 90–135. Women were well aware of the greater freedom accorded to the Jesuits and eager to join the adventure. See Elizabeth Rhodes, "Join the Jesuits, See the World: Early Modern Women in Spain and the Society of Jesus," in *The Jesuits II: Cultures, Sciences and the Arts, 1540–1773*, ed. Johann Bernhard Staudt (Toronto: University of Toronto Press, 2006), 33–49.

5 For a fuller exploration of this topic and visuals, see Strasser, *Missionary Men in the Early Modern World,* chapter 2.

6 Barbara H. Rosenwein, "Worrying about Emotions in History," *American Historical Review* 107 (2002), 821–845. She defines "emotional communities" as "systems of feeling." They reveal "what these communities (and the individuals within them) define and assess as valuable or harmful to them; the evaluations that they make about others' emotions; the nature of the affective bonds between people that they recognize; and the modes of emotional expression that they expect, encourage, tolerate, and deplore." Ibid., 842.

7 See, for example, Ute Frevert, *Men of Honour: A Social and Cultural History of the Duel,* trans. Anthony Williams (Cambridge, MA: Blackwell, 1995).

8 The notion of "emotional regime" comes from William Reddy, *The Navigation of Feeling: A Framework for the History of Emotions* (Cambridge: Cambridge University Press, 2001). On emotions as practice, see Monique Scheer, "Are Emotions a Kind of Practice (and What Makes Them Have a History)? A Bourdieuan Approach to Understanding Emotions," *History and Theory* 51 (2012): 193–220.

9 Notable exceptions include: Liam Brockey, "Largos Caminhos e Vastos Mares: Jesuits Missionaries and the Journey to China in the Sixteenth and Seventeenth Centuries," *Bulletin of Portuguese/Japanese Studies* 1 (2000): 45–72; Tobias Winnerling, *Vernunft und Imperium: Die Societatis Jesu in Indien und Japan, 1542–1574* (Göttingen: Vandenhoeck & Ruprecht, 2014).

10 See, for example, Allyson M. Poska, *Gendered Crossings: Women and Migration in the Spanish Empire* (Albuquerque: University of New Mexico Press, 2016). On attempts to restrict women's travel aboard Portuguese ships to Asia as well as exceptions for female family of high-ranking officers, see Franz Halbartzschlager, "Menschen und Schiffe auf der portugisieschen 'Carreira da India'", in *Seefahrt und frühe europäische Expansion,* ed. Alexander Marboe and Andreas Obenaus (Vienna: Mandelbaum, 2009), 154–178, here 167–69.

11 Winnerling, *Vernunft und Imperium,* 56.

12 The classic, four-volume biography seeking to resolve all these contradictions is Georg Schurhammer, *Francis Xavier, His Life, His Times,* 4. Vols. (Rome: The Jesuit Historical Institute, 1973–82).

13 Rita Haub, and Julius Oswald, *Franz Xaver, Patron der Missionen: Festschrift zum 450. Todestag,* 1. Aufl. ed., Jesuitica (Regensburg: Schnell + Steiner, 2002).

14 On emotives, see Reddy, *Navigation of Feelings,* 63–111.

15 Martin Mulsow, "Exemplum und Affektenlehre bei Georg Stengel, S. J.," *Archiv für Kulturgeschichte* 72 (1990): 313–350. See especially pp. 313–314 and p. 318.

16 Mulsow, "Exemplum", 320.

17 Massimo Leone, *Saints and Signs: A Semiotic Reading of Conversion in Early Modern Catholicism* (New York: De Gruyter, 2010), 325–326.

18 Leone, *Saints and Signs,* 331.

19 Leone, *Saints and Signs*, 374; Torsellini's biography of Xavier was often bound and published together with his edition of Xavier's letters, 371.
20 For various vernacular editions, see Leone, *Saints and Signs*, 369–70. Also, Rachel Miller, "Patron Saint of a World in Crisis: Early Modern Representations of St. Francis Xavier in Europe and Asia" (PhD Dissertation, University of Pittsburgh, 2016), 46.
21 Cited after the German version of 1615. All translations are mine. Torsellini Orazio, *Vom Tugentreichen Leben, Vnd Grossen Wunderthaten B. Francisci Xaverii der Societet Iesv, So den Christlichen Glauben in India Sehr Erweitert, Vnd in Iapon Anfänglich Eingeführt Sechs Bücher* (München: Nicolaus Henricus, 1615), 65.
22 Ibid.
23 Torsellini, *Vom Tugentreichen Leben*, 65–66.
24 Torsellini, *Vom Tugentreichen Leben*, 67.
25 Torsellini, *Vom Tugentreichen Leben*, 71.
26 Torsellini, *Vom Tugentreichen Leben*, 153, 199, 226. Various other prophecies regarding the sea are also associated with him. See Torsellini, *Vom Tugentreichen Leben*, 427ff.
27 Torsellini, *Vom Tugentreichen Leben*, 226.
28 Torsellini, *Vom Tugentreichen Leben*, 342.
29 Miller, "Patron Saint of a World in Crisis," 91 and 94; Leone, *Saints and Signs*, 459. For a depiction of this image, see Strasser, *Missionary Men in the Early Modern World*, chapter 2.
30 Torsellini, *Vom Tugentreichen Leben*, 342.
31 Torsellini, *Vom Tugentreichen Leben*, 342.
32 "How Christ Our Lord Calmed the Storm" is the title of this meditation. Ignatius of Loyola, *Ignatius of Loyola: Spiritual Exercises and Selected Works*, ed. George E. Ganss (New York: Paulist Press, 1991), 189.
33 Jerome Nadal, *Adnotationes et meditationes in Evangelia*, Antwerp, 1607, "Dominica IIII. Post Epiphan." 29.
34 Leone, *Saints and Signs*, 466.
35 KJV, Mark 4:35–441, quote from Mark 4:40.
36 KJV, Mark 4:41.
37 The comprehensive account of early modern conceptions of fear is Andreas Bähr, *Furcht und Furchtlosigkeit. Göttliche Gewalt und Selbstkonstitution im 17. Jahrhundert*, (Göttingen: Vandenhoeck & Ruprecht, 2013). This summary is based especially on pages 79–83.
38 See Bähr, *Furcht und Furchtlosigkeit*, 85–95 on confessional differences, but with disproportionate attention to Protestant arguments.
39 Scheer, "Are Emotions A Kind of Practice?," 195–199.
40 Ignatius, *Spiritual Exercises*, ed. Ganss, Rule 18 on pp. 213–214.
41 Brockey, "Largos caminhos e vastos mares," 45.
42 Brockey, "Largos caminhos e vastos mares," 64.
43 The *Neue Welt-Bott* appeared in a series of single issues between 1725 and 1758, which were subsequently bound together in five volumes. Each volume contained eight issues or 'Teile' (Parts) of 100 to 150 folio pages. Each Part was numbered separately. The missionary letters, treatises, and other materials were numbered consecutively throughout the *Der Neue Welt-Bott*. There is some variation in binding, especially with regards to the images included. I consulted the edition housed in the Herzog-August-Bibliothek in Wolfenbüttel, Germany. Stöcklein, Joseph. Peter Probst, Franz Keller, eds., *Der Neue Welt-Bott oder Allerhand so Sehr als Geistreiche Brief/Schrifften und Reisbeschreibungen, welche von denen Missionaris der Gesellschaft Jesu aus Indien und andern weit-entfernen Ländern seit 1642 bis auf das Jahr 1726 in Europa angelangt seynd. Jetzt zum ersten male Theils aus handschrifftlichen Urkunden, theils aus denen französischen Lettres edifiantes*, 5 vols. Graz/Augsburg 1726–1736 (Verlag Philipp, Martin, und Johann Veith) and Vienna 1748–1761 (Leopold Johann Kaliwoda).
44 Brockey, "Largos caminhos e vastos mares," 46–47.
45 For example, Stöcklein, *Der Neue Welt-Bott*, vol. 1, part 7, Letter 160, 857–876.

46 Stöcklein, *Der Neue Welt-Bott*, vol. 1, part 7, Letter Nr. 172, 75.
47 Stöcklein, *Der Neue Welt-Bott,* Vol. 1, Part 2, Letter 39, 15.
48 Stöcklein, *Der Neue Welt-Bott,* Vol. 1, Part 2, Letter 39, 14.
49 Stöcklein, *Der Neue Welt-Bott*, Vol. 1, Part 2, Letter 39, 16–17; here 17.
50 Stöcklein, *Der Neue Welt-Bott,* Vol. 1, Part 2, Letter 39, 17.
51 Stöcklein, *Der Neue Welt-Bott,* Vol. 1, Part 2, Letter 39, 18.
52 Ibid.
53 Stöcklein, *Der Neue Welt-Bott*, Volume 1, Part 3, Letter 65, 2–3.
54 Stöcklein, *Der Neue Welt-Bott*, Volume 1, Part 3, Letter 65, 3.
55 Stöcklein, *Der Neue Welt-Bott*, Volume 1, Part 3, Letter 65, 5.
56 Stöcklein, *Der Neue Welt-Bott*, Volume 1, Part 3, Letter 65, 6.
57 Stöcklein, *Neue Welt-Bott,* Volume 1, Part 3, Letter 65, 3.
58 Stöcklein, *Der Neue Welt-Bott*, Volume 1, Part 3, Letter 65, 7.
59 Stöcklein, *Der Neue Welt-Bott*, Volume 1, Part 3, Letter 65, 8.
60 Stöcklein, *Der Neue Welt-Bott*, Volume 1, Part 3, Letter 65, 9.
61 Stöcklein, *Der Neue Welt-Bott*, Volume 1, Part 3, Letter 65, 9.
62 Stöcklein, *Der Neue Welt-Bott*, Volume 1, Part 3, Letter 65, 11.
63 Stöcklein, *Der Neue Welt-Bott*, Volume 1, Part 3, Letter 65, 11.
64 Stöcklein, *Der Neue Welt-Bott*, Volume 1, Part 3, Letter 65, 12–13.
65 Catherine Newmark, "Weibliches Leiden - Männliche Leidenschaften. Zum Geschlecht in älteren Affektenlehren," *Feministische Studien* 26, no. 1 (2008): 7–18. For a comparison between Jesuits and examples of religious women aboard ships, see Strasser, *Missionary Men in the Early Modern World*, chapter 2.

18
SPANISH WOMEN, WORK, AND THE EARLY MODERN ATLANTIC ECONOMY

Allyson M. Poska

Evaluating the substance and meaning of work has been critical to the study of early modern European women. Indeed, some of the field's most influential scholars have debated the ebbs and flows of women's labor, including whether women's work suffered a decline in status and how the relationship between expectations and realities played out in women's work lives.[1] However, despite the fact that during the early modern period the Atlantic economy connected markets in Europe, Africa, and the Americas and transformed labor systems with the rapid expansion of African slavery, few scholars have engaged the Atlantic economy from a gendered perspective.[2] Influential scholars of European economic history who have considered the role of gender in economic change tend to do so only within a European context and with an eye towards the industrialization of the nineteenth century. For instance, neither Sheilagh Ogilvie nor Jan de Vries engages the Atlantic world in their discussions of women and preindustrial work. Both Deborah Simonton and Daryl Hafter hint at the connection to the Atlantic economy in their research, but their analyses remain focused on the role of women in the urban economy without making broader Atlantic connections explicit.[3] Other scholars, including Carmen Sarasúa, have analyzed how Enlightenment economic reforms transformed or attempted to transform the gendered division of labor, but again without connecting those policies or their consequences to the Atlantic world.[4]

Similarly, historians of the Atlantic economy have largely neglected the gendered implications of that expansion on European women. For instance, none of the essays in either of the two major collections on the issue devote any significant discussion to European women as such, but only to European women living in the Americas.[5] Scholars of women and gender have explored the impact of Atlantic economic growth on West African women, as well as white, indigenous, and enslaved women in the Americas, but only a few have even considered European women in Europe as a part of the Atlantic economy.[6] One of the only works to deal with issues of European women's work in an Atlantic context is Catterall and Campbell's collection of essays, *Women in Port: Gendering Communities, Economies, and Social Networks in Atlantic Port Cities, 1500–1800*.[7]

There are significant implications for understanding the impact of the Atlantic economy on European women's work. Across Atlantic Europe, scholars have noted the prevalence of female-headed households, including not only households headed by single women and widows, but also women with absent husbands. In these homes, in which women's labor was the sole income generator, the ramifications of changes in women's work were critical, but those changes affected male-headed households as well. The expansion of women's economic activities and their integration into broader economies increased familial wealth and women's economic authority, thus altering gender expectations and familial roles. Moreover, changes in women's work improved the basic living circumstances for women and their families from the wealthiest to the poorest. Indeed, during the eighteenth century, as early modern nation-states focused on economic growth and industrialization, women's work became central to government economic policy precisely because of its broad social implications.

The eighteenth-century expansion of the Atlantic economy affected European women's work in at least three key ways. First, government-driven economic policies led to the establishment of new industries based on cheap female labor, which often tied women and the goods that they produced directly into the Atlantic economy. Second, the growth of the service economy in port cities further linked women to the Atlantic world as they provided housing, retail goods, and domestic service for the growing commercial sector and the men and women who transited through the ports. Finally, the Atlantic economy redefined expectations of European women's work in a diversified and global labor system, as state policy and the expansion of slavery privileged women's engagement in preindustrial work over agricultural labor.

Spanish Enlightenment economists regularly engaged issues relating to women's work and the port at La Coruña in northwestern Spain, which was opened to the trading monopoly with the Americas in 1764 and to free trade with the Indies in 1778, provides an excellent opportunity to analyze the interaction between economic policy and the transformations in Spanish women's work in an Atlantic context. However, there is little unique about La Coruña and the changes women there experienced in terms of work, and hopefully other scholars will find that this argument has resonance in European port cities beyond the Iberian Peninsula.

Spanish economic policy and women's labor

During the second half of the eighteenth century, the connections between European women's work and the Iberian Atlantic economy were grounded in a series of Enlightenment policy initiatives known as the Bourbon reforms. From the Crown's perspective, Spain was beset by crises, unable to keep pace with the industrialization of its imperial rivals, struggling with an array of social problems, and losing its global dominance. The Bourbon reforms attempted to remedy Spain's crises by revitalizing the economy, expanding industrialization, and strengthening the relationship between the peninsular and American economies. For many Enlightenment thinkers, women were at the core of Spain's economic ills and thus its economic revival supposedly because large numbers of healthy, adult women remained "idle" rather than contributing to Spain's economic development.

What did these men mean by idle? Despite the rhetoric, in reality, most women did work. Across northern Spain, most peasant men and women worked side by side in the fields with very little evidence of any particular gendered division of labor.[8] Indeed, some Spanish Enlightenment thinkers and foreign travelers even commented on northern peasant women's agricultural labor. For instance, royal minister and Enlightenment thinker, Pedro Rodríguez Campomanes, noted that in northern Spain women cared for livestock, guided the carts, harvested and gleaned, and even worked the land when men were absent.[9] Enlightenment economist Eugenio Larruga (1747–1803) acknowledged that women first completed their agricultural tasks and then engaged in spinning "during unoccupied hours and at night, and the shepherdesses while they are in the mountains."[10] Nevertheless, in the next breath, Campomanes and others bemoaned Spanish women's "idleness," by which they meant not the failure to work, but the failure to engage primarily in preindustrial labor.[11]

For these economists and policymakers, women's textile work was key to Spain's economic revival. First and foremost, the profits generated by women's labor would do much to fill state coffers. Economist Bernardo Ward (d. 1779) counted two million idle women and estimated that if women and girls would only spin more, the Crown would take in around 20 million *escudos* per year, "almost three times as much as the King collects from all of the Indies."[12] A decade later, Campomanes upped the ante, figuring that there were four million able-bodied adult women who could spin during their "free time." At twenty pesos per woman, this home industry could generate 80 million pesos per year—"more than the value of the Indies."[13] Moreover, women's work would help reestablish some economic equilibrium between the metropole and its vast American territories.[14] In response, Bourbon bureaucrats and intellectuals promoted the development of the textile and related industries across Spain as a means to put millions of these women to work.

In addition to economic growth, integrating women into the preindustrial economy would have critical ramifications for Spanish society. Putting women to work helped resolve a perceived problem with female morality, as many asserted that steady work prevented women from falling into prostitution and that the state could reform prostitutes and other problematic women through retraining in state workhouses.[15] Economists also believed that putting women to work would help increase the peninsula's population, as the perceived imbalance between Spain and its American territories could be quantified in people as well as pesos. Both Ward and Campomanes believed that women were marrying later and therefore having fewer children because they felt that they could not afford the extra mouths to feed.[16] Women's preindustrial labor would solve an array of social ills.

In response, both Campomanes and Ward proposed significant policy changes, not all of which were explicitly gendered, but all of which had gendered implications and tied women's labor directly into the Atlantic economy. For instance, Campomanes proposed the extension first of the trade monopoly and later free trade with the Indies to the port of La Coruña, a change in trade policy which, among other things, allowed for the direct imports of American cotton to Galicia. He then advocated setting up spinning wheels and teaching Galician women how to spin the imported cotton.[17] He noted that free trade would not only slow migration from the region, but that the cotton, linen, and hemp spun by Galician women could then be exported back to the Americas.[18] These textile exports would fill a critical consumption need and help Spain's balance of trade, as the importation of woolen goods to both the peninsula and the Indies was costing the nation millions of pesos annually.[19]

Bernardo Ward proposed an even more direct connection between peninsular women's textile work and that of their counterparts in the Americas. According to Ward, the considerable handiwork that linen and hemp required to get it ready to be spun occupied "many Indian women," and once it was cleaned, much of it could be brought to Spain to be spun by Spanish women, as well as "knit, whitened, and in other ways worked."[20] In this way, women's textile work would become a truly transatlantic industrial process.

The implementation of some of these policies led to the creation of new economic institutions, including the establishment of the Real Consulado de La Coruña in 1785. This organization created Escuelas de Hilaza, schools to teach women and children how to spin.[21] As a result, across the region, the number of looms expanded considerably.[22] The Real Consulado also attempted to expand the planting of hemp and flax across the region to supply these women with the requisite raw materials. However, even when the agricultural side of this expansion floundered, women's integration into the broader economy did not.[23] Women quickly altered their place in the production process, working cloth imported from the Baltic and other parts of northern Europe for sale on the peninsula as well as for reexport to the Indies.[24]

In the last decades of the eighteenth century, the push to capitalize on the growth of the Atlantic economy led to the opening of new enterprises, often by French and Catalan entrepreneurs, many of which were supported by the Real Consulado. Among others, José Codercq employed many women in the manufacture of calicos and linens beginning in 1790 and the firm of Salabert y Barrié (1796/97) came to employ 135 to 140 women (and some men) in the production of more than 20,000 hats each year, mostly for export.[25] Catalan merchants also established a number of factories for salting fish and meats, which employed mostly or exclusively women and made up the bulk of non-textile exports from Galicia to places like Cuba.[26] In addition, at the beginning of the nineteenth century, the Crown established the Royal Tobacco Factory in La Coruña. The goal was to produce more tobacco products than were readily available more cheaply than the imports (usually from Cuba), using tobacco imported from Cuba and the United States. Most of the employees were young women, between the ages of 12 and 20, who for the first time had to leave home to work in the factory.[27] As a result of these policy initiatives, in the following decades, transatlantic industry provided work for thousands of Galician women.

Late eighteenth-century Spanish economic policy and state-driven attempts at industrialization focused on women's employment in these emergent industries. They brought thousands of Spanish women into the Atlantic economy, working products made for export and reexport to the Americas, as well as transforming American products like cotton and tobacco for domestic consumption.

Women and the Atlantic service economy

The growth of the Atlantic economy also created an extensive service economy dedicated to supplying goods and services for the growing numbers of merchants, sailors, soldiers, migrants, and travelers making the transatlantic journey, especially after the Crown opened La Coruña to direct maritime commerce with the Americas. In response, women, both natives of La Coruña and immigrants from across northern Spain, became the purveyors of the goods and services upon which the expanding port depended.

With the opening of Atlantic trade, the population of La Coruña increased significantly and much of the growth in the permanent population came from an influx of women. The city's population nearly doubled in less than forty years, from 7,457 in 1752 to more than 13,000 in 1787. Moreover, throughout the last half of the eighteenth century, the city had a substantial excess of adult women, only about 82 men for every 100 women.[28] Most of these women had migrated from nearby rural areas. By the end of the century, 75% of the women who sought aid from La Coruña's Hospital de la Caridad were migrants and more than 80% were from other parts of Galicia, a majority of whom were single women who hailed from within 60 kilometers of the city.[29] However, the hospital admissions lists also indicate that women came to the city from quite far away, including Asturias, but also the Basque Country, Cataluña and Valencia.[30] The employment possibilities of the Atlantic economy were strong enough to attract women from nearly 1000 kilometers away.

The growth in the city's population meant an increase in the opportunities for work in domestic service and caregiving labor. Not surprisingly, half of the women admitted to the Hospital de la Caridad who listed an occupation were servants.[31] In addition, as increasing numbers of families lingered at port before making the transatlantic crossing, they required an array of temporary services, including nursing, wet nurses, and childcare. Among others, in 1779, royal officials paid María del Carmen, the wife of a nurse at the Royal Hospital, eighty *reales* for having cared for a sick man waiting to leave for the Americas.[32] Around the same time, Francisca Lamela, a twenty-six-year old from outside of Santiago de Compostela, was hired as wet nurse for a family who had enlisted as colonists to Patagonia.[33] As the numbers of transatlantic travelers increased, the economic possibilities for women increased as well.

With the influx of people, the thriving port city needed more and more temporary housing, and women were frequently owners of taverns and inns. Castilian law not only allowed adult women to engage in business contracts, but coastal inheritance laws that tended to favor women also provided them with the economic resources and real estate that they could easily put to use in the service economy. Already by 1752, 14 of the 22 tavern and innkeepers in La Coruña were women.[34] In addition, over the next few decades, the demand for temporary housing gave other women the opportunity to rent out rooms to travelers. In the summer of 1779, as the Spanish Crown used the city as its base for a project to colonize Patagonia, the bureaucrats in charge regularly approved payments to women like Ana Caamero, who provided housing to one of the colonists and his family, and to Doña María Ygnés Rodríguez for the families that she housed.[35] La Coruña's city council also looked to women to provide housing for troops. In fact, a list of housing for soldiers from May 1778 reveals the extent of women's participation in this temporary housing market. Among others, Teresa Manso housed soldiers in five *ranchos*—small, one-story habitations, near the chapel of San Roque—and Joaquina Manso housed soldiers in 46 ranchos located around the city.[36] These women's access to real estate provided a key resource in the Atlantic service economy.

Well before the expansion of the Atlantic trade, women dominated some sectors of the retail economy, including the sale of fresh fish and fruit. According to the 1752 census, 15 of the 18 fresh fish merchants and 20 of the 24 fruit vendors were women.[37] Moreover, women took advantage of the expanded military presence in the city. Female entrepreneurs like Antonia Diaz, whose husband was absent, provided food and other supplies to the army and navy.[38] Although the late eighteenth-century census data does not exist for La Coruña, as the population grew, their role in basic provisioning would have only increased. When royal bureaucrats needed 74 bedframes for the peasants enlisted in a project to colonize Patagonia, they contracted with Doña Sebastiana Sánchez, the widow of Don Joachim Varela, for the items.[39]

The Atlantic economy also provided new investment opportunities for women of means. Rosa de Abelenda, from La Coruña, was the primary investor in the mail frigate "El Colon," which shipped sardines to Havana in 1783. The Basque María de Cabieces funded the mail frigate "El Aguila" that carried shirts to Montevideo in 1788, an opportunity that Josefa Bengoechea took advantage of a year later.[40] In fact, of the 31 Basque merchants in La Coruña who primarily traded with the Americas, five were women.[41] These women moved the capital that they acquired either through their own hard work or through inheritance beyond the confines of the local economy into the Atlantic world.

Increases in trade and immigration at the port of La Coruña meant new opportunities in the Atlantic service economy. As one scholar of eighteenth-century La Coruña has noted, "The benefits from the demand for labour and supplies cannot be overestimated, nor can the resulting stimulus for demographic, professional, manufacturing and market growth."[42] That demand for labor and supplies was met in large part by women, as was at least some of the increased need for investment capital.

Atlantic slavery and the redefinition of European women's work

Enlightenment economic policies aimed at intensifying Spain's industrialization integrated women into the Atlantic economy, and the growth of the Atlantic service economy provided more employment opportunities for women. However, these changes did more than alter the substance and quantity of women's work. As they coincided with an expansion of slavery in the Spanish empire, they also altered expectations about women and work. During the last decades of the eighteenth century, Bourbon reform rhetoric that advocated for moving lower-class European women away from agricultural labor and into preindustrial work combined with an increased association of agricultural labor with slavery. This intersection led to a gradual but critical redefinition of European women's place in the transatlantic labor system.

Key to this transformation was the fact that the last decades of the eighteenth century witnessed a significant expansion of slavery across the Spanish empire. In 1789, the Spanish Crown opened the traffic in enslaved Africans to the Spanish in New Spain, Cuba, Puerto Rico, Santo Domingo, and Caracas. Six years later, the royal decree was extended to include Perú, the Rio de la Plata, Nueva Granada, and Cartagena.[43] In fact, of the more than twelve million enslaved Africans transported to the Americas during the colonial period, more than half made the journey between 1750 and 1825.[44] For Cuba and the Rio de la Plata, this expansion was transformative. From 1790 to 1820, as many as 300,000 enslaved people may have been imported to Cuba. Between 1778 and 1810, the enslaved population of Buenos Aires grew more than 100%, and during those same decades, the enslaved population of Montevideo increased 486%.[45] Unlike their predecessors, these enslaved men and women were almost entirely bound for work in agriculture, especially in the Caribbean.[46] Thus, especially with the transition to plantation agriculture, basic agricultural tasks that had been largely or exclusively done by white women and free women of color were increasingly taken over by enslaved men and women. In fact, even beyond plantations, families with a minimal economic surplus regularly purchased enslaved men and women to plant, hoe, glean, harvest, and care for livestock, all of which was traditionally women's work.[47]

On the peninsula, the fact that the expansion of slavery was most intense in the very places with which La Coruña had direct trade (Cuba and the Rio de la Plata) may have quickly influenced perceptions of what was considered desirable women's work and what kinds of labor were no longer deemed appropriate for white women. In addition to the extension of direct trade with both Cuba and the Rio de la Plata during the last decades of the eighteenth century, more and more women from northwestern Spain traveled to the Americas, learning firsthand of the changing expectations of enslaved people and white women. Take, for instance, the experience of peasant woman Antonia Seijas. Born just outside of La Coruña, she later traveled to Montevideo with her husband, a soldier who served as a drummer in the 29th Battalion of Mallorca. The couple was sent back to Spain with the regiment in 1772 but quickly volunteered to return to the Rio de la Plata as colonists in 1778, along with their two young children.[48] Her transatlantic travels were not unique. By the eighteenth century, it was increasingly common for both men and women to travel to and from the Americas with military deployments, colonization projects, and to attend to family affairs. During those sojourns, peninsular women witnessed how a racial division of labor was superseding the expectations about women's agricultural labor with which they had been raised. Moreover, in the succeeding decades, the connection between the slave trade and Galicia only strengthened. Between 1816 and 1820, 32 merchants from La Coruña participated directly in the slave trade, making more than seventy-five slaving expeditions. The economic impact was intense enough that economic historian Luis Alonso Alvarez has referred to the new triangle trade between La Coruña, West Africa, and Cuba.[49]

Those connections between Galicia and the slave trade had important social and cultural ramifications. Earlier in the eighteenth century, travelers and Enlightenment thinkers regularly referred to northern Spanish peasants as "slaves." In 1757, Englishman James Bruce declared the inhabitants of Galicia to be "indigent and miserable to a point difficult to imagine, slaves of the rest of the provinces of Spain and Portugal,"[50] and Padre Sarmiento called them "the unhappy poor who are slaves of all and of the land." In 1769, the Junta of the Kingdom of Galicia wrote to the Crown that the people of Galicia "certainly are the most enslaved of the Spanish world, there is no comparison between their misery and suffering and that of both Castiles."[51] At this point, as Michel Trouillot has pointed out, slavery was an easy metaphor, casually used to describe an array of evils. However, with the intensification of the slave trade at the end of the century, "slave" was no longer a term that would be meaningfully applied to white men or women, and the agricultural labor done by enslaved Africans and people of African descent certainly would not be associated with white women anywhere in the Spanish empire.

The expansion of the Atlantic economy and slavery did not have the same effect on peninsular men, primarily because state policy did not set out to reorganize men's work in the same ways that it focused on women's work. According to Carmen Sarasúa, Spanish state policy was "reshaping the gender division of labor, facilitating women's work in manufactures and men's work in agriculture, public works and the armies." In fact, moving women out of the fields ensured an abundant supply of agricultural work for men.[52] Indeed, state policy not only reasserted traditional expectations of men's work, Spain's Economic Societies, prompted by Enlightenment economists, also extolled peninsular men's ability to "perfect" agriculture.[53] Thus, both Enlightenment economics and the European culture of racial dominance and control distinguished between European men's labor and enslaved people's labor in ways they did not for women.

Understanding women's connections to the Atlantic economy provides the basis for a more complex understanding of the evolution of women's work. Although I have focused on women in northern Spain, Dutch, French, English, and Portuguese women also experienced dramatic changes in both the substance and the expectations of work at the end of the eighteenth century. Moreover, gendered analysis of the Atlantic economy reveals the degree to which women's work was a critical link between colony and metropole and central to the economic dynamism of the early modern Atlantic world.

Notes

1 Many scholars have contributed to these debates, but Merry Wiesner-Hanks has played a central role. Among other works, her *Working Women in Renaissance Germany* (New Brunswick, NJ: Rutgers University Press, 1986) and "Spinning Out Capital: Women's Work in Preindustrial Europe, 1350–1750," in *Becoming Visible: Women in European History*, ed. Renate Bridenthal, Susan Mosher Stuard and Merry E. Wiesner (Boston: Houghton Mifflin, 1998), 203–232 have been critical to the field. Moreover, she has been critical in pushing for a revival of interest in early modern women's work in the context of the 100th anniversary of the publication of Alice Clark's *Working Life of Women in the Seventeenth-Century* (London: Routledge, 1919).
2 This article follows up on ideas presented in Susan D. Amussen and Allyson M. Poska, "Shifting the Frame: Trans-imperial Approaches to Gender in the Atlantic World," *Early Modern Women: An Interdisciplinary Journal* 9, no. 1 (October 2014): 3–23.
3 Among her many works on urban women's labor, see Deborah Simonton, "Widows and Wenches: Single Women in Eighteenth-Century Urban Economies," in *Female Agency in the Urban Economy* ed. Deborah Simonton and Anne Montenach (New York: Routledge, 2013), 93–115; Daryl M. Hafter, *Women and Work in Preindustrial France* (University Park, PA: Penn State Press, 2007).
4 Carmen Sarasúa, "Technical innovations at the service of cheaper labour in pre-industrial Europe. The Enlightened agenda to transform the gender division of labour in silk manufacturing," *History and Technology*, 24, no. 1 (2008): 23–39 and "Una política de empleo antes de la industrialización: paro, estructura de la ocupación y salarios en la obra de Campomanes," in *Campomanes y su obra económica*, ed. F. Comín and P. Martín Aceña, (Madrid: Instituto de Estudios Fiscales, 2004), 171–191.
5 John J. McCusker and Kenneth Morgan, eds., *The Early Modern Atlantic Economy* (Cambridge: Cambridge University Press, 2000) and Peter A. Coclanis, ed., *The Atlantic Economy during the Seventeenth and Eighteenth Centuries: Organization, Operation, Practice, and Personnel* (Charleston: University of South Carolina Press, 2005). For an example of a brief discussion of European women in the Atlantic economy, see Nuala Zahediah, *The Capital and the Colonies: London and the Atlantic Economy, 1660–1700* (Cambridge: Cambridge University Press, 2010), 59.
6 Among others, Philip Havik, *Silences and Soundbytes: The Gendered Dynamics of Trade and Brokerage in the Pre-colonial Guinea Bissau Region* (Munster: Lit. Verlag, 2004); Ellen

Hartigan-O'Connor, *The Ties that Buy: Women and Commerce in Revolutionary America* (Philadelphia: University of Pennsylvania Press, 2009); Lisa Norling, *Captain Ahab Had a Wife: New England Women and the Whalefishery, 1720–1870* (Chapel Hill: University of North Carolina Press, 2000); Jennifer L. Morgan, *Laboring Women: Reproduction and Gender in New World Slavery* (Philadelphia: University of Pennsylvania Press, 2004); Jane Mangan, *Trading Roles: Gender, Ethnicity, and the Urban Economy in Colonial Potosi* (Durham: Duke University Press, 2005). For instance, Amy Froide, *Silent Partners: Women as Public Investors during Britain's Financial Revolution, c. 1690–1750* (Oxford: Oxford University Press, 2016); Nicole Dufournaud and Bernard Michon, "Les femmes et le commerce maritime à Nantes (1660–1740): un rôle largement méconnu," *Clio. Histoire, femmes et sociétés* [on-line], 23 (2006), last modified June 1, 2008, accessed November 26, 2017, http://clio.revues.org/1926; Jennifer L. Palmer, *Intimate Bonds: Family and Slavery in the French Atlantic* (Philadelphia: University of Pennsylvania Press, 2016).

7 Douglas Catterall and Jodi Campbell, eds., *Women in Port: Gendering Communities, Economies, and Social Networks in Atlantic Port Cities, 1500–1800* (Leiden: Brill, 2012).

8 Serrana Mercedes Rial García, "Trabajo femenino y economía de subsistencia: el ejemplo de la Galicia moderna," *Manuscrits* 27 (2009): 86. On Asturias, Patricia Suárez Álvarez and Alberto Morán Corte, "Más allá del telar: el mundo del trabajo femenino en la Asturias del siglo XVIII," *El Futuro del pasado: revista electrónica de historia* 2 (2011): 483–498.

9 Pedro Rodríguez Campomanes, *Discurso sobre la educación popular* sección *de los artesanos y su fomento* (1775) sección XVII, available at www.cervantesvirtual.com.

10 Eugenio Larruga, *Memorias políticas y económicas sobre los frutos, comercio, fábricas y minas de España: con inclusion de los reales decretos, ordenes, cedulas, aranceles y ordenanazas expedidas para su gobierno y fomento. Tomo XLIII, Pesca, monedas, pesas, medidas, ferias, mercados, contribuciones y comercio de Galicia* (Madrid: Oficina de Don Joseph Espinosa, 1798), 178.

11 For a recent discussion of and an extensive bibliography on women and textile production in eighteenth-century Madrid, see Victoria López Barahona, *Las Trabajadoras en la sociedad madrileña del siglo XVIII* (Madrid: Editorial ACCI ediciones, 2016). On women, families, and Catalan textile production, see the work of Marta Vicente, including *Clothing the Spanish Empire: Families and the Calico Trade in the Early Modern Atlantic World* (Houndsmills, UK: Palgrave Macmillan, 2006).

12 Bernardo Ward, *Proyecto económico: en que se proponen varias providencias dirigidas á promover los intereses de España...* (Madrid: Joaquin Ibarra, 1779), xvi. There is considerable debate over Ward's authorship and/or plagiarism of the text. According to David Brading, José del Campillo y Cossío's *Nuevo sistema para el gobierno económico para la América* (Madrid: Benito Cano, 1789) circulated in manuscript form between 1743 and 1762 when it was then incorporated into Ward's text. D.A. Brading, *Miners and Merchants in Bourbon Mexico: 1763–1810* (Cambridge: Cambridge University Press, 1971), 25. According to Barbara and Stanley Stein, the true author is Melchor Rafael de Macanaz. *Silver, Trade, and War Spain and America in the Making of Early Modern Europe* (Baltimore, MD: Johns Hopkins University Press, 2000), 222.

13 Pedro Rodríguez Campomanes, *Discurso sobre el fomento de la industria popular* (1774), VIII, available at www.cervantesvirtual.com.

14 Stanley J. Stein and Barbara H. Stein, *Apogee of Empire: Spain and New Spain in the Age of Charles III, 1759–1789* (Baltimore: Johns Hopkins University Press, 2003), 69.

15 On these issues, see López Barahona, *Las Trabajadoras en la sociedad madrileña* and María Luisa Meijide Pardo, *La mujer de la orilla: visión histórica de la mendiga y prostituta en las cárceles, galeras de hace dos siglos* (A Coruña: Ediciós do Castro, 1996).

16 Ward, *Proyecto económico*, 59.

17 Manuel de Castro, O.F.M., "Informe de Campomanes sobre la emigración e industrialización de Galicia," *Cuadernos de Estudios Gallegos* 13, no. 40 (1958): 251.

18 Manuel de Castro, O.F.M., "Informe de Campomanes," 252.

19 Campomanes, *Discurso sobre el fomento*.
20 Ward, *Proyecto económico*, 266.
21 María del Carmen Sánchez Rodríguez de Castro, "El Real Consulado de La Coruña: impulsor de la Ilustración en Galicia," in *Censura e ilustración: XX Aniversario da Fundación da Facultade de Filosofía e CC. da Educación*, ed. Xosé Luis Barreiro Barreiro, Martín González Fernández, and Luis Rodríguez Camarero (Santiago de Compostela: Universidad de Santiago de Compostela, 1997), 79–93, esp. 86.
22 Pegerto Saavedra, "Desenvolvemento e crisis da industria textil Galega: A fabricación de lenzos, 1600–1840," in *Das casas de morada ó monte comunal* (A Coruña: Xunta de Galicia, 1996), 279 and Joám Carmona Badía, *El atraso industrial de Galicia. Auge y liquidación de las manufacturas textiles (1750–1900)* (Barcelona: Ariel, 1990), 128.
23 Rodríguez de Castro, "El Real Consulado," 83. Luis Alonso Álvarez, *Comercio colonial y crisis del antiguo régimen en Galicia (1778–1818)* (A Coruña: Xunta de Galicia, 1986), 88–89 and 97–99.
24 Ofelia Rey Castelao, "Casas y cosas en la Galicia occidental en el siglo XVIII," *Cuadernos de historia moderna* 14 (2015): 231. The reasons for the decline and/or stagnation of the linen industry in Galicia are complex and hotly debated, see Carmona Badía, *El atraso industrial* and Saavedra, "Desenvolvemento."
25 Ofelia Rey Castelao, "Del noroeste español a América: oportunidades y medios de fraude y de corrupción," *e-Spania* (Dec. 2013): paragraph 30; José Lucas Labrada, *Descripción económica del reyno de Galicia* (Ferrol, 1804), 35.
26 Antonio Meijide Pardo, *El puerto de La Coruña en el siglo XVIII* (La Coruña: Editorial la Vox de Galicia, 1985).
27 Luis Alonso Álvarez, "De la manufactura a la industria: la Real Fábrica de Tabacos de La Coruña (1804–1857)," *Revista de Historia Económica—Journal of Iberian and Latin American Economic History* 2, no. 3 (1984): 13–34.
28 Baudilio Barreiro, *La Coruña 1752 Según las respuestas generales del Catastro de Ensenada* (La Coruña: Tabapress, 1990), 8 and 16. Antonio Eiras Roel, "Demografía rural en la España moderna: evolución, variantes y problemas" in *El mundo rural en la España moderna*, ed. Francisco José Aranda Pérez, (Cuenca: Ediciones de la Universidad de Castilla-La Mancha, 2004), 2:28. It is important to note that a series of agricultural crises also acted as important factors in the intense migration to La Coruña.
29 Eva Sampayo Seoane, "Un refugio tan preciso como interesante a la república: el hospital de la Caridad de Coruña, 1796–1805," *Cuadernos de Estudios Gallegos* 46, no. 111 (1999): 128. Interestingly enough, the Hospital de la Caridad was established by a woman, Doña Teresa Herrera. Alfredo Vigo Trasancos, *A Coruña y el siglo de las luces: la construcción de una ciudad de comercio (1700–1808)* (A Coruña: Universidade de A Coruña, 2007), 278–285.
30 Sampayo Seoane, "Un refugio," 137.
31 Sampayo Seoane, "Un refugio," 140.
32 Archivo Municipal La Coruña (AMLC), Colección de la familia de Cayo Acha de Patiño, caja 5 (1) 1, Libro de Cuentas, agosto 1779.
33 Juan Alexandro Apolant, *Operativo Patagonia: Historia de la mayor aportación demográfica masiva a la Banda Oriental* (Montevideo: Ediciones El Galeón, 1970), 320. On gender and the colonization project, see Allyson M. Poska, *Gendered Crossings: Women and Migration in the Spanish Empire* (Albuquerque: University of New Mexico Press, 2016).
34 Barreiro, *La Coruña, 1752*, 148-9. On the status of women with absent husbands, see Allyson M. Poska, *Women and Authority in Early Modern Spain: The Peasants of Galicia* (Oxford: Oxford University Press, 2005).
35 AMLC, Colección de la familia de Cayo Acha de Patiño, caja 5 (1)1, Libro de cuentas, Mayo 25–Julio 31, 1779 and Dec. 1779. On female landlords in Galicia, see Serrana M. Rial García, *Las mujeres en la economía urbana del antiguo régimen: Santiago durante el siglo XVIII* (A Coruña: Ediciós do Castro, 1995), 166-67.
36 AMLC, Fondo Ayuntamiento Coruña, Libro de Actas 1778, fol. 301.

37 Barreiro, *La Coruña 1752,* 143–147.
38 Barreiro, *La Coruña 1752,* 108.
39 AMLC, Libro de Cuentas, Caja 5 (1) 1, Nov. 1780.
40 Alonso Álvarez, *Comercio colonial,* 107, 109, and 177.
41 Alonso Álvarez, *Comercio colonial,* 177.
42 Jesus Angel Sánchez Garcia, "Commerce and Harbour Development in the town of Corunna (Spain) during the Eighteenth Century," *International Journal of Maritime History* 22, no. 1 (2010): 145.
43 Elena Schneider, "African Slavery and Spanish Empire: Imperial Imaginings and Bourbon Reform in Eighteenth-Century Cuba and Beyond," *Journal of Early American History* 5 (2015): 26.
44 Alex Borucki, "The Slave Trade to the Río de la Plata, 1777–1812: Trans-Imperial Networks and Atlantic Warfare," *Colonial Latin American Review* 20, no. 1 (2011): 81.
45 Matt D. Childs, "'The Defects of being a Black Creole': The Degrees of African Identity in the Cuban *Cabildos de Nación,* 1790–1820," in *Slaves, Subjects, and Subversives: Blacks in Colonial Latin America,* ed. Jane G. Landers and Barry M Robinson (Albuquerque: University of New Mexico Press, 2006), 214; Borucki, "The Slave Trade to the Río de la Plata," 83–88.
46 On the transition to plantation agriculture, especially in the Caribbean, see Schneider, "African Slavery," 12ff.
47 On people of modest means owning slaves, see Lyman L. Johnson, *Workshop of Revolution: Plebian Buenos Aires and the Atlantic World. 1776–1810* (Durham: Duke University Press, 2011), 39. On enslaved people doing women's work see Poska, *Gendered Crossings,* 179–180.
48 Apolant, *Operativo Patagonia,* 244; Juan Alexandro Apolant, *Génesis de la familia uruguaya: los habitantes de Montevideo en sus primeros 40 años, filiaciones, ascendencias, entronques, descendencias* (Montevideo: Imprenta Vinaak, 1966), 658–659.
49 Alonso Álvarez, *Comercio colonial,* 227–228.
50 Jacobo García Blanco-Cicerón, *Viajeros angloparlantes por la Galicia de la segunda mitad del siglo XVIII* (A Coruña: Fundación Pedro Barrie de La Maza, 2006), 206.
51 Cited in Antonio Meijide Pardo, "La emigración Gallega intrapeninsular en el siglo XVIII," *Estudios de historia social de España* 4, no. 2 (1960): 463–606, esp. 481. On the uses of the word "slave" in the eighteenth century, see Michel Trouillot, *Silencing the Past: Power and the Production of History* (Boston: Beacon Press, 1995), 85–86.
52 Sarasúa, "Technical innovations," 35 and Ruth Mackay, *"Lazy, Improvident People:" Myth and Reality in the Writing of Spanish History* (Ithaca: Cornell University Press, 2006), 165 n. 5.
53 Mackay, *Lazy, Improvident People,* 118.

AFTERWORD

Looking backwards and forward

Susan Karant-Nunn

I. Women's and gender history

This book-length tribute to Merry Wiesner-Hanks draws together the essays of a number of Merry's longest-term colleagues who have become her friends. Several of us matured as scholars together, in interaction with one another. The majority of these works reflect indeed their authors' bonds with her in that they take up new aspects of the first cast and attainment of Merry's career, namely to draw our attention to the ubiquitous presence, the varied attainments, and even the influence of women throughout early modern European society. The contributors came to this fundamental shift in vision under the pioneering stimulus of Merry and a few of her similarly imaginative peers such as—apropos of the longer sixteenth century—Heide Wunder, Natalie Zemon Davis (who has graced this volume with an introduction), and Lyndal Roper. No doubt, Merry drew some impetus too from the explorations of Miriam Usher Chrisman and Nancy Lyman Roelker. Robert Kingdon was creditably willing to bless Merry's own voyages of discovery—and even, in the latter part of his scholarly career, took up the subjects of divorce and sexual transgression in Geneva. Both the times and his increasingly distinguished student goaded the eminent teacher as well! Learning is ever reciprocal.

Merry gladly embraced the feminist theory that was emerging and sank her *bona fides* deeper. She has nonetheless never wielded that theory obtrusively. I take her to be laughing at its extremes when she writes,

> ...[M]y title implies that I might be doing an intertextual reworking of post-Certeauian explications of the interactivity between event and structure combined with a neo-Althusserian privileging of structure over agency set in the context of a Foucaultian paradigm of phallologocentric self-referential discourse pre/overdetermined by positionalities of subjectivity and authority.[1]

She has stated again and again that historians of women should never consider that, having focused on a neglected populace for two generations, they have now amassed sufficient familiarity with the conditions of life and outlook of the objects of their study. Whatever trends may bear on their interpretation, they should go on collecting from that inexhaustible wellspring of what we do not know. Perhaps *The Marvelous Hairy Girls: The Gonzales Sisters and Their World* (a *New Yorker* "Briefly Noted" book[2]) is a manifestation of her own determination to keep doing precisely that.[3] The theme of omitting, or forgetting about, or alternatively, engaging in prejudicial or stereotyped ways of remembering women permeates her work down to today.[4]

Even as most of the writers here mark Merry's impression upon them as from her initial and ongoing identity as a specialist on women's past, they demonstrate the novel historiographic currents that continue to shape the questions we pose. This innovation, echoing her own, is part of their offering to Merry. Seven concentrate on the German-speaking lands in which she began. David Whitford finds that Martin Luther's estimation of Eve, as measured by his expositions of Genesis 1 in 1523 and 1535, improves after his marriage and becoming a father. Joel Harrington features people's ongoing belief—indeed, into the nineteenth century—in the signals concerning guilt or innocence that corpses, by bleeding or moving, could give. A dead wife reveals with her effusions of blood her husband's identity as her murderer. Amy Leonard, like Harrington, reflecting recent interest in the body as well as in sexuality, considers the evidence of a continued affirmation of the superior honorability inherent in especially female virginity. Although this was more decisive within early modern Catholicism, even Martin Luther, the great advocate of marital (sexually active) chastity, presented mixed messages in insisting on the perpetual physical virginity of Mary. Leonard concludes that virginity "becomes a blank slate on which historical actors could express their deepest sexual and societal views" (p. 32). Beth Plummer asserts the hybridity and changeability of Saxon nuns' decisions for and against the Reformation in contrast with the clean "yes or no" alignments that some past historians have totted up. Where possible, she pursues individuals during key years (1525, 1533–1534, 1540–1560) and finds vacillation in their arguments. Some who had left their convents desired to return. Using letters and diaries, Sigrun Haude describes the calculations of Bavarian nuns, members of major families, during the Thirty Years' War. Should they flee the encroaching Swedish troops or try to negotiate with them? Whatever their ploy, the outcome was often unhappy. Haude stresses the disturbance the sisters suffered in their sense of space.

Marc Forster observes the centrality of sexual honor in defining women's status in the village courtrooms of the island of Mainau in the seventeenth and eighteenth centuries. Strong wives were valued in Catholic rural society but needed to avoid the tainture of accusations of being whores or witches. Such slanders were rampant. John L. Thompson portrays another facet of the supremely learned, theologically adept Anna Maria van Schurman: that revealed in portions of her small corpus of vernacular verse. She may have presented these stanzas to the

"Utrecht Circle" of her Reformed friends. Thompson finds them characteristically Reformed in content and lacking in mystical eroticism.

Other contributors to this festschrift, while adhering to the subject of women, bring in their research on other parts of Europe as befits their specializations. Carol Levin shows how James I's contempt for—fear of—women played out after his succession as he banned expressions of mourning for Elizabeth. Certain high-ranking women, Mary Lake and Ann Cecil (Lady Roos), were regarded as, respectively, Eve and the serpent. Levin points out that James's court was "rife with scandal," yet the king was apparently ready to impute evil calculation to many women, of whom she gives other examples. Jeffrey Watt uses the Geneva consistory records to prove that more women than men remained attached to Catholic practices such as the veneration of Mary and the celebration of Christmas. Nonetheless, most women were eager to conform to the new regime. Raymond Mentzer argues that in post-Edict of Nantes France, elite women subtly sustained Reformed tradition as much as possible even as their husbands presented an image of Catholic fidelity. Emigration, however, gave Huguenot women greater opportunities for religious expression, even as preachers and prophetesses.

Dutch women emigrées in Emden are visible in that city's poor-relief registers of 1569–1575. Timothy Fehler observes that even as *femmes soles*, as widows and other heads of households, they are listed without their own occupations. Christine Kooi detects numerous ways that Catholic women within the officially Reformed Netherlands managed to retain and perpetuate their faith. Female sociability helped them to fade into the broader populace. Some lived as *klopjes* or semi-nuns and managed to fill a priestly numbers-gap.

Elizabeth Lehfeldt compares Spanish and English visitations of convents on the eve of the Reformation. Mainly clergy oversaw nuns in Spain, and they avidly sought their religious enclosure. In England, laity too could apply for membership on a visitation panel. One Thomas Legh was especially bent on rigid discipline. North and south, nuns regarded outside incursion into their long-standing practices with hostility. Nicholas Terpstra features the communal nature of Jewish exile from Spain in and after 1492. In this setting, women, who were influential in the domestic liturgical and spiritual setting, continued to wield some authority.

A further essay is not about women and gender but rather one man's particular spiritual cause. Jodi Bilinkoff writes about Alonso de la Madre de Dios (d. 1636), a Discalced Carmelite who made the beatification of John of the Cross his special cause. Alonso joined the fray over John's relics and gathered stories about the future saint's suffering and miraculous deeds, which he collected in his biography.

II. The Wider world

Merry continues to leave her imprint on the composite field of world history. Three of the contributions to this festschrift echo the shift in Merry's circumspection from Europe to the broader planet. The essays here have strong implications for Europe's subsequent and ongoing interactions with other peoples and environments. Ulrike Strasser incorporates the sea voyage of every mission-minded member of the Society of Jesus as an ordeal that compelled the brethren to hone their faith and overcome their fear of death by foundering. Modeling themselves on the first-generation paragon, Francis Xavier, Jesuits established their credentials as *men* by undergoing this ordeal of outreach beyond contiguous Europe. In so far as their actual knowledge of distant lands extended, Kathleen Comerford finds that the lists of holdings of seven major Jesuit libraries reveal a surprising ignorance of the fathers' geographic destinations. Only 2.5% of the titles were global in their content. The men were, she concludes, poorly prepared for missions and yet suffused with religious zeal.

Allyson Poska in one sense returns to Merry's initial book-length foray into history by considering women's work and its decline in status, only now in the Iberian world and during the eighteenth century. Writers of that era regarded women as idle and advised their confinement to domestic labor and gainful skills related to it, such as spinning imported cotton and domestic flax. Some rich women were nonetheless engaged in trade with South America. Overall, women's labors underwent revision downward in those parts of Europe that were affected by the Atlantic economy.

Today, Merry herself lays strong emphasis on Europeans' activities and reactions outside their homelands. She threw down the gauntlet not later than 2000, when the first edition of *Christianity and Sexuality in the Early Modern World: Regulating Desire, Reforming Practice* appeared.[5] Merry is explicitly comparative here, featuring official teachings and popular practices inside Europe and also the colonizers' efforts to extend their values into Latin America, Africa and Asia, and North America. Her jointly authored textbook, *A History of World Societies*, was in its tenth edition in 2015[6]; and in that year, her own *Concise History of the World* made its debut.[7] In the Division for Late Medieval and Reformation Studies at the University of Arizona, Merry gave the Reformation quincentennial (2017) Town and Gown Lecture. She was invited to select her own favored topic, and it proved to be intercultural and comparative. The title was "To the Ends of the Earth: Religious Transformations in the Age of the Reformation." She began by asking what emerging religious leader "renounced traditional religious practices and beliefs, particularly those observances that promised salvation; who promoted education for a wider swath of people and supported the printing of religious texts in the vernacular language, so that the educated elite would no longer have sole control of religious practices and worship."[8] Although these might also have characterized Martin Luther, the religious revolutionary whom she meant to describe was Guru Nanak (1469–1539), the founder of Sikhism. She noted, too the spread of Jewish mysticism in the sixteenth century, and the spread of Sufism in certain Islamic centers. She briefly took up the Safavid and Songhay empires. Her unifying message was, and often is, that we should look beyond our smaller settings and acquire familiarity with the broader contemporaneous ranges of human thought and aspiration. Merry stressed that she was not suggesting a relational link between Nanak and Martin Luther but that it is valuable to be aware that other impulses toward religious reform existed and were articulated by powerful voices beyond those on whom we, with our ethnic and confessional links, happen to focus. Neither Luther nor Europe was the hub of the universe.

Merry does not entertain illusions about the abilities of mere mortals to master multiple fields with their respective languages and research sources. It nevertheless behooves and serves us to expand our vision. This would seem to be the principle at which Merry has arrived as she prepares to retire from formal teaching. We may all look forward with her; she has left us a rich legacy, and she will doubtless continue to build it. She is a colleague of unflagging energy and enthusiasm; her model and the expansive corpus of her work will endure.

As I write this, Merry Wiesner-Hanks is president of the World History Association. It is surely appropriate that in that capacity, and over her signature, a letter has gone out to Mr. Trevor Packer of the College Board in response to the Board's decision to chronologically and thematically curtail aspects of the Advanced Placement World History program. She, the other officers, and numerous other signatories argue coherently:

> The change you announced erases one of the few opportunities that students have to engage meaningfully with non-Western cultures in the current K-12 landscape .... The sub-discipline of world history differs from regional and national histories in challenging students and practitioners to think on multiple scales .... Only by examining the human past over the very long term can we discern the shared history of our humanity, interactions between humans and the environment, patterns of state-building and governance, similarities and differences in social structures such as gender or class, changes in cultural practices such as religion or architecture, and major ruptures such as the development of agriculture or the fossil fuel revolution .... We want students at every level to have exposure to this broad panorama, to allow them to better understand and function in their increasingly interdependent world.[9]

This festschrift honors Merry Wiesner-Hanks for the whole of her attainment, which encompasses her early path-breaking enterprise as well as that work that points us into a future that is global and interrelated. If this book were to include a *tabula gratulatoria*, the names of numerous non-North American, non-early-modernist colleagues would be appended here. We who have written for this festschrift acknowledge the breadth of her present audience and the effects for future students of history that her message will prove to have.

Notes

1 "Women's History and Social History: Are Structures Necessary?" in *Time, Space, and Women's Lives in Early Modern History*, edited by Anne Jacobson Schutte, Thomas Kuehn,

and Silvana Seidel Menchi, Sixteenth Century Essays and Studies 57 (Kirksville, MO: Truman State University Press, 2001), pp. 3–16, here at p. 3.
2 (July 27, 2009), p. 75.
3 (New Haven: Yale University Press, 2009).
4 Merry Wiesner-Hanks, "Confessional Histories of Women and the Reformation from the Eighteenth to the Twenty-First Century," in *Archeologies of Confession: Writing the German Reformation 1517–2017*, edited by Carina L. Johnson, David M. Luebke, Marjorie E. Plummer, and Jesse Spohnholz (New York and Oxford: Berghahn, 2017), pp. 89–110.
5 Published in the series, Christianity and Society in the Modern World (London and New York: Routledge); a second (revised) edition appeared in 2010.
6 John P. McKay is the first-listed author of several (Boston: Bedford-St. Martin's).
7 Cambridge, Eng., and New York: Cambridge University Press.
8 A slightly modified quotation from the summary of Rachel Davis Small in "Desert Harvest," 25, 1 (spring 2017), p. 5, biannual newsletter of the Division for Late Medieval and Reformation Studies, University of Arizona. Accessible on-line at https://dlmrs.arizona.edu/desert-harvest-newsletter.
9 www.thewha.org. Merry's term ran from 2018 through 2019.

INDEX

Abé, Takao 197
Abelenda, Rosa de 228
Acquavia, Claudio 199
Act of Supremacy 1534 (United Kingdom) 112–13
Actes and Monuments (Foxes) 181
Adam 38–41
addled Parliament 74
Adnotationes et Meditationes in Evangelia (Jerome) 214
Adolphus, Gustavus 97–8, 100
adultery 27
Adultery and Divorce in Calvin's Geneva (Kingdon) 1
Adventures of Tom Sawyer (Twain) 20
Agartha, Saint 30
Age of Voyages, 1350–1600 (Wiesner-Hanks) xvi
Agnes, Saint 30
aiguillette 140
Albabata, Ambrosius de 99
Alberti, Michael 20
Algonquin 201
almshouses 153
Altenburg convent 89
American Historical Review 2
Amphitrite (ship) 216–19
Anabaptists 178; disbursements 193
anti-Catholic laws 149
Antolín, Fortunato 48
anxious masculinity 6
Ap Rice, John 115, 116, 117
Apostles' Creed 139
Aquinas 30
The Araignment of Lewd, Idle, Froward and Unconstant Women (Swetnam) 71
arbitration 59

Arjó, Joseph de 199
Arte, y bocabulario de la lengua guarani (Ruiz de Montoya) 200
Atlantic economy: cotton trade 226; and European women's work 224; expansion in 18th century 224; investment opportunities for women in 228; new enterprises by French and Catalan entrepreneurs 226–7; retail trade 228; and slavery 229–31; and Spanish Enlightenment 224–7; textile trade 226; tobacco trade 227; women in service economy 227–9; women's roles in 223–31
Attending to Early Women (symposium) 5
Augustine 30, 38–9
Ave Maria 139
Avellaneda, Diego de 199
Avendaño, Diego de 203

Bainton, Roland 1
Ballard, Antoine 162
Bambergensis 16
bandeirantes 202
baptism 138, 152–3
Bauchlin, Barbara 60
Bavaria, Swedish invasion of 97–8
Beane, John 19
beatas 162
Bengoechea, Josefa 228
Bernard of Clairvaux 125, 128
Besold, Christoph 20
Bethune, Maximillian de (Duke of Sully) 70–1
Beuditz convent 93
Beweismittel 16
Beza, Theodore 163–4

bier test; *see* cruentation
"Birth, Death, and the Pleasures of Life: Working Women in Nuremberg, 1480–1620" (Wiesner-Hanks) xiv
Bishop of Salisbury 109
Blanc, Clauda 161
Blancus, Marcus Antonius 16
bleeding corpse 13–21
body xv; bleeding corpse 13–21; and legal judgment 6; overview 6; power of 6
body wars 4
Boerious, Nicolas 16
Bommerin, Barbara 65
Bonauerin, Ursula 61, 62
Books of Martyrs (Crespin) 181
Bora, Katharina von 92
born-again virgins 25, 30; *see also* virgins/virginity
Brehna convent 91
Brent, Charles 91
Bresen, Ana 91
Bressani, Francesco Giuseppe 201
Breul, Elisabeth 93
Breve relatione d'alcune missioni de' PP. della Compagnia di Giesù nella Nuova Francia (Bressani) 201
Brief Compendium of the Life of the Blessed Father Friar John of the Cross (Madre de Dios) 52
Brockey, Liam 202–3
Brouet, Simon 162
Brown, Peter 25
Bruce, James 230
bruderhofen 179, 181
Brunner, Michael 65
Bruno, Giordano 175–84
Burkhardt, Jacob 2

Cabieces, Maria de 228
Calvin, John 136, 138, 155, 160–9
Calvinists 149, 150, 153, 155, 160
Cambridge World History xvi, xvii
Canisius, Peter 202
Canticles 125
Cantimori, Delio 176
Caracas 229
Carleton, Dudley 71, 74–5
Carolina 15–6
Carpentiers,. Josijn 155
Carpzov, Benedict 20
Carr, Robert (Earl of Somerset) 72
Cartagena 229
Castellio, Sebastian 176
Castle, John 76

Cataluña 227
Catherine of Aragon 177
Catholic Church 25, 26–7, 30, 149–53, 197, 210
Catholic League 97
Catholic women: in 17th-century Dutch Republic 148–57; baptism of children 152–3; domestic roles 150–1; exercise of faith 153–4; marriage 151–2; and patriarchal culture 148; under regime of toleration 149–50; spiritual maidens 154–6; spousal relationship 151–2
Catholicism: conversion to 141–2, 180; Dutch 148, 157, 183; overview 7; privatization of 157; and Reformed families in France 141; and spiritual maidens 155, 157
Catholics: and anti-Catholic laws 149; Dutch 149–50, 179; edification of pious 154; on Exodus 184; and sexuality 25; on spiritual virginity 27; on symbolic revirginization 30
Cats, Jacob 122
Cecil, Robert (Earl of Salisbury) 73
Cecil, Thomas (1st Earl of Exeter) 74
Cecil, William (Lord Roos) 74–6
celibacy 31
Chamberlain, John 71, 72, 76, 78
chambre de l'Édit of Castres 141
Charlemagne 14
Charles V 15
chastity 26
Cheke, Mary 74
child support 61
childbirth 42–3
children: baptism of 152–3; and Catholicism 141–2; illegitimate 61; mater familias as protector of 138; of mixed/interfaith marriages 151; of *moriscas* 180; of refugee deacons 191–2; of refugee relief recipients 188, 190; of refugee women 181; religious instruction 138–9
Chrisman, Miriam 1
Christian exiles 7
Christianity and Sexuality in the Early Modern World: Regulating Desire, Reforming Practice (Wiesner-Hanks) 4, xv–xvi
Church of England 112
Church of Saint-Gervais 138
City of Ladies (de Pizan) xvii
Claes, Annetge 154
Clark, Alice xiv
Claro, Giulo 20

Claver, Peter 202
Clifford, Lady Anne 78
Codercq, José 226
Collado, Diego 200
Colladon, Nicolas 161, 167
A Companion to Gender History (Wiesner-Hanks and Meade) xvi
A Concise History of the World (Wiesner-Hanks) xvii
concupiscendo 40
concupiscentia 41
confession 43
conquistadores 197
Consistory of Geneva 160, 161–2, 165, 166, 169
Convent of Saint Claire 144
convents 6, 85–94
Convents Confront the Reformation: Catholic and Protestant Nuns in Germany xvi
conversa/converso 177, 180, 183
Corpus Christianorum 180
cotton trade 226
Council of Trent 210
created tradition 14
Crenshaw, Kimberlé 4
Cromwell, Thomas 112–13, 116–17
Cronschwutz convent 89
cruentatio cadaverum 17
cruentation 14–21
Cuba 227, 229
Cuijper, Philips de 151
cultural confessionalism 7
cupiditas 41

d'Afflitto, Matteo 16
d'Agnon, François 164
d'Albret, Jeanne 136
Danelsz, Abram 153
Dathenus, Peter 124
Davis, Natalie Zemon 168
Daza, Juan 114
de Ceglia, Francesco Paolo 17
De Jussie, Jeanne 167–8
De la Madre de Dios, Alonso 48–55; brief encounter with John of the Cross 48, 53; death of 52, 53; as guardian and manager of John's relics 50–1; post-mortem surgery on John of the Cross 50; as *procurador* 51–2; as promoter of John's cult 51
de Medici, Catherine xvii
de Pizan, Christine xvii
debt payment 59
del Carmen, María 227–8

Delft consistory 151–2, 155
Demonology (James VI) 15
Dentière, Marie 136, 167–8
Désert 143
Devereux, Robert (3rd Earl of Eassex) 72, 74
Diaz, Antonia 228
Díaz, Pedro 199
disbursements 188–91, 193
Discalced Carmelite 48–54
Dommitzsch, Wolf von 87
dowry 27–8
Duran, Marie 144
Dutch Republic: anti-Catholic laws 149; Catholic women in 148–57; Peace of Westphalia of 1648 150; regime of toleration 149–50; Twelve Years Truce (1609–1621) 152
Dutch Revolt 187, 192

early modern self 198
Early Modern Women: An Interdisciplinary Journal 5
Eckhart, Meister 129
Edict of Nantes 141, 175
een vertoog 124
Egipte, Jacquème 167
El Aguila frigate 228
El Colon frigate 228
Elizabeth, death of 70
Emden, Dutch refugees in 187–95
emergency baptism 138
Entscheidungsmittel 16
Epistre tres utile (Dentière) 136
Ernestine Saxony convents 86, 88
Escuelas de Hilaza 226
Esholt convent 112
Essenes 25
Essex, Countess of 72
Eukleria (Van Schurman) 130
European women: and Atlantic economy 223–31; in Atlantic service economy 227–9; conflicts in German villages 59–67; court cases 59–67; as investors 228; in retail trade 228; in service economy 227–9; in slave trade 229–31; and Spanish economic policy 224–7; in textile trade 226; during the Thirty Years' War 97–105; tobacco trade 227
Eve 37–41, 43; malediction of 42–4; punishment 43–4
exegetes 38–9, 42
Exeter, Countess of 72, 77–80
exiles, religious 175–84; Anabaptists 178;

conventional model 176–7; deacons 191–2; disbursements 188–91, 193; in Emden, Germany 187–95; gendered nature of 177; Huguenots 182; Jews 179–80; male intellectuals 176; Münster Catholics 178–9; Muslims 180; record-keeping 187–95; relief recipients 187–95; Walloonians 182; widows 187–95; women as 176
Exodus 184

Farel, Guillaume 139, 168
Farinseius, Propsero 20
Favre, Jean 161
Favre, Jeanne 161
fear: in Catholic theology 214–15; filial 214–15; servile 214–15; and ship voyages 210–11
female agency 6
female body 6, 13–21
female religious communities, during Thirty Years' War 97–105
female sexuality 6
femme divineresse 141
Fenals, Miguel 114
Ferdinand II, Emperor 98
Ferdinand of Aragon 110–11
Feren, Peter 13
Festial 43
filial fear 214–15
forced monachization 30–1
Francis I, King of France 168
Franciscans 198
Franck, Sebastian 176
Frater Ildephonsus a Matre Dei, Procurator beatificationis 52
Frederick, John 85, 86
Freiburg convent 93
Freisinger Rechtsbuch of 1328 14
Frenckl, Catharine 93
Froment, Antoine 136, 168
frühzeitige Beischlaf 61
Fuchs, Johan Georg 99
furor 40–1

Galicia 230
Gannerel, Marguerite 162–6
Gebhardt, Katharine 93
gender history 37
gender research 3–4
Genesis 1:27–28 38–42
Genesis 3:16 42–4
Geneva, female religious expression in 160–9

Gerard, George 74–5
Gernrode 86
gesang: sections (§§1–3) 125–6; sections (§§4–15) 126–7; sections (§§15–24) 127; sections (§§26–34) 127; sections (§§35–51) 127–8; sections (§§52–end) 127–8; structure and content of 125–8; text and character 124
Gezang over het geestelyk huwelyk van Christus met de gelovige ziele; see Hymn (Van Schurman)
Ghosh, Durba 4
Glischhen, Conrad 91
global turn 4, 8
globalism 197
Glossa Ordinaria 40
Golterin, Elizabeth 60
Gómez, Antonio 20
Gonzales, Petrus xvii
Goodard, Peter 201
Gouda consistory 152, 153–4, 155–6
Gowing, Laura 59
Grave, Hermes de 192–3
Great Men 176–7
Gregory of Nyssa 38–9
Gresham, Elizabeth 78
Greyerz, Kaspar von 99
Grosse, Ave von 92
Grüner, Veronica 90
guilt, indicators of 16
Günther, Count of Schwarzburg 93

Hafter, Daryl 223
Hagenbach, Valentin 63
Hagenbacherin, Catherina 63
Hatton, Luke 78
Hausen, David 65
Hebraer, Jacob Mater 60–1
hegemonic masculinity 5
Heiliggrab by Bambberg convent 98, 103–4
Hendriks, Elysbeth 155
Henri II xvii
Henry IV 70, 136
Henry of Navarre 136
Henry VIII 112–13
Hessen-Darmstädtische Landesordnung of 1639 20
Hillenzoen, Aggeus 191
Hoff, Joan 2
Hofmeister 103
Holeugffer, Elisabeth 90
Holland Mission 149, 152, 154
"Holy Household" ideology 181
Holzfrevel 61

Hosne, Ana Carolina 197
Hospital de la Caridad 227
Howard, Frances 72, 75
Howard, Georgi-Anna 75
Howard, Katherine (Countess of Suffolk) 72
Howard, Thomas (Earl of Suffolk) 72, 73
Hsia, Ronnie 179
Huber, Marie 136–7
hueren bueben (whore's boys) 65
Huerzin, Magdalena 63–4
Hufton, Olwen 1, xiv
Huguenots 142, 175, 182, 218, 237
Hunt, Lynn 3
Hurons 201
Hymn (Van Schurman) 123–31; 1732 edition 123; handwritten copy 123; sections (§§1–3) 125–6; sections (§§4–15) 126–7; sections (§§15–24) 127; sections (§§26–34) 127; sections (§§35–51) 127–8; sections (§§52–end) 127–8; structure and content of 125–8; text and character 123, 124–5; themes and influences 128–31; translations 124
hypertrichosis xvii

Ichtershausen convent, storming of 93
Ignatius of Loyola 177, 210, 214, 215
Ignatius winds 216
Imago Dei 38–9, 40
Imperial Chamber Court 89
indicia 15
indicium falsum 16
indicium perfectum 16
indicium remotum 16
inheritance 59
Inquisition 162, 166
interconfessional marriage 151–2
interdisciplinary turns 4
interfaith marriages 151–2
Iroquois 201
Isabel of Castile 110–11
ius cruentationis; *see* cruentation

Jacobs, Margarita 155
James I 70–80; contempt toward Elizabeth 72; humiliation of Bathsua Reginald Makin 72; scandals in court of 72
James VI 15, 70
Janssen, Geert 179
Janssen, Grietje 156
Jerome 39, 214
Jesuits: annual letters 201; in Asian colonies 200; conversion of heretics 201; descriptions of everyday business 200–1; emotional community 210; fear as moral guide 210–11; global studies 197–204; libraries 198–200; manhood 212; masculinity/femininity in missions 210; mission-related texts 202, 202–3; in New France 200; in New Spain 199–200; overview 8; *praeceptum-exemplum-imitatio* 212; reports from missions 201; return of lapsed believers 201; ship voyages 210–19; in Southeast America 201–2; in Vietnam 201
Jews 179–80
John of the Cross 48–55; Alonso's brief encounter with 48; biographies 52; death in Ubeda 49; post-mortem surgery on 50; relics of 50–1; sepulcher for the remains of 50; theft of body 50
Joris, David 176
Jungfrau (virgin) 26
Junius, Maria Anna 98, 103
Jussie, Jeanne de 139

Karant-Nunn, Susan 180, xv, xvi
Kelly, Joan 2
Kempis, Thomas à 125, 128
Keyser, Gijsbert de 153
King, John 71
Kingdon, Robert 1, xiv
Kington Priory 109
kloppjes/kloppen (spiritual maidens) 154–6, 183
Knechtin, Magdalena, slander complaint by Barbara Bommerin 64–5
Knowles, David 118
Koppe, Leonhard 87
Kostka, Stanislaus 202
Kurz, Maria Magdelena 100–1

La Coruña port 224, 226, 227–9
Labadie, Jean de 124, 128
laicization 93
Lake, Anne 74–9
Lake, Arthur 73, 74
Lake, Mary 70, 73–80
Lake, Thomas 73–80
Lamela, Francisca 228
Larruga, Eugenio 225
Las Puellas 115
Lateran IV 14
Layton, Richard 114–15, 116, 117
Le sisteme des anciens et des modernes (Huber) 136
Lebenzeiche (body signs) 15

Lee, Edward 112
Legh, Thomas 114, 117, 119
Lemnius, Levinus 18
Lettres édifiantes et curieuses 216
Leupold, Margarethe Zedwitz 85
Levet, Claudine 167
Li, Shenwen 197
Libavius, Andreas 17–8
libraries 198–200
Lieberin, Anna 65
Life, Virtues, and Miracles of the Holy Father Friar John of the Cross (Madre de Dios) 52–3
ligature 140
Litterae annuae provinciae Paraquariae Societatis Iesu 203
Litterae indípetae 198, 202
Livius, Andreas 18
Lohausen, Wilhelm Geroge von 103
Longland, Bishop of London 112
Lord's Prayer 138–9, 162, 166
Lorkin, Thomas 76
Louis XIII 142
Louis XIV 143
Loyola, Ignatius 216
Luoder 62
lust 41
"'Lustful Luther': Male Libido in the Writings of the Reformer" (Wiesner-Hanks) 37
lusts of the flesh (*cupiditates carnis*) 41
Luther, Elisabeth 37
Luther, Hans 36
Luther, Katherina 36–7
Luther, Martin: attacks on the Catholic Church 27; on the Catholic Church and virginity 26–7; dismissal of spiritual virginity 28; as father 6, 36–7; as husband 6, 36–7, 44; lectures 6; on marriage and virginity 29; marriage to Katherine 37; on material value of virginity 28; on nuns' departure from convents 85–94; pastoral importance of confession 43; preaching on Genesis 1 40–2; on pregnancy and childbirth 42; sermons 6; views on virginity 6, 26–32
"Luther and Women" (Wiesner-Hanks) xv
Luther on Women: A Sourcebook xvi
Lutherans 141, 149

Maggi, Girolamo 20
Maggius, Hieronymus 16
Makin, Bathsua Reginald 71
mala fama (bad reputation) 17

Malleus Maleficarum 17
Manso, Joaquina 228
Manso, Teresa 228
Marguerite of Navarre 168
María Ygnés Rodríguez, María Ygnés 228
Mariastein by Eichstätt convent 98
marital sisters 182
marriage 27–9; Catholic women in Dutch Republic 151–2; court complaints 61; interconfessional 151–2; pregnancy before 61; as remedy to lust and sin 39; reneged promises of 61
Martin, Loys 140
Martínez Fernández, Alonso 49
Martínez Fernández, Fernando 49
martyrs 30, 181
Martyrs Mirror (Van Bracht) 181
The Marvelous Hairy Girls: The Gonzales Sisters and their Worlds (Weisner-Hanks) 236, xvii
Mary, Virgin 26, 29–30, 161, 169
Mary Magdalene 30
Matthijs, Jan 178, 180
Maximilian, Elector 97, 100
Meade, Teresa xvi
Meckler, Margarethe 92
Medici, Cosimo de 177
Melanchthon, Philip 18
memories, creation of 91–3
Mengin, Jerg 60
Mennonites 149
Menologio di pie memorie d'alcuni religiosi della Compagnia di Gesù (Patrignani) 202
Mercado, Luis de 50
Merckhen, Georg 61
Mergin, Anna Maria 61
Merzch, Dorothea 88
Messmerin, Catherina 62
migration 7
Mirk, John 43
Mission Hollandica 149
Molina, J. Michelle 198
monachization, forced 30–1
monastic space 6, 102–3
monastic subjects, masculine relationships 6
Monoculus, Peter 14
Montevideo 229
Montjoye, Anne 143
Moravian radical communities 179
More, Thomas 177
Morgengabe ("morning-gift") 28
moriscas/moriscos 180, 183
Mosaic Law 15
Mosis, Adriaentje 156

Mottu-Weber, Liliane xiv
Münster 178
Münsterberg, Ursula von 86, 88, 89
Muratori, Ludovico Antonio 201
murder trials 13–21
Musa virginea (Reginald) 71
Muslims 180

Nadere Reformatie 124, 129, 131
Nahuatl 199
Navarre, Marguerite de 136
New France 200, 201
New Spain 199–200, 229
Newton, Adam 77
Nguyen Phúc Lans 201
Niebelungenlied 14
Niedergericht (lower court) 60–1
Nimbschen convent 89, 90
Norton, Anne 72
Nueva Granada 229
Nunburnholme convent 112
nuns: conflicts with male Reformers 109–19; creation of memories 91–3; decisions to leave convents 86–7; departure from convents 87–9; early Reform propaganda and 87–9; monastic space 102–3; overview 6–7; and papacy's bulls on visitors' powers 110–11; and Reformation 85–94; self-reported memories 87; in Thirty Years' War 97–105; visitations 89–91, 111–15
Nuovi avisi delle Indie di Portogallo 203

oath-helpers 14
Oberamtsgericht 62
Oberweimar, Florentina von 88
Oberweimar convent 92
old maid 25
omnes 41
Oran fatwah of 1504 180
ordo salutis 127
orphanages 153
Overbury, Thomas 72
overseas travel 7

papacy 110–11
papist ceremonies 90
Parenti, Marco 177
Park, Katherine 17
Patagonia, colonization of 228
patriarchy 5, 6, 148
Patrignani, Giuseppe 202
Peace of Westphalia of 1648 150

Peasants' War (1524–1525) 86, 88, 89
Pellet, Marianne de 144
Peñalosa, Ana de 50
Pernin, Antoine 162
Pernin, Monet 161
Peronet, Marquet 161
Peronet. Tevene 161
perpetual virgins 25–6, 31
Perry, Mary E 180
Perú 229
Petersberg convent 86
Philip III 74
Philipp of Hesse 178
physical virginity 26
Pierre, Louis de la 162
Pierre, Marie de la 162–6
placards (anti-Catholic laws) 149
plague 36–7
Pole, Reginald 176
Pollman, Judith 166
Poor Clares convents 98, 99, 100–2, 139, 144, 167
Poska, Allyson 5
Potts, Thomas 17
prêcheuse 143
Prémare, Joseph de 211, 215–16, 216–17
Preston, Jennet 16–7
Privy Council 74
procreation 38–9, 40
procurator 51–2
Professed House of Antwerp 199
property rights 59
Protestantism 7; abandonment of 142; anticlericalism 25; and Edict of Nantes 141; Italian 176; and sacral systems 137; and shift to Catholicism 142; suppression in late 17th century 143; themes 123; women in 137–8, 141
protoevangelion 123, 126
Psalm 146:7-8 140
Puckering, Sir Thomas 76
Puerto Rico 229

Ranchin, François 18
Real Consulado de La Coruña 226
Rebdorf 99
Reformation 6, 24–32; nuns confronting 85–94; women in 135–45
Reformed Church 148; and anti-Catholic laws 149; and baptism of children 152–3; Delft consistory 151–2, 155; Gouda consistory 152, 155–6; and regime of toleration 150

248 Index

Refuge movement 142
refugees, religious 175–84; Anabaptists 178; conventional model 176–7; deacons 191–2; defined 7; disbursements 188–91, 193; in Emden, Germany 187–95; gendered nature of 177; Huguenots 182; Jews 179–80; male intellectuals 176; Münster Catholics 178–9; Muslims 180; record-keeping 187–95; relief recipients 187–95; Walloonians 182; widows 187–95; wives 187–95; women as 176
Reginald, Henry 71
Régis, Jean François 202
register 144
Reich, Barbara 91
Reichman, Catharina Schöpperitz 92
Reinigungseid 16
Reinoso, Andre 213–14
relief from credit 59
religious actors 7
religious instructions 138–9
religious persecutions 7
religious refugees 175–84; Anabaptists 178; conventional model 176–7; deacons 191–2; disbursements 188–91, 193; in Emden, Germany 187–95; gendered nature of 177; Huguenots 182; Jews 179–80; male intellectuals 176; Münster Catholics 178–9; Muslims 180; record-keeping 187–95; relief recipients 187–95; Walloonians 182; widows 187–95; women as 176
religious tribunals 7
Remse convent 90
Rens, Guillaume 2, 166
Rens, Philippa 166
réparation 161
Revels, Jan 190
revirginization 30
Revius, Jacob 122, 125
Revocation of Edict of Nantes 142–3
Richelieu 142
Rider, Mary 73
Rievaulx Abbey 115
Rio de Plata 229, 230
Rochefoucauld, Marie de La 142
Rodney, George 79
Rodney, Sir John 79
Rodriguez, Alfonso 202
Rodríguez Campomanes, Pedro 225–6
Roelker, Nancy 1
Roland, Bainton 176–7
Roman Superstition 89
Roos, Lady 74–9
Roos, Lord (William Cecil) 74–6
Roper, Lyndal 180, xv
Rörer, Hanna 36
Rothenham, Hans Georg van 103
Rotnmann, Bernhard 178
Rousseau, Jean-Jacques 136–7
Royal Tobacco Factory 227
Ruíz de Montoya, Antonio 200
Russell, Camella 203

Saalburg convent 90
Sabean, David 66
Sachsenspiegel 15
sacral systems 135–45; emergency baptism 138; female preachers 143–4; religious instructions 138–9; and sorcery 140–1; women in 135–45
Saint-Martin, Damoiselle de 140
Salisbury, Earl of (Robert Cecil) 73
same-sex relationships 25
Sánchez, Sebastiana 228
Sanders, Katharina 89
Santa Clara convent 109
Santa María, Francisco de 53–4; as biographer of John of the Cross 52
Santo Domingo 229
Sarasúa, Carmen 223, 230
Sarmient, Padre 230
Satan 162
Saxe-Weimar, Bernhard von' 103–4
Schilling, Diebold 13
Schmerzensgeld (damages) 60–1
Schmidt, Frantz 17
Scott, Joan 2, xiv
sermons 6, 19
Servetus, Michael 175–84
servile fear 214–15
sex, sinfulness of 39
sexual deviance 179
Shakespeare, William 19
ship voyages 210–19; and adverse weather events 216; and fear 210–11; Ignatius winds 216; Jesuits 210–19; male-dominated spaces in 211; threats to 216; Xavier as go-to Jesuit saint 216–19
Short Chronicle 139
Siejas, Antonia 230
Silberin, Johanna 62–7; relationship with soldiers 63–4; slander complaint against Barbara Steüerin 63–4; slander complaint against Catherina Messmerin 62; slander complaint by Catherina Hagenbachein 63
Simonton, Deborah 223

Sinningthwaite convent 112
Skocir, Joan xvi
slander 62–5, 117
slavery 229–31
Sluhovsky, Moshe 183
Small Council 160, 162, 165
Smith, Bonnie xvi
Smith, Frances Brydge 74
Society of Jesus 197, 198, 210, 212; *see also* Jesuits
Socino, Fausto 176
Socino, Lellio 176
Somerset, Countess of 72, 75
Somerset, Earl 72
Somerset, Earl of 72
Song of Songs 129
sorcery 140–1
South Africa 176
Spanish Enlightenment 224
spatial turns 4
Spiess, Hans 13, 16
Spiessin, Margarete, murder of 13, 20
spinsters 25
spirit xv
Spiritual Exercises (Ignatius of Loyola) 214
spiritual maidens 154–6
spiritual virgins 26–7, 28, 30
St. Katharina's convent 86, 98, 100
Staiger, Clara 98, 99, 100
Star Chamber 72–3
Steinbrecher, Elisabeth 92–3
Steüerin, Barbara 63
St.John of the Cross 6
Stockman, Gillis 190, 192
Stranger Church 182, 183
Strigel, Simon 65
Strozzi, Alessandria Macinghi 177
Strozzi of Florence 177
Suffolk, Countess of (Katherine Howard) 72, 75–7
Suffolk, Earl of (Thomas Howard) 72, 73
Sully, Duke of (Maximillian de Bethune) 70–1
Summary of the Life and Miracles of the Venerable Father Friar John of the Cross (Madre de Dios) 52
Swarton, Sarah 77
Sweden, in Thirty Years' War 97–105
Swetnam, Joseph 71

Tartre, Vincent de 211, 215–16, 217–19
Tauler, John 128
Teelinck, Willem 128, 129, 130

Tell-Troth, Thomas 71
Teresa of Avila 49, 166
textile trade 226
the Fall 38–9
Theatre of the Cruelties of the Heretics of our Age (Verstegen) 181
Thesaurus Indicus, seu, Generalis instructor pro regimine conscientiae, in iis quae ad Indias spectant (de Avendaño) 203
Thirty Years' War 7, 97–105
Thomas, Keith 19
Thuringia 89
Tilly, Louise xiv
timor filialis (filial fear) 214–15
timor servilis (servile fear) 214–15
tobacco trade 227
Torsellini, Orazio 211, 212–13
torture 15, 16
Tour de Constance 144
"Towards a Gender Analysis of the Reformation" (Wiesmer-Hanks) xv
Tregonwell, John 115
Truillot, Michael 230
Twain, Mark 20
Twelve Years Truce (1609–1621) 152

Uitbreiding 123
Ursach und antwort (Luther) 87
Utrecht Circle 125

Valdaura, Margarita 177, 182
Valencia 227
Valignano, Alessandro 198
Valldonella convent 115
Valor Eclesiasticus 112
Van Beek, Pieta 123
van den Heede, Hans 189
Van Lodenstein, Jodocus 123, 125
Van Schurman, Anna Maria 7, 122–31; 1638 "dissertation" 130; Catholic persecution 122; classical education 122; Dutch poetry 123; *Hymn* 123–31; mastery of biblical languages 122
Varela, Joachim 228
Verhörprotokolle 60
Vermigli, Peter Martyr 176
vertoog 124
Verwer, Elysbeth Hendriks 155
A Very Useful Epistle (Dentière) 168
Vestal Virgins 25
Villet, Jacquème 162
Viret, Pierre 139, 168
Virgin Mary 26, 29–30, 161, 169

virgins/virginity: born-again virgins 25, 30; categories of 25; chastity, compared with 26; as commodity 27–8; and dowry 27–8; Luther's views on 6, 24–32; and marriage 27–9; Mary 29–30; material value of 28; as metaphor for Christians and the church 26; old maid 25; perpetual 25–6, 31; physical virginity 26; and Reformation 24–32; revirginization 30; saints and martyrs 30; spiritual 28, 29–30, 30; young maid 25
visitations 89–91, 111–15
Vives, Juan Luis 176, 177–8
Voetius, Gisbert 122, 128

Waldensians 143
Waldpardt, Mathias 61
Wallis., Thomas 76
Walloonians 182
Waltzer, Michael 149–50
Ward, Bernardo 225–6
Warham, William 112
A Warning to Fair Women 19
Webster, John 18
Weibergeschwätz (women's gossip) 59, 62
widows 187–95
Wiesner-Hanks, Merry 1–5, 37, 85, 104, 137, 175, 180, 204, xiv–xviii
Willemsz, Jan 151
Williams, George 78, 176
Wilson, Christine 16–7
Wintney convent 117
Winwood, Sir Ralph 74
Wirtin 62
witches 16–7
Wolframsdorf, Margarethe 91
Wolsey, Cardinal 114
women: and Atlantic economy 223–31; in Atlantic service economy 227–9; Catholic nuns during Reformation 85–94; Catholics in 17th century Dutch Republic 148–57; conflicts in German villages 59–67; female body 13–21; forced monachization of 30–1; incarceration 143–4; preachers 143–4; in Protestantism 135–45; in Reformation 109–19, 135–45; religious expression in Reformation Geneva 160–9; religious lives of 85–94; religious refugees 175–84; in sacral systems 135–45; scandals in court of James I of England 70–80; in slave trade 229–31; and Spanish economic policy 224–7; during the Thirty Years' War 97–105; virgins/virginity 24–32
Women and Gender in Early Modern Europe (Wiesner-Hanks) 1–3, 85, 104, xv
women in courts: family disputes 60–1; Johanna Silberin 62–7; marriage disputes 61; *Niedergericht* (lower court) 60–1; as plaintiffs and defendants 59; property disputes 60; slander 62–5
Women in Port: Gendering Communities, Economies, and Social Networks in Atlantic Port Cities, 1500–1800 (Catterall and Campbell) 224
Women in the Reformation: Germany and Italy (Bainton) 1
Women of the Reformation (Bainton) 176
women's history 2–3
Working Life of Women in the Seventeenth Century (Clark) xiv
Working Women in Renaissance Germany (Wiesner-Hanks) 1, xiv
World Spirit 176
Wunder, Heide xiv
Württemberg Criminal Ordinance (1609) 20
Wyandotte 201

Xavier, Francis 202, 211; biography 211; death on 1552 211; hagiological identity 212; mastery of fear 213; as patron saint of ship voyages 216–19; transit from Malacca to India 213; voyage from Japan towards China 213–14

young maid 25

Zarri, Gabriella 183
Zedwitz, Margarethe von 85
Zemon Davis, Natalie 1, 2
Zitter, Martha Elizabeth 86, 89

Printed in the United States
By Bookmasters